Algeria

Anthony Ham
Nana Luckham, Anthony Sattin

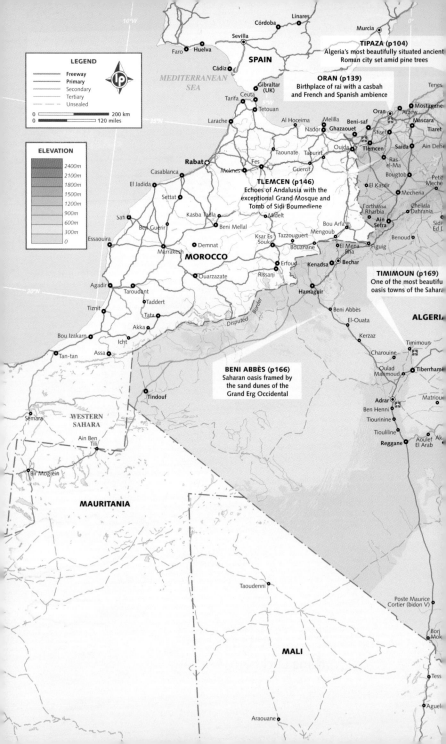

LEGEND

Freeway
Primary
Secondary
Tertiary
Unsealed

0   200 km
0   120 miles

ELEVATION

2400m
2100m
1800m
1500m
1200m
900m
600m
300m
0

TIPAZA (p104)
Algeria's most beautifully situated ancient
Roman city set amid pine trees

ORAN (p139)
Birthplace of rai with a casbah
and French and Spanish ambience

TLEMCEN (p146)
Echoes of Andalusia with the
exceptional Grand Mosque and
Tomb of Sidi Boumediene

TIMIMOUN (p169)
One of the most beautifu
oasis towns of the Sahara

BENI ABBÈS (p166)
Saharan oasis framed by
the sand dunes of the
Grand Erg Occidental

MEDITERRANEAN
SEA

SPAIN

Córdoba   Linares
Murcia
Sevilla
Faro   Huelva
Cádiz
Gibraltar
(UK)
Ceuta
Tarifa
Tetouan
Larache
Al Hoceima
Nador
Melilla
Beni-saf
Ghazaouet
Arzew
Oran
Mostagane
Tenes
Taounate   Tapurirt
Oujda
Tlemcen
Sfisel
Saida
Ain Deh
Rabat
Fes
Guercif
Meknes
Casablanca
El Jadida
Settat
Kasba Tadla
Midelt
Beni Mellal
Bou Arfa
Ain
Sefra
El Kasdir
Mecheria
Chellala
Dahrania
Safi
Ben Guerir
Ksar Es
Souk
Tazzouguert
Mengoub
Figuig
Benoud
Sidr
Ed L
Essaouira
Demnat
Bouanane
El Mena
Bha
Marrakesh
MOROCCO
Erfoud
Kenadsa   Bechar
Rissani
Ouarzazate
Agadir
Taroudant
Taddert
Hamaguir
Beni Abbès
El-Ouata
Kerzaz
Timimoun
Tiznit
Tata
Akka
Charouine
ALGERI
Bou Izakarn
Icht
Oulad
Mahmoud
Tiberrham
Assa
Tan-tan
Matriou
Adrar
Ben Henni
Tiourinine
Tindouf
Tiouiline
Reggane
Aoulef
El Arab
Ak
Sémara
WESTERN
SAHARA
Ain Ben
Tili
Bir Mogrein
MAURITANIA
Taoudenni
Poste Maurice
Cortier (bidon V)
Bor
Mok
MALI
Tess
Aguel
Araouane

Forthassa
Rharbia
Bougtob
Ras
el-Ma
Petit
Meche
Mascara
Tiaret
Taourirt
Bou
Arfa
Kenitra

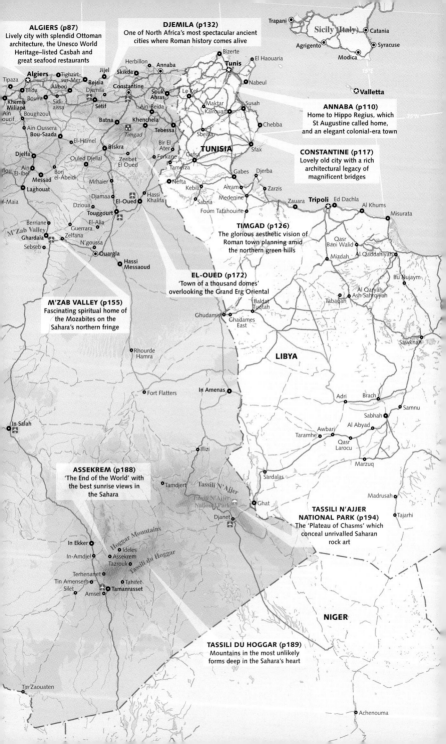

ALGIERS (p87)
Lively city with splendid Ottoman architecture, the Unesco World Heritage–listed Casbah and great seafood restaurants

DJEMILA (p132)
One of North Africa's most spectacular ancient cities where Roman history comes alive

ANNABA (p110)
Home to Hippo Regius, which St Augustine called home, and an elegant colonial-era town

CONSTANTINE (p117)
Lovely old city with a rich architectural legacy of magnificent bridges

TIMGAD (p126)
The glorious aesthetic vision of Roman town planning amid the northern green hills

EL-OUED (p172)
'Town of a thousand domes' overlooking the Grand Erg Oriental

M'ZAB VALLEY (p155)
Fascinating spiritual home of the Mozabites on the Sahara's northern fringe

ASSEKREM (p188)
'The End of the World' with the best sunrise views in the Sahara

TASSILI N'AJJER NATIONAL PARK (p194)
The 'Plateau of Chasms' which conceal unrivalled Saharan rock art

TASSILI DU HOGGAR (p189)
Mountains in the most unlikely forms deep in the Sahara's heart

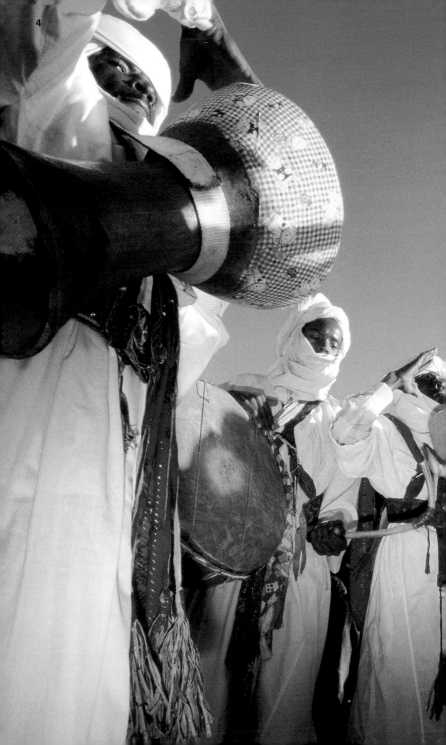

Wheat is harvested in the oasis of Timimoun (p169)

Rock paintings (p80) in Tassili N'Ajjer date back thousands of years

Opposite: The Tuareg celebrate for three days at Le Tafsit (p186), a festival which culminates in a camel race

Sunrise over Assekrem (p188), 'the End of the World', is not to be missed

TED PINK/ALAMY

Algiers (p87), the whitewashed capital on the Mediterranean coast

Ghardaïa, first among the five ancient cities of the M'Zab (p155)

FRANS LEMMENS/DAS FOTO

TRIP/ALAMY

Touchstones of Berber identity (p40) are language and culture

Traditionally, blacksmiths (p55) hold a unique place in Tuareg society

FRANS LEMMENS

TRIP/ALAMY

Bountiful dates grow in the Saharan oasis of the M'Zab Valley (p155)

8

Timgad (p126), an entire Roman town, laid out in a grid pattern

Survey the Sahara astride a camel (p75)

Contents

Regional Map Contents

Algiers & Around pp88–9

Northeast Algeria p109

Northwest Algeria p138

Ghardaïa & the Grand Ergs p154

Tamanrasset, Djanet & the Sahara p180

The Authors

ANTHONY HAM
Coordinating Author

Anthony's first encounter with Algeria was as a refugee lawyer in Australia in the 1990s when he worked on behalf of Algerian and other asylum seekers. While working as a lawyer he obtained a Masters degree in Middle Eastern politics. His second encounter came in 2001 when he (illegally) walked across the Algerian border from an isolated corner of the Libyan Sahara and back again. He has since returned, both legally and illegally. Now a full-time writer and photographer based in Madrid, Anthony has written Lonely Planet's *Libya* and the Mauritania, Mali and Niger chapters of *West Africa*, as well as contributing to *Morocco* and *Tunisia*. Whenever he can, he heads for the Sahara.

The Coordinating Author's Favourite Trip

I love the uproar and the unspoken secrets of the Algiers Casbah (p93) and rai rhythms of Oran (p139). But all the while I'm dreaming of the Sahara and as the bus rambles out across the High Plateaus, I can feel my spirits lift. From Taghit (p165) I can look out across the sands of the Grand Erg Occidental (p162). Beni Abbès (p166) could keep me detained for days, as could Timimoun (p169). Any place with a name like Assekrem ('the End of the World'; p188) is my sort of place and I'd spend as much time as I had in the Tassili du Hoggar (p189). I couldn't leave Algeria without visiting Djanet (p191) and the utterly compelling rock art of the Tassili N'Ajjer National Park (p194).

NANA LUCKHAM
Ghardaïa, Tamanrasset, Directory & Transport

Nana was born in Tanzania to a Ghanaian mother and English father. Childhood in England followed, punctuated with periods in Ghana, Zimbabwe, Australia and France. After a degree in French and history and a Masters in international relations, Nana headed off solo to see the world, also working as a press officer for the United Nations. She has spent the past couple of years as a freelance writer based in London, travelling in and writing about Africa. She has contributed to numerous publications including guides to Kenya and West Africa and Lonely Planet's *Africa* and *Southern Africa* books. She jumped at the chance to explore southern Algeria, where she began a love affair with the Sahara.

LONELY PLANET AUTHORS

Why is our travel information the best in the world? It's simple: our authors are independent, dedicated travellers. They don't research using just the internet or phone, and they don't take freebies in exchange for positive coverage. They travel widely, to all the popular spots and off the beaten track. They personally visit thousands of hotels, restaurants, cafés, bars, galleries, palaces, museums and more – and they take pride in getting all the details right, and telling it how it is. Think you can do it? Find out how at lonelyplanet.com.

ANTHONY SATTIN
Algiers, Northeast & Northwest Algeria

Since his first visit as a teenager, Anthony has spent much of his adult life travelling around and writing about North Africa and the Middle East. He is the author of several highly acclaimed books about Africa, including *The Pharaoh's Shadow,* in which he searched for Egypt's surviving ancient culture, and he edited Lonely Planet's *A House Somewhere: Tales of Life Abroad.* His most recent book, *The Gates of Africa,* tells the history of early exploration in Africa and the search for Timbuktu. Now based in London, he is a regular contributor to the *Sunday Times* and *Conde Nast Traveller.*

CONTRIBUTING AUTHORS

Jane Cornwell wrote the rai music boxed text in the Culture chapter. Australian-born, UK-based Jane writes on world music and arts for a variety of publications including the *Telegraph,* the *Evening Standard* and the *Australian.* Her fascination with the rai music of Algeria began when she attended the 1997 Khaled concert at London's Astoria and witnessed a spectacle involving flashing lights, loud music, and bare-chested men holding the Algerian flag aloft and/or storming the stage to try to touch the hem of their hero's trousers. Jane frequently travels to and writes about North Africa.

Zahia Hafs wrote the *hittistes* boxed text in the Culture chapter, the Shanghai Blue boxed text in the Algiers chapter and the *taxieurs* boxed text in the Transport chapter. Of Kabylian descent, Zahia was born and raised in Paris. After few years at the UN in New York, she joined a press agency in Paris before setting up the French office of Lonely Planet. A decade later, she created her own little publishing company, Jalan Publications. Zahia discovered Algiers in 2004. Together with artist Elsie Herberstein, she published, in 2005, a book about the white city, *Alger: Simples Confidences.*

Destination Algeria

Algeria is the most fascinating country you never thought of visiting.

Off limits for decades, Algeria is again struggling to its feet, resilient and ready to show you just why the country is becoming many travellers' favourite North African destination. Like all countries along the southern Mediterranean rim, Algeria has two primary drawcards: outstanding Roman ruins and the exceptional landscapes of the Sahara. The difference is that Algeria has them in almost embarrassing abundance.

Algeria's catalogue of ancient Roman cities is astonishingly varied. Tipaza, a favourite of Albert Camus, weaves among the palm trees and down to the shores of the Mediterranean. Djemila, nestled amid the hills, stunningly evokes northeastern Algeria's ancient past, while Hippo Regius is alive with the echoes of St Augustine. A further four Roman sites, all in the country's mountainous northeast, make Algeria a paradise for the amateur archaeologist in you.

Further from the coast, you don't have to travel too deep into the Sahara to be swept up in its magic. The oases of the west – Taghit, Beni Abbès and Timimoun – are surrounded by palm trees and the dunes of the Grand Erg Occidental (Great Western Erg) and are home to glorious mud-brick architecture. Intriguing Ghardaïa stands at the heart of the M'Zab Valley, home to one of the world's few remnant Ibadi Muslim communities. Deep in the desert's heart in Algeria's far south, Assekrem (the End of the World), Atakor and the Tassili du Hoggar, where the otherworldly rock formations are the spiritual home of the Tuareg, are the stuff of legend for even the most experienced of Saharan travellers. Away to the remote southeast is the mythical terrain of the Tassili N'Ajjer where superbly rendered, millennia-old rock art tells the Sahara's story in shades of ochre and other earth tones.

It all comes together in Algiers, a city that's as alive as any in the world. When deciding to include Algiers' Casbah on its World Heritage list, Unesco described it as 'one of the finest coastal sites on the Mediterranean' and we're inclined to agree. Also on the northern coast are Algeria's most beautiful cities. Constantine is stunning. Oran, the birthplace and home of rai, Algeria's world-famous musical export, is an intriguing marriage of France and Spain. And Tlemcen could easily be one of Andalusia's most beautiful cities were it not in Algeria.

There's something about Algeria that has always given it the quality of an epic and perhaps that's why so many great travellers of the past have sought to know it, and from St Augustine in Hippo Regius to Isabelle Eberhardt in the oases of the Sahara, from Red Beard the pirate-king to Charles de Foucauld the desert hermit somewhere close to the End of the World.

Algeria's troubled recent past may have slowed the arrival of travellers and the mere thought of Algeria can be daunting. There's no doubting that visiting here is a challenge. But Algeria has never lost its mystique and armed with this book, as well as the latest updates on the security situation in Algeria, you'll quickly discover that there are so many world-class places to visit in Algeria and that almost all of them are not only safe but crying out for the visitors they so richly deserve.

There are not many destinations left in the world that still possess an edgy cachet, that showcase landscapes of rare beauty and promise the joy of discovering ancient sites of world significance. Algeria is such a place and the time to visit is now.

Getting Started

Algeria can be a challenging destination and many of your pretrip thoughts are likely to centre around arranging a visa (see p206), checking out the security situation (see p200 and the boxed text, opposite) and deciding which is the best time to visit (below). But tracking down books and films before leaving home is a great way to whet your appetite for the journey ahead. Algeria is a fascinating country with a thriving cultural life and landscapes of unrivalled beauty that have drawn writers and travellers down through the centuries.

WHEN TO GO

The best time to visit Algeria is in October and November when the skies are clear, the temperatures are mild and, depending on end-of-summer rains, the desert may even have a greenish tinge in places. The next best alternative is from March through to early May, although there's a higher chance of sandstorms in April and, by May, temperatures are really starting to rise. December through to February is also a good time, although temperatures can be surprisingly cool and night-time temperatures in the Sahara routinely drop below zero. In summer (mid-May to September), temperatures can be unbearably hot – don't even think of a desert expedition at this time.

See Climate Charts (p199) for more information.

Apart from the weather and a sprinkling of local festivals (see the boxed text, p16), the most important consideration for when to visit is the holy month of Ramadan. Few countries take the month of fasting as seriously as Algeria does and the simple fact of closed restaurants alone – most Algerians break the daily fast in private homes and many restaurants close for the month – should make you think seriously about avoiding travelling in Algeria for the duration. Only in five-star hotels in Algiers are you likely to find a place to eat. For details on upcoming dates for Ramadan, see p202.

COSTS & MONEY

Algeria is not the region's most expensive destination and travellers on a tight budget could get by on €35 per day by staying in youth hostels,

---

DON'T LEAVE HOME WITHOUT...

- A visa firmly ensconced in your passport (p206)
- Travel insurance (p202) – accidents do happen
- Driving licence, car documents and appropriate car insurance (p215) if bringing your own car
- Extremely warm clothes for winter (above)
- A universal bathplug – you'll thank us when you emerge from the desert
- An MP3 player – the desert can be beautiful but there are days when epic distances and empty horizons can do your head in
- Mosquito repellent – that unmistakeable high-pitched whine in the ear is death to sleep in many Saharan oases
- A small size-three football (soccer ball) – a great way to meet locals

For more advice on what to bring for travelling in the Sahara, see p68.

OFF LIMITS

As you set about planning your Algerian itinerary, remember that uncertain security in some parts of the country means some regions remain off limits to travellers.

For the foreseeable future, you should definitely avoid overland travel through the Kabylie region in Algeria's northeast. Consider flying into places such as Sétif or Annaba; many of the towns are relatively safe. The town of Bejaïa and the coastal area east to Jijel was particularly volatile and dangerous at the time of research. For more information on the security situation in this region see the boxed text, p110. In the northwest, Mascara and Chlef should also be avoided.

In southern Algeria, concerns remain about security for travellers in some desert regions, which is why independent travel is forbidden in desert regions south of Ghardaïa. In practice, this means that the spectacular Saharan landscapes around Tamanrasset (p180) and Djanet (p190) can only be visited in the company of a professional guide. For more information see the boxed text, p181.

travelling in shared taxis and eating cheap. Staying in midrange accommodation and eating in decent sit-down restaurants will blow the budget out, but only to a reasonable €60 per day. If you add in car hire, a few internal flights, the odd local tour and a bit of shopping, your daily spend is more likely to approach €100 or more. For advice on the expected cost of accommodation, see p196.

The rule when it comes to money in Algeria is simple: bring cash, preferably in euros or British pounds, as ATMs that accept foreign cards are extremely rare and credit cards and travellers cheques will rarely (if ever) have a chance to leave your wallet. For more information on money matters, see p203.

TRAVEL LITERATURE

The Sword and the Cross (Ian Fleming) This wonderfully readable account of the lives of Charles de Foucauld and Henri Laperrine is a like a journey through French historical fantasies about the Sahara and Algeria in particular.

The Conquest of the Sahara (Douglas Porch) Porch tells a rollicking, even sensationalist tale of the often ill-fated French attempt to seize control of the Sahara and their battles with the equally ill-fated Tuareg.

Sahara Unveiled (William Langeweische) One of the most carefully written narratives of modern Saharan exploration, this fine book combines sparing prose and an epic journey that begins in Algeria.

Tangier to Tunis (Alexandre Dumas) In 1846 Alexandre Dumas was asked by the Ministry of Public Instruction in France to travel and write his way around Algeria and the result is a fascinating window into 19th-century circumstances.

The Tuareg and **Sahara Man** (Jeremy Keenan) There is no finer academic authority on the Algerian Tuareg than Jeremy Keenan, whose anthropological work in southern Algeria began in the 1960s and is updated with an enlightening return decades later.

The Oblivion Seekers (Isabelle Eberhardt and Paul Bowles) Paul Bowles provides a biography of this most iconic of travellers as a precursor to Eberhardt's 11 enthralling stories that vividly bring to life late-19th- century Algeria.

The Star of Algiers (Aziz Chouaki) This fast-paced novel of cultural conflict in 1990s Algiers is set against the backdrop of music and civil war, two of the driving forces of recent Algerian history.

The Great War for Civilisation (Robert Fisk) This weighty tome by the doyen of Western Middle East correspondents includes one of the most searing and compelling studies of the Algerian civil war.

INTERNET RESOURCES

153 Club (www.the153club.org) One of the best sites for Saharan enthusiasts with a pleasing mix of the aspirational and the practical, and plenty of Algeria-specific information.

HOW MUCH?

Algiers–Tamanrasset air ticket DA14,000

Algiers–Ghardaïa bus ticket DA650

1 hour's internet access DA80-150

Tour from Tamanrasset DA4800-7750

Museum entry DA20

See also inside front cover.

TOP PICKS

Algerian Music

The following albums will provide a marvellous soundtrack to your Algerian visit; they're widely available throughout Europe and elsewhere.

- *Deb – Heart Broken* (Souad Massi)
- *Forever King* (Khaled)
- *Diwan* (Rachid Taha)
- *Meli Meli* (Cheb Mami)
- *Rai Roots* (Cheikha Rimitti)

Algerian Festivals

There's no boring time to visit Algeria, but organising your visit around one or more of the following festivals will add an extra dimension to your trip.

- Fête du tapis (March/April; Ghardaïa; p158)
- Le Tafsit (end April; Tamanrasset; p186)
- S'bou de Timimoun (dates vary; Timimoun; p170)
- Festival National de la Chanson du Rai d'Oran (August; Oran; p144)
- Sebiba (Djanet; p193)

Algerian Films

These films should give you a taste of one of Africa's most innovative and respected film industries (p53).

- *The Battle of Algiers* (directed by Gillo Pontecorvo; 1966)
- *Bab el-Oued* (directed by Merzak Allouache; 1994)
- *Chronicle of the Years of Embers* (directed by Mohamed Lakhdar-Hamina; 1975)
- *Barakat!* (directed by Djamila Sahraoui; 2006)
- *Days of Glory* (directed by Rachid Bouchareb; 2006)

Algeria.com (www.algeria.com) At first glance a little light-on for information, but its range of topics (tourism, news, business and culture) is hard to beat.

Lonely Planet (www.lonelyplanet.com) Includes background information on Algeria with links to travellers' reports on visiting the country.

Sahara Overland (www.sahara-overland.com) Companion to the excellent desert guidebook of the same name with up-to-date travel reports and news.

Wanadoo – Algérie (www.wanadoo.dz in French) A multipurpose French-language portal that takes a contemporary and tech-savvy look at Algerian culture from writers and traditional costumes to the latest news.

Yakeo (www.yakeo.com/fr/algerie/) One of the most extensive listings of (mostly French-language) links to Algerian news, music and sport sites.

Itineraries

CLASSIC ROUTES

THE BEST OF THE COAST
Two Weeks/Tlemcen to Annaba

Travelling along Algeria's Mediterranean coastline is like a journey through the Algerian soul, with all the clamour, historical influences and home-grown creativity on show. There's no better place to start than **Tlemcen** (p146) with its touch of Andalusia and the Almoravid twist that is Tlemcen's trademark. On no account miss the **Grand Mosque** (p148) and the **Mosque & Tomb of Sidi Boumediene** (p149). Just up the road, **Oran** (p139) suggests a Spanish aesthetic grafted onto Algerian soil, but with a French ambience and an irresistible soundtrack of rai music that began in Oran. You could stop off in **Cherchell** (p106) and **Tipaza** (p104) as you head for Algiers, but most people visit these as a day trip from the capital. **Algiers**, (p87) the bustling white capital, can be overwhelming. Fly to evocative **Constantine** (p117) and use it as a base for visiting the Roman cities of **Timgad** (p126) and **Djemila** (p132). **Annaba** (p110) is one of Algeria's most agreeable cities, not least because it boasts **Hippo Regius** (p113).

This route covers around 820km by road, plus the flight from Algiers to Constantine – the flight avoids the roads east of Algiers where the security situation can be unpredictable.

DEEP INTO THE SAHARA   Three Weeks/Algiers to Tassili N'Ajjer National Park

Algiers (p87) has long been one of the most important gateways into the interior of Africa and it can turn your head for as long as you let it, but you've a long journey ahead of you. You could fly to Tamanrasset or Djanet (and you should do so for the return journey), but travelling the first leg of the Trans-Saharan Hwy is one of Africa's great road trips. By the time you reach the five oasis towns that make up **Ghardaïa** (p155), you're already deep into the northern Sahara. Take the opportunity to explore the town itself, but the real fascination here lies in the oases of the M'Zab, home to one of Islam's smallest minorities, the Mozabites (see the boxed text, p160) who are Ibadi Muslims (see the boxed text, p48). You get a real sense of this community at **Beni Isguen** (p160) which is surrounded by ramparts. **Melika** (p161) offers splendid views, while **El-Atteuf** (p162) is the oldest of the M'Zab villages. The dune-surrounded town of **In Salah** (p181) is another convenient place to break up the journey, before pushing on to **Tamanrasset** (p183). From here, the excursions into the wonderful world of the Ahaggar are endless, with **Atakor** (p188), **Assekrem** (p188) and the **Tassili du Hoggar** (p189) some of the most extraordinary vistas anywhere in the Sahara. If you time it right, catch the weekly flight to the often-sleepy, sometimes overrun oasis town of **Djanet** (p191). The **Tassili N'Ajjer National Park** (p194) – the world's most astonishing open-air gallery of millennia-old **rock art** (p80) – is close by and you should spend as much time as you have exploring it.

From Algiers to Tamanrasset is just under 2000km – ideally take a week so you can break up Algeria's longest journey. The excursions from both Tamanrasset and Djanet will require an organised tour using a mixture of 4WD and walking. Flying between Tamanrasset and Djanet is essential.

ROADS LESS TRAVELLED

THE OASES OF THE WEST
Two to Three Weeks/Oran to Ghardaïa

All great desert journeys begin beyond the Sahara's borders in your last taste of civilisation before entering the wilderness. There are no more civilised cities in Algeria than **Oran** (p139) and **Tlemcen** (p146). After crossing the High Plateaus, pause at **Aïn Sefra** (p162), one of the most agreeable oasis towns of the northern Algerian Sahara. It shouldn't be too difficult to avoid the fate of Isabelle Eberhardt (see the boxed text, p163), that great 19th-century traveller who drowned here in 1904. The road winds through the western reaches of the Saharan Atlas and then down around the silent gravitas of the **Grand Erg Occidental** (p162), one of the great sand seas of the Sahara. There are few more evocative Saharan villages on the edge of a sand sea than little **Taghit** (p165) – the dune-fringed oasis town you always imagined as a child. **Beni Abbès** (p166) is equally beautiful. As magical as these places are, nothing quite prepares you for **Timimoun** (p169), which would be many travellers' favourite oasis town in all the Sahara (if they made it this far) and which combines abandoned villages, an escarpment perch and sand dunes. It's the sort of place to relax and soak up the silence for a few days. If you've an extra week up your sleeve, you could make a dash down the Route du Hoggar to **In Salah** (p181) and the rarely visited **Tassili d'Immidir** (p182). Most of you will, however, be more than satisfied to complete a partial circuit of the southern Grand Erg Occidental and on into the oasis towns of the **M'Zab** (p160) and **Ghardaïa** (p155) .

You can make the entire journey (1715km if you don't visit the Tassili d'Immidir, almost 2900km if you do) by public transport (mostly bus, with an occasional shared taxi). If you stay longer in the oasis towns, you easily add a week to your journey.

EASTERN TRAILS   Two to Three Weeks/Ghardaïa to Tassili N'Ajjer National Park

Ghardaïa (p155) and the oasis towns of the **M'Zab** (p160) are fascinating in their own right and are the starting point of many Saharan expeditions, but a less-frequented and very intriguing road to take from there is the one that heads east. **Ouargla** (p176) is a moderately interesting town and **Touggourt** (p175) won't win any beauty contests, but the latter is central to the spirit of modern Saharan exploration – it was here that the first motorised crossing of the Sahara to Timbuktu began in 1922. Touggourt also makes a good base for visiting the ruined mud villages of **Temacine** (p176), which has a *ksar* (castle; fortified stronghold), and **Tamelhat** (p176). The road east passes amid the dunes of the **Grand Erg Oriental** (p172) to **El-Oued** (p172), the 'Town of a Thousand Domes' and one that sees far fewer travellers than it deserves. Returning the way you came, leave the main road south of Touggourt and pass through the oil-service town of **Hassi Messaoud** (p178), whereafter a long, lonely road with almost no public transport bisects the Grand Erg Oriental and finally leaves you in **Illizi** (p191). Deliciously remote, Illizi is for those who love the desert but without the crowds and who love the possibilities inherent in surveying the empty horizons. Short excursions are possible to the impressive rock-art site of **Tamdjert** (p191), but true desert aficionados will want to set out to cross the northern Tassili N'Ajjer en route to **Djanet** (p191). Here you'll rejoin the tourist trail, but after so long off the beaten track you may welcome the company. The extraordinary rock art and twisted rock formations of the **Tassili N'Ajjer National Park** (p194) are your reward for one of the most challenging but worthwhile Algerian journeys.

You'll need your own vehicle to travel south of Hassi Messaoud and you must travel with a guide and an organised expedition from Illizi to Djanet and into the Tassili N'Ajjer National Park. This route covers around 2000km.

TAILORED TRIPS

ROMAN ALGERIA

There's nothing Roman about modern **Algiers** (p87), apart from the **National Museum of Antiquities** (p96) and the fact that Romans took the town in AD 146 and held it for almost four centuries. However, it provides the ideal base for visiting the charming last vestiges of Roman **Tipaza** (p104), which was a favourite of that great Franco-Algerian writer Albert Camus and which meanders amid the pine trees down to the beach. **Cherchell** (p106) doesn't quite have Tipaza's enchanted air, but even Tipaza plays second fiddle to **Djemila** (p132), one of Algeria's most appealing drawcards and one of the most beautiful extant Roman cities in Africa. The setting among the Petit Kabylie hills and the well preserved state of the ruins make this the premier Roman site in Algeria. **Timgad** (p126) also makes it easy to imagine a lively and prosperous Roman city, while the ruins of **Lambèse** (p125) scattered around the village of Tazoult require a lot more imagination. **Tiddis** (p122) is similarly modest but not-to-be-missed if Roman ruins are your thing, while **Hippo Regius** (p113) is Djemila's rival for the title of Algeria's most spectacular Roman site, not to mention a place forever associated with the spirit of St Augustine (see the boxed text, p113).

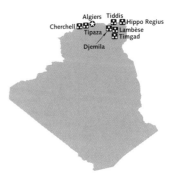

UNESCO WORLD HERITAGE SITES

The gritty, labyrinthine and quintessentially Algerian Casbah in **Algiers** (p93) is the most recent addition to Unesco's list of World Heritage sites in Algeria; it's a worthy member of what is an exceptional group of signature Algerian attractions. **Tipaza** (p104) has also charmed its way onto the list and there was no way that the doyens of the world's most important cultural sites could resist **Timgad** (p126) and **Djemila** (p132) – Roman Algeria clearly caught the eye when Unesco sat down to revise its catalogue in 1982. In the same year, the incomparable rock-art sites and extraordinary natural beauty of the **Tassili N'Ajjer National Park** (p194) were inscribed on the list. Few places in the Sahara can quite match the Tassili N'Ajjer for its exquisite rock art that tells the strangely compelling story of the Sahara's journey from green and pleasant land to the world's largest desert. The **M'Zab Valley** (p155) similarly tells a strange story of survival and isolation, home as it is to one of the last remaining communities of Ibadi Muslims (see the boxed text, p48) anywhere in the world. **Al-Qal'a of Beni Hammad**, the ruined 11th-century seat of the Hammamid emirs, rounds out the list, although the security situation meant that we were unable to visit this time around.

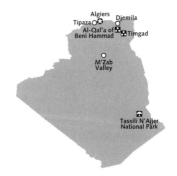

Snapshot

Peace and prosperity, that's all Algerians ask for. Having not had a lot of either for the last 60 years, it's scarcely surprising that these are the two topics that dominate most conversations in Algeria.

For a start, one generation of Algerians is still waiting to hear an apology from France for the estimated one million Algerians who died during the 1954–62 Algerian War of Independence. They've been waiting a long time and aren't exactly holding their breath, but many still live in hope. As bitter as the memories are, looking longingly out across the water towards France is something of a national pastime. So many Algerian immigrants have made their homes in France (and so many more would like to) that the old enemy still holds their attention, with every Algerian desperate for France to take notice in return.

Meanwhile, the next generation of Algerians with its own recent memories of war is hoping against hope that the relative peace of recent years will hold. Scarred by the terror that rained down upon them from all sides during the 1990s, most Algerians you meet will express misgivings about the 2005 amnesty law, even as they proudly tell you that they were among the 97% of Algerians who voted in favour. Yes, criminals have walked free, but for most Algerians that's a necessary evil to help the war recede further into history with every passing day. A resumption of isolated attacks in 2006 and the perennially simmering conflict with the Berber (Amazigh) people of the Kabylie, , and the April 2007 Al-Qaeda attacks nonetheless ensure that Algerians can't imagine relaxing for some time yet.

As the thriving Algerian music, film and literature scenes attest, Algerians are some of North Africa's most imaginative and creative people if given the chance and that chance is all that most Algerians ask for. What's the point in having an education or staying in Algeria if there aren't nearly enough jobs to go around, most Algerians ask. What's the point of democracy if the best option is President Bouteflika, they wonder. And just what is the government so afraid of that they have to crack down on media freedom, causing Algerians to tune in to satellite channels beamed in from elsewhere, they question. What is the good of oil wealth if life never gets any better, they plead.

For the most part, however, they've become tired of asking the same questions over and over again. The cynicism, despair and social dislocation sweeping the country's young do not bode well for Algeria's immediate future.

Algerians are desperate for good news, but it's hard to see from where such good tidings could come. From the banal (Algeria's much-loved and once-successful national football team seems to have lost the art of winning) to the bleak (the Salafist Group for Call and Combat, the GSPC, changed its name to Al-Qaeda in January 2007), Algerians just can't take a trick.

The only consolation is that if the travails of Algeria's recent history have taught Algerians one thing, it is the art of survival.

FAST FACTS

GDP per capita: US$6603

Unemployment: 25%

Inflation: 3%

Life expectancy at birth: 73.26 years (men 71.68; women 74.92)

Oil production: 1.373 million barrels per day

Adult/youth literacy rate: 69.9/90.1%

Population: 33 million

Population under 15/over 65: 30.4/4.5%

Doctors per 100,000 people: 113 (UK: 164)

Under-five mortality rate per 1000 live births: 40 (1970: 220)

History

Although Algerians have always been the mainstay of the story that is Algerian history, it was the great empires of the Mediterranean – the Phoenicians, Romans, Byzantines and Ottoman Turks – the armies of Islam from the east and finally the French who wrote the script. It is only since the second half of the 20th century that Algerians have been given a chance to make history for themselves.

THE GREEN SAHARA

Hundreds of millions of years ago, the Sahara was covered by expansive inland seas. Tens of millions of years ago, the Sahara was a desert larger than it is today. When the Sahara again turned green tens of thousands of years ago, and Europe shivered under the Ice Age, the Sahara became home to lakes and forests and a pleasant Mediterranean climate. Perhaps drawn by this idyllic climate, two distinct races appeared in North Africa between about 15,000 and 10,000 BC: the Oranian and then the Capsian (the former named after Oran in Algeria and the latter after Qafsah – ancient Capsa – in Tunisia). Their integration with indigenous peoples resulted in the spread of Neolithic (New Stone Age) culture and the introduction of farming techniques. The earliest evidence of lasting or semipermanent settlements in Algeria dates from this time.

Rock paintings and carvings in the Tassili N'Ajjer National Park (p194) and elsewhere (see p83) in Algeria, and across the borders in neighbouring Libya and Niger, are the greatest source of knowledge about this time when the Sahara was one of the nicest places to live in all the world. For more information on the Sahara's climatic periods, see p81.

It is from these Neolithic peoples that the Berbers (the indigenous peoples of North Africa; for more information see p40) are thought to descend. Taking into consideration regional variations and the lack of hard evidence, they appear to have been predominantly nomadic pastoralists, although they continued to hunt and occasionally farm. By the time of contact with the first of the outside civilisations to arrive from the east, the Phoenicians, these local tribes were already well established.

Archaeological evidence of human habitation in Algeria has been dated back as far as 200,000 BC, and some scholars believe that the presence of *Homo erectus* goes back further still.

THE PHOENICIAN FOOTHOLD

The strategically located North African coast attracted the attention of the competing seagoing powers of Phoenicia and Greece, and the area's fortunes became inextricably linked to those of its conquerors.

The Phoenicians first came cruising the North African coast around 1000 BC in search of staging posts for the lucrative trade in raw metals from Spain. These ports remained largely undeveloped and little was done to exploit the interior of the continent. From the 7th century BC settlements were established all along the southern rim of the Mediterranean, including at Hippo Regius (in Annaba; p113), Saldae (in Bejaia) and Cesare (in what was formerly Iol, now Cherchell; p106) in Algeria.

The foundation of the major settlement of Carthage is traditionally given as 814 BC. Long politically dependent on the mother culture in

TIMELINE	200,000 BC	15,000–10,000 BC
	The first sign of human habitation in Algeria	The Oranian and Capsian people appear in North Africa

Tyre (in modern Lebanon), Carthage eventually emerged as an independent, commercial empire partly because Tyre came under increasing pressure from the Babylonians, but largely in reaction to Greek attacks on Carthage launched from Sicily. By the 6th century BC, the Phoenicians had established a settlement at Tipaza (p104), with further ports and market towns following at Hippo Regius and Ruiscade (now Skikda).

By the 4th century BC, Carthage controlled the North African coast from Tripolitania (northwestern Libya) to the Atlantic and although the Algerian ports were important, the real power lay in Carthage. Indeed, the ongoing viability of Carthaginian Algeria depended very much on events in Carthage and beyond. The Carthaginians did develop the hinterland, but this extended little beyond the mountains shadowing the Algerian coast. Always, the primary Carthaginian concern was maintaining a safe chain of ports and guarding trade routes.

The Carthaginians are credited with teaching the Numidians and Mauri (who were later called Berbers) advanced agricultural methods. For the most part, however, the Carthaginians uprooted the local tribes and forced them into the desert and mountain hinterland. Trade links between the Carthaginians and the small handful of Berber states grew in importance, but Carthage was not averse to demanding tributes and forcibly recruiting Berber conscripts for their massive army. Berbers made up the largest single group in the Carthaginian army in the 4th century BC.

The rise of the Roman Empire saw the Carthaginians and Romans clash in Sicily, which lead to the Punic Wars and, ultimately, the downfall of Carthage. The first of the Punic Wars lasted from 263 to 241 BC, during which the Carthaginians lost numerous naval battles and finally accepted Roman terms and abandoned Sicily, Sardinia and Corsica. Carthage consolidated its position in Africa but Roman armies landed at Utica (Tunisia) in 204 BC. Carthage capitulated and paid an enormous price, giving up its fleet and overseas territories.

With Carthage weakened by the failure of its overseas conquests, Berber kingdoms grew in power. These included Numidia, which encompassed much of northeastern Algeria, where the powerful King Massinissa held sway from his capital at Cirta Regia (modern Constantine) in the 2nd century BC.

Carthage hung on, despite incessant threats from Massinissa. In 149 BC, during the Third Punic War, the Roman army again landed in Utica, laid siege to Carthage and then overran the city in 146. It is unlikely that the Berbers mourned Carthage's demise. In the meantime, in 148 BC, King Massinissa died and the Berber kingdoms fell into disarray.

ROMAN ALGERIA

Rome quickly brought Carthage under its control and by 64 BC the whole of northern Libya was in Roman hands. Roman attention turned to the west when the Numidian ruler Jugurtha, Massinissa's grandson, massacred a number of Romans who were helping a Roman ally, Adherbal, defend the town of Cirta Regia. Jugurtha managed to resist several attempts by Rome to uproot him, but he was finally betrayed by Bocchus I, a Mauretanian king, in 105 BC. The boundaries of the Roman colony were extended and settlers (mostly veterans) were given land in the area.

Library of Congress – Country Studies (http://lcweb2.loc.gov/frd/cs/dztoc.html) provides a detailed overview of Algerian history in manageable, bite-sized portions.

When the Romans defeated Carthage, they were so afraid of the Carthaginians returning to power that the city was totally destroyed, sprinkled with salt as a symbol and damned forever.

4500–3000 BC	1000 BC
The last regular rain falls in the Sahara whereafter it becomes a desert	The Phoenicians arrive along the Algerian coast

Over the next 50 years, a trickle of Roman settlers moved in, and, after Julius Caesar crushed the last Numidian king, Juba I, in 46 BC, more organised state expansion got underway, fuelled by the realisation that North Africa could become the expanding empire's breadbasket.

When Bocchus II of Mauretania died in 33 BC, bequeathing his kingdom to Rome, Augustus fostered local rule by installing Juba II (a renowned scholar married to the daughter of Cleopatra and Mark Antony). After the murder of Juba's son, Ptolemy, in about AD 40, the kingdom was split into two provinces – Mauretania Caesariensis, with its capital in Caesarea (in modern Algeria), and Mauretania Tingitana, with its capital at Tingis (Tangier).

From this time until the decline of Rome in the 4th century AD, Algeria proved a stable and integral part of the empire. Agriculture was all important, and by the 1st century AD, Africa was supplying more than 60% of the empire's grain requirements. From African ports, too, came the majority of the wild animals used in amphitheatre shows, as well as gold, olive oil, slaves, ivory, ostrich plumes and *garum* (a fish-sauce delicacy in Ancient Rome).

By the middle of the second century, Roman veterans had founded settlements at Tipasa (now Tipaza; p104), Cuicul (Djemila; p132), Thamugadi (Timgad; p126) and Sitifis (Sétif; p128).

The period of Roman rule witnessed increasing urbanisation and prosperity in northern Algeria. The Roman presence saw some Berbers prosper. Some were granted Roman citizenship and many prominent Roman citizens were of Algerian origin; it was these wealthy locals who donated the monumental public buildings that graced the Roman cities of the region. The evidence of their patronage is particularly in evidence at Djemila.

At the same time, Roman encroachment created massive upheaval for the Berber tribes, with many losing agricultural lands and former autonomy. Berber uprisings were frequent. In response, the emperor Trajan (r AD 98–117) built a line of forts surrounding the Massif de Aurés and Nemencha mountains and from Vescera (modern Biskra) to Ad Majores (Hennchir Besseriani, southeast of Biskra) to mark out the southern limits of Roman rule. The southernmost point in Roman Algeria was at Castellum Dimmidi (modern Messaad, southwest of Biskra). Although it would later do so, Roman rule in the 2nd century did not extend west beyond Sitifis (modern Sétif).

With the spread of Christianity following the conversion of the emperor Constantine in AD 313, many of the Roman and Berber inhabitants embraced the new religion. Doctrinal schisms later gave prominence to one of the most famous figures of the early church, St Augustine (see the boxed text, p113), who became Bishop of Hippo Regius.

By the 4th century, tribal rebellion was endemic across the region, a sign that the end was near for Roman Algeria.

Until the end of the 1st century AD, Rome's North African colonies produced one million tonnes of wheat every year, of which a quarter was exported to Rome. By the 2nd century, the levels of olive oil production and export reached similar levels.

THE VANDALS & BYZANTINES

In AD 429, king Gaeseric (or Genseric), who had been busy marauding in southern Spain, decided to take the entire Vandal people (about 80,000 men, women and children) across to Africa, in one of the largest-scale mass migrations in history. By 430, Gaeseric had reached the gates of

814 BC	263–241 BC
The Phoenicians' North African capital is founded at Carthage	The First Punic War between the Romans and Phoenicians

Hippo Regius – St Augustine died during the ensuing siege. Much of northeastern Algeria was soon in the Vandals' possession and by the middle of the century Gaeseric's ships were in control of much of the western Mediterranean. Rome was all but a spent force.

The Vandals confiscated large amounts of property and their exploitative policies accelerated North Africa's economic decline. The Vandals, more adept at pillage and overseas conquests than in administering their colonies, fortified themselves in armed camps and the outlying areas fell once again under the rule of tribal chieftains. The Berbers became increasingly rebellious and, as the Vandals recoiled, small local kingdoms sprang up.

The Byzantine emperor Justinian, based in Constantinople (modern Istanbul), had in the meantime revived the eastern half of the Roman Empire and had similar plans for the lost western territories. His general Belisarius defeated the Vandals in 533. With Byzantine control limited to coastal cities and a few hinterland towns such as Timgad, Berber rebellions in the hinterland reduced the remainder of Algeria to anarchy and the potential prosperity of the provinces was squandered. Byzantine rule was deeply unpopular, not least because taxes were increased dramatically in order to pay for the colony's military upkeep while the cities were left to decay.

THE ARRIVAL OF ISLAM

The Cambridge Illustrated History of the Islamic World by Ira M Lapidus and Francis Robinson is comprehensive and beautifully illustrated, and contains references to Algeria.

With tenuous Byzantine control over Algeria restricted to a few poorly defended coastal strongholds, the Arab horsemen under the command of Amr ibn al-As swept all before them as they made their way across North Africa after having taken Egypt in 640. However, it was not until Uqba bin Nafi al-Fihri began his campaign of conquest that the full military force of Islam was brought to bear on North Africa.

For three years from 669 he swept across the top of the continent, establishing Islam's first great city in the Maghreb, Al-Qayrawan (Kairouan in modern Tunisia). With an army of Arab cavalry and Islamised Berber infantry, he marched into the Atlas and is said to have reached the Atlantic. By 698, the last remnants of Byzantine rule had disappeared and by 712 the entire region from Andalusia to the Levant came under the purview of the Umayyad caliphs (r 661–750) of Damascus.

Abu al-Muhajir Dina, Uqba's successor, cemented Islamic rule in Algeria, converting large numbers of Christian Berbers, especially around Tlemcen. Umayyad governors based in Al-Qayrawan administered eastern Algeria, with less rigorous control to the west.

Despite the rapid success enjoyed by the forces of Islam, the social character of Algeria remained overwhelmingly Berber. While largely accepting the arrival of the new religion, the Berber tribes resisted the Arabisation of the region. Although Arab rule flourished in coastal areas, the enmity between the Berbers (who saw their rulers as arrogant and brutal) and the Arabs (who scorned the Berbers as barbarians) ensured that rebellions plagued much of Algeria's hinterland. A mass rebellion, in reaction to the tyrannical behaviour of the occupying troops and inspired by the Muslim heresy of Kharijism (see the boxed text, p48), set out from Morocco in 740 and conquered the Umayyad armies west of Al-Qayrawan.

148 BC	146 BC
Massinissa, king of the Numidians (Berbers), dies	The Romans defeat and destroy Carthage, bringing Phoenician rule in North Africa to an end

With the shift of the caliphate from the Umayyads in Damascus to the Abbasids in Baghdad in 750, the Muslim west (North Africa and Spain) split from the east. Three major Islamic kingdoms finally emerged in North Africa: the Idrissids in Fès, the Aghlabids in Kairouan and the Rustamids in Tahart in Algeria.

Abd al-Rahman ibn Rustum and his elected successors ruled a vast swathe of central and northern Algeria from Tahirt, southwest of Algiers, from 761 until 909. One of history's few examples of Kharijite or Ibadi rule (see the boxed text, p48), the Rustamids were also some of the most enlightened Islamic rulers of Algerian history, renowned for their patronage for the arts and scholarship in mathematics and astronomy, and for their justice and lack of corruption. Their enlightened ideals didn't extend to forming a permanent army and they were easily swept away by the more powerful Shiite Fatimids. Finding many supporters among the Kabylie Berbers, the Fatimids defeated the Aghlabids before marching on Egypt and founding Cairo in 972.

Before leaving for Egypt, however, the Fatimids entrusted their North African territory (Ifriqiyya, or roughly modern Tunisia and parts of Algeria and Libya) to the rule of the Berber Zirids (972–1148) who founded Algiers and made Algeria the centre of regional power almost for the first time in history. Bejaia also became one of the most important ports in North Africa. However, like the Berber Hammadids (1011–1151), their neighbours to the west, the Zirids were unable to resist pressure from within for religious orthodoxy and officially returned to Sunnism in open defiance of the Fatimids in Cairo.

The reply from Cairo was devastating: the Bani Hilal and Bani Salim (also known as the Bani Sulaim) tribes of Upper Egypt and the Arabian Peninsula were encouraged to invade the Maghreb, and over the following century North Africa was slowly reduced to ruins. The Zirids managed to hang on to a few coastal cities until 1148, while the Hammadids retreated to the coastal town of Bejaia, but northern Algeria had effectively been Arabised.

A Traveller's History of North Africa by Barnaby Rogerson is history made accessible and an ideal companion to your Algerian visit.

BERBER DYNASTIES

As Idrissid power in Morocco expired, a new force emerged from the Sahara. Inspired by a Quranic teacher, Abdallah bin Yasin, the Sanhadja confederation of various Berber tribes began to wage wars throughout the southern and central Sahara in a bid to retain control over trans-Saharan trade routes that were under pressure from the Zenata Berbers in the north. The Sanhadja were known as 'the veiled ones' *(al-mulathamin)* because of their dress, and later as the 'people of the fortress' *(al-murabitin)* – the Almoravids. In 1062 their leader, Youssef bin Tachfin, founded Marrakech as his capital and led troops on a march of conquest that, at its height, saw a unified empire stretching from Senegal in Africa to Zaragoza in northern Spain and reaching east as far as Algiers.

Almoravid rule brought a measure of prosperity to the region and prompted a flourishing of the arts in Andalusia and elsewhere. It was during Almoravid rule that the Grand Mosque of Tlemcen (p148) was built; it would later be used as a prototype for the Grand Mosque of Córdoba.

46 BC	Mid-2nd century AD
Juba I, the last of the Numidian kings, is defeated by the Romans	Rome establishes Algeria's major Roman cities: Djemila, Tipasa and Timgad

Another Moroccan movement, 'those who proclaim the unity of God' *(al-muwahhidin)*, known as the Almohads, denounced the religious laxness of the Almoravids and by 1160, Algeria was in Almohad hands. However, the empire grew too fast and soon began to crumble under its own weight. As it caved in, the Maghreb split into three parts: Ifriqiyya (Tunisia and parts of Libya) came under the Hafsids; Algeria under the Banu Abd al-Wad from Tlemcen; and Morocco under the Merenids. Although borders have changed and imperial rulers have come and gone, this division remains more or less intact today. The Abd al-Wadids (also known as the Zayanids) transformed Tlemcen into a major regional centre. They later formed an alliance with Granada in an effort to survive, but fell to the greater power of the Merenids in 1352.

OTTOMAN ALGERIA

Having successfully driven out the Muslims by 1492, Spain became a leading power in North Africa. They did so by establishing fortified outposts *(presidios)* along the coast from where they exacted tribute from passing ships and the tribes of the interior. Some of their strongholds in Algeria included Mers el-Kebir (1505), Oran (1509), Tlemcen (1510) and Algiers (1510); the Spanish Fort of Santa Cruz (p142) remains to this day.

At around the same time, the Turkish pirate Barbarossa (or Kheireddin; see the boxed text, opposite) and his brother Arudj were permitted to settle on the island of Jerba (Tunisia). Arudj captured Algiers from the Spanish, but they retook the city and killed Arudj in 1518. Thereupon Barbarossa allied himself with the Ottoman Turks in order to protect his Barbary possessions. With Ottoman support he secured control the entire Algerian coast from Oran to Constantine, making Algeria the most powerful foothold for the Ottomans in North Africa.

There was a flurry of activity as Spaniards and Turks fought for supremacy in North Africa. Tripoli fell to the Turks in 1551, followed by Tunis in 1574. Together with Algeria, the three provinces were governed by a pasha, assisted by a dey (administrative chief), a bey (military chief) and janissaries (soldiers, known as *ojaq* in Algeria). Power in fact resided more in the dey in Algeria and the bey in Tunisia, and the pashas were little more than figureheads. The dey's power declined in Algeria with the assassination in 1671 of the last dey elected directly from Turkey.

During Ottoman rule, Algiers was the bastion of direct Ottoman power while the rest of the country was divided into three provinces with their capitals at Constantine, Médéa (south of Algiers) and later, after the Spanish abandoned it in 1791 after a massive earthquake, Oran. Further inland, local tribes enjoyed considerable autonomy and nowhere was this more true than in the Kabylie region.

In fact, almost from the beginning, Turkey's rule over its North African possessions was little more than a formality, although it was sufficiently powerful to exclude Arabs and Berbers from any significant positions. The sultan's name was used in the weekly sermons and new leaders sought confirmation of their nominations from Constantinople, but to all intents and purposes Algeria, Tunisia and Tripolitania acted independently, and frequently attacked one another.

The Ottoman deys (administrative chiefs) were elected for life, but between 1671 and 1830, 14 of the 29 rulers were assassinated before completing their turn.

393–430	430
St Augustine serves as bishop of Hippo Regius	Vandals take control of northern Algeria

---

THE PIRATES OF THE MEDITERRANEAN

In the 16th and the 17th centuries, the secluded harbours and coastal cities from Morocco to Libya were havens for pirates who terrorised seagoing traffic in the southern Mediterranean and exacted tribute (ie protection money) from foreign governments to leave some ships alone.

Also known as corsairs, the pirates even had their own trade union or *taifa* (community) which sought to lobby on behalf of the pirate cause. Businessmen themselves, they understood that their survival depended upon a string of safe ports where no pursuers could track them down. Algiers and Tripoli in particular were cities where the entire economy came to revolve around the profiteering of pirates. Local rulers provided sanctuary and, together with otherwise legal merchants in the home ports, took their cut of the loot.

One of the most picaresque pirates of legend was the Turkish pirate Barbarossa ('Red Beard' or Kheireddin) who changed the course of North African history by securing the region for the Ottoman Turks. Born on the Greek island of Lesbos in 1483, Barbarossa and his brother Arudj quickly showed that they were destined for far greater things than mere pirating.

By 1510, the brothers were some of the richest North Africans of their generation and they seized control of Algiers in 1515. After Arudj was killed in 1518 at Tlemcen, the shrewd Barbarossa sniffed the political wind and realised that Ottoman power was on the rise. After he offered them Algiers, they returned the favour and appointed him governor. Suddenly the pirate-king had become respectable. In 1533, Süleyman the Magnificent was so impressed that he summoned Barbarossa to Constantinople and proclaimed him admiral of the Ottoman fleet. Until his death in 1547, he mounted successful raids on Tunis, Majorca, Italy and Nice on behalf of his Ottoman bosses.

And the name? Although historians hold to the fact that Barbarossa beard was indeed red, there remains some speculation that 'Barbarossa' was simply a mispronunciation of 'Baba Arudj'.

In all three, piracy played a pivotal role in the local economies, and the Barbary pirates, operating mainly from Algiers, Tunis and Tripoli, were the scourge of Europe's Mediterranean shipping. European fleets occasionally blockaded North African ports and attacked the corsairs, but rarely with any lasting effect.

FRANCE TAKES CONTROL

The French presence in North Africa started in earnest in 1830, when they blockaded and attacked Algiers, supposedly because the dey of Algiers had insulted the French consul, but a more likely motive was the need at home for a military success to revive the flagging fortunes of Charles X.

Within three weeks of the French landing, 34,000 French troops took Algiers and the government of the dey had capitulated. The victorious French soldiers wreaked havoc on the Algerian capital, killing and raping thousands of locals, desecrating mosques and cemeteries and looting more than 50 million francs from the Treasury which was located in the Casbah. The French quickly took control of prime real estate and agricultural lands, further alienating and marginalising the local population.

A couple of weeks later, Charles X himself had been overthrown, although by then the French had become entrenched in Algiers and a French parliamentary committee ruled that the occupation should be maintained for no reason other than what it called 'national prestige'.

The Barbary Corsairs: Warfare in the Mediterranean, 1480-1580, by Jacques Heers, is filled with the skulduggery and picaresque adventures of the pirates that raided with impunity from Algeria.

533

Byzantine forces led by Belisarius take North Africa from the Vandals

642

Armies of Islam arrive in Algeria

France annexed occupied Algeria in 1834 and administration (the *régime du sabre,* or 'government of the sword') of the colony was vested in a military governor-general.

Opposition came from Oran in 1832 and most notably from the bey of Constantine who shrewdly replaced Turkish officials with local Arabs and made Arabic the official language. When the French marched on Constantine in 1836, they were roundly defeated, although they finally took the city a year later.

Abdelkader was a Tlemcen-based sherif (descendant of the Prophet) who had been elected locally as the leader in the conflict with the invading European Christians. He was recognised by the French in the Desmichels Treaty of 1834, which effectively gave him control of western and inland central Algeria. Such was his charisma and ability to rally people that, by late 1838, the area under his control stretched from Biskra to the Moroccan border in the south, and from the Kabylie region east of Algiers to Oran in the north – almost two thirds of Algeria. This area virtually constituted a separate state, with its own judicial and administrative system.

By 1840, the French general Bugeaud had 108,000 soldiers in Algeria and one third of the French army was now on Algerian soil. By starving the local population, destroying crops and depopulating the countryside, the French began to claw back territory.

Algeria, by JR Morell, is an enlightening account of a journey through French-occupied Algeria in the 1850s with plenty of 19th-century sniffling and wide-eyed curiosity at local customs.

After a six-year struggle against the French, Abdelkader was forced into Morocco, where he called on the sultan, Abd ar-Rahman, for support. This was provided, but the army was trounced by the French at Isly (near Oujda in Morocco) in 1844. Abdelkader finally surrendered to the French in 1846 on condition that he be allowed to live in the Middle East. Despite this, he was imprisoned in Toulon, Pau and Amboise until 1852; he was finally allowed to settle in Damascus.

By 1847, General Bugeaud had conquered the greater part of the country and had been proclaimed governor-general of Algeria.

ABDELKADER'S LAST YEARS

Abdelkader was by far the greatest figure in Algeria's nationalist movement and is a national hero today, with many streets named after him and a major statue commemorating him in central Algiers. But few Algerian nationalists in the past few centuries have enjoyed such an unlikely retirement as did Abdelkader.

After he surrendered in 1846, he was imprisoned despite having been promised exile. The reason? The French minister of war had once been a French general in Algeria and had bitter memories of having been trounced by Abdelkader. In 1852, Louis Napoleon set him free and even granted him an annual pension of 150,000 francs. Abdelkader moved to Damascus where, in 1860, he acted quickly to avert a planned massacre of Christians by the Ottomans in the Syrian capital, in the process saving an estimated 12,000 lives, including the French consul. And so it was that the French awarded a man who was once one of France's most bitter enemies the Grand Cordon of the Legion of Honour.

He died in Damascus in 1883 after 36 years in exile. After independence, in 1966, Algeria's government brought his remains back to Algeria to mark the 136th anniversary of the French invasion of Algeria. Two years later, the Mosque of Emil Abdelkader (p120) was also built in Constantine in his honour.

761–909	972–1148
The Ibadi Rustamids rule Algeria from Tahirt	Berber Zirid dynasty rules over much of northern Algeria

French domination of the entire north of the country was not achieved until 1871, when the people of the mountains of the Kabylie region were finally subdued.

AN UNHAPPY OCCUPATION

During the first 50 years of French occupation, land was appropriated and European settlers – mainly of French, Italian, Maltese and Spanish origin – established their domination over the local inhabitants. Local culture was actively eliminated, and the Arab casbahs were replaced with streets laid out in grids. The Djemaa el-Kebir of Algiers (p93) was converted to the Cathedral of Saint Philippe, complete with a cross atop its minaret.

At a government level, the administration was dominated by Arabists who were generally more sympathetic towards the local population, a stance which led to increasing tensions between the French government and the *pieds-noirs* (see p42) or ordinary settlers. Napoleon III, who visited Algeria in the 1860s, found a fellow nobility in local tribal chieftains and he began to grow tired of the radicalism and racism of many European settlers in Algiers. His motives were hardly pure – he dreamed of a mostly-Muslim *royaume arabe* (Arab kingdom) with himself as *roi des Arabes* (king of the Arabs). Thwarted by colonial officials sympathetic to the settlers, Napoleon's plans came to nothing and French rule over the local population became increasingly exploitative and repressive.

When Napoleon III was defeated by the Prussians in 1870, French and other European colonists seized power in Algeria. A year later, the Kabylie region began a rebellion that quickly spread across a country that had become impoverished under the French. The French response was to confiscate massive tracts of tribal land, and military rule became even more repressive. Muslim Algerians had essentially become bystanders in their own country and their only permissible contribution to the running of Algeria came in the form of paying high taxes. Needless to say, few of the benefits of tax revenues were enjoyed by locals.

Apart from the wholesale appropriation of the best agricultural land, Algerians were imprisoned without trial and the school system for Algerian children was neglected, something which the sending of a handful of (mostly upper-class) Muslim children to France to further France's 'civilising mission' did nothing to conceal. This latter policy was one which the French would later regret, as the *évolués* (literally 'the evolved ones') began to wonder why French ideals of freedom only applied in France. This group of educated Algerians would plant the seeds of an Algerian nationalist movement in the lead-up to WWII. The more-than-170,000 Algerians who had fought for France during WWI also came to increasingly question French rule in Algeria. One of the most popular leaders was, for a time, Khaled ibn Hashim, the grandson of Abdelkader.

Calls for independence grew louder as predominantly younger Algerians formed nationalist groups and began agitating for autonomy or independence. These efforts culminated in the formation in 1937 of the Parti du Peuple Algérien, which was followed by the establishment of the Association of Algerian Ulama, a largely religious body, in Algeria itself. Although the first nationalist leaders pushed a largely secular line,

The Conquest of the Sahara, by Douglas Porch, is a rollicking tale of French ambitions to conquer the Sahara, with evocative reconstructions of the last days of the ill-fated Flatters mission.

In 1909, Muslims represented 90% of the Algerian population and produced just 20% of the country's income, but paid at least 45% and up to 70% of the taxes levied by the French.

At the end of the 19th century, the French authorities were spending five times more on educating European schoolchildren than they were on the Muslim children who made up 85% of students. In 1870, just 5% of Algerian children attended school.

11th century

Bani Hilal and Bani Salim (Bani Sulaim) sweep across North Africa, completing Algeria's cultural Arabisation

1529

Kheireddin (Barbarossa) establishes Ottoman regency at Algiers

SUBJUGATING THE SOUTH

By 1871, the French had secured effective control over all of northern Algeria, but Algeria's vast south was a different matter altogether. For centuries, the isolated oases of the Algerian Sahara had been largely untouched by events in the north.

The Sahara was the domain of the Tuareg (p41), the nomadic people of the desert, and they survived by serving as both the raiders and protectors of trans-Saharan caravans. Although dispersed throughout the Sahara, they formed loose confederations watched over by sultans who only had as much power as the disparate Tuareg tribes allowed them. From their capitals in Agadez in Niger and the Tassili du Hoggar (p189), the sultans mediated in disputes between Tuareg tribes. The Tuareg known as Kel Ahaggar (the People of the Ahaggar) were, by some accounts, the largest and most powerful Tuareg in all the Sahara.

Having established northern Algeria as their own, the French decided that it was time to seize control of the Sahara and the supposed riches of Central Africa that lay beyond. With dreams of building a railway across the Sahara, the French government sent two expeditions led by Colonel Paul Flatters deep into the Sahara. After the first was turned back by menacing Tuareg and a shortage of supplies, a second reached Amguid at the northwestern limits of the Tassili N'Ajjer escarpment, east of In Salah and north of Tamanrasset. A Tuareg ambush was lying in wait and those who weren't killed in the initial attack died slow and painful deaths on the long trek north. Just 12 out of 97 men survived the expedition. Colonel Flatters was not among them.

This attack bought the nomads time – two decades in fact – but in the first decade of the 20th century, French military expeditions succeeded in defeating the Tuareg and, for the first time, all of Algeria was under French sovereignty.

Islamic groups also grew in popularity, thereby revealing the first signs of a major fault line in Algerian society and one which would, decades later, have a devastating impact upon the country.

Despite ongoing repression, after WWII the French president, Charles de Gaulle, offered citizenship to certain categories of Muslims. This was considered inadequate, and an uprising near Sétif saw the massacre of more than 100 Europeans. Up to 45,000 Algerian Muslims were killed in response. By 1947, however, all Muslims had been given full French citizenship rights and the right to live and work in France. For the French, however, independence was a road too far.

THE ALGERIAN WAR OF INDEPENDENCE

On 1 November 1954, the young guerrillas *(maquisards)* who had formed the new National Liberation Front (FLN) – a body whose stated aim was to bring down the French administration by military means at home and diplomacy abroad – launched a series of attacks across Algeria against a host of French government installations. On the same day, the FLN broadcast a message exhorting Algerians to join the fight for the 'restoration of the Algerian state, sovereign, democratic, and social, within the framework of the principles of Islam'. France's minister of the interior, one François Mitterrand, replied that 'the only possible negotiation is war'. The Algerian War of Independence had begun.

In addition to conventional French forces, the FLN found itself up against colonial farmers vigilante groups whose brutality during *ratonnades* (literally 'rat-hunts') was largely ignored by the French authorities.

Throughout the 1954–62 Algerian War of Independence, the National Liberation Front (FLN) was active among Algerian immigrants in France, and its feuds with other opposition groups led to what were known as the 'café wars' in which nearly 5000 people died.

1671	1791
Assassination of the last dey elected directly from Turkey	The Spanish abandon Oran

With the countryside in turmoil, hundreds of thousands of colons fled to Algiers.

In a bid to curtail the war, Charles de Gaulle sent Jacques Soustelle to Algeria as governor-general with proposals for improving economic conditions for ordinary Algerians, but the FLN massacre of 123 French civilians near Philippeville (near Constantine) in August 1955 and the French retaliation that claimed up to 12,000 Muslim lives announced the outbreak of full-scale war.

By 1956, the fight for Algerian independence was being actively supported by Morocco and Tunisia, both former French protectorates, as well as Egyptian president Gamal Abdel Nasser, the great emerging voice of Arab nationalism. Such support led to the construction by the French of a series of massive barbed-wire fences and observation posts to separate Algeria from both Morocco and Tunisia. The fence along the Moroccan border was over 1000km long, and the remnants can still be seen today.

In 1956, the FLN also began to take guerrilla warfare onto the streets of Algiers and other cities, as immortalised in the classic cult movie *The Battle of Algiers* (p53). The following year, the FLN, who had more than 40,000 guerrillas under arms, called a national strike and in spring alone carried out 800 gun attacks. Their trademark became night raids and ambushes on military and civilian targets. The Massif de Aurès, the Kabylie and the mountainous areas surrounding Oran, Algiers and Constantine became FLN strongholds. In-fighting within the nationalist movement was also a feature of the war and many Muslims suspected of ties to France were also increasingly the subject of FLN attacks.

The French response was equally brutal. French troops were granted permission to use any tactics necessary to quell the rebellion and this blanket immunity was manifested in the torture of prisoners and a policy of collective punishment for villages and families suspected of supporting the FLN. More than two million Muslim Algerians were forcibly resettled. Fighting alongside the 400,000 French troops in Algeria were as many as 150,000 *harkis,* Muslim irregulars loyal to France.

In 1958, with the colons demanding an even stronger French response, Charles de Gaulle took power again and it seemed as if the colons' wish had come true. De Gaulle was seeking an alternative to the FLN and proposed measures favourable to Muslim Algerians. By 1959, the French had secured military control over Algeria, but widespread opposition in France to the war was taking its toll, and former colonies across Africa soon began to gain independence.

The colons had meanwhile come to believe rumours that Charles de Gaulle was moving towards Algerian independence, and they led brand their erstwhile hero as a traitor. Two failed coup attempts and an escalation in terrorism by a settler terrorist organisation, the Organisation de l'Armée Secrète (OAS), were the last throws of the dice by the colons.

Their worst fears were confirmed when the French government opened negotiations with the FLN in Évian in May 1961. The result was a ceasefire due to take effect on 19 March 1962, and a referendum on independence followed in Algeria the same year. The result was six million in favour of independence and only 16,000 against. De Gaulle proclaimed

Frantz Fanon, who wrote *The Wretched of the Earth,* was internationally recognised as the FLN's leading political theorist. His theories included an eloquent justification for the use of violence in achieving national liberation.

The Battle of the Casbah, by Paul Aussaresses, is an unprecedented exposé of French brutality and government complicity during the Algerian War of Independence as told by a former French army officer.

1830	1871
French army invades Algeria and takes control of Algiers	French defeat Berber rebels in the Kabylie region and extend control over all of northern Algeria

Algerian independence on 3 July and it took effect on 25 September. The trickle of French settlers returning to France turned into a flood.

During eight years of war, as many as one million Muslim Algerians were killed (including 70,000 at the hands of the FLN), along with 18,000 French soldiers and 10,000 European civilians.

THE INDEPENDENCE YEARS

Ahmed ben Bella, a leading figurehead of opposition to French rule, became independent Algeria's first elected president. He pledged a 'revolutionary Arab-Islamic state based on the principles of socialism and collective leadership at home and anti-imperialism abroad'.

A Savage War of Peace: Algeria 1954-1962, by Alistair Horne, is detailed and highly readable, and one of the best accounts of Algeria's struggle to be free of French rule.

Despite the euphoria surrounding independence and Ben Bella's popularity, many of the old rivalries that simmered away during the war continued to plague the country and Ben Bella's leadership style did not foster orderly administration in a country still devastated by war. He was overthrown in 1965 by the defence minister and FLN chief of staff, Colonel Houari Boumedienne. Ben Bella spent many years in exile in Switzerland, but he would later return to lead his party, the Movement for Democracy in Algeria (MDA), in 1990.

Boumedienne was a cautious pragmatist. He set about rebuilding the country's economy, which had come unstuck at the time of independence with the departure of the majority of the country's administrators and technical experts, all of whom were Europeans. Unemployment and underemployment remained serious problems and many Algerians were forced to work in France, despite the ill-feeling which existed there towards them.

There was very little political change in Algeria under Boumedienne. The FLN was the sole political party, pursuing basically secular, socialist policies. Bad planning by the lumbering centralised bureaucracy saw agricultural production fall below levels achieved under the French. The economy was saved by the discovery of large gas and oil reserves in the Sahara, but few of the proceeds reached ordinary Algerians.

THE ROAD TO WAR

Colonel Boumedienne died in December 1978 and, at a meeting of the FLN in Algiers, Colonel Chadli Benjedid was elected president. Chadli inherited a country brimming with discontent.

Berber university students and others from the Kabylie region increasingly agitated against the government's Arabisation of government and education. When the government made extremely limited concessions to the Berbers, however, Islamists mounted vociferous protests. A deteriorating economy also pushed many Algerians into the Islamist fold, although how many did so out of disaffection with the failed promises of the independence-era elite rather than genuine religious conviction is not known. Once-liberal Algeria became a social battleground as conservative activists took their protests to the streets, targeting 'indecency' and what they saw as the country's moral decline.

The police cracked down hard on the Islamists. At the same time, the government sought to highlight their own Islamic credentials and drain popular support from the Islamists by opening new mosques and introducing family laws that seriously diminished the rights of women.

1881	1947
Tuareg raiders ambush and massacre the French military expedition of Colonel Paul Flatters in the Sahara	Muslim Algerians receive full French citizenship rights and the right to live and work in France

With the economy in freefall, Chadli abolished the central planning authority, the bastion of socialist economic control. The new legislation removed most public companies from direct government control and freed up the banking system. Chadli moved slowly for fear of opposition within the ruling FLN, as the party's old-timers regarded any moves away from central control of the economy with deep suspicion.

Massive strikes in October 1988 in Algiers quickly turned into riots and spread to Annaba, Blida and Oran. More than 500 people were killed in the resulting violence in what is still remembered as 'Black October'.

The government tried further changes and the 1989 reforms blew through Algerian society like a breath of fresh air. New press freedoms were married to a liberalising of the political system and in 1989, Abbassi Madani and Ali Belhadj founded the Islamic Salvation Front (Front Islamique du Salut; FIS). The FIS quickly outpolled the ruling FLN in local elections.

The first round of Algeria's first free multiparty elections, held on 26 December 1991, produced another landslide for the FIS. Of the 231 seats decided (out of 430 in the National Assembly), the FIS took 188. The FLN won just 15 seats, 10 fewer than the Socialist Forces Front (FFS) – a Berber party.

The army stepped in, dissolving parliament, persuading Chadli to step down and replacing him with a five-man Haut Conseil d'Etat (HCE) led by President Mohammed Boudiaf. The second round of elections was cancelled, FIS leaders Abbas Madani and Ali Belhadj were arrested and others fled into exile.

Boudiaf lasted barely six months before he was assassinated in bizarre circumstances while opening a cultural centre in Annaba. The official line was that Boudiaf had been shot by a lone gunman, who also managed to wound 40-odd members of the audience before escaping undetected by the legions of security guards at the scene. Adding that the gunman had acted out of religious conviction didn't make the story any more plausible. There were suggestions that Boudiaf was the victim of an establishment plot hatched by people opposed to his attempts to tackle institutionalised corruption.

Whatever the truth of the matter, he was replaced by a hardliner in former FLN stalwart Ali Kafi, who remained at the helm until he was replaced by a former general, Liamine Zéroual, on 31 January 1994, with the country on the brink of civil war.

London-based Darf Publishers (www.darf publishers.co.uk) should be your first stop when trying to track down hard-to-find travellers' accounts of North Africa; there's a Libya focus but plenty available on Algeria.

CIVIL WAR OR THE 'SECOND WAR OF LIBERATION'

Initial reports that Islamic leaders had rejected violence as a means of taking power from the military soon proved ill-founded. By the end of April 1994, more than 3000 people had died in the civil war that militants were calling the second war of liberation.

The rising death toll included a growing list of foreigners, most of them resident in the country. Among the victims were 12 Croatian engineers whose throats were slit after their attackers confirmed that the victims were Christians. Eight others were spared after convincing their attackers that they were Bosnian Muslims. Attacks against foreigners have been justified on two grounds: firstly, to sabotage Algeria's already

1954–62	25 September 1962
Algerian War of Independence	Algeria becomes independent

troubled economy – which many regard as being propped up by the West; and secondly, as vengeance on the 'spies of the unbelievers in the land of Islam'.

The vast majority of victims, however, were Algerians. Particularly targeted by guerrillas were policemen, mayors, judges and Francophile intellectuals. The attacks were claimed by various underground groups such as the Groupes Islamiques Armés (GIA) and the Mouvement Islamique Armé (MIA). The government responded with displays of force and the mass arrests of suspects. There was also irrefutable evidence that the government set up its own shadowy paramilitary groups which operated like South American–style death squads as they carried out (often collective) revenge killings.

The blood-letting peaked at 300 deaths a week in early 1994, signalling the failure of a so-called commission of national dialogue to have any impact on proceedings. It also signalled the end of the road for President Kafi.

President Liamine Zéroual proved unable to stem the tide of violence and in July 1995, the GIA exploded a bomb on the Paris Metro and in December hijacked an Air France airliner in Algiers. A November 1996 referendum approved constitutional reforms but for Algeria at the time it was one step forward, two steps back. During the first two weeks of Ramadan in 1997, more than 300 people were killed and grisly ritual massacres, reportedly by both sides, kept the country in a state of terror. In elections in 1997, legal Islamist parties such as the Movement of Society for Peace and the Islamic Renaissance Movement won around 22% of the vote.

With the population exhausted by almost a decade of war in which nearly 100,000 people were killed, the FIS offered to disband its military wing, although another group, the Salafist Group for Call and Combat (GSPC) vowed to continue the reign of terror. In April 1999, the military's preferred candidate, Abdelaziz Bouteflika, won elections boycotted by opposition parties.

The killings continued.

ALGERIA TODAY

Although no-one can say for certain when the war ended, by 2002 the main guerrilla groups had either been defeated or had accepted the offers of a government amnesty. That's not to say that Algeria's problems are over.

Modern Algeria, by John Ruedy, is one of few English-language histories of Algeria to have been updated in recent years (make sure you have the second edition published in 2005) and includes the 2004 elections.

The Algerian economy has been devastated by war and unemployment, and social dislocation remains high. In the predominantly Berber (Amazigh) Kabylie region, there is increasing discontent over unheeded demands for autonomy and recognition of Berber languages and culture. Security forces clashed repeatedly with the Kabylie Citizens' Movement into 2003 with a mounting death toll the only discernible result.

President Bouteflika consolidated his hold on power in parliamentary elections in May 2003 and in 2004 he became the first-ever Algerian president to be re-elected by popular vote. The elections were, however, marred by allegations of vote-rigging.

A feature of President Bouteflika's rule has been attempts to heal the deep scars that still divide Algeria. Although there was some disquiet

26 December 1991	1992
Algeria's first multiparty elections won by FIS Islamist party	Algerian army dissolves parliament and cancels second round of elections

about such moves among human rights groups and victims' groups, the Civil Harmony Act and Charter for Peace and National Reconciliation were approved by 97% of voters in a referendum in September 2005. The laws provided an amnesty for most crimes committed in the course of the war, and under the law Ali Belhadj, one of the founders of the FIS, was released.

The spectre of terrorism also remains a primary concern for Algerians. Although the GSPC announced in March 2005 that it could be prepared to disarm and accept the government's offers of amnesty, it then formally allied itself with Al-Qaeda in September 2006. In January 2007, the GSPC formally changed its name to Al-Qaeda. GSPC militants were responsible for kidnapping 32 European travellers in the Algerian Sahara in 2003 and Al-Qaeda claimed responsibility for the serious bomb attacks of April 2007 which killed dozens and injured more than 100 people. They are believed to still have their base in Algeria's extreme southwest, close to the border with Mali.

AllAfrica.com (www
.allafrica.com) is the
place to go for non-
mainstream news cover-
age of Algerian history as
it happens.

1994–2002	September 2005
Civil war	Some 97% of Algerians vote for government amnesty for crimes committed during the civil war

The Culture

THE NATIONAL PSYCHE

Although exceptions exist, Algerians are a forthright, passionate people who can seem to carry within them all the optimism, vision and conflict that the country itself possesses. Few require much prompting to voice what they see as the ills of their country, whether it be the president and his shortcomings or the Islamists and their fanaticism. Anger is a common emotion as Algerians look around at the country's abundant natural wealth and compare it with their own poverty – they're tired of official excuses and politicians of every ilk squabbling over riches that never seem to reach people like them.

Another common response to the perceived ills of the country is a sense of defeat. It is not unusual in Algiers and Oran in particular to find men of any age simply staring out to sea, dreaming of a better life in Europe; the women are most likely too busy to have time. Among these are the *hittistes* (see the boxed text, below), the vast numbers of young, sometimes educated men – almost a third of the population is under 30 and the youth literacy rate stands at 90% – who have grown tired of waiting for the promises of a new Algeria to become real and have been left with nothing to do and nowhere to go. As one Algerian told us, Ramadan was quite easy for him because he didn't get to eat during the day during any other month of the year anyway.

At the same time, the Algerian middle class is as sophisticated as any in the Arab world, their refined sensibilities, creativity and love of intellectual debate as evident as their dream that Algeria will one day be a tolerant, wealthy and peaceful society.

As Algerian passions repeatedly spill over and subside, home-grown music (most likely rai) provides the soundtrack, tracing the frenetic, roller-coaster ride that is the Algerian existence and reminding people just why, in spite of everything, they are so proud to be Algerian.

LIFESTYLE

Life for the ordinary Algerian revolves around the family, a bond that took on added significance during the years of conflict surrounding independence and the 1990s. Such has been the exodus of Algerians to Europe, especially France, that these bonds became infinitely more

---

WHAT ARE 'HITTISTES'? *Zahia Hafs*

On busy streets, you will see young men standing around, leaning against walls, idling the day away. These are referred to as *'hittistes'*, from *'hit'*, meaning wall. Literally they are said 'to hold the wall'. They are jobless young men in their 20s, struggling to make a few dinars each day, if they are lucky, by selling small items. About 80% of the unemployed are under 30 and most of them are unqualified, which makes the search for work almost impossible. Most of the time they have nothing to do besides hanging around, talking to friends, watching girls go by and trying to chat them up. They usually stick to the same wall, making it their territory. Maybe it is a way to have their own space when they lack privacy at home. They all dream of greener pastures, somewhere on the other side of the Mediterranean.

When the Berlin wall fell in 1989, the running joke was: 'Instead of breaking down the wall, the Germans should send it to us…'. No matter how hard a situation is, Algerians always find a way to make light of it with their sense of humour.

complicated in the second half of the 20th century. However, the massive strain on social services ensures that family support networks – including remittances from overseas – nonetheless remain as important as ever.

Grafted onto the immediate family are multiple layers of identity, among them extended family, tribe and village, with an overarching national component of which every Algerian is proud, albeit with reservations. The nuclear family was traditionally large with numerous children, although some, mainly urban, Algerians now opt for a more manageable Western-style number of offspring.

Men generally marry later than women (for men the average age is 33, for women 29, the relative lateness of which is partly attributable to the high cost of staging weddings) and arranged marriages still frequently take place between the children of male cousins. This is, however, becoming increasingly rare in urban areas and in particular among families where members have returned to Algeria after years of living in Europe. This amalgam of Algerian and European values is one of the most fundamental changes determining the Algerian future, although the results are far from clear.

Life expectancy (73.26 years) is one of the highest in Africa and literacy (approaching 70%) is respectable, but these figures conceal overloaded health and education systems that many Algerians see as boding ill for the country's future. Housing is another major problem, particularly with the movement of people from rural areas into the larger cities in recent decades.

> Each adult woman now gives birth to an average of 1.89 children, a far cry from the early 1990s when population growth rates were out of control and the country's population was doubling every 20 years.

ECONOMY
The Good News
Algeria is one of the richest countries in Africa and in 2006 Algeria ranked third (behind neighbours Libya and Tunisia) among mainland African countries on the UN's Human Development Index, which ranks countries according to a range of economic and quality-of-life indicators. Such apparent wealth reflects the country's formidable natural resources: Algeria has the seventh-largest natural gas reserves in the world, is the second-largest exporter of natural gas and has the 14th-largest reserves of oil. High oil prices in recent years has meant that Algeria has a significant trade surplus, its external debt has been considerably reduced, inflation is low and GDP per capita sits at a comfortable US$6603.

In pre-oil days and during the French occupation, agriculture was the mainstay of the Algerian economy and it remains an important feature of the domestic market, even as it contributes little to the country's export earnings.

> Just 3% of Algeria is suitable for agriculture, but somehow Algeria manages to be 70% self-sufficient in food, up from just 40% 15 years ago. Major crops include wheat, barley, grapes, olives and citrus fruits.

The Bad News
That the Algerian economy is on the upswing only partially hides the fact that it has a long way to climb. The damage done to the economy by the years of civil war is still being felt and although investors are starting to return, unemployment remains high and general living standards are taking a long time to reach the potential that the Algerian economy undoubtedly has. As such, the issue of more equitably distributing Algeria's considerable wealth to ensure that all Algerians benefit – a quarter of Algerians live below the poverty line – is a matter of daily concern for Algerians.

The other major issue confronting the country's economic planners is how to diversify an economy that is almost wholly dependent on oil. High oil prices, promising results from recent oil and gas prospecting and high demand among Western countries for Algeria's low-sulphur oil conceals the fact that oil and natural gas account for 95% of export earnings. That's fine for the present, but the day that Algeria runs out of oil is one that most Algerians prefer not to think about.

POPULATION

Together, Arabs and Berbers make up 99% of the population. Historically these two groups have intermarried, making demarcation difficult, although most estimates suggest that 75% of the population consider themselves to be Arab, with a further 20% to 25% Berber. Other groups include the Tuareg and a small handful of *pieds-noirs* (French Algerians).

Algeria's population density stands at 13.8 people per sq kilometre, although so vast is Algeria's largely uninhabited desert region that population density in northern regions is much higher than these figures suggest. Around 60% of Algerians live in cities, but this figure is rising.

Arabs

The question of who the Arabs are exactly is still widely debated. Are they all the people speaking Arabic, or only the residents of the Arabian Peninsula? Fourteen centuries ago, only the nomadic tribes wandering between the Euphrates River and the central Arabian Peninsula were considered Arabs, distinguished by their language. However, with the rapid expansion of Islam, the language of the Quran spread to vast areas.

The first wave of Arab migration came in the 7th century as the armies of Islam spread rapidly across North Africa and established Arab-Muslim rule as far afield as Andalusia in what is now southern Spain. But it was not until the 11th century that vast numbers of Arab settlers from the Bani Salim and Bani Hilal tribes on the Arabian Peninsula arrived and the cultural Arabisation of the region began. The reason behind the migration was an attempt by the Fatimid dynasty ruling Egypt at the time to increase its hegemony over the outlying reaches of its empire. The Bani Salim largely remained in the eastern Libyan region of Cyrenaica, while it was the Bani Hilal who colonised large parts of northern Algeria.

Although the Arabs were relatively few in number in Algeria, their culture quickly became established through language and intermarriage. The term 'Arab' came to apply to two groups: in addition to the original nomadic Arabs, the settled inhabitants of newly conquered provinces such as Algeria also became known as Arabs.

Berbers

Berbers claim to be the descendants of North Africa's original inhabitants and most historians believe this to be true, arguing that the Berbers descend from the Neolithic peoples who arrived in the area up to 17,000 years ago. Other historians claim that the Berbers are descended from the remnants of the great Garamantian empire, which flourished in the Fezzan region of southern Libya from around 900 BC to AD 500. Otherwise, little is known about their origins.

The name 'Berber' has been attributed to a collection of communities by outsiders, but rarely, until recently, by the Berbers themselves. The name is thought to derive from the Latin word '*barbari*', the word used in Roman times to classify non-Latin-speakers along the North African coast. 'Berber' is used as a loose term for native speakers of the various Berber dialects, most of which go by the name of Tamazigh. In fact, many Berbers do not even use a word that unites them as a community, preferring instead to define themselves according to their tribe.

A History of the Arab Peoples, by Albert Hourani, is the definitive text when it comes to Arab history painted in broad brush strokes. Better still, it's written in a lively style and is easy to dip into or read in full.

Amazigh Online (www .amazighonline.com) lists links to a host of interesting websites dedicated to the Berber (Amazigh) people, from scholarly articles to lively social and cultural debates.

When Arab tribes swept across North Africa in the 7th and 11th centuries, many Berbers retreated into the mountain and desert redoubts which they continue to occupy. In Algeria, by far the largest concentration of 'Berbers' are the Kabyles who inhabit the Kabylie Mountains in northeastern Algeria. Most often, groups from this region do not call themselves Berber at all, but, like the Tuareg, prefer to be known as Imazighen (singular: Amazigh), which means 'the noble and the free'. Other 'Berber' groups include the Chaouia in the mountains south of Constantine, as well as communities throughout the Atlas Mountains from Blida to the Moroccan border and beyond, and in the M'Zab region close to Ghardaïa.

Historical Dictionary of the Berber (2006) by Hsain Ilahiane is the most comprehensive study of the history and culture of the Berber people of North Africa, with a range of alphabetical entries and maps.

The key touchstones of Berber identity are language and culture, although most Berbers are now bilingual, speaking their native language and Arabic. Within the Berber community, loyalty is primarily to the family or tribe. Households are organised into nuclear family groups, while dwellings within a village or town are usually clustered in groups of related families.

In keeping with their centuries-long resistance to foreign domination and to the imposition of religious orthodoxy, many Berbers belong to the Kharijite or Ibadi sect (see the boxed text, p48). True to their religious beliefs, Berber communities have long prided themselves on their egalitarianism. The traditional Berber economy consists of farming and pastoralism, meaning that most people live sedentary lifestyles, tied to their particular patch of land, while a small minority follows seminomadic patterns, taking flocks to seasonal pasturelands.

The Tuareg, by Jeremy Keenan, is considered one of the best and most readable anthropological studies of the Algerian Tuareg.

Although Berber agitation for sweeping autonomy in Algeria is unlikely to be granted any time soon, recent years have seen an increase in Berber-language education in Berber areas and Tamazigh is now recognised as a 'national language', although not an official one.

Tuareg

The Tuareg are the nomadic, camel-owning bearers of a proud desert culture who traditionally roamed across the Sahara from Mauritania to western Sudan.

The two main Tuareg groups in Algeria, whose members number an estimated 75,000, are the Kel Ahaggar from the Tassili du Hoggar and the Kel Ajjer from the area around Djanet, although within each group there are various subgroups which have slightly different languages and customs.

TUAREG ORIGINS

The origins of the Tuareg are not fully understood, although it is widely agreed that the Tuareg were once Berbers from regions stretching from southeastern Morocco to northeastern Libya. There are indeed marked similarities between many words in the Tuareg language of Tamashek and those in the Berber language of Tamazigh. When the Arab armies of Islam forced many Berbers to retreat into the desert in the 7th century, and when waves of Arab migration swept through the region in the 11th century, those who would become Tuareg fled deep into the desert where they have remained ever since.

Tuareg stories about their origins largely concur with this version of history, although most Algerian Tuareg claim to be descended from a single noblewoman, Tin Hinan, who arrived in the Tassili du Hoggar astride a white camel having journeyed from the Tafilalt region of southeastern Morocco. Finding the land to be largely uninhabited, the Tuareg say, Tin Hinan decided to stay and she became the mother of all Tuareg.

The Tuareg traditionally followed a rigid status system with nobles, blacksmiths and slaves all occupying strictly delineated hierarchical positions, although the importance of caste identity has diminished in recent years. Until the early 20th century, the Tuareg made a fiercely independent living by raiding sedentary settlements, participating in long-distance trade and exacting protection money from traders passing across their lands.

The veils or *taguelmoust* that are the symbols of a Tuareg's identity – the use of indigo fabric which stained the skin has led them to be called the 'Blue People of the Sahara' – are both a source of protection against desert winds and sand, and a social requirement. For more information on the *taguelmoust,* see the boxed text, p68.

Traditionally, Tuareg women are not veiled, enjoy a considerable degree of independence and play a much more active role in the organisation of their society than do their Arab or Berber counterparts. Descent is determined along matrilineal lines.

The name 'Tuareg' is a designation given to the community by outsiders and it is only recently that the Tuareg have begun to call themselves by this name. The name is thought to be an adaptation of the Arabic word *'tawarek',* which means 'abandoned by God' – a reference both to the hostility of the land the Tuareg inhabit and to what other Muslims consider their lax application of Islamic laws. The Tuareg themselves have always, until recently, preferred to be known as 'Kel Tamashek' (speakers of the Tamashek language), 'Kel Taguelmoust' (People of the Veil) or 'Imashaghen' (noble and the free).

Traditional Tuareg society is rapidly breaking down, mainly due to the agrarian reform policies of the government, the influx of large numbers of Arabs from the north and a series of crippling droughts which have forced many people into the towns to search for work. For more information on the changes to Tuareg life, see the boxed text, p77.

The Pastoral Tuareg, by Johannes and Ida Nicolaesen, is a two-volume, encyclopaedic study of the Tuareg, especially those of southern Algeria. It's a great addition to your reference library.

Pieds-Noirs

Although few remain, the *pieds-noirs* (singular: *pied-noir*) are crucial to any understanding of Algeria's population mix. They are the 'Black Feet' or predominantly French settlers and their descendants in Algeria; the name is also used to refer to Algerian Jews.

After France occupied Algeria in the first half of the 19th century, settlers from all over southern Europe began arriving en masse. At first called colons, they planted deep roots in Algerian soil and by the 20th century most considered themselves to be more Algerian than French (except, it must be said, for many cases, when dealing with Muslim Algerians). By 1926, over 15% of the population were *pieds-noirs.* By 1959, there were more than one million *pieds-noirs* in Algeria – 10% of the population – and they accounted for more than 30% of the population of Algiers and Oran. There was also a large *pied-noir* population in Annaba.

The name *'pied-noir'* has been attributed to the fact that people of French origin in Algeria wore black boots, although in the early 20th century the name referred to all indigenous Algerians.

From 1954, as the country descended into a war of independence, the *pieds-noirs* fiercely supported France and were in turn targeted by Algerian nationalist forces. When President Charles de Gaulle effectively sanctioned Algerian independence in 1962, the *pied-noir* community levelled accusations of betrayal at the French government, but to no avail: 900,000 *pieds-noirs* fled Algeria in 1962, thereby gutting government administration in many places such as Oran. Many also laid waste

FAMOUS FRENCH PEOPLE WITH ALGERIAN ROOTS

Although not all considered themselves to be *pieds-noirs* (Black feet; descendants of French settlers), the following are some of the most famous French people to have been born on Algerian soil.

■ Louis Pierre Althusser (1918–90) One of the leading Marxist philosophers of the 20th century.

■ Albert Camus (1913–60) A leading light in the existentialist school of thought (although he rejected the designation), Camus won the Nobel Prize for Literature in 1957 and some of his novels are set in Algeria.

■ Jacques Derrida (1930–2004) The father of deconstruction theory was another of the most eminent philosophers of the 20th century.

■ Yves Saint-Laurent (1936–) The exclusive French fashion designer was born in Oran and served briefly as a conscript in the French army during the Algerian War of Independence.

■ Edith Piaf (1916–1953) One of the iconic French voices of the 20th century, Mme Piaf's maternal grandmother came from the Kabylie region of northeastern Algeria.

■ Zinedine Zidane (1972–) Although the three-time World Footballer of the Year was born in Marseille and played for France, his parents were from the Kabylie region and many Algerians still claim him as their own; in 2006 he returned for a visit to the region.

to their properties so that they would be useless to Algerians. The effect on the Algerian economy was catastrophic.

Once they arrived in France – a place many *pieds-noirs* had never visited – most *pieds-noirs* were left to fend for themselves. Embittered by what they saw as France's rejection and angered by criticism of the *pieds-noirs'* often brutal tactics during the 1954–62 war, many chose to migrate to the Americas, Spain or New Caledonia. The *harkis* – Muslim Algerians who had supported French rule – fared even worse, as thousands were refused visas for France and were massacred by the National Liberation Front (FLN) after the French left. Around 100,000 *pieds-noirs* elected to remain in Algeria, but by the 1980s there were fewer than 3000 left.

The Architecture of Memory: A Jewish-Muslim Household in Colonial Algeria 1937-62, by Joelle Bahloul, is an intimate portrait of the last days of the Algerian Jewish community who had lived in Algeria for millennia.

Jews

Although Algerian Jews were often historically called pieds-noirs, they occupied a distinctive place in Algerian society from Roman times until 1994. Following their expulsion from Spain (especially Andalusia) in 1492, many Jews settled in Algeria, with particularly large communities putting down roots in Algiers and Oran. Algerian Jews were granted French citizenship in 1870 and by 1931 Jews made up 2% of Algeria's population and more than 10% of the populations of Constantine, Ghardaïa, Sétif and Tlemcen.

Algeria's postindependence government bestowed Algerian independence only upon Muslims and the overwhelming majority of the 150,000 Jewish Algerians fled to France. Following the Armed Islamic Group's declaration of war on all non-Muslims in Algeria in 1994, all but a handful of the last remaining Jews left the country and the final functioning synagogue in Algiers closed down. Many fled to Israel where they were granted instant citizenship. It is believed that fewer than 100 Jews remain in Algeria, with most of these living in Algiers.

SPORT

When Lakhdar Belloumi fired home Algeria's second goal to defeat West Germany in the first game of the 1982 World Cup, hopes were high that Algerian football (soccer) was entering a golden age and that Algeria was on the verge of becoming a major footballing power. Those hopes continued as Algeria again qualified for the World Cup finals in 1986 and went on to win the African Nations' Cup in 1990. The promise was never realised and Algerian football has been in decline ever since, a state of affairs made all the more sad by the fact that football is wildly popular in Algeria and it is difficult to overestimate the passions which the sport inspires here. In a sign of how far the Algerian national team (known as the Desert Foxes) has fallen, in 10 qualifying matches for the 2006 World Cup, Algeria won just one game and finished behind Angola, Nigeria, Zimbabwe and Gabon. As a result, Algerian football fans are largely restricted to cheering for Algerian footballers plying their trade in Europe – Madjid Bougherra, Ali Benarbia and Brahim Hemdani are among the better-known – or staking a claim for three-time World Footballer of the Year Zinedine Zidane who in return is quite publicly proud of his Kabylie Algerian roots.

Another important sport among Algerians is athletics. The Algerian national team came third at the 1999 African Games. Algeria's plans to host the 2007 African Games were thrown into disarray when Algeria was suspended from international track and field competitions due to government interference in the sport.

Other popular sports include volleyball, handball, boxing and martial arts, including a Maghrebi martial art known as El-Matreg in which two players fight using long sticks. In southern desert regions, horse and camel racing are popular, especially among the Tuareg during local festivals.

> In 1992 Hassiba Boulmerka won Algeria's first-ever Olympic Gold Medal in the women's 1500m running. Boulmerka's feat was emulated four years later by Noureddine Morceli, who won gold in the men's 1500m.

MEDIA

Radio and TV stations are government-owned and content is strictly controlled, which is the major reason why most Algerians tune into satellite TV stations from France and across the Arab world. When it comes to newspapers, many are privately owned and do – somewhat bravely, it must be said – criticise the government on a regular basis. That said, it is a criminal offence punishable by prison sentence to 'insult' or 'defame' the president, members of parliament, judges or the army; Algerian newspapers mark the passage of this law with an annual 'day without newspapers'. The government has proved itself more than willing to abuse this law and in 2005 alone, 114 journalists were prosecuted under the law, of whom 111 were fined or sent to prison. Newspapers that openly campaigned against the re-election of President Bouteflika are particularly targeted.

Internet censorship is less prevalent, although the Paris-based Reporters Without Borders speculates that this may be more to do with government ignorance than any new spirit of openness.

> According to Reporters Without Borders (www.rsf.org), Algeria ranks 126th out of 167 countries in a ranking of world press freedom.

Algerian journalists not only have to run the gauntlet of government paranoia, but have also been targeted by Algeria's militant Islamist opposition. Between 1993 and 1997, 57 journalists were killed, with most murders blamed on armed Islamist groups. Although the situation has improved, journalism is still a perilous occupation in Algeria.

RELIGION

Sunni Islam is the official state religion in Algeria, adhered to by an estimated 99% of the population and one of the few things which unites Algeria's often fractious population. There are also Christian communities that are more historically than numerically significant.

Islam

THE BIRTH OF ISLAM

Abdul Qasim Mohammed ibn Abdullah ibn Abd al-Muttalib ibn Hashim (the Prophet Mohammed) was born in AD 570 in Mecca in what is now

Saudi Arabia. Mohammed's family belonged to the Quraysh tribe, a trading family with links to Syria and Yemen. By the age of six, Mohammed's parents had both died and he came into the care of his grandfather, the custodian of the Kaaba in Mecca. When he was around 25 years old, Mohammed married Khadija, a widow and a merchant and he worked in running her business.

At the age of 40, in 610, Mohammed retreated into the desert and began to receive divine revelations from Allah via the voice of the Archangel Gabriel – the revelations would continue for the rest of Mohammed's life. Three years later, Mohammed began imparting Allah's message to the Meccans. Mohammed soon gathered a significant following in his campaign against Meccan idolaters and his movement appealed especially to the poorer, disenfranchised sections of society.

Islam provided a simpler alternative to the established faiths which had become complicated by hierarchical orders, sects and complex rituals, offering instead a direct relationship with God based only on the believer's submission to God ('Islam' means submission).

Among Mecca's ruling families, however, there was a dawning recognition of the new faith's potential to sweep aside the old order. By 622, these families had forced Mohammed and his followers to flee north to the oasis town of Medina. There, Mohammed's supporters rapidly grew in number. In 630, Mohammed returned triumphantly to Mecca at the head of a 10,000-strong army to seize control of the city. Many of the surrounding tribes quickly swore allegiance to him and the new faith.

When Mohammed died in 632, the Arab tribes spread with missionary zeal, quickly conquering all of what is now the Middle East. By 670, the armies of Islam had arrived in Algeria and they had established themselves in Andalusia by 710, an astonishing achievement given the religion's humble desert roots.

THE QURAN

For Muslims, the Quran is the word of God, directly communicated to the Prophet Mohammed; unlike the Torah and Bible, which are the interpretative work of many individuals, the Quran is believed by Muslims to be the direct word of Allah. It contains 114 suras (chapters) which govern all aspects of a Muslim's life, from their relationship with God to minute details about daily living (p47).

In addition to drawing on moral ideas prevalent in 7th century Arabia, some of the Quran's laws closely resemble those of the other monotheistic faiths, particularly the doctrinal elements of Judaism and the piety of early eastern Christianity. The suras contain many references to the earlier prophets – Adam, Abraham (Ibrahim), Noah, Moses (Moussa) and Jesus (although Muslims strictly deny his divinity) are all recognised as prophets in a line that ends definitively with the greatest of them all, the Prophet Mohammed; 21 of the 28 prophets are mentioned in the Bible.

It is not known whether the revelations were written down during Mohammed's lifetime. The third caliph, Uthman (644–656), gathered together everything written by the scribes and gave them to a panel of editors under the caliph's aegis. A Quran printed today is identical to that agreed upon by Uthman's compilers 14 centuries ago.

Another important aspect of the Quran is the language in which it is written. Some Muslims believe that the Quran must be studied in its original classical Arabic form ('an Arabic Quran, wherein there is no crookedness', sura 39:25) and that translations dilute the holiness of its sacred texts. For Muslims, the language of the Quran is known as *sihr*

Muslims attribute a place of great respect to Christians and Jews as *ahl al-kitab*, the People of the Book (sura 2: 100–115). However, Muslims believe the Quran is the final expression of Allah's will and the definitive guide to his intentions for humankind.

halal (lawful magic). Apart from its religious significance, the Quran, lyrical and poetic, is also considered one of the finest literary masterpieces in history.

THE FIVE PILLARS OF ISLAM

To live a devout life and as an expression of submission to Allah, a Muslim is expected to adhere to the Five Pillars of Islam.

Profession of Faith (Shahada)

This is the basic tenet of Islam: 'There is no God but Allah and Mohammed is his prophet' *(La illaha illa Allah Mohammed rasul Allah)*. It is commonly heard as part of the call to prayer and at other events such as births and deaths.

Prayer (Sala)

Ideally, devout Muslims will pray five times a day when the muezzins call upon the faithful, usually at sunrise, noon, mid-afternoon, sunset and night. Although Muslims can pray anywhere (only the noon prayer on Friday should be conducted in the mosque), a strong sense of community makes joining together in a mosque preferable to praying elsewhere.

Alms-Giving (Zakat)

Covering Islam (1981), by Edward Said, is a searing study of how stereotypes have shaped our view of Islam, Muslims and the Middle East. Although the examples used are dated, the book remains as relevant today as when it was written.

Alms-giving to the poor was, from the start, an essential part of Islamic social teaching and was later developed in some parts of the Muslim world into various forms of tax to redistribute funds to the needy. The moral obligation towards one's poorer neighbours continues to be emphasised at a personal level, and it is not unusual to find exhortations to give alms posted up outside some mosques. Traditionally Muslims are expected to give a 40th of their annual income as alms to the poor.

Fasting (Sawm)

Ramadan, the ninth month of the Muslim calendar, commemorates the revelation of the Quran to Mohammed. In a demonstration of a renewal of faith, Muslims are asked to abstain from sex and from letting anything pass their lips from sunrise to sunset every day of the month. This includes smoking. For the dates when Ramadan commences over the coming years, see the boxed text, p202.

Pilgrimage (Haj)

The pinnacle of a devout Muslim's life is the pilgrimage to the holy sites in and around Mecca. Every Muslim capable of affording it should perform the Haj to Mecca at least once in their lifetime. The reward is considerable – the forgiving of all past sins. Ideally, the pilgrim should go to Mecca in the last month of the lunar year, and the returned pilgrim can be addressed as Haji, a term of great respect. In villages at least, it is not uncommon to see the word 'Al-Haj' and simple scenes painted on the walls of houses, showing that their inhabitants have made the pilgrimage.

THE MOSQUE

Embodying the Islamic faith, and representing its most predominant architectural feature, is the mosque, or *masjed* or *jama'a*. The building was developed in the very early days of Islam and takes its form from the simple, private houses where believers would customarily gather for worship.

The house belonging to the Prophet Mohammed is said to have provided the prototype for the plan of the mosque. The original setting was an enclosed, oblong courtyard with huts (housing Mohammed's wives) along one wall and a rough portico providing shade. This plan developed with the courtyard becoming the *sahn,* the portico the arcaded *riwaqs* and the haram the prayer hall. The prayer hall is typically divided into a series of aisles; the centre aisle is wider than the rest and leads to a vaulted niche in the wall called the mihrab – this indicates the direction of Mecca, which Muslims must face when they pray.

Islam does not have priests as such. The closest equivalent is the mosque's imam, a man schooled in Islam and Islamic law. He often doubles as the muezzin, who calls the faithful to prayer from the tower of the minaret – except these days recorded cassettes and loudspeakers do away with the need for him to climb up there. At the main Friday noon prayers, the imam gives a *khutba* (sermon) from the minbar, a wooden pulpit that stands beside the mihrab. In older, grander mosques, these minbars are often beautifully decorated.

Before entering the prayer hall and participating in communal worship, a Muslim must perform a ritual washing of the hands, forearms, face and neck. For this purpose, mosques have traditionally had a large ablutions fountain at the centre of the courtyard, often carved from marble and worn by centuries of use. These days, modern mosques have rows of taps.

The mosque also serves as a kind of community centre, and often you'll find groups of children or adults receiving lessons (usually in the Quran), people in quiet prayer and others simply dozing – mosques provide wonderfully tranquil havens from the chaos of the street.

Most Algerian mosques are officially off limits to non-Muslims, although permission can often be obtained from the imam between morning and noon prayers. You must dress modestly.

THE CALL TO PRAYER
Allahu akbar, Allahu akbar
Ashhadu an la Ilah ila Allah
Ashhadu an Mohammed rasul Allah
Haya ala as-sala
Haya ala as-sala

The soundtrack to your visit to Algeria will be this haunting invocation, a ritual whose essential meaning and power remain largely unchanged in 14 centuries.

Five times a day, Muslims are called, if not actually to enter a mosque to pray, at least to take the time to do so where they are. The noon prayers on Friday, when the imam of the mosque delivers his weekly *khutba,* are considered the most important. For Muslims, prayer is less a petition to Allah (in the Christian sense) than a re-affirmation of Allah's power and a reassertion of the brotherhood and equality of all believers.

The act of praying consists of a series of predefined ablutions and then movements of the body and recitals of prayers and passages of the Quran, all designed to express the believer's absolute humility and Allah's sovereignty.

ISLAMIC CUSTOMS
In everyday life, Muslims are prohibited from drinking alcohol (sura 5:90–95) and eating carrion, blood products or pork which are considered unclean (sura 2:165), the meat of animals not killed in the prescribed

Islam: A Short History (2006), by Karen Armstrong, is an accessible and sympathetic record of the world's fastest-growing religion without the sensationalism.

manner (sura 5:1–5) and food over which has not been said the name of Allah (sura 6:115). Adultery (sura 18:30–35), theft (sura 5:40–45) and gambling (sura 5:90–95) are also prohibited.

Islam is not just about prohibitions but also marks the important events of a Muslim's life. When a baby is born, the first words uttered to it are the call to prayer. A week later follows a ceremony in which the baby's head is shaved and an animal is sacrificed in remembrance of Abraham's willingness to sacrifice his son to Allah. The major event of a boy's childhood is circumcision, which normally takes place between the ages of seven and 12. When a person dies, a burial service is held at the mosque and the body is buried with the feet facing Mecca.

ISLAM IN ALGERIA

Although Islam arrived in northern Algeria in AD 670, it was not until 711 that the north of the country yielded to the new faith. The initial conquests, which included the taking of Algeria, were carried out under the caliphs, or Companions of Mohammed, of whom there were four. They in turn were followed by the Umayyad dynasty (AD 661–750) with its capital in Damascus and then the Abbasid line (AD 749–1258) in Baghdad (in modern Iraq). Given that these centres of Islamic power were so geographically removed from Algeria, the religion of Islam may have taken a hold, but the political and administrative control which accompanied Islamic rule elsewhere was much more tenuous in Algeria.

THE IBADIS OF ALGERIA

Algeria may be almost universally Sunni in outlook, but the M'Zab, close to Ghardaïa, is famous for being home to a small community of Ibadi Muslims.

The Ibadis are an offshoot of the Kharijite sect, whose name literally means 'seceders' or 'those who emerge from impropriety'. The Kharijites' origins lie in the bitter struggle for leadership over the Muslim community in the wake of the Prophet Mohammed's death. Kharijites, who recognise only the first two Muslim caliphs as legitimate and believe in the absolute equality of all Muslims regardless of race, became renowned for their fierce and uncompromising belief in the primacy of the Quran rather than in loyalty to corrupt, supposedly Muslim authorities. As such, Kharijism has always been an ideology of rebellion.

Not surprisingly, the egalitarian Kharijite theology appealed almost instantly to the Berbers of Algeria. In particular, the doctrine that any Muslim could become caliph, which questioned the Arab monopoly over Muslim legitimacy, was of great appeal. Thus it was that the Kharijite missionaries who actively courted the Berbers in Islam's early days in Algeria enjoyed great success.

One of the leading strands of Kharijite thought was developed by one Abdullah ibn Ibad. This founder of the Ibadis espoused many Kharijite teachings, such as anti-authoritarianism and the strictest adherence to the Quran, but also developed a more tolerant outlook than his somewhat fanatical Kharijite predecessors, especially in his dealings with other Muslims. Ibadism quickly became a major power in Algerian life. From AD 778 until 909, much of Algeria was ruled by the Ibadi imams known as the Rustamids. The Rustamids presided over a period of stability, encouraged scholarship and the arts, and were notable for their piety and lack of corruption.

After the Rustamids were swept away by the Shiite Fatimids, Ibadi refugees retreated to the five oases of the M'Zab in the 11th century, where they have remained until this day. They are now frequently known as the Mozabites; for more information on this community, see the boxed text, p160. Many Algerian Ibadis or Mozabites now reject the use of the term Kharijite to describe their community.

Ibadism is now extremely rare in the Middle East. Apart from the M'Zab oases, other small Ibadi communities are found only in Jerba (Tunisia), the Jebel Nafusa (northwestern Libya), Oman and Zanzibar.

Islam took longer to spread to the far south of Algeria, whose history is to a large extent separate: only in the 15th century were the Tuareg finally converted to Islam.

The leading strands of Islamic thought brought transformations to Algerian life, many of which survive to this day. The orthodox Sunnis divided into four schools (*madhab*) of Islamic law, each lending more or less importance to various aspects of religious doctrine. In Algeria, as elsewhere in the Maghreb, the Maliki rite of Sunni Islam came to predominate and still does. Founded by Malik ibn As, an Islamic judge who lived in Medina from AD 715 to 795, it is based on the practice which prevailed in Medina in the 8th century. The generally tolerant Maliki school of Islamic thought preaches the primacy of the Quran (as opposed to later teachings).

The holy fasting month of Ramadan (see p46) is taken extremely seriously in Algeria and is universally and very publicly observed. For details on the implications of travelling in Algeria during Ramadan, see p14.

In addition to mainstream Sunni practice, there are also small communities of Ibadis (see the boxed text, opposite) in the M'Zab region. As with elsewhere in North Africa, there have been significant communities of Sufis in the country for much of Algeria's history; the many Algerian town names beginning with 'Sidi' testify to this fact. Current figures regarding Sufi adherence are not known, although its influence waned in the wake of the Islamic scholar Abdelhamid ben Badis who preached against traditional marabouts, established a network of Sunni schools and demanded a return to orthodoxy in the early 20th century.

Islam also provided a rallying cry for opposition to a succession of governments in the second half of the 20th century. During the Algerian War of Independence, nationalist fighters called themselves *mujahedin* (warriors of jihad), Algerian dead were routinely referred to as *chouhada* (martyrs) and a return to Islamic principles was central to the independence movement's platforms.

Mindful of the mobilising power of Islam in Algeria, successive postindependence governments sought to monopolise public Islam and keep the Islamic establishment firmly within its control by appointing imams and keeping a close eye on all mosques. Such policies proved useless in holding back the march of militant Islam and when the Islamic Salvation Front (FIS) won the first round of the 1991 elections, the resulting tension spilled over into outright war; see p35 for more information.

Although the war has largely ended, Islam remains at the centre of public life and has come to be the fault line at the heart of Algerian society – between adherents of militant Islam and predominantly middle-class, moderate Muslims. In elections in 2002, legal Islamist parties won 20% of the vote.

'The holy fasting month of Ramadan is taken extremely seriously in Algeria'

Christianity

Although exact figures can be difficult to come by, it is estimated that there are fewer than 5000 Christians in Algeria, most of whom are Europeans or nationals of other Western countries. The Algerian constitution forbids discrimination based on religious belief, although a 2006 law makes proselytising for Christianity a criminal offence punishable by a one- to three-year jail term and prohibits non-Muslim worship outside of state-approved churches.

The fact that Algeria now has a tiny Christian community belies the fact that two towering figures in Christian church history spent much of their lives in what is now Algeria.

THE WHITE FATHERS

One of the most enduring Christian presences in Algeria is the missionary society which is popularly known as the Pères Blancs (White Fathers). Founded by Cardinal Lavigerie, the Bishop of Algiers, as the Missionaries of Our Lady of Africa of Algeria in 1868, the society for teaching Arab orphans quickly evolved into a society with grand plans for the conversion of Africa. In 1876, and again in 1881, two caravans of missionaries set out from southern Algeria but they were massacred en route to Sudan. An 1878 caravan proved more successful and laid the groundwork for missions in 42 African countries.

One year after founding the White Fathers, Cardinal Lavigerie founded a sister group for nuns, known as the Congregation of the Missionary Sisters of Our Lady of Africa.

The White Fathers, who still have their headquarters in Algeria, are unusual in that the rules of their mission require that members live in community homes of no fewer than three people, speak the language of the local people among whom they live, eat local food and wear local dress. Therein lies the reason behind the group's unusual name: their dress closely resembles the robes of Algerian Arabs, with a cassock and a burnous.

The first mission by the White Fathers was established among the Berbers of Jurjura, and missions throughout the Sahara later became their trademark. Visitors are welcome to visit the White Fathers hermitage and library in Ghardaïa (p158).

St Augustine served as the Bishop of Hippo Regius (now Annaba) from AD 393 to 430 and it was during this period that he developed the theology that would become so influential in the teachings of the early church. He was also one of the first Christian theologians to espouse the idea of 'just war'. For more information on the saint's life, see the boxed text, p113.

One of the most singular figures of 20th-century Christianity was Charles de Foucauld (see the boxed text, p189), who retreated into the Sahara where he worked among the Tuareg and lived an ascetic life as a Trappist monk. His simple stone hermitage at Assekrem (p188), whose name means 'the End of the World', is still home to a small number of monks from his order and can be visited.

WOMEN IN ALGERIA

Despite having played a leading role in Algeria's struggle for independence, life since then has been difficult for Algerian women.

In official terms, the situation is reasonable by regional standards. The Algerian constitution guarantees gender equality and Algeria ratified the Convention on the Elimination of All Forms of Discrimination against Women (Cedaw) in 1996, albeit with reservations. Later legislative provisions, particularly in relation to work, extended the principle of equality into the labour market.

That's the good news.

The bad news is that violence against women is rife and women have been targeted by Islamist militants since the early 1990s. A strong tradition of female activism meant that the Algiers of a few years ago is recalled as a place where dress codes were relatively relaxed. What to wear has, however, become a much tougher decision since Islamic militants in the early 1990s shot dead a schoolgirl in the street for not wearing a veil – and two veiled students were killed in retaliation as they waited for a school bus. 'You'll die if you don't wear the veil. You'll die if you do wear the veil, too. So shut up and die', wrote poet Tahar Djaout before he himself was killed in 1993. The cycle of violence may have abated, but Algeria's public face is now extremely conservative and the majority of women wear veils,

Women make up 27% of civil servants and almost 60% of secondary school teachers, and a record number of women candidates contested the 2002 elections.

even in once liberal Algiers. These vary from the lacy, white handkerchief-type ones worn in the north, which cover just the lower half of the face, to the robes worn by the women of the M'Zab (the area around Ghardaïa), which are held together in such a way that only one eye is visible.

Apart from violence, it was the 1984 Family Code that set back the cause of women's rights by decades. Effectively reducing women to the status of minors, the law has not been amended in the decades since. President Bouteflika ordered a review of the law in 2003, but like so many presidential promises of gender equality, the results have been a severe disappointment for Algerian women. Despite assuring Algerian women in 2004 that the government was ready to help them break free from the social constraints of a patriarchal society and enjoy their full constitutional rights, the president has let the review disappear without a trace after conservative critics of the government opposed it.

In January 2007, the UN sent its Human Rights Council's Special Rapporteur on violence against women on a fact-finding mission to Algeria. The Special Rapporteur's report is not expected to bring back much positive news.

ARTS
Architecture
From the claustrophobic clamour of Algiers' Unesco World Heritage–listed Casbah to the red and white earth tones of the Saharan oases, Algerian architecture is a highlight of any visit to Algeria. Particularly in the north of the country, much of what you'll see is a fusion of styles – Roman, Byzantine, Spanish, Ottoman, French and indigenous Islamic to name a few.

Examples of this often incongruous but always eye-catching combination, the Souk el-Ghazal Mosque (p119) and Grand Mosque (p119) in Constantine date from the 18th and 14th centuries respectively and include Roman-era granite columns and Corinthian capitals as essential elements of their structures.

OTTOMAN ARCHITECTURE
The rise of Christian Spain in the late 15th century brought to bear two important influences on the Algerian architectural landscape. The first was the arrival of Muslim refugees from Andalusia who brought with them new ideas regarding architecture. The second was less direct: in a bid to counter growing Spanish influence, rulers in the Maghreb turned

---

ALGERIAN ARCHITECTURE – THE HIGHLIGHTS

■ Roman – Tipaza (p104); Hippo Regius (p113); Timgad (p126); and Djemila (p132)

■ Byzantine – Djemaa Ali Bitchine (p93) and Notre Dame d'Afrique (p95) in Algiers

■ Early Islamic – Mosque and Tomb of Sidi Boumediene (p149) and Grand Mosque (p148) in Tlemcen

■ Spanish – Bey's Palace (p142) and Fort of Santa Cruz (p142) in Oran

■ Ottoman – Dar Khedaoudl el-Amia (p94), Dar Hassan Pacha (p94) and the Palais des Raïs Bastion 23 (p95) in Algiers; Palace of Ahmed Bey (p119) in Constantine

■ French – Place du 1 Novembre (p141) in Oran

■ Saharan – Ghardaïa (p156); Beni Abbès (p166); Timimoun (p169); El-Oued (p172); In Salah (p181); Djanet (p191)

■ Modern – Sidi M'Cid Bridge (p119) in Constantine and Makam Echahid (p96) in Algiers

east towards the Turkish Ottoman Empire, and Algiers in particular benefited from this shift in focus. Ottoman architecture remained the dominant force until the arrival of the French in the 19th century.

The first building erected by the Ottomans was the Djemaa el-Djedid (p93) in 1660. Its Ottoman-style dome is still the most recognisable Ottoman landmark in Algeria, although the Andalusian influence evident in the minaret is typical of the time when a Moorish style still held sway. Much of the Islamic architecture in northern Algeria would later be destroyed or, more often, converted by the French to serve a Christian purpose. Although these buildings were returned to their original functions after independence, many now bear traces of colonial meddling. The Djemaa Ketchoua (p94), also in Algiers, was used as a cathedral by the French, although, thankfully, they made few alterations. The Djemaa Safir was one of the last Ottoman-built mosques in the capital.

The Ottomans left largely unscathed the overhanging buildings, wooden bay windows and delicate stucco work of the Casbah, primarily because they settled largely in the lower part of the city. Elsewhere most Ottoman palaces and townhouses featured an L-shaped entrance which led into an interior marble-paved courtyard surrounded by porticoes, horse-shoe arches and mosaic tiles on four sides. The Dar Hassan Pacha (p94), also in Algiers, is a particularly fine example.

Islam: Art & Architecture, by Markus Hattstein and Peter Delius, is comprehensive and beautifully illustrated and contains numerous references to the architecture of Algeria and its historical context.

SAHARAN ARCHITECTURE

Although new towns have grown up alongside them, the huddled dwellings of the oasis towns of the Sahara still use ancient building methods – sun-baked mud, straw and palm products, flat roofs – that are well suited to the harsh demands of desert life. In smaller settlements, many traditional flat-roofed Saharan houses have been neglected to the point of dereliction as a result of the relocation of their residents to modern housing elsewhere. Many such houses are vulnerable to rare but devastating downpours.

TRANSFORMING ALGIERS

Algiers long ago expanded seemingly beyond the capacity of its traditional architecture to cope. The Casbah, for example, is believed to have lost more than a thousand homes since independence because its cramped conditions can no longer meet the growing needs of the population. This is a major reason why Unesco inscribed the Casbah on its World Heritage list of endangered sites in 1992.

But there is also something about Algiers that captures the imagination – its clamour, its Mediterranean fusion of French refinement with Arab-Islamic aesthetics – and it has drawn some of France's most eminent architects. Le Corbusier spent much of the 1930s developing 12 ambitious projects for the rejuvenation of Algiers, only to discover that this is a difficult city to tame – not one of the 12 came to fruition.

More successful was Fernand Pouillon, whose sympathetic incorporation of traditional architectural styles in urban Algiers won him plaudits in France and Algeria alike. His reconstruction of the entire neighbourhood of Diar Essada in the mid-1950s was followed by simliar success in the neighbourhoods of Diar Mahçoul and Climat de France. Pouillon later renovated one of the churches he built in Diar Essada as part of its postindependence conversion back into a mosque. Although commissioned by the French, Diar Essada became a postindependence icon for confidence in doing things the Algerian way to such an extent that it appeared on one of independent Algeria's first banknotes. Elsewhere, Pouillon was also extremely active in seeking to build tourist resorts along the Algerian coast that were both environmentally sustainable and incorporated into the local landscape. The Hôtel Gourara in Timimoun is another Pouillon creation.

Cinema

From *Chronicle of the Year of Embers* (directed by Mohammed Lakh-dar-Hamina), which won the prestigious Palme d'Or at the Cannes Film Festival in 1975, to Rachid Bouchareb's Oscar-nominated *Days of Glory* in 2007, Algerian film has been charming international critics for decades. That doesn't necessarily translate into regional audience numbers to match Egypt's blockbuster industry. Nor does it convert into the government funding the industry deserves – like so many film industries the world over, Algeria's is facing a shortage of funds that is crippling the creative works of its directors. But if quality is the touchstone, the Algerian film industry is in rude health.

The first sign that Algerian film would become one of the most inventive in the world came in 1965 with *The Battle of Algiers*. Written and directed by the Italian Gillo Pontecorvo, this relentlessly compelling representation of urban guerrilla warfare on the streets of Algiers nonetheless owed much to Algerian creativity and suggested that Algerians had a natural affinity with the silver screen. The film, which remains a cult hit, was funded by the Algerian government and almost all of the actors were ordinary Algerians.

Algerian directors would quickly show that they, too, were capable of tackling the big themes and doing so with panache. Not surprisingly, given its impact on Algerian society, the 1954–62 Algerian War of Independence would become a recurring muse for Algerian directors. This cluster of war films served as a platform for later directors to tackle the serious issues of Algerian society and exile with an unflinching gaze – one of the defining characteristics of Algerian film. It can make for harrowing viewing but it's the sort of cinema that has the power to change the way you think about the world.

A case in point was Mohamed Rachid Benhadj's *Desert Rose* (1989), which has an almost claustrophobic intensity and which some critics see as a coming-of-age for Algerian cinema. The film recounts the story of a seriously handicapped man in a remote oasis village. Benhadj has described Mousa, the main character, as 'a symbol of Algeria, of the Third World in general, formed by rigid beliefs and intolerance, but now having to redefine itself as all the alibis on which its place in the world depended begin to fall away.'

Another fine example is the critically acclaimed *Rachida* (2002) by Yamina Bachir-Chouikh, in which a young teacher is shot by terrorists after she refuses to plant a bomb in a school. *Rachida* also represented the directing debut for this highly talented female director, who had written the screenplay for the 1976 classic *Omar Gatlato* by Merzak Allouache (see the boxed text, p54).

Similarly, the French-born Algerian director Bourlem Guerdjou won awards for *Living in Paradise* (1997) which looks at the dislocated lives of Algerian exiles living in France. His 2005 offering, *Zaina: Rider of the Atlas,* is also outstanding.

The Palestinian tragedy has also proved to be the perfect subject matter for Algerian directors, most notably in *Nakhla* (1979) by Farouk Beloufa. Few Algerian movies have been as warmly praised by critics and so fiercely targeted by government censors.

The already mentioned Mohammed Lakhdar-Hamina has had one of the most distinguished careers, gaining no fewer than four nominations (one successful) for the Palme d'Or at Cannes. His filmography began with *The Winds of the Aures* (1966) and drew to an equally impressive close with *La Dernière Image* (1986).

La Guerre sans Nom (The War Without a Name), by director Bertrand Tavernier, is a documentary which consists entirely of meaningful interviews with French veterans of Algeria's War of Independence.

Arab Film Distribution (www.arabfilm.com) has a good list of Algerian films with plot synopses and details of how to buy them on DVD.

MERZAK ALLOUACHE

Amid Algeria's star-studded film industry, there is one director who stands out above all the rest: Merzak Allouache.

Born in Algiers in 1944, the award-winning Merzak Allouache witnessed first-hand the devastation caused by Algeria's War of Independence before studying film-making at the renowned Institut des Hautes Études Cinématographiques (Idhec) in Paris. Known for his searing realism and the use of Algerian street dialect, he made the first of 16 feature films, *Omar Gatlato,* which marked him out as a special talent. That film is widely seen as having definitively proved – both to critics and an Algerian audience – that Algerian cinema could combine both serious issues and popular appeal. Allouache chose to shoot the movie in the Bab el-Oued district of Algiers, a location to which he returned for *Bab el-Oued City* (1994), which won the International Critics' Prize at Cannes. The highlights of his glittering career include the following films:

Omar Gatlato (1976) The aimless lives of young Algiers men are the subject of Allouache's first feature and the empty bravado, dislocation and hollow dreams of North African youth have never been better depicted.

Following October (L'Après-Octobre; 1989) One of his rare forays into the world of documentary film-making to recount the riots in the suburbs of Paris in 1988.

Bab el-Oued City (1994) The creeping violence and fear gripping Algeria in 1993 as Allouache was filming infuse every moment of this landmark film about two conflicted, flawed, utterly human young fundamentalists.

Hey Cousin (Salut Cousin; 1996) The in-between-cultures angst of the children of Algerian immigrants in France is interspersed with rare flashes of humour in one of Allouache's best films of the 1990s.

The Other World (L'Autre Monde; 2001) Algerians in exile and the worrying but irresistible call of the homeland provide the most enlightening and heart-rending moments of the Algerian civil war yet captured on film.

One of the most impressive recent debuts came with Djamila Sahraoui's 2006 debut *Barakat!*. This excellent film follows the travails of an emergency doctor who returns home in 1991 to find that her husband has disappeared and has most likely been kidnapped by Islamist rebels. She is accompanied on her search by an older nurse who is a veteran of the independence struggle and the story becomes an intergenerational exploration of modern Algeria. It is outstanding.

Tony Gatlif, who was born as Michel Dahmani in Algiers in 1948, is one of France's most respected directors. His *La Terre au Ventre* (1979) is a story of the Algerian War of Independence, while *Exils* (2004), about Algerian exiles on their journey home, won a Best Director award at Cannes.

'Tuareg silver jewellery is highly sought after'

Jewellery

Although largely functional in purpose, Tuareg silver jewellery has evolved into an art form in its own right which is highly sought after by Western collectors.

The most unusual item is the *croix d'Agadez* (a stylised Tuareg cross of silver with intricate filigree designs) named after Agadez in Niger. Every town and region with a significant Tuareg population has its own unique version of the cross and by some estimates there are 36 different versions. Although European explorers saw the design as evidence of prior Christianity, traditional Tuareg see them as powerful talismans designed to protect against ill fortune and the evil eye. Some also serve as fertility symbols. The crosses are still used by Tuareg men as currency (eg for buying camels), although these days this is rare in Algeria. At other times, the crosses are worn by their wives as a sign of wealth.

Other silver items include: a wide range of silver necklaces (those containing amber are generally from across the border in Niger); striking, square, silver amulets that are worn around the neck by elders as a symbol of status (some are also used in weddings by women); and ornamental silver daggers with leather hilts.

Almost as interesting as the silverwork are the 'artists' who create it. Tuareg blacksmiths (Inaden) have always occupied a special place within Tuareg society, perhaps because of their dark communion with fire, iron and precious metals. At one level, the Inaden were traditionally looked down upon by noble Tuareg because the blacksmiths are darker-skinned than other Tuareg and they lived on the margins of Tuareg villages and encampments. At the same time, the Inaden were purveyors of traditional medicines, custodians of oral traditions and go-betweens in marriage negotiations. As such, they are essential figures in most Tuareg ceremonies. Shunning a blacksmith is considered taboo in Tuareg society.

Literature

Algerian writers first made a name for themselves during the French colonial period when many found a market in France for their novels. Foremost among them was Tlemcen-born Mohammed Dib (1920–2003), who wrote more than 30 novels, plus works of poetry, short stories and children's books. Although writing in the language of the occupiers, Dib and his contemporaries reclaimed the language as their own. Awarded the Grand Prix de la Francophonie de l'Academie Francaise in 1994, Dib is seen by many as the father of modern Algerian literature. Sadly, few of his works have been translated into English, but *The Savage Night*, a 13-storey compendium, is an excellent window on Dib's world.

Kateb Yacine (1929–89) was a contemporary of Dib and was also considered one of North Africa's finest writers of the 20th century. His landmark novel *Nedjma* interweaves family history with the Algerian War of Independence and is considered one of the most important French-language novels ever written in the Maghreb. Jean Amrouche (1907–62) was another important pioneer of Algerian writing in French.

It is also impossible to talk of Algerian literature of the period without paying homage to Albert Camus (1913–60), a *pied-noir* (see p42) who won the Nobel Prize for Literature in 1957 and is considered one of the towering figures of French literature and existentialist thought.

Frantz Fanon (1925–61) was born in Martinique but will be forever associated with Algeria for his work *The Wretched of the Earth,* which was based on his experiences during the Algerian War of Independence and is considered an important revolutionary book.

After independence, Algerian writers found themselves confronted with the highly political question of which language to write in. French ensured a wider audience but was tarnished with a colonial brush. Arabic was politically correct, but limited the author to a small, local book-buying market. Tamazigh was itself a fraught choice for both political and economic reasons.

The highly regarded Rachid Boudjedra (b 1941) chooses to write in Arabic and produce his own translations into French. Mohamed Khaireddine chooses to write in French as an act of cultural resistance because Tamazigh is forbidden. Other writers from the Kabylie region and for whom Berber identity plays a critical role include Marguerite Taos Amrouche (1913–76) and Mouloud Mammeri (1917–89). Across the cultural divide, Tahir Wattar chooses to write in Arabic, although his work *The Earthquake* is widely available in English.

The perils faced by Algerian writers are by no means restricted to language. In 1993, Tahar Djaout (*The Watchers* and *The Last Summer of Reason*), a proudly secular novelist from the Kabylie region, was assassinated.

Art of Being Tuareg – Sahara Nomads in a Modern World (2006) is a stunning pictorial study of Tuareg life with informative essays on Tuareg culture, including poetry, music and the role of women.

TOP FIVE CONTEMPORARY ALGERIAN NOVELS

■ *So Vast the Prison* by Assia Djebar

■ *The Star of Algiers* by Aziz Chouaki

■ *The Lovers of Algeria* by Anouar Benmalek

■ *Sherazade* by Leila Sebbar

■ *The Last Summer of Reason* by Tahar Djaout

One of the assassins later told police that Djaout was targeted because 'he wrote too well, he had an intelligent pen, and he was able to touch people; because of this he was a danger to the fundamentalist ideology'.

Women are among the leading crop of current Algerian writers whose works have been translated and are widely available in English. Assia Djebar is the most widely known and her novels (*Fantasia: An Algerian Cavalcade* and *So Vast the Prison*) and nonfiction (*Algerian White* and *Women of Algiers in their Apartment*) explore the role of women in Algerian society through beautifully told stories. Another leading light is Leila Sebbar who moved to France aged 17 and whose novels (*Sherazade* and *Silence on the Shores*) centre around the lives of Algerian women living in France.

Other important contemporary Algerian novelists include Anouar Benmalek *(The Lovers of Algeria)*, Aziz Chouaki *(The Star of Algiers)* and the prolific Yasmina Khadra (the pen name of Mohammed Moulessehoul) who made his name with *The Swallows of Kabul* but whose *Autumn of the Phantoms* deals with more Algerian themes.

Music

For a full run-down on the enduring Algerian music sensation that is rai, see the boxed text, opposite.

KABYLIE MUSIC

Although not as well known beyond Algeria's shores, the music of the Berber (Amazigh) people of the Kabylie region of northeastern Algeria is a mainstay of the local music scene. With its roots in the music and poetry of the Kabylie villages and in the exile and disaffection felt by many Amazigh in post-independence Algeria, Kabylie music has always provided something of a barometer for the health of Algerian society.

Kabylie singers from the colonial era such as Slimane Azem (1918–83) were, like many Kabylie, strong supporters of the push for Algerian independence. Azem's song 'Locusts, Leave My Country' became a de facto anthem for a generation of Algerians, both at home and in France. Western icons of the 1960s such as Bob Dylan later influenced liberal-minded Kabylie musicians who longed for their own counterculture revolution in Algeria. The Kabylie uprising of the early 1980s heard voices such as Djamel Allam's (b 1947) and Matoub Lounès' (1956–98) emerge as the soundtrack for a new generation of rebels; Lounès was to pay for his passionate advocacy for secularism and Amazigh rights in Algeria when he was assassinated soon after he returned home from France in 1998.

Female singers with Kabylie roots have also taken the world by storm, most notably Paris-based Souad Massi (b 1972) whose debut *Raoui* (Storyteller) was an instant hit in 2001. Her follow-up *Deb – Heart Broken* (2003) was, if anything, even better. Iness Mêzel is another important female Kabylie singer, while male Kabylie singers to watch out for are Akli D, Cheikh Sidi Bemol (www.louzine.net), Aït Menguellet and Takfarinas.

Azawan.com (www.azawan.com) is an extremely comprehensive website dedicated to showcasing the talents of Kabylie musicians.

RAI MUSIC   *Jane Cornwell*

Want to know what Algerians on the street are thinking? Check out the country's most popular music genre: rai. Meaning 'state an opinion', rai – rhymes with eye – is ubiquitous in Algeria. Danceable, infectious and buoyed by synthesisers and drum machines, it pulses through windows, from car stereos, around markets and beyond. Lyrics in Arabic and French tell of the pain and joy of daily life, of betrayal and exile, lust and love. It's hardly surprising, then, that rai turns conservative Islamic groups apoplectic. Cassettes have been confiscated at road blocks, performers threatened and worse. But for Algeria's MTV-watching youth – the genre's largest consumers – modern rai is as rebellious and compelling as American rap.

Rai originated in the 1930s in Oran, a metropolis then divided into Jewish, French, Spanish and Arab quarters. French colonisation saw these cultural influences mix with traditional Bedouin music and its flowery poetic singing, *malhun*. Many early rai singers were *cheikhas* – women who'd bucked Oran's strict code of conduct and become entertainers and outcasts. The most infamous of these was Cheikha Rimitti. An illiterate, feisty orphan who sang of sex and poverty and recorded her first album in 1936, Rimitti (who drew a bird as an autograph) paved the way for singers such as the reggae-and-funk-loving Khaled. She died in Paris in 2006, aged 83, having performed just two days beforehand.

Mass migration into the cities of western Algeria plus the attendant world depression cemented rai as a genre – a blend of traditional Arabic elements, Western production and whatever else took its fancy. Back then rai appealed to an underclass eager to be heard, its *chebs* and *chabas* (young men and women) articulating their *mehna* (hardship and suffering).

Rai came into its own in the '70s and '80s. Fadela's outspoken 1979 hit 'Ana ma h'lali ennoum' gripped the country. Rachid Baba Ahmed threw in modern pop and became rai's most important producer. The first state-sanctioned Rai Festival in Oran in 1985 marked its emergence as a nationally accepted genre. Then came civil war and encroaching fundamentalism. Cheb Hasni, the great star of rai love, was gunned down in Oran in 1994; Rachid Baba Ahmed was killed a few months later. Khaled, the King of Rai, whose song 'El-Harba Wayn?' became an anthem for protestors, left Paris after death threats. Others followed suit; France (and Egypt) is now home to a wealth of Algerian musicians including rai (ish) rocker Rachid Taha; chaabi-rai innovator Bilal; and rai fusionist Cheb Mami, who recorded a duet, 2000's 'Desert Rose', with Sting.

Second-generation Algerians including Faudel, the self-styled Prince of Rai, continue to make waves in Paris. The historic 1998 *1,2,3 Soleil* concert at Bercy stadium saw Khaled, Faudel and Rachid Taha (respectively the King, Prince and Rebel of Rai) entertain a 15,000-strong crowd; the excellent live album is released by Barclay. Rai continues apace in Algeria: Houari Dauphin, Hasni's successor, is huge. *Chebs* and *chabas* and their older, more traditional equivalents, *cheikhs* and *cheikhas,* sing in clubs and cabarets, and at festivals including Oran each August. Their lyrics may be more benign than those of their exiled, politicised colleagues, but their music still combines the best of all worlds.

Must-have Albums

- *Sahra* by Khaled (Polygram 1997)
- *1,2,3 Soleil* (Barclay France 1999)
- *Dellali* by Cheb Mami (Ark 21 2001)
- *N'ta Goudami* by Cheikha Rimitti (Because 2006)
- *Takitoi* by Rachid Taha (Wrasse 2004)
- *Baida* by Faudel (Ark 21 1997)
- *Lovers Rai* by Cheb Hasni (Rounders Select 1997)

TUAREG MUSIC

Although Algeria's Tuareg have made few contributions to the desert blues music that has become a cause célèbre for world music fans in 2005 and beyond, the country does have a claim to fame in this regard. The

**'Tin Hinan...
definitely
a name to
watch out
for'**

celebrated Tuareg group Tinariwen hail from the remote Kidal region of
northeastern Mali, but they spent much of the 1980s and 1990s in exile
as famine and then rebellion raged in their homeland. Part of that exile
was spent in Tamanrasset and later in Libya. It was there that the band
members learnt to play the guitar and much international success has
followed.

Inspired by the success of groups such as Tinariwen and, more recently, Etran Finatawa from Niger, Tin Hinan is a young Algerian Tuareg
group for whom critics are predicting great success and they're definitely
a name to watch out for.

Painting

Most discussions of Algerian painting centre around French artists,
among them Delacroix, Renoir, Matisse and Fromentin, who visited
Algeria in the 19th century or early 20th century and whose work was
transformed by a new approach to light and colour as a result.

This Eurocentric view of Algerian art reflects the fact that French colonial rule in Algeria did little to provide education or support for local Muslim Algerian artists. One artist who emerged during the colonial period
was Mohammed Racim (1896–1975), who began his career as a craftsman
illuminator in the Casbah of Algiers and went on to become a celebrated
artist at home and in France. After meeting a French patron of the arts
at a workshop, Racim was commissioned to illustrate a lavish edition of
Arabian Nights and the project enabled him to move to Paris where he
lived for eight years. Developing his skill as a miniaturist, he made stirring
if somewhat idealised representations of aristocratic Algiers.

However, it was not until after independence in 1962 that Algerian
artists truly began to flourish, most notably those known as the 'Generation of 1930' – artists born in and around that year. One of the most
celebrated was Baya Mahieddine (1931–98) who was born in Algiers and
was adopted by a French couple at age five. Never taught to read or write,
Baya, as she is best known as a painter, instead taught herself to paint
using gouache on paper and held her first exhibition in France aged just
16. She came to the attention of such luminaries as André Breton and
Pablo Picasso and her stellar career never looked back with exhibitions of
vivid colours and abstract figures in Paris, Washington and Algiers.

Mohammed Khadda (http://khadda.yellis.net/) was another eminent
Algerian abstract painter (1930–91) who emerged in the post-independ-
ence period after he, too, emigrated to Paris and worked under Picasso's
careful eye. In the euphoria of independence, he turned his back on the
Western figurative tradition of fine arts in favour of representations of
Arabic letters in creative calligraphic forms.

Other artists of note from the period include M'Hamed Issiakhem
(1928–85) and Choukri Mesli (b 1930) who both learned their trade at
the Ecole des Beaux-Arts in Paris.

More recent artists to take up Khadda's calligraphic mantle include
Majhoub ben Bella (b 1946) and Rachid Koraïchi (b 1947). Other painters
representative of the post-independence period include Ali Silem (b 1947),
Redha Chikh Bled (b 1949), Hamid Tibouchi (b 1951), Samta Benyahia
(b 1949) and Akila Mouhoubi (b 1953), while Slimane Ould Mohand
(b 1966), Philippe Amrouche (b 1966), Raouf Brahmia (1965–) and Kamel Ya-
hiaoui (b 1966) are the great hopes for the next generation of Algerian art.

For an excellent overview of Algerian art and works by European
Orientalist painters who visited Algeria, visit the Musée des Beaux Arts
(p97) in Algiers.

FOOD

The food you're likely to eat as a traveller in Algeria is unlikely to live long in the memory. Couscous with a meat or vegetable sauce, salads, rotisserie chicken, pizza and vegetable or lamb stews will be your staples.

Meal times in Algeria are broadly similar to what you may be used to at home. Breakfast is eaten generally until 9am or 10am, while lunch can be any time from 1pm onwards. Dinner can begin any time between 6pm and 8pm, although it's more likely to be the former.

In restaurants, etiquette is mostly identical to what you'd find back home. Many restaurants have separate family sections where unaccompanied men are not permitted. You should avoid eating with the your left hand. At home, Algerians usually spread out a plastic tablecloth atop a carpet on the floor and eat with their hands from a communal bowl. Prior to eating, the host will usually bring a jug of water, soap and a small plastic receptacle and will then proceed to pour so that each guest can wash their hands. At home, Algerian families eat together, but when guests arrive, men and women usually eat separately; Western women are generally considered honorary men and in such circumstances the traditional rules of segregation probably don't apply. As the meal commences, many say *'bismillah'* (a form of asking Allah to bless the meal). During the meal, the best morsels of meat will be gently pushed in the direction of an honoured guest. When sated, Algerians will say *'al-hamdu lillah'* (thanks be to God) whereupon other diners will encourage the person to eat more; if the person truly has finished, someone will say *'Saha, Saha'*, meaning 'good health'.

'when sated, **Algerians say** *'al-hamdu lillah'* **(thanks be to God)'**

If you're lucky, you may also come across tagine (a stew cooked in a ceramic dish of the same name), while seafood provides some much-needed variety in the north. Grilled meats are also something of a recurring theme (in the south, it may be camel meat), while the Spanish rice dish paella makes a surprising (and downright welcome) appearance on a few menus in better restaurants. Eggplant salads are also something of an Algerian speciality, while the spicy *harissa* (a red-chilli paste) gives considerable zest to many dishes.

Like in most Middle Eastern and North African countries, vegetarianism is something of an alien concept for Algerians. Vegetarians should always specify their requirements as soon as they arrive in the restaurant (ask for *bidoon laham*, without meat). Although most restaurants are obliging and keen to make sure you don't leave hungry, many won't be able to offer more than bread, salad, French fries, plain rice and perhaps an omelette. Many soups are precooked and include meat as a matter of course; often no substitute is available.

Other dishes you won't come across often, but you'll be glad when you do, include *harira* (thick, rich soup with chickpeas, lentils, meat and coriander), *merguez* (spicy seasoned lamb or goat sausages), *brik* (a flaky, deep-fried envelope of pastry stuffed with all manner of things), *chorba* (vegetable soup with noodles and meat) and *kefta* (meatballs made from seasoned, minced lamb). In Oran, the local speciality of *brannieh* (stew of lamb or beef with courgettes and chickpeas) is definitely worth seeking out.

French-inspired dishes make an appearance in some top-end restaurants of the north, and a coffee and a croissant have become a typically Algerian way to start the day. Sweet pastries of myriad other descriptions are also popular.

Environment

THE LAND

Algeria is one of geography's grand epics. At 2.38 million sq km, this is the world's 11th-largest country and the second biggest in Africa (Sudan is the largest). To help imagine Algeria's scale, consider this: most of Western Europe – including Germany, France, Spain, Italy, Poland, the UK and Portugal – would fit inside Algeria with room to spare. If that's just too big to contemplate, Algeria is almost equivalent in size to Western Australia, is 3.5 times the size of Texas or almost 10 times the size of the UK.

Most of Algerian territory is consumed by the Sahara Desert – over 90% by most estimates – although the northern, non-Saharan section of Algeria contains a surprising range of other landscapes. Just 0.9% of Algeria is covered by forests.

The Tell & the Northeast

The distance from Algiers to Tamanrasset is more than 2000km, which is greater than the distance from Algiers to Paris.

Pushed up hard against the Mediterranean Coast, the Tell region of Algeria consists of the narrow coastal strip and its mountainous hinterland. Not surprisingly, this is the most densely populated area of the country. Apart from the coastal littoral, the Tell is dominated by the east–west Atlas Mountains, which are a continuation of the Moroccan Atlas and cut right across the north and into Tunisia. It is not an unbroken chain: it consists of a number of separate ranges, and so does not constitute an impenetrable topographical barrier.

There is some fantastic mountain scenery here, particularly in the many different subranges of the Atlas that make up the Kabylie region east of Algiers. In the Massif du Djurdjura lies northern Algeria's highest point at 2308m; the Petite Kabylie and Grande Kabylie ranges also plunge down to the Mediterranean from a great height. South of Constantine, the Massif de l'Aurès is another signature massif of the northeast. Between the peaks lie numerous high plains – both Sétif and Constantine sit atop the plains – and valleys making for a region of the country that is rarely short on topographical interest.

Most of Algeria's agricultural possibility – just 3% of the land is arable – lies within the Tell, especially the Mitidja Plain west of Algiers and around Bejaïa to the east.

As might be expected, the only major river systems are in the north of the country, and many of these are seasonal. The main reservoirs for irrigation are in the mountains to the west of Algiers, while those in the northeast produce the 5% of the country's power which is generated by hydroelectricity.

The High Plateaus & Saharan Atlas

Before reaching the Sahara proper, Algeria descends ever so slightly from the Atlas into what is known as the High Plateaus (Hauts Plateaux), arid, steppelike plains that run east for almost 600km from the Moroccan border. With an average height of around 1200m above sea level, these plains gradually drop down to around 400m around Bou-Saada. It's only geographers who, on a technicality, would deny that the High Plateaus differ from the Sahara and a quick look at a map of the region confirms that the low rainfall and barren soil is incapable of supporting more than a handful of settlements.

Separating the plateaus from the Sahara, the Saharan Atlas (Atlas Saharien) consists of three massifs – Monts des Ksour, the Djebel Amour and Monts des Ouled – stretching from the Moroccan border near Béchar to Biskra. The highest point is 1927m. Serving as the final barrier between the Sahara Desert and northern Algeria, the Saharan Atlas gets reasonable rains and is home to a number of large oases such as Béchar, Aïn Sefra, Laghouat and Biskra.

Sahara: A Natural History, by Marq de Villiers and Sheila Hirtle, is a lively biography of the desert with sections on the Sahara's climate, wildlife and human inhabitants and much more.

The Algerian Sahara

As Marq de Villiers and Sheila Hirtle write in *Sahara: A Natural History,* 'In Morocco you can taste the desert, but Algeria is full immersion'. Although the Sahara runs from the Atlantic Coast to the Red Sea, from the coastal hinterland of the Mediterranean to the Sahel deep in Africa, Algeria is one of the few countries where both the vast scope and infinite variety of the world's largest desert is on full, unrelenting display.

Sand seas the size of European countries – the Grand Erg Occidental and Grand Erg Oriental – rise hundreds of metres in an ever-changing landscape of pristine lines sculpted by the wind. The Grand Ergs of central Algeria are slowly making their way across Algeria – north towards the Saharan Atlas and the Massif de Aurès and south towards the Tassili du Hoggar – engulfing the country in a seemingly unstoppable march of desertification. Although many regions of the Sahara received regular rains until 3000 years ago (see p81), it is believed that the Grand Ergs have not received meaningful rainfall for 12,000 years.

Geomorphology in Deserts, by Robert Cooke and Andrew Warren, may have been written in 1973, but it remains the definitive work on the Sahara's geography.

Despite the common misconception, the Sahara is not just one big expanse of sand. Gravel plains such as the impossibly barren Tanezrouft in southwestern Algeria and Mali and barren plateaus such as the Plateau du Tademaït (north of In Salah) provide some of the most featureless horizons in the Sahara. In Algeria's far southeast are some of the signature massifs of the central Sahara, especially the Hoggar (or Ahaggar) Mountains and the Tassili N'Ajjer, surrounded by vast sandstone or granite plateaus otherwise known as the Mid Sahara Rise. It is in the Hoggar, at Mt Tahat (2908m), where you'll find Algeria's highest point, although peaks

---

THE FORMATION OF SAND DUNES

Sand dunes are among the great mysteries of the Sahara. In the desert, sand particles are relatively heavy so even the strongest winds can rarely lift them much higher than an adult's shoulders. The slightest bump in the landscape can cause a phenomenon known as cresting, where an accumulation of drifting sand builds up. The slopes facing the wind are generally more compacted and less steep than those that lie on the other side of the ridge-line. The actual formation takes place where there were originally favourable land formations (often surprisingly small) and a constancy in the direction of the winds. Over time, with a base of ever more densely compacted sand, they become a 'permanent' feature of the landscape. Individual or small groups of dunes inch forward with time, pushed by consistent winds, although sand seas are relatively stable, having formed over millennia as rock is scoured and worn down to individual grains of quartz or sand.

Some of the most common types of dune are barchan or crescent dunes (the shape of the ridge-line); *seif* (Arabic for sword), which have long, sweeping ridges; and *akhlé,* a haphazard network of dunes without any discernible pattern. Unique combinations of all of these can be found in both the Grand Erg Occidental (p162) and Grand Erg Oriental (p172), as well as smaller sand seas elsewhere.

For more information on sand dune formation, the 1973 *Geomorphology in Deserts* by Robert Cooke and Andrew Warren is dense but comprehensive, while Ralph Bagnold's *Libyan Sands – Travels in a Dead World* (1935; see the boxed text, p66) is more accessible.

regularly approach 2000m. Owing their weird-and-wonderful shapes to volcanic eruptions millions of years ago, these otherworldly mountain ranges are a tortured terrain of soaring monoliths and deep canyons. The Hoggar alone occupies an area roughly equivalent to France.

The Sahara may cover more than 90% of Algeria, but it is home to less than 10% of its human population.

For advice on exploring the Sahara in an environmentally responsible manner, see p71; for some of the most important statistics of Saharan geography see the boxed text, p67.

WILDLIFE
Animals
The prehistoric rock paintings of the Tassili N'Ajjer and elsewhere suggest that elephants, giraffes and rhinoceroses once roamed the region. Not surprisingly, none remain and Algeria has few surviving mammal species. Most of the animal species which do remain have been pushed into ever-more-remote areas and you're extremely unlikely to see more than a handful of species (if any) during your visit.

Algeria is home to 92 mammal species, of which 15 are officially classified by the International Union for the Conservation of Nature (IUCN) as threatened. More common species which survive include gazelles, porcupines, antelopes, golden jackals, Egyptian mongooses, spotted hyenas and European genets. In northern Algeria European wild boar and Barbary red deer remain reasonably prevalent, although both are a favourite of hunters.

In the Sahara the painfully shy waddan, a large goatlike deer whose agility is perfectly suited to its steep mountain domain, hides in remote mountain wadis in the Tassili N'Ajjer and Hoggar Mountains. The fennec fox is a gloriously adapted, largely nocturnal species with fur-soled feet to protect against scorching sands and comically large ears; it spends most of the hot daylight hours underground. The largest rodent in the Libyan Sahara is the gundi, which can stop breathing for up to a minute to hide itself from prey. Wolves are also present. The four-toed jerboa is a small rodent that sometimes hops through desert camps at night in search of food and is a favourite meal of the fennec. The extremely shy sand cat is also present in southern Algeria, while other species found in the Hoggar region in reasonable numbers include Cape hares, Ruppell's foxes and, to a lesser extent, Barbary sheep.

Lizards, snakes (the striped sand snake, the horned viper and the Saharan sand snake) and scorpions are also quite common; you'd have to be extremely unlucky to encounter snakes in winter.

Of the marine wildlife along Algeria's Mediterranean Coast, dolphins, porpoises and whales are all common.

La Vie Sauvage au Sahara, by Alain Dragesco-Joffe, is the finest study (in French) of the Sahara's wildlife, including rare photos and analysis of the Saharan cheetah.

ENDANGERED SPECIES
The addax is a large antelope that once frequented the Hoggar and Tassili N'Ajjer regions but may have become extinct in Algeria. Remarkably, it never drinks water. The scimitar-horned oryx (a long-horned antelope) was officially declared extinct in Algeria in 1996. Other species for which it may be too late include the Barbary hyena and Barbary leopard. The dorcas gazelle is considered threatened, while the dama gazelle may have gone the way of the addax in Algeria due to hunting and human encroachment.

One of the most curious survivors in all the Sahara is the Saharan cheetah, of which between 200 and 500 are thought to survive in the whole

Sahara. Surveys in 2005 found that a small community of cheetahs – the world's fastest land animal – continues to hide out in the Hoggar Mountains. What makes their survival even more remarkable is the fact that the Saharan cheetah – whose colours have dulled in the Saharan sun – is extremely susceptible to stress and heat exhaustion.

In the north the Barbary ape (Barbary macaque) and Algerian wild dog are also considered at risk of extinction.

The Mediterranean monk seal is Europe's most highly endangered marine mammal, with just 600 surviving worldwide; a small colony remains in the caves and on rocky outcrops along Algeria's far northeastern coast. Over-fishing by commercial fleets in the Mediterranean and coastal pollution have reduced their numbers in Algeria to just 10. The leopard-like serval, which has the longest legs in the cat family, may survive in northern Algeria, but only in similar numbers to the monk seal.

BIRDS

At last count, Algeria had 183 endemic bird species, of which eight are considered endangered. In addition to these, hundreds of millions of migrating birds cross the Sahara every year, escaping the European winter for the warmth of equatorial Africa. Some have been known to cross the Sahara in just 40 hours, although the toll is considerable – up to half will not return. The same species are believed to have been following trans-Saharan migratory routes for millennia, from since before the Sahara was a desert.

Birds that you may come across include the Lanner falcon, Marbled teal, Barbary partridge, blue rock thrush, Greylag goose, golden eagle, Common or Red crossbill and desert sparrow as well as shrikes, larks, crows, turtle doves, vultures, herons, bitterns, woodpigeons, eagles and bulbuls. The sociable moula moula bird, with a black body and striking white face and tail, is a constant companion in the far south; the Tuareg call it the messenger bird or the deliverer of happiness.

In the Kabylie region, the Kabylie nuthatch, with its russet-coloured breast, is sometimes spotted above 1000m, although it is considered threatened, as is Audouin's Gull.

Sahara Conservation Fund (www.saharaconserva tion.org) is an excellent website detailing efforts underway to protect Saharan wildlife and the Saharan environment.

Plants

Along the coast of Algeria, the usual array of Mediterranean flora thrives, with large areas given over to the cultivation of olives and citrus fruit. You may also come across eucalyptus, bougainvillea and oleander. Other species include gall oak and cork oak.

Inland, the only vegetation is largely confined to the oases, where the date palm reigns supreme, along with fig, tamarisk and oleander trees. Outside the oases, Acacia arabica (acacia) often provides the only shade in the middle of the desert wilderness. Alfalfa grass and salt bushes often appear as if by miracle after rains.

Like the Sahara's few surviving mammal species, a few holdouts of Mediterranean plant species – such as Mediterranean olive, Saharan myrtle and tarout cypress trees – can be found at high altitudes in the Hoggar and Tassili N'Ajjer regions.

NATIONAL PARKS

Algeria has 11 national parks in addition to a host of other protected areas that encompass a total of between 5% and 10% of the country's land area. That said, although the Algerian government's record in setting aside protected areas has improved in recent years, these are rarely national parks in the traditional sense – there are few park wardens, locals continue to live within most park boundaries and there are rarely official entry gates, all of which means you may end up visiting one of the parks without realising it.

Ahaggar National Park

The Ahaggar National Park (Parc National de l'Ahaggar) covers an astonishing 450,000 sq km, making it one the largest protected areas in the world. Created in 1987, the park runs from In Salah to the Mali and Niger borders and encompasses the Hoggar Mountains (p188) and the Tassili d'Immidir (p182). There's an **information office** (☎ 029 734117; pl du 1er Novembre) in Tamanrasset.

Tassili N'Ajjer National Park

Covering 80,000 sq km, the Tassili N'Ajjer National Park (Parc National de Tassili N'Ajjer; (p194) is Algeria's other major park and arguably the most effectively run. The Office National du Parc Tassili in Djanet controls entry to the park, with a DA100 entry fee per person.

In addition to the rock art for which the park is famous, the park was set up to protect 28 endangered plant species such as Mediterranean olive, Saharan myrtle and tarout cypress, as well as threatened animal species such as the Barbary sheep, sand cat, cheetah and dorcas gazelle. The Tassili N'Ajjer National Park is also an important waystation for migrating bird species, while up to 10,000 people, mostly nomadic Tuareg, live within the park's confines.

Other National Parks

Two of the most important national parks in Algeria are located in the country's northeast, although facilities for travellers are practically nonexistent.

Taza National Park (Parc National de Taza), which was set aside in 2004, is situated on the Mediterranean Coast in the Kabylie region and its stunning cliffs and precipitous valleys (the landscape soars from sea level to over 1100m) are home to the endangered Barbary ape and the Kabylie nuthatch, as well as the largest stands of gall oak and cork oak in Algeria. The region is especially popular for raptor bird species.

Also of significance is the El-Kala National Park (Parc National d'El-Kala), which is hard-up alongside the Algerian–Tunisian border, close to Annaba. The park is home to two of Algeria's 26 entries on the Ramsar List of Wetlands of International Importance. An important stopover for migrating birds on their trans-Saharan odyssey, these wetlands play host to rare waterfowl such as the tufted duck, white-headed duck, Ferruginous duck and purple gallinule.

In addition to these parks, there is one further coastal park (Gouraya National Park), five parks covering mountain regions (Theniet el-Had National Park, Djurdjura National Park, Chrea National Park, Belezma National Park and Tlemcen National Park) and one national park on the High Plateaus (Djebel Aissa National Park).

ENVIRONMENTAL ISSUES

Algeria's record on environmental protection is patchy, with daunting challenges and the primacy of oil production and consumption on the list of government priorities proving a destructive combination. Despite some public willingness to tackle the big environmental issues, the government has not, for example, signed the 1997 Kyoto Protocol.

Desertification

The major environmental issue facing Algeria is undoubtedly desertification – by some estimates, the Algerian Sahara grows by hundreds of square kilometres every year and the Sahara is now just 200km from the shores of the Mediterranean. The stripping of vegetation for firewood and soil erosion from overgrazing have meant that once-fertile soil has begun to unravel, hastening the desert's irresistible march.

Successive Algerian governments have tried a range of responses to combat desertification with limited impact. In 1975 the government planted what it called a 1500km-long, 20km-wide 'green wall' along the northern boundary of the Sahara and the cost of maintaining it drained US$100 million from government coffers every year for two decades, only for further overgrazing and human encroachment to strip away much of the good work. Despite such efforts and some successes – some environmentalists claim that 26,000 sq km of pastureland have been reclaimed from the desert on the High Plateaus – the Department of Agriculture estimates that 130,000 sq km have become desert in Algeria in the last 10 years. In December 2006 President Bouteflika earmarked a further US$2.5 billion for the fight against desertification.

The government also has ambitious plans to develop southern regions not only for environmental reasons, but also to stem the rising urban migration of peoples from southern Algeria. Algerian environmentalists have targeted the Taghit region in western Algeria for a possible national park and ecotourism project as a means of regenerating desert life in harmony with the environment. The government has also redoubled its efforts to plant desert-friendly trees in Saharan areas and develop agricultural regions in the south to arrest the region's environmental and economic decline.

Water

With more than 90% of Algerian territory covered by desert, water is not surprisingly a major environmental issue. Water shortages are common and pollution of water sources, especially in the north, from both domestic and industrial sources is a serious problem in many areas. Techniques for water purification are substandard, and rivers are being increasingly contaminated by untreated sewage, industrial effluent and wastes from petroleum refining.

Droughts are an increasing feature of Algerian life, even in relatively fertile areas in the north. These dry spells have not only fuelled an exodus from the rural south to the industrialised north, they have also left the land susceptible to devastating fires such as those that swept through the northeast in 1999.

Water shortages are particularly acute in the south where people rely on underground water sources for human consumption and crop production. It was ever thus in the Sahara – underground water channels known as *foggara* and dating back centuries discovered in the Adrar region were found to extend over 2000km.

The Mediterranean has also been contaminated by the oil industry, fertilizer runoff and soil erosion.

The deforestation that has denuded so much of Algeria wasn't helped by the French, who repeatedly bombed northern regions with napalm during the 1954–62 Algerian War of Independence.

Algerian carbon dioxide emissions amount to 5.1 tonnes per capita, which makes it the 76th worst environmental villain in the world. US figures are 19.8 tonnes, while carbon dioxide emissions from the average Malian are just 0.04 tonnes.

Recent radiocarbon dating suggests that the water currently stored beneath the Sahara has been there for between 14,000 and 38,000 years, with smaller deposits from 7000 years ago.

Travelling in the Sahara

Exploring the Algerian Sahara offers the traveller the ultimate challenge, not to mention some of the last great wilderness adventures in the world. You may see some of the most beautiful scenery on earth – Algeria is famed among experienced Saharan travellers as a true landscape of the soul – but the process of getting there along the long, dusty, rocky trails is something that you'll remember almost as long as you will places like Tassili N'Ajjer National Park, Tassili du Hoggar, Assekrem or Tanezrouft.

The home page of Alain Sèbe (www.alainsebe images.com), arguably the finest photographer currently working in the Sahara, is filled with inspirational desert shots.

A Saharan expedition is definitely not for those who value their creature comforts, as transport can be uncomfortable, conditions are often primitive, the climate is almost always extreme and the range of food limited. There will surely come a moment when the arduous nature of travel in the Sahara makes you wonder why on earth you decided to come.

But then you'll catch a glimpse of a distant sand dune of pristine, sculpted perfection, stumble upon a slash of green in a remote canyon of desolate black rocks, discover a wall adorned with rock art so exquisite as to qualify as a masterpiece or find yourself in patient conversation with a Tuareg keen to initiate you into the Sahara's secrets. These are the moments when all memories of the hardship disappear and you begin to wonder how you can ever bear to leave.

We can also promise you one thing: once you have visited the imagined territory of the Sahara, the Sahara will fill your dreams and you'll spend the rest of your life longing to return.

BEFORE YOU GO

Visiting the Sahara, whether it be in Algeria or elsewhere, requires careful planning. While much of this involves practical preparation, it also entails catching a sense of the Sahara's magic, and dreaming a little before you go.

Some aspects of travelling in the Algerian Sahara are covered elsewhere in this book. In addition to the destination chapters – Ghardaïa and the Grand Ergs, and Tamanrasset, Djanet and the Sahara – detailed coverage of Saharan rock art can be found on p80, while descriptions of the Sahara's geography (p61) and the wildlife (p62) you may see there form a central part of the Environment chapter.

READING UP

When it comes to preparing for a Saharan expedition, a little inspiration can take you a long way. The following books will help you to catch the spirit of the Sahara and whet your appetite for what awaits you in Algeria:

Wind, Sand and Stars (Antoine de Saint-Exupéry) The existentialist bible of Saharan travel, filled with all the wisdom and gravitas of the world's largest desert.

The Sahara (The World's Wild Places, Time-Life Books) An unlikely desert classic which combines a wealth of information with evocative text that captures the essence of Saharan travel.

Libyan Sands – Travels in a Dead World (RA Bagnold) A beautifully written 1920s exploration of the Egyptian and Libyan deserts that overflows with the joy of discovery, a sensation that is still possible today.

The Gates of Africa: Death, Discovery and the Search for Timbuktu (Anthony Sattin) No book about the Saharan explorers of old so beautifully evokes the reasons why they (and perhaps we) felt so called by the desert.

SAHARA STATS

It is a notoriously unwieldy beast to quantify, but most estimates put the Sahara's size at 9.065 million sq km, which is comparable to the continental United States. Almost a quarter of the Sahara lies within the borders of Algeria.

Contrary to popular misconceptions, sand covers just 20% of the Sahara's surface and only a ninth of the Sahara rises as sand dunes.

More typical of the Sahara are the vast gravel plains and plateaus such as the Tanezrouft of southeastern Algeria. Improbably, plains such as these owe their existence to water. When the rains ceased and the Sahara began to dry out around 4000 years ago, the rivers which once flowed from the mountains of the central Sahara to the sea dried out. They left behind mountain debris carried down onto eroded plains such as the Tanezrouft. These great tablelands of sedimentary limestone, newly exposed to unimpeded Saharan winds, were thereafter polished smooth as all loose debris was scoured away by wind and sand.

The Sahara is also home to barren mountain ranges of sandstone and granite such as the Jebel Acacus (Libya), Aïr Mountains (Niger), Tibesti (Chad), Adrar-n-Iforhas (Mali) and the Algerian ranges of the Hoggar and Tassili N'Ajjer. These dark apparitions of the central Sahara were formed by volcanic activity, beginning 570 million years ago with the Great African Episode, which formed the mountains of Africa, and culminating in the last volcanic activity a mere two million years ago. Most of these mountains are basalt to the core, with underlying foundations of granite.

Although there are places where life can seem impossible, the Sahara is home to 1400 plant species, 50 species of mammal and 18 species of bird.

Impossible Journey: Two Against the Sahara (Michael Asher) Epic tales of Saharan exploration aren't the preserve of 19th-century travellers and this crossing of the Sahara from west to east is extraordinary.

Desert Divers (Sven Lindqvist) A deeply meditative text on the peoples of the Algerian Sahara and the strange mysteries of the desert.

Mysterious Sahara (Byron Khun de Prorock) A stirring 1920s account of journeys into the Sahara (including extensive sections on Algeria) by one of the most intrepid Saharan travellers of the 20th century.

Call of the Desert (Philippe Bourseiller) A weighty coffee-table tome that you won't want in your suitcase, but which has one of the most exceptional collections of Saharan photos.

Sahara: An Immense Ocean of Sand (Paolo Navaresio and Gianni Guadalupi) A kilo or two less than Bourseiller's book, but similarly exceptional photos and lively, informative text.

Sahara: The Atlantic to the Nile (Alain and Berny Sèbe) Award-winning photos of the Sahara's signature landscapes with a heavy focus on Algeria.

Sahara: The Forbidding Sands (Jean-Marc Durou) is a stunningly photographed addition to your library, with text by Tuareg writers and some of France's most respected Saharan travellers.

WHEN TO GO

The season during which you visit the Sahara will have a strong bearing on what you're able to achieve and what type of memories you'll take home.

The best time to visit the Sahara is in October or November when daytime temperatures can be surprisingly mild and the nights won't have fallen below zero as they tend to do in the months that follow. If you're lucky and there have been late-summer rains in the preceding months, some desert landscapes will still be alive with flowers and soft tinges of green.

Winter (December through to February) in the Algerian Sahara will also mean that you're free to explore just about anywhere without too much difficulty, although you may be surprised at just how cool the days can become, and nights can be bitterly, interminably cold. Having 'slept' outdoors in the central Sahara in just a light sleeping bag when the temperatures dropped more degrees below zero than we care to remember, we can only exhort you to come well prepared; see p68.

'people
survive by
staying
indoors
for most
of the
daylight
hours'

From March until the middle of May are also good months for visiting the Sahara, although in April there is a greater risk of strong winds and sandstorms, which can reduce visibility to just a few metres and be extremely unpleasant if you find yourself in open country. By late April and early May, temperatures have begun to rise and given that your car is unlikely to let you use air-conditioning when traversing tough terrain, you may be a little more restricted in how deep into the desert you want to travel.

Don't even think of travelling in the Sahara from late May until mid-September when temperatures are fierce. In any event, given that you have to visit the Algerian Sahara in the company of a guide, you'll struggle to find one willing to leave the shade and accompany you at such times. For people who live in the Sahara, these are months to be endured and the people survive by staying indoors for most of the daylight hours. One day in the open desert and you'll feel like doing the same.

WHAT TO BRING

Although we've provided some general advice on what to bring on your visit to Algeria (see the boxed text, p14), there are further things that are specifically necessary for Saharan travel that you should consider carrying in your backpack.

Clothes & Camping Equipment

If you're visiting the Algerian Sahara as part of an organised tour, check what equipment the operator will be sending with you. A warm sleeping

---

TYING YOUR TAGUELMOUST

The Tuareg turban (known as an *ashaersh* or *taguelmoust*) has puzzled ethnographers for centuries. The Tuareg are one of the few societies in the world where men, but not women, must wear the veil. One functional purpose is as protection against wind and sand.

However, it also serves a social purpose in the rigid hierarchy of social relationships. A Tuareg man is not supposed to show his face to one of higher status, and Tuareg who still follow the traditional way of life will rarely expose the lower half of their face in company. When such men drink tea, they are supposed to pass their glass under their *taguelmoust* so as not to reveal the mouth.

There are many ways of tying the *taguelmoust*. Although it's likely to take a while for you to gain the casual ease with which Tuareg men accomplish the task, one relatively easy way to do it is as follows:

Step 1 Fold the cloth so that it remains the same length but half the width.
Step 2 Drape the folded cloth flat over your head so that three quarters of its length hangs down in front of your right arm and the shorter length over your left.
Step 3 With your right hand, hold the cloth about halfway down its length.
Step 4 Place your left hand across your body, and tense it so that your four fingers are pointing out to your right and your thumb is pointing to the sky.
Step 5 Holding your left hand just below your right shoulder, about chest high and about 15cm out from your body, grasp the nearest fold of the long length of cloth in your left hand between the thumb and flattened forefinger.
Step 6 With your right hand, quickly take the length of cloth in a full circle in front of your face and around the back of your head until you return to where you started.
Step 7 Repeat as many times as necessary.
Step 8 Tuck any remaining strands of cloth into the folds on the top or back of the head.
Step 9 Ask your Tuareg guide to sort it out.

There; we told you it was easy.

bag and tent are essential in colder weather, while blankets should also be provided. A portable stove is also a must, as are kitchen and eating utensils.

No tour operator can be held responsible, however, if you find yourself freezing on a cold desert night because you didn't bring enough warm clothes. For all but summer months, we advise you to bring a jacket or coat which is effective at keeping out the wind and keeping you warm. Other warm clothes should also be considered, depending on the time of year. Thermal underwear, for example, takes up little space.

Good, sturdy boots are another must for the uneven trails of the Tassili N'Ajjer in particular.

Sunscreen is necessary, as is some form of head protection to help guard against getting sunburn or, worse, heat exhaustion. You should definitely bring a hat, but many travellers don traditional Tuareg headgear – the *taguelmoust* (see p42) or other cloth – which not only shields you from the sun, but also keeps out wind-borne sand. For advice on the complicated fun of tying your new Tuareg *taguelmoust* in nine easy steps, see the boxed text, opposite. Moisturising cream for dry skin is also recommended.

A medical kit (see p219) is a near-essential item, while you should also make sure that your travel insurance (see p202) covers you for trekking, camel trekking and 4WD expeditions in the Algerian Sahara. Some form of mosquito repellent is also recommended – that unmistakeable high-pitched whine in the ear is death to sleep in many Saharan oases.

Useful items to have around the camp site at night include a Swiss army knife, a torch (some people prefer a head lantern) and spare batteries. Some travellers like to also carry a short-wave radio with them, although most prefer the silence of desert nights to knowing what's happening in the world beyond the desert. A small telescope for studying the night sky is something of an indulgence, but one that you'll appreciate if you have room in your backpack or vehicle.

'good, sturdy boots are a must'

Documents

Be sure to carry all your documents – passport, *carnet de passage* (passport or travel permit for your vehicle), vehicle registration and insurance papers for your vehicle – with you at all times and keep them easily accessible. The Algerian security services are known to pop up in the most remote and unlikely places and, although they're primarily there for your own protection, they'll want to make sure that everything is in order before they let you continue on your way.

Maps

Navigating the Sahara requires good maps and an experienced local guide. A satellite-generated Global Positioning System (GPS) can also come in handy, but it's no substitute for the local knowledge of an experienced guide – a GPS can point you in the right direction but can't tell what lies in your path, and hence the most appropriate route.

For an overview of the area, the regularly updated Michelin map *Africa: North and West* (sheet 953, formerly 153, scale 1:4,000,000) is one of the best and most detailed, and something of a classic. It has lent its name to the 153 Club (www.the153club.org) whose members have driven across the Sahara and around West Africa. That said, don't rely solely on the Michelin map as its scale makes it insufficiently detailed for most desert navigation. Expect also a few discrepancies between the map and reality, especially regarding road information, because old tracks get upgraded and once-smooth highways become potholed disasters.

STUCK IN THE SAND   *Anthony Ham*

There's no feeling like it, that sense of being so deep in the Sahara and so far from civilisation that you wonder whether you've fallen off the end of the earth. The glorious sense of solitude and the gravitas of a desert landscape sculpted by the wind are among the many rewards of travelling in the Sahara. That is until something happens to your vehicle. And so it was that we awoke one morning in the sands of the Sahara to find that the car's battery was a complete nonstarter.

I have become accustomed over the years to drivers in this area being able to fix anything – for them necessity is indeed the mother of invention. I have watched, 300km from the nearest town, as my driver dismantled a Land Rover's suspension and then rebuilt it in just over two hours. I have marvelled as my guide and driver changed the entire gear system of a Toyota Landcruiser in a deep valley of a sand sea. So I wasn't worried at first.

We dug the wheels from the sand and pushed. When that failed, my driver and two guides jacked up the car and tried to spin the wheels, hoping that would coax the engine to life. They dismantled the fan belt and tried to charge the battery by hand. They talked excitedly and with purpose which suggested that things were not as bad as they seemed to me. Then came the moment when my two guides and driver stopped peering into the engine and, as one, began to look hopefully towards the horizon. That's when I knew we had problems and began to wonder just how much trouble we were in.

And so it was that one guide and one driver set out to walk 25km across the sand to the nearest police post, leaving us to contemplate what it truly meant to be stuck in the sand with no prospect of passing traffic in one of the most remote corners of the Sahara. As the hours passed, with the sun overhead, we crawled under the car for shade. What if they got lost and never returned? What if the police vehicle was under repair or away on patrol? We knew we had enough food and water for at least a week, but the sense of helplessness soon morphed into morbid thoughts.

Although my usual rule is to venture into the Sahara only with two or more 4WDs, I often break it when I am with an experienced driver who knows his car. Off the beaten track, I also always travel with a satellite phone. In this case, I had no phone and no second car.

Finally, after six hours, a police car with mounted machine guns appeared over the horizon, bearing our guide and driver and the means to restart our car.

A happy reunion. Relief that you could almost taste. And one of the most important lessons of Saharan travel learnt – always know your vehicle before taking it into the desert.

The most detailed topographical maps are the old Russian satellite survey maps (1:200,000) from the 1970s. They may be in Cyrillic script but they're still the best maps for Saharan navigation, at least when it comes to topographical features.

If you can't find the Russian maps, your next best bet is probably the series of maps produced by the Institut Géographique National (IGN). IGN's extensive series of *Carte Internationale du Monde* sheets (1:1,000,000) covers the Algerian Sahara and the most relevant sheets are likely to be *In-Azaoua, Djanet, Tamanrasset* and *In-Salah*. The only problem with these maps is that they were surveyed in the 1960s and don't seem to have been updated since. As such, they're generally excellent for topographical features, but of little use for road detail.

To try to track down these and other Saharan maps, your first stop should be **Stanfords** (☎ 020-7836 1321; www.stanfords.co.uk; 12-14 Long Acre, Covent Garden, London WC2E 9LP, UK), the world's largest supplier of maps. It also has stores in Manchester and Bristol.

In France, **IGN** (☎ 01 43 98 80 00; www.ign.fr; 107, rue de La Boétie, 75008 Paris) sells its sheet maps at stores in Paris and Dijon.

Another excellent resource, especially for preparing your vehicle for the Sahara and advice on desert driving, is the 2nd edition of *Sahara*

Overland: A Route and Planning Guide by Chris Scott. It includes 16 detailed route descriptions for the Algerian Sahara, often including GPS coordinates.

For general advice on good country maps of Algeria, see p203.

Vehicle Equipment

If you're travelling in your own 4WD, you should make sure that your engine has been rigorously checked and any potential problems either fixed or noted. If you choose the latter option, and even if you don't, a close to full set of spare parts is essential. Your tyres (including spares) must be in excellent condition, while spare inner tubes and repair kits are also a must. A spare battery can also be a good idea. Your vehicle should be equipped with either an additional petrol tank or petrol containers, as well as a number of large water containers or jerry cans – you'd be surprised at how many inexperienced desert travellers set out into the Sahara with the idea that a few water bottles will see them through.

'equip your vehicle with additional petrol and water'

Sand ladders (also known as sand plates), tow ropes and shovels are staples of Saharan 4WD expeditions, while electric compressors (air pumps that run from your car's engine and pump up your tyres) are useful for reinflating tyres after a journey through soft sand. An airbag jack is also an excellent thing to have on hand.

A satellite phone is another near-essential accessory, although if you're travelling with a tour company a satellite phone for the group *may* be part of the service.

RESPONSIBLE SAHARAN TRAVEL

Despite appearances, the Sahara can be an extremely fragile environment and the only evidence of your visit that you should leave behind is footprints in the sand. Some general rules to keep in mind so as to minimise your impact while travelling in the Sahara include the following:

- Carry out all your rubbish. If you've carried it in, you can carry it out. Most Algerian tour companies are sensitive to these concerns and leave behind little rubbish but you can make sure of it.

ENVIRONMENTALLY PISTE-OFF

Before you decide to explore the Algerian Sahara by 4WD, it is worth considering the environmental cost of what is known as the 'Toyotarisation' of the Sahara. With their large wheels, 4WDs break up the surface of the desert which is then scattered into the air by strong winds. By one estimate, the annual generation of dust has increased by 1000% in North Africa in the last fifty years. And in case you thought that your 4WD tracks across the sands would soon be erased by the winds, remember that tracks from WWII vehicles are still visible in the Libyan Desert six decades after the cessation of hostilities. Airborne dust is a primary cause of drought far more than it is a consequence of it, as it shields the earth's surface from sunlight and hinders cloud formation.

The consequences of our impatience in the desert extend far beyond Algeria and its desert communities. The stirred-up sand threatens to envelop large tracts of the world in dust, with serious consequences for human health, coral reefs and climate change. Plankton on the surface of the world's oceans is being smothered by sand with devastating implications for marine life. Dust storms are increasingly common in cities, such as Madrid and the dust-laden winds threaten to transform 90% of Spain's Mediterranean regions into deserts. Sand from the Sahara has even reached as far away as Greenland, settling on icebergs and causing them to melt faster. The process of desertification is extremely difficult and costly to reverse.

Travelling by camel or on foot may be more restricting, but it's the best way to ensure that you leave behind nothing but footprints in the sand.

- Minimise the waste you must carry out by taking minimal packaging and instead take reusable containers or stuff sacks.
- Never bury your rubbish. Digging disturbs soil and ground cover, and encourages erosion. Buried rubbish will more than likely be dug up by animals, who may be injured or poisoned by it. It may also take decades to decompose in the dry desert air.
- Don't rely on bought water in plastic bottles. Disposal of these bottles is creating a major problem as a quick look at the outskirts of many oasis towns or travellers' former camp sites will attest.
- Sanitary napkins, tampons and condoms should also be carried out despite the inconvenience. They burn and decompose poorly.
- Where there's no toilet, bury your waste. Dig a small hole 15cm (6 in) deep. Cover the waste with soil and a rock. Use toilet paper sparingly and bury it with the waste, or burn it.
- If you light a fire, don't surround it with rocks, as this creates a visual scar.
- When collecting firewood, only use dead wood and never take from a living tree.

'The most significant risks for travellers in the Sahara are dehydration and heat exhaustion'

TREKKING SAFETY

Apart from questions of vehicle maintenance (see p71 for details), there are two major safety aspects to trekking in the Algerian Sahara.

Security

The first thing that you must take into consideration is the question of security, because militant Islamist groups continue to operate in remote stretches of the Sahara and have targeted foreign travellers in the past, most spectacularly in 2003; see the boxed text, p181, for further details. After 31 of the 32 hostages were finally freed (one died of heat exhaustion while in captivity), few people back in Europe showed any sympathy for the former captives, instead calling on the released hostages to pay back the costs of the massive search. For its part, the Algerian government maintains that the groups would not have been kidnapped had they been travelling with an official Algerian guide.

The rules surrounding expeditions into the Algerian Sahara have since been tightened and all off-road travel south of Ghardaïa must be undertaken in the company of a professional local guide, which can be arranged in Tamanrasset, Djanet or Adrar.

The most important preparation you can undertake is to carefully check the prevailing security situation for the area in which you wish to travel. One source of such information is your own government (see p201), either from their travel advisory websites or from their embassies in Algiers.

Another important information stream to monitor is forums set up for Saharan travellers. The most comprehensive of these is the **Sahara Overland** (www.sahara-overland.com), the companion website to the book of the same name.

Apart from adhering to the requirement that you travel with a professional Algerian guide, other important precautions include notifying your embassy of your plans and providing a detailed itinerary to the police in Tamanrasset, Djanet or another regional centre before you set out.

Desert Health

The most significant risks for travellers in the Sahara are dehydration and heat exhaustion. These potentially serious conditions are best combated by drinking plenty of water, doing so often and keeping your head covered; for the latter, a hat is good, but a Tuareg *taguelmoust* (see p69 for more information) is even better. Resist the temptation to strip down to shorts and T-shirt at every available opportunity, because long sleeves and light trousers actually help to keep the body cool. Given that sweat usually evaporates in the desert before you realise it has appeared, you may not always be aware that your body is losing fluids. Don't wait until you're thirsty before drinking. You should aim to consume 6L of water per day – more if you're engaged in strenuous activity. You should also avoid direct sunlight between 10am and 3pm to minimise the burning and dehydrating effects of the sun. Remember also that the sun can be extremely powerful even on cloudy days.

Dehydration is a particular danger if you're struck down with diarrhoea, when the necessity of replacing lost bodily fluids and salts is even greater. It's also a good reason to ensure that food is properly prepared and cooked and that you, along with all those involved with your food preparation, are washing hands and cooking utensils regularly.

Another small but serious risk to your health in the Algerian Sahara is bites from snakes and scorpions. The Sahara has many poisonous snakes although the vast majority of travellers never see one. In winter and other colder months, snakes are a rarity. If you're camping in a rocky area, consider sleeping in a tent and avoid leaving any food scraps littered around the site. If that all sounds scary, remember that the incidence of snakebite is exceptionally rare and that snakes are probably more afraid of you than you are of them and will clear out long before you arrive.

If you do get bitten, remain calm, thoroughly wash the affected area and keep it below the level of your heart. Paracetamol, rather than aspirin, is recommended for the pain and you should get medical treatment as soon as possible.

Of less gravity, the hot, dry conditions can also lead to dry skin which is more uncomfortable than serious.

The most dangerous snake in the Sahara is the horned viper which buries itself almost completely beneath the sand so as to conceal itself from prey – avoid walking too far away from your camp without shoes.

Safety Guidelines

Before embarking on a walking trip, consider the following points to ensure a safe and enjoyable experience:

- Be sure you are healthy and feel comfortable walking for a sustained period.
- Obtain reliable information about physical and environmental conditions along your intended route. In practical terms, this means contacting the Office National du Parc Tassili (OPTN; p191) in Djanet or the Office du Parc Nationale de l'Ahaggar (L'OPNA; p185) in Tamanrasset.
- Be aware of local laws, regulations and etiquette about wildlife and the environment.
- Before entering the Tassili N'Ajjer National Park, pay the DA100 permit in Djanet; see p191 for details.
- Walk only in regions within your realm of experience and on tracks that suit your level of fitness.
- Be aware that weather conditions and terrain vary significantly from one region, or even from one trail, to another. Seasonal changes can significantly alter any trail. These differences influence the way walkers dress and the equipment they carry.
- Avoid camping in what seems like a dry riverbed *(oued)* because rain, even kilometres away, can transform the *oued* into a raging torrent within no time.

ON THE GROUND

You've dreamed a little, filled your backpack with all the necessaries, thought about responsible Saharan travel and informed yourself as to the risks. Now's the time to explore the Sahara for real and put the theory into practice.

REACHING THE SAHARA

If you stick to the major routes, the road network is fairly well developed. Without a vehicle, you can take any of the routes (p76) normally followed by the overland crowd by using public transport to reach the start of off-road desert trails. Transport on some of the routes is, however, infrequent so you'll need to be prepared to take a plane to get out or else sit around for a week or more waiting for a shared taxi to leave. This applies mainly to the eastern route from Hassi Messaoud down through In Amenas, Illizi and Djanet to Tamanrasset. The Route du Hoggar presents no such problems, although you may end up on a bus between In Salah and Tamanrasset.

TYPES OF EXPEDITION

Most people explore the Algerian Sahara using a mixture of 4WD and trekking by foot, but for those in no hurry camel-trekking is the most environmentally responsible manner to explore the Sahara. Believe it or not, cycling is also a possibility.

4WD

There's almost nowhere that you can't reach in the Algerian Sahara in a 4WD and you're almost certain to travel by 4WD at some point in your journey, even if it's only to reach the trailhead from which you commence your trek on foot. The advantage of travelling in this way is that you will be able to range much wider than you can on foot or by camel (unless you have months to spend on the latter). You will be able to reach a more varied range of sites and traverse a more representative sample of Saharan landscapes, leaving the Algerian Sahara with a better appreciation of its scale. Travelling in this way does, however, come at a significant environmental cost (see the boxed text, p71, for details), which is something that you should take into account when deciding how best to travel in the Sahara.

Even if you are a small group or a party of one, you should never travel into the Sahara without at least two vehicles (the guide or driver brings the other). For longer expeditions, an additional vehicle is always necessary for carrying food supplies, kitchen and camping equipment and your additional water and petrol.

Desert driving requires a whole new set of skills and if you're feeling as if you could use some instruction from the experts, **Timtar Expeditions** (☎ 029 346038; www.timtar.com) in Djanet offers courses from October to May.

For advice on equipping your 4WD vehicle for a foray, see p71.

> Organising a 4WD expedition through one of the travel agencies in Tamanrasset or Djanet should cost €50 to €80 per person per day.

Hiking

The desire to walk in the hot Saharan sun may seem like a strange form of madness, but there's no other way to reach and explore the fine rock art that is such a feature of the Tassili N'Ajjer National Park (p194). Remember, however, that this and other treks in the Algerian Sahara are almost always restricted to rocky mountain areas and no-one's expecting you to walk amid the sands of the Grand Ergs. Sturdy hiking boots are essential.

The overwhelming benefit of exploring the Sahara on foot is that it's just you and nature and that your impact upon the environment will likely be minimal.

Hiking tours can be arranged through all of the travel agencies in Djanet (p191). Tours organised through an international tour company (see p78) can also include walking components with the cost incorporated into the overall cost of your tour.

Camel-Trekking

Surveying the Sahara from high atop a camel is desert travel at its most atmospheric, allowing you to cover reasonable distances (20km to 40km per day) but at the same time slow down to a loping desert pace. It also enables you to truly experience the solitude of the desert without engine noise and to discover an intimacy with the landscape that simply isn't possible by 4WD. By camel, you may not see great swaths of the desert, but you'll see it in far greater detail and come to appreciate its subtleties far more than you could by motorised transport. Camel safaris are

Djanet travel agencies generally charge from €50 to €60 per person per day for treks into the Tassili N'Ajjer, which should include all water, food and camping equipment, a national park permit, a guide and pack animals for carrying your luggage and supplies.

THE GREAT CARAVANS OF THE SAHARA

People have been travelling through the Sahara by camel since the 1st century BC and the great trans-Saharan caravans once created some of the most lucrative trade routes in Africa.

For centuries, there were two principal kinds of Saharan caravan. The first were the caravans organised by wealthy merchants of the oasis towns of the Sahara and trading cities along the North African coast, such as Tripoli, or in the African interior such as Kano. The merchants rarely travelled themselves, but instead paid trusted cameleers to ferry their goods across the Sahara to distant towns where the merchants' agents sold the goods and bought new ones for the return journey. In this way, goods from the interior of Africa – precious stones, gold, silver, ivory, dates and ostrich plumes – headed north to the coast while items as unusual as glass necklaces, paper from Venice for use in religious texts and linen from Marseille passed through en route south. Trade caravans such as these were, for example, the only connection that the Roman cities of North Africa had with the interior of the continent.

The prosperous trading towns of the Sahara such as Timbuktu, Agadez, Murzuq and Ghadames actually produced few goods of their own, but their merchants became adept at profiting from passing trade and ultimately controlling it. The Tuareg, too, learned how to extract their profits, alternately looting the caravans and serving as paid protectors of the travelling salesmen.

The arrival of European traders and armies on the West African coast from the 15th century onwards marked the death knell for trans-Saharan caravans. Trade was reoriented away from the Sahara and the caravans became ever less frequent over the subsequent centuries, before finally disappearing altogether.

The second type of trans-Saharan caravan were the salt caravans, which were the exclusive domain of the Tuareg who ventured deep into the salt mines of the Sahara – mines at Taoudenni in northern Mali and Bilma in northeastern Niger were the most important. Many Tuareg then travelled to towns on the Saharan fringe where they traded the salt for foodstuffs, cloth and tea. For centuries, salt was so highly prized that it traded ounce-for-ounce with gold in the lands south of the Sahara. By the time the salt caravans returned home to their bases in the Hoggar Mountains of Algeria or the Aïr Mountains of Niger, they had been away for seven or eight months, during which time the difficulties of Saharan travel – daily, 18-hour forced marches were the norm – had taken their toll on humans and camels alike. Many never returned.

As late as the 19th century, caravans consisting of more than 20,000 camels would set out for the salt mines amid great fanfare. Salt caravans do still cross the Sahara, especially in Mali and Niger where camels remain the cheapest way of transporting salt, but they're a shadow of their former glories and the last salt caravans are a distant memory in Algeria.

also the most environmentally friendly way to see the Sahara – for more information see the boxed text, p71.

The major drawback of travelling by camel is that you will be restricted to seeing a relatively small corner of the desert – so vast are the distances of the Algerian Sahara that exploring several regions astride a camel would take more time than you probably have.

Travel agencies in Tamanrasset (p185) can organise camel treks into the Hoggar Mountains (p189) and Assekrem (p188), while international tour operators (see p78) can similarly make the arrangements.

If you're setting out on a camel expedition, consider buying Tuareg pants *(akerbai)*, with their exquisitely brocaded hems. These loose-fitting pants are very comfy and ideal for minimising the chafing of riding a camel.

Cycling

Cycling in the Sahara seems about as likely as skiing (see p198). But think about it a little more and you'll quickly come to the realisation that the arduous but infinitely rewarding trails of the Hoggar Mountains (p189) could be a mountain-biker's paradise.

Asking Algerian travel agencies about cycling tours is likely to inspire blank looks, and suitable two-wheeled transport is almost impossible to find in Algeria so you'll need to bring your own bicycle or mountain bike and spare parts. For international tour companies offering advice and/or cycling tours to the Hoggar Mountains, see p79.

ROUTES

The possibilities are endless. What follows is our pick of the best.

Cyclists planning to travel through the Algerian Sahara should consider contacting Bicycle Africa through www.ibike.org /bikeafrica; it has some information on cycling in the country.

Western Oases & Grand Erg Occidental

For those of you with a passion for desert oasis towns and sand seas of incomparable beauty, but with no desire to mount a major expedition, the road from Aïn Sefra to Ghardaïa (see above) could be for you. The road encircles the southern half of the Grand Erg Occidental and expeditions into the sands can be arranged from both Taghit (p165) and Timimoun (p169). The Grand Erg Occidental itself is one of the largest and most beautiful sand seas in the Sahara.

The Grand Erg Oriental

The northern limits of the Grand Erg Oriental can be seen from the road between Ouargla and El-Oued and this section can be travelled by public transport. The paved road south from Touggourt bisects the erg as it runs all the way down to Illizi (for an itinerary see p20), although you would really need your own vehicle for this journey.

Like its western counterpart, the Grand Erg Oriental is a signature Saharan sand sea, and international tour operators can organise journeys south from Hassi Messaoud. After crossing the erg, the routes diverge, with some heading for Illizi (three days) and the Tassili N'Ajjer, while others pass through Amguid – the site of a Tuareg massacre of a French military expedition in 1881 (see p32) – before entering the Hoggar Mountains from the north (three days). Another possibility is to cross an arm of the erg by leaving El-Oued bound for Deb Deb (three days).

One area of the Algerian Sahara that is considered off-limits at present is the Tanezrouft, the desolate and often trackless area of the Sahara west of Tamanrasset and south of Reggane and across the border into Mali.

The Trans-Saharan Highway

Although the Trans-Saharan Hwy sees far fewer travellers than it used to, the route from Ghardaïa down into Niger is part of Saharan travelling legend and completing it remains a significant notch on the belt of seasoned Saharan travellers. 'Highway' is something of a loosely applied term as wind-blown sand and the impossibility of regular maintenance have meant that the road can be difficult even to find. Although in theory this route can be completed using public transport, we don't recommend it because of the uncertainties of the journey and the bureaucratic formalities at the Niger border. In your own vehicle, allow four days to reach Arlit in northern Niger, whereafter there's a well-paved road.

Hoggar Mountains

The deep valleys and soaring, bizarrely shaped peaks of the Hoggar Mountains represent the magnificent heartland of the Algerian Sahara and are the spiritual home to the Kel Ahaggar, one of the major Tuareg confederations of the central Sahara. The most popular – and undoubtedly most spectacular – route climbs steeply up from Tamanrasset to the plateau of Atakor and Assekrem (p188); it's possible to take this route by either camel or 4WD. If your time is short, you can go as far as Assekrem and return to Tamanrasset the following day; even if the crowds that make this trek fill the route with anything but a desert solitude, don't miss it. If you've more time, there are countless opportunities to leave the crowds behind and explore further afield.

Tassili N'Ajjer

The rocky plateau that makes up the Tassili N'Ajjer National Park is only accessible on foot and you could easily spend a week trekking atop the plateau and down into the deep rocky valleys for which the region

> If the sands of the Grand Erg Oriental were laid out flat, the sand would still rise 26m above the earth. The Grand Erg Oriental is believed by geologists to have been a sand sea for at least 4000 years.

ENCOUNTERS WITH THE TUAREG

Although many travellers encounter the Tuareg as guides or drivers, there are still small numbers of Tuareg families who live a traditional life across southern Algeria. Most live in semipermanent shelters, although it's not uncommon to find young Tuareg girls or boys herding their goats in remote *oueds* (dry riverbeds) or old Tuareg men similarly far from home.

If you do encounter the Tuareg in this manner, there are a few things to remember. The most important is that these families live in the Hoggar or Tassili N'Ajjer because they choose to pursue a traditional lifestyle, not for the benefit of tourists. An increasingly exploitative relationship threatens that choice and Tuareg families are in danger of becoming a tourist sideshow as foreigners seek to meet an 'authentic' Tuareg family. It's a difficulty faced by indigenous peoples the world over and the most important thing to remember is to behave with the utmost discretion. If you meet an elderly Tuareg man, address him as 'Sheikh' or 'Haj' as a mark of respect. The Tuareg are a mine of information about the region and its history and spending time talking with them is far more important than sneaking a photo.

The Tuareg have, of course, learnt the ways of the world. Many will only allow their photos to be taken if you pay money or buy something from them, while one old Tuareg man said that he allowed photos to be taken by those with a digital camera so that he could then see himself! To avoid it becoming a one-way encounter, consider making a small contribution to fuel or firewood stocks, or purchasing one of the small items they offer for sale.

Some nomadic Tuareg openly wonder whether this will be the last generation of their people who live a traditional life. Older Tuareg lament the loss of traditional ways and you'll come across Tuareg men who know how to drive a 4WD but for whom the camel is a relative mystery. Many Tuareg have been forced to move into the cities of the Sahara and further afield by government policies, droughts and decades of war and rebellion.

Perhaps moving with a changing world is merely a continuation of the Tuareg's innate adaptability, which they learnt through the centuries while coping with the world's most hostile environment. And yet, the gradual erosion of traditional Tuareg ways as a result first of colonial invasion, then government and tourist intrusion into the Tuareg realm has led many to worry that an entire way of life is in danger of disappearing. If it does, it would be one of the great tragedies of Saharan history.

is famous. It's also possible to trek for shorter periods. For descriptions of possible routes, see p195.

Tamanrasset to Djanet

Sahara Unveiled by William Langeweische is a beautifully told account of his journey along the Trans-Saharan Hwy with a uncomfortable detour to the Tassili N'Ajjer before tourism arrived.

The 676km-, three-day route from Tamanrasset takes you via Assekrem and Ideles to Djanet. If you add on an exploration of the Tassili N'Ajjer, you will have covered the stand-out attractions of Algeria's southern Sahara. Travel agencies in Tamanrasset (p185) and Djanet (p191) can organise 4WD expeditions along this route. To complete this trek astride a camel would take a minimum of two weeks one-way.

TOUR OPERATORS

If this is your first journey to the Sahara, or if you can't face the logistics of organising your own expedition, there are dozens of recommended Algerian and international tour operators to choose from.

Algerian Operators

Akar Akar (☎ 029 344638; www.akar-akar.com in French; Tamanrasset) Long-established Tamanrasset agency with tours around the Hoggar.

Club d'Aventure Africaine (☎ 021 697922; www.caa-dz.com in French; 7 rue des Frères Oughlis, Algiers) Allows you to organise everything from Algiers.

Essendilène Voyages (☎ 029 475295; www.essendilene-voyages.com; Djanet) Has strong local contacts and is especially good if you're planning to cross into Niger, but also offers tours that include yoga, art therapy and family-friendly activities.

Hoggar Soleil (☎ 029 346972; www.hoggarsoleil.com in French; Tamanrasset) Four- to 14-day treks through the Hoggar and Tassili N'Ajjer.

Immidir Voyages (☎ 029 344468; www.immidir-voyages.com; Tamanrasset) Offers 4WD treks and tours around the Immidir region.

Mer de Sable (☎ 049 902595; www.agence-merdesable.com; rue Abd el-Kader Ziadi, Timimoun) Trips in camel caravans and by 4WD into the Grand Erg Occidental.

M'Zab Tours (☎ 029 880002; mzabtours@hotmail.com; ave du 1er Novembre, Ghardaïa)

The Tuaregs by Karl G Prasse is one of the most accessible reads about the Tuareg of Algeria and their history of occupying the Algerian south.

Tailored tours around the M'Zab and the Grand Ergs.

Tarakeft Voyages (☎ 029 342007; www.tarakeft.com; Tamanrasset) Runs 4WD and trekking tours in the Hoggar and Mali.

Timbeur Voyages (☎ 029 475270; www.voyages-timbeur.com; Djanet) Short trips around Djanet and into the Tassili N'Ajjer.

Timtar Expeditions (☎ 029 346038; www.timtar.com; Djanet) Creative camel treks and 4WD expeditions.

Walene Voyages (☎ 029 344229; www.walene-voyages.com in French; Tamanrasset) Range of tours including camel treks to Assekrem.

Zeriba Voyages (☎ 061 382853/346924; www.zeribavoyage.com in French; Djanet) Tassili N'Ajjer treks and the Djanet–Tamanrasset route.

International Operators

All of the following agencies can arrange treks through the Hoggar Mountains and Tassili N'Ajjer.

Adventures Abroad (www.adventures-abroad.com) Small group tour.

Cheche Tours (www.chechetours.com) Excellent range of tours, some of which extend into Niger and Mali.

Explore Worldwide (www.explore.co.uk) Limited range of small-group tours.

Hommes et Montagnes (www.hommes-et-montagnes.fr in French) Eight- to 22-day treks ranked according to difficulty.

La Route du Sahara (www.laroutedusahara.com) Cultural tours to Djanet, and de Foucauld 'spiritual treks'.

Les Matins du Monde (www.lesmatinsdumonde.com in French) Tours and rock-climbing.

Lost Frontiers (www.lostfrontiers.com) Three-week tour.
Point Afrique (www.point-afrique.com in French) Extensive range of personally tailored and group tours.
Sablé0 (www.sableo.com) Regular cycling trips to the Hoggar Mountains.
Sahara Travel (www.saharatravel.co.uk) Self-drive 4WD expeditions.
Terres d'Aventure (www.terdav.com in French) Tours and family-friendly trips suited to kids.

Saharan Rock Art

Algeria shares with neighbouring Libya and Niger one of the finest collections of prehistoric rock art in the world, and seeking out the finely rendered paintings and carvings of Algeria's south is one of the undoubted highlights of a visit to the country. These are more than mere paintings on remote rock walls. Many date back 12,000 years. Many depict animals that haven't been seen in these parts for millennia and which are impossible to imagine in the barren heart of the world's largest desert. Indeed, there is something at once poignant and improbable about standing amid the splendid, parched cathedrals and finding images that tell the story of when the Sahara was a green and fertile land rich in water and wildlife.

Many thoughts spring to mind as you contemplate the extraordinary detail, the whimsical beauty that the images portray. The most obvious response is one of wonder. In many ways the wonder we feel when viewing rock art may not be so dissimilar from the wonder when confronted with the improbability of a giraffe, for example, which prompted the artists to paint the images in the first place.

How on earth have such seemingly fragile works of art survived the considerable ravages of time? How is it that the artists who left behind these masterpieces were able to capture a sense of childlike simplicity in their conception of the natural world but do so with such exceptional skill? How different was the Saharan world they inhabited that creatures, such as the elephant, giraffe and lion once roamed these wadis? And who were they, these great artists whose work still captivates us?

Most of the answers we know, but like any great mystery in this Saharan landscape of the imagination, there are many about which we can only speculate.

African Rock Art, by David Coulson and Alec Campbell, is the definitive text on the rock art of Africa, with informative narrative sections on the Sahara and lavish photographs and illustrations.

THE DISCOVERY OF SAHARAN ROCK ART

Although the indigenous Tuareg inhabitants of the Sahara have known about the rock art in their midst for centuries, it has only recently captured

---

WHO WERE THE ARTISTS?

The question of who sat on rocky ledges mixing their paints or chipping painstakingly away at the rock is one that continues to baffle archaeologists and rock-art specialists, inviting speculation that has intrigued European travellers for centuries. In 1850 the great German explorer Heinrich Barth visited the Tassili N'Ajjer of southwestern Algeria and wrote that 'No barbarian could have graven the lines with such astonishing firmness, and given to all the figures the light, natural shape which they exhibit'.

Some archaeologists attribute the images to the Neolithic ancestors of the modern Tuareg, the people who remained in the Sahara as the climate dried. Others claim that the Garamantes people, who inhabited Wadi al-Ajal across the border in Libya to the northwest from 900 BC to AD 500, were responsible, for they were a sophisticated people who made the desert bloom long after the rains stopped and other Saharan peoples fled south. Both claims may indeed be true, but the fact that much of the art predates these groups suggests that they were merely following a tradition set in motion by earlier indigenous inhabitants of the region.

The local Tuareg believe that the ancient artists saw their art as a school for their descendants, a history book of what they saw and how they lived. Or as one Tuareg told us, 'perhaps they were people like we are today, because human beings always like to leave their mark, to leave something behind that will remain long after we have gone.'

the attention of the outside world. Two German explorers of the Sahara, Heinrich Barth and Gustav Nachtigal, reported their findings and even made sketches of some of the pieces in the 19th century, but it was not until the middle of the 20th century that serious studies of the art were carried out. Frenchman Henri Lhote visited the Tassili N'Ajjer in the 1930s and was so intrigued that he returned two decades later, in 1956, to undertake a major catalogue of the region's art. Although it would be left to later archaeologists to investigate the meaning of what he saw, Lhote was the first to delineate the distinct periods from which the art dates and to realise that the images told of the 'spiritual and religious existence of the different peoples which followed on, one after another'. At the same time, just across the border in the Jebel Acacus of Libya, a team from the University of Rome led by Professor Fabrizio Mori performed a similar task, proving that borders have never been a barrier to the flourishing of artistic creativity. The work done by these specialists and their successors was critical in ensuring that the Tassili N'Ajjer, like the Jebel Acacus in Libya, was inscribed on Unesco's World Heritage List of Endangered and Protected Sites.

Travels and Discoveries in North and Central Africa, by Heinrich Barth, includes the author's 1850s discovery of the rock art of the Tassili N'Ajjer.

THE CLIMATIC CONTEXT

When the Ice Age was at its coldest in the northern hemisphere, around 20,000 years ago (18,000 BC), it ushered in a period of low rainfall and barren landscapes across the Sahara – much the same as prevails today.

With the thaw of the Ice Age 12,000 years ago (10,000 BC), the climate of the Sahara again became temperate and wild animals and people returned to occupy most of the region. This was the Sahara's golden age, when the region was bathed in what we would now call a Mediterranean climate, when vegetation and water were as plentiful as the wild animals that now adorn so many rock walls. At such a period in history the Sahara must have been a great place to live, with ample prey for hunters and a natural world that provided more than enough food for the small numbers of people spread across this immense land.

The English Patient (directed by Anthony Minghella): yes, it's pure Hollywood and no, it wasn't filmed in Algeria, but no film captures the excitement of the discovery of Saharan rock art quite like this.

Another possible dry spell approximately 8000 years ago (6000 BC) saw the introduction of domesticated cattle from the west, but for the next 3000 years the Sahara continued to be covered with savanna, year-round lakes, pastureland and acacia trees. The temperate, often humid climate continued until 4500 years ago (2500 BC), when the last transition commenced and the Sahara began to become the vast, arid desert that it is today, a process that was drawn out over 1500 years. Perennial lakes were replaced by more-seasonal water sources and, as the region became progressively drier, oases replaced lakeside and mountain villages as the sites of settlements and agricultural or pastoral activity. It was also the period in which trans-Saharan trade became the dominant economic activity, fostered by an increased reliance on chariots, then horses and finally camels, which were introduced to the Sahara 2200 years ago (200 BC).

One painting discovered by Henri Lhote in the Tassili N'Ajjer and called *The Negro Mask* bears a striking resemblance to the masks later used by the Senoufo people of West Africa.

In addition to providing a human complement to geological studies of the Sahara's history, the Saharan rock art provides an invaluable resource depicting humankind's changing relationship with nature. The shift from a time when wild animals were dominant over humans towards domestication and a taming of the natural environment through food production and more intensive land-use practices could be Saharan rock art's most enlightening legacy.

TYPES OF ROCK ART

The two main types of rock art in the Sahara are paintings and carvings (also known as petroglyphs).

WHY ROCK ART MATTERS

When the rock art of the Sahara was discovered by the outside world in the 19th century, few Europeans could believe that the paintings and engravings were the work of what were at the time believed to be the primitive cultures of Africa. Subsequent studies have proved such assumptions to be wrong and this is perhaps one of rock art's greatest legacies: African civilisations may not have left many written records, but their civilisations were as advanced as any in Europe at the time. As such, Saharan rock art is a priceless record of an otherwise undocumented period of African history, representing as it does the earliest known form of African communication.

The evidence of symbolic and religious inspiration behind the art – many studies point to religious symbolism as the primary motivation behind the art – suggests that the natural world was central to the spiritual life of the ancients, thereby deepening our understanding of the ancient world.

By providing a detailed snapshot of the region's human, geographical and climatic history, the rock art also provides a salutary lesson to the modern world in these days of creeping environmental catastrophe. After all, the artists of the green and pleasant land that the Sahara once was almost certainly never imagined that their world would one day become a desert. Not only is Saharan rock art a powerful reminder to not assume that the natural world as we know it will last forever, how well we protect art work that has survived the millennia but is now under threat from our supposedly advanced civilisation (see p84) will also provide important signs as to whether we are capable of protecting the human heritage of those who went before us.

Rock-art specialists are also keen to point out that the human history represented in the Sahara is our own heritage with strong links to the artistic influences of the Western world. For example, in *African Rock Art*, David Coulson and Alec Campbell argue that the breaking down of boundaries in European art in the early 20th century, which led to genres such as the Cubism of Picasso and others, was inspired by the masks and statuettes of sub-Saharan Africa, art forms which may have themselves derived from the artists of the Sahara before they were driven south by a drying climate.

There is also a belief among some archaeologists that it was from the Sahara that such art spread to Ethiopia, Kenya and Egypt; and the Egyptian artists possibly drew on the Saharan art for inspiration in the great subsequent flourishing of Egyptian art.

Rock Art in Africa: Mythology and Legend, by Jean-Loic Le Quellec, is another wonderful book that will have you imagining remote desert worlds and the people who once inhabited them.

The paintings (also called pictographs) were usually applied using a brush made of feathers or animal hair, a spatula made of stick or bone or the fingers of the artist. To ensure accurate proportions, the artists are believed to have painted the images in outline and then coloured them in. Most of the paintings in Algeria are red, which was achieved through the use of a wet pigment thought to have been derived from ground-and-burned stone; the colouration came from soft rock containing oxidised iron (hematite or ochre). A liquid binder was then applied, most often egg-white or milk, although urine, animal fat and blood were also used on occasion. It is to these binding agents that we owe the remarkable longevity of the paintings.

The carvings were achieved through a method known as 'pecking', which involved the use of a heavy, sharp stone. A second stone was sometimes used to bang the sharp stone like a pick. Like the paintings, the outline was usually completed first, often by scratching. Upon completion, some of the lines were ground smooth and, on occasion, the rock face was smoothed first as a form of preparation. After metal was introduced to the Sahara around 3200 years ago (1200 BC), a metal spike may have been used.

Although the varieties of subject matter across the many open-air galleries of Saharan rock art are endless, the two most common forms are human and animal figures. Often stylised, the human figures are shown in many different poses, from what may have been portraits to scenes of hunting, celebration and even making love, while animals are most frequently shown in motion, often pursued by hunters.

PERIODS OF SAHARAN ROCK ART

The rock art of North Africa is thought to have its origins almost 12,000 years ago (10,000 BC) in the central Sahara, although some historians believe that many paintings or carvings could date back even further. Although centuries of exposure to the elements have made it difficult to precisely date much of the rock art, most of the examples to be found in the Algerian Sahara fall within five relatively discrete historical periods.

The first of these is most commonly known as the Wild Fauna Period (10,000–6000 BC); other names include the Early Hunter Period and the Bubalus Period after a species of giant buffalo that became extinct 5000 years ago. This era is characterised by the portrayal of elephants, giraffes, crocodiles, hippopotamuses, rhinoceroses and lions from the time when the Sahara was covered by the plentiful savanna.

The Round Head Period (8000–6000 BC), overlapping its forerunner, is known for human figures with formless bodies and painted, circular heads devoid of features. Paintings from this period are found only in the Tassili N'Ajjer and nearby Jebel Acacus in Libya, and often take on enormous proportions. Women are often shown with arms raised, perhaps calling for blessings from the massive male figures alongside. During this period the people of the central Sahara are believed to have been foragers in the era prior to the appearance of domesticated stock. Its later stages feature more decorative figures adorned with headdresses and unusual clothing.

The next era was the Pastoral Period (5500–2000 BC), also known as the Bovidian Period, which coincides with the gradual transition from a temperate to arid climate. As such, this period in some ways marks the beginning of the modern Saharan world. Accordingly, human figures are shown in positions of dominance over the natural world, with spears, domesticated cattle, diminishing wild animals and ceremonies in keeping with more settled communities. Paintings of boats and the arrival of people with less Negroid features in the Tassili N'Ajjer also feature. Curiously, experts also believe that this was when the skill of the artists began to show a decrease in quality.

The Horse Period (1000 BC–AD 1) followed, with many images of horses or horse-drawn chariots, some seemingly propelled through the air, reflecting the fact that transport and movement became more sophisticated and enabled relatively long-distance travel. Cattle are by far the dominant forms. Human figures from this period are represented by two triangles, one upright and one upside down, joined at the apex with a circular head on top. Much of the Tuareg writing (Tifinagh) alongside the paintings is from this period.

The final era of Saharan rock art was the Camel Period (200 BC–present). Camels became the Sahara's beast of burden and they are shown in abundance during this period. Paintings from the earliest part of this period are of the highest quality while more recent ones are nowhere near as finely conceived.

WHERE TO SEE ROCK ART IN ALGERIA

The desert realm of remote massifs in the far southeast of Algeria is littered with rock paintings and carvings, but it is the Tassili N'Ajjer National Park (p194) that qualifies as the premier rock-art site anywhere

It is believed that in 18,000 BC the Sahara was larger than it is today, reaching far into West and even Central African regions that we now know as the Sahel.

Met Museum – Timeline of Art History (www .metmuseum.org/toah /hd/nroc/hd_nroc.htm) is a compact introduction to the art of the Sahara, with a section dedicated to the Tassili N'Ajjer.

The strange letters which appear on some rock walls are from the Tifinagh alphabet of the Tuareg, although many modern Tuareg are unable to read the letters in their ancient form.

in the world. Home to more than 15,000 petroglyphs and pictographs spread over 80,000 sq km, the Tassili N'Ajjer is the Louvre, Prado and Uffizi of the rock-art world rolled into one and if you came to Algeria and saw only the Tassili N'Ajjer, you'd leave more than satisfied.

That's not to say that there are not impressive rock art sites elsewhere, and in most cases you'll find them to be less overrun with large groups of tourists. In addition to the neighbouring national park, there are some fine sites close to Djanet, especially the iconic engraving of *la Vache qui Pleu* (Crying Cows) at Tagharghart (p194), while the paintings are also outstanding at Tamdjert (p191), close to Illizi.

Elsewhere, the Tassili du Hoggar (p189) provides an even more spectacular backdrop to the paintings and engravings, with the latter especially fine at Tin Tarabine (p190).

Away to the northwest, the rarely visited Tassili d'Immidir (p182) has hundreds of fine paintings, a wildly beautiful landscape and scarcely a tourist in sight. The Tassili d'Immidir can be accessed from either In Salah or Tamanrasset.

There are also some rock engravings at Taghit (p165) on the western fringe of the Grand Erg Occidental.

THE PROTECTION OF ROCK ART

The rock art of the Sahara may have proved to be extraordinarily durable down through the millennia, but it has never been endangered like it is today. While the local Tuareg proudly seek to safeguard the art forms and have lived alongside them for millennia, the same can't be said for tourists and oil companies prospecting in desert areas – their increasing encroachment into the rock-art world is the major threat to the art's survival.

Although oil companies have caused some damage through their prospecting, one company has set up plans for the art's preservation.

While the vast majority of tourists respect the rock art and leave it as they found it, a greedy few have decided that it would make a beautiful (or lucrative) souvenir of their visit to Algeria. Other than security concerns, the subsequent belief by the Algerian authorities that tourists cannot be trusted is central to the requirement that visits to southern Algeria can only be undertaken with a professional guide.

Algeria's suspicion of travellers on this score has not been misplaced. One of the most publicised cases came in 2004, when five German tourists went missing. Fearing a terrorist abduction, the Algerian authorities mounted a massive search, only to discover that the tourists in questions had deliberately escaped their guide to go rock art hunting. They were finally discovered with a distressing array of 130 rock art pieces in their bags. They were sentenced to three months in prison and fined UK£262,000.

Sadly, such stories are all too common in Algeria, as well as in neighbouring Libya and Niger. Acts of vandalism have included chipping away sections of the rock wall and throwing water on the paintings to enhance the light for taking photographs, as well as using complex silicon processes designed to copy the paintings, all of which have placed in jeopardy the survival of art forms that have existed for over 12 millennia.

In addition to damage caused by humans, the impact of the Sahara's harsh climate is also playing a part. On a recent visit to the Jebel Acacus of Libya, we found a badly faded painting that was vividly colourful just five years ago. The cause? Unusually heavy rains that caused water to run down the rock, thereby erasing the painting.

The carving known as *la Vache qui Pleu* (Crying Cows) at Tagharghart is considered one of the masterpieces of Saharan rock art and experts believe that the artist spent months studying the site before beginning.

Le Grand Dieu du Sefar (The Great God of Sefar) in the Tassili N'Ajjer rises over 3.25m tall and, according to Henri Lhote, dates back 8000 years and belongs to the Round Head Period of Saharan rock art.

Bradshaw Foundation (www.bradshawfoundation.com/africa/) contains up-to-date news on rock-art protection, as well as galleries of photos from Saharan rock-art sites.

ROCK ART RULES OF ENGAGEMENT

It seems extraordinary that we should have to say this, but the basic rule of observing rock art is to leave the paintings and engravings as you find them.

More specifically, the various organisations dedicated to studying and protecting rock art (see below) have laid out a number of guidelines that you should follow in order to avoid accelerating the natural deterioration of the art:

- Never touch the rock art – sweat and your skin's natural oils speed up the process of fading, while the wearing down of rock by touching is similarly damaging.
- Never throw liquids on a painting or outline an image in chalk to enhance its photogenic qualities – the damage to desert varnish is irreparable.
- Never remove even the most ordinary stones from a rock art site – these may be critical for future scientific studies of the site; this is Algeria's national heritage and not yours to steal.
- Never for a minute imagine that you are improving the open-air gallery by adding your own graffiti – what you're observing is art, what you add is vandalism.
- Never walk atop an engraving or painting in order to get a better view or enable a more favourable photographic angle – pieces can break off and the loss of desert varnish inhibits future study of the site.
- Try to avoid getting too close to the rock and leaving a mass of footprints and tyre tracks alongside – it spoils it for everyone else, especially photographers, and will continue to scar the environs for years.
- Take out with you all rubbish (including cigarette butts, water bottles and cans) that you carry to the site.
- If camping in a rock-art area, never set up camp closer than 100m to a rock-art site.
- Respect the right of other travellers to view the rock art in silence and free from human toilet refuse.

ROCK ART ASSOCIATIONS

If you want to learn more about Saharan rock art or about efforts being undertaken to preserve rock art across Africa, contact the outstanding **Trust for African Rock Art** (TARA; ☎ 254-20-884467; www.africanrockart.org; PO Box 24122, Nairobi, Kenya). It's also worth keeping an eye on its upcoming expeditions to see if the association is heading to Algeria and whether you can join it.

In Germany the **Heinrich-Barth-Institut** (☎ 0221-556680; fst.afrika@uni-koeln.de; www.archaeoafrica.de) at the University of Köln is also dedicated to the study of rock art, while the **American Rock Art Research Association** (www.arara.org) flies the flag in the USA.

In France the excellent nonprofit **Association des Amis de l'Art Rupestre Saharien** (http://aars.fr/index_en.html) promotes studies of Saharan rock art and has a range of publications and forums for discussion.

Algiers

Algiers & Around

Algiers 'la blanche', the white one, is what the French called the capital of Algeria. A big, bustling, whitewashed city, with the Mediterranean out front, hills and rich farmland behind, Algiers (El-Djazaïr in Arabic) is an exciting destination and the gateway to the country's interior.

Algiers was the most successful of all the Barbary pirate bases, especially in the 16th century under the most remarkable pirate of all, Kheireddin Barbarossa. It was also the most cherished of all French colonial centres. And since independence in 1962, it has been the political, economic and cultural hub of an extremely large and culturally and geographically diverse country. The largest port in northwest Africa and the largest city too, it now spreads far to accommodate a population that has doubled in 20 years.

Algiers suffered along with the rest of the country during the 'black years' of the 1990s. Since then, it has seen a strange split in its fortunes. You don't have to walk far in the centre to see people hanging around with nothing to do. All capitals have their jobless and homeless, but they look out of place in a country that has just paid off its foreign debt. Thanks mainly to oil and gas revenue, there has never been so much cash in the city – the state is spending large sums and there is a sense among some individuals that money is there to be made. The number of new cars choking the main roads is a sign of growing personal prosperity.

Yet, in its rush to modernise Algiers has still preserved some of its old mystique; it has a strong sense of identity and is still dazzlingly white.

HIGHLIGHTS

- Lie low in the **Casbah** (p93) – follow pirates and princes through the lower part of Algiers' old town

- Sip a cold drink in the garden of the **Hôtel el-Djazaïr** (p102), the old St Georges

- Visit the ruins of **Tipaza** (p104) to see how sweet life must have been here 2000 years ago

- Roll up your sleeves to enjoy a plate of seafood at one of the many **seafood restaurants** (p100)

- Live like a king, or at least a prince, at the **Palais des Raïs** (p95)

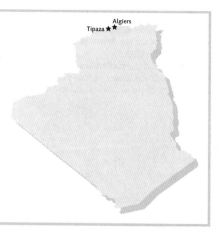

Algiers
Tipaza ★★

ALGIERS الجزائر

☎ 021 / pop 3.3 million

HISTORY

The beginning could not be more romantic: legend tells that 20 companions of the hero Hercules sailed into the bay and settled here. The truth of the city's earliest origins is lost in the sand or still buried beneath modern buildings, but there are clear signs that the bay, with its perfect natural harbour, attracted early settlers. The Phoenicians used it as a staging post between Carthage in the east and the pillars of Hercules to the west. For many centuries it was a convenient anchorage fought over by passing powers – the Romans took it in 146 BC, the Vandals swept through in the 5th century AD, during the 6th century the Byzantines retook it and developed a small Christian community, and in 650 it came under Arab control – but it remained insignificant until the 10th century and the emergence of a strong ruler. The local Berber leader Bologhin ibn Ziri took control of the region in the 970s, after the Fatimid moved their capital from Mahdia (Tunisia) to Cairo, and named the city El-Djezaïr, as it is still called today.

Successive Maghrebi rulers – the sultans from Tlemcen, Fès and elsewhere – always ensured they had control of the port, which still only had local strategic importance. All this changed in the 16th century when the great powers of the Mediterranean, the Spanish, French, Venetians, Genoese and Ottomans, fought for control of the sea. In 1510 the proselytising Spanish took control, but eight years later in an inspired move, the inhabitants declared themselves subjects of the Ottoman sultan and called on the Greek pirates, Aroudj and his younger brother Kheireddin Barbarossa to protect them. After Aroudj was killed fighting the Spanish, Barbarossa led the fight and finally defeated his more powerful adversary in 1529, establishing the regency of El-Djezaïr and becoming High Admiral of the Ottoman navy.

Barbarossa established the city as we can see it – the harbour with its protective arm, tipped with a lighthouse; the huddled houses of the Casbah sloping up the hill; the lookout and fortifications on the hilltop where the citadel now stands. The site was ideal, the place well planned and for 300 years, El-Djezaïr remained the pre-eminent Mediterranean pirate base that even the mighty British navy proved unable to destroy. Under Mohamed ben Osmane Khodja, dey from 1766–91, El-Djezaïr flourished into a well-fortified city of 100,000 inhabitants. The city became increasingly rich as one of the trailheads for the trans-Saharan caravans, as well as from demanding tribute from passing ships and taking action if the tribute was denied: there are many stories of both Christian and Muslim ships being captured by Algerian pirates, with all hands on board either being ransomed or pressed into slavery. It was during this period that many of the most interesting buildings in the city were constructed.

British Admiral Nelson bombarded the port in 1804, hoping to slow the movement of slaves; it didn't work. In 1815 it was the turn of Commodore Decatur and his American squadron: they captured the Algerian flagship and forced the dey of El-Djezaïr into an agreement to end tribute and slavery. Decatur was dubbed the 'conqueror of the Barbary pirates'. In August the following year a British and a Dutch squadron were sent to secure the release of the British consul and more than 1000 other Christians held captive in the city. The commander of the British ships, Admiral Pellew, again bombarded the city into submission, and forced the dey to abandon his palace for the safety of the citadel.

The continuing threat of piracy in the southern Mediterranean provided a resurgent France with the pretext it needed to move south. Their hope was to counterbalance British influence in the Mediterranean by controlling the southern straits of one of the sea's more narrow passages. On 14 June 1830, a force of 37,612 Frenchmen landed on the beach of Sidi Ferruch, just north of the city. The French claimed they had no initial plan to establish a colony, but in 1834 they officially annexed much of northern Algeria, making Algiers the capital of their new colony.

The city was rebuilt under French rule. The citadel, with its strategic position, was strengthened to ensure security and a large area of the lower Casbah was demolished to make way for new roads. After the French

ALGIERS

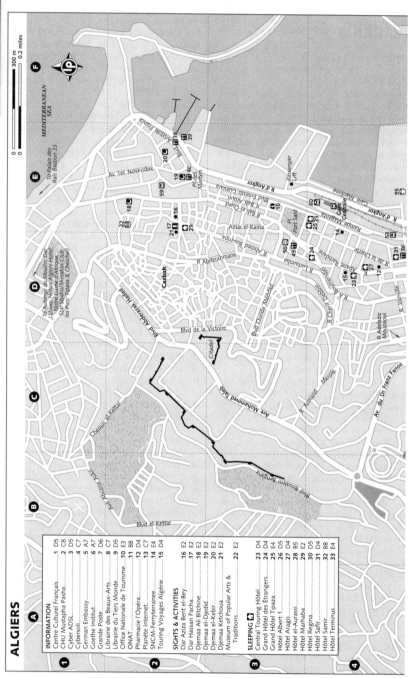

INFORMATION
Centre Culturel Français...........	1 D5
CHU Mustapha Pasha...............	2 C8
Cyber ADSL...........................	3 D5
Cybersoll.............................	4 C7
German Embassy.....................	5 A7
Goethe Institut.......................	6 A7
Grande Poste.........................	7 D6
Librairie des Beaux-Arts...........	8 C7
Librairie du Tiers Monde..........	9 D5
Office Nationale de Tourisme....	10 E3
ONAT..................................	11 B8
Pharmacie l'Opéra...................	12 D4
Planète Internet......................	13 C7
SNCM-Ferryterranee...............	14 E4
Touring Voyages Algérie...........	15 D4

SIGHTS & ACTIVITIES
Dar Aziza Bent el-Bey..............	16 E2
Dar Hassan Pacha...................	17 E2
Djemaa Ali Bitchine................	18 E2
Djemaa el-Djedid...................	19 E2
Djemaa el-Kebir.....................	20 E2
Djemaa Ketchoua...................	21 E2
Museum of Popular Arts &	
Traditions...........................	22 E2

SLEEPING
Central Touring Hôtel..............	23 D4
Grand Hôtel des Étrangers........	24 D4
Grand Hôtel Tipaza.................	25 E4
Hôtel Albert 1.......................	26 D5
Hôtel Arago..........................	27 D4
Hôtel el-Aurassi.....................	28 B5
Hôtel Marhaba.......................	29 E2
Hôtel Regina.........................	30 D5
Hôtel Safir...........................	31 D4
Hôtel Samir..........................	32 B8
Hôtel Terminus......................	33 E4

300 m
0.2 miles

MEDITERRANEAN
SEA

To Palais des
Raïs Bastion 23

Av. 1er Novembre

Pl. des
Martyrs

To Auberge du Moulin; Dar
Jablou; Hilton Algiers Hotel;
Notre Dame d'Afrique;
Star Studio/Sheraton Club
les Pins; Tipaza & Cherchell

R. Abderahmane

Casbah

Blvd Abderrazak Hadad

Blvd de la Victoire

Citadel

Ave Mohammed Taleb

Blvd Bouzrina Benghana

Blvd el-Kettar

Chemin el-Kettar

Ave Arsène Aklii

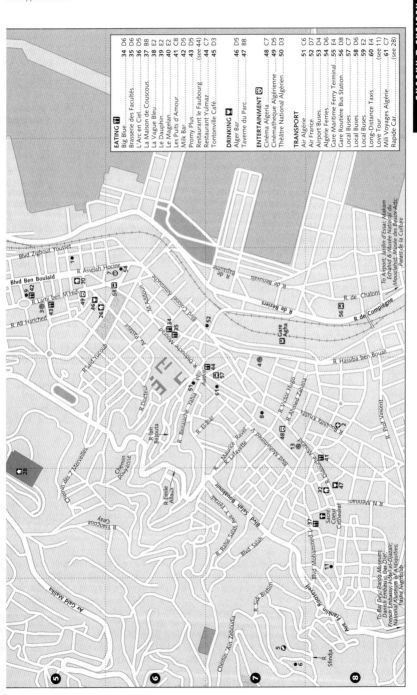

Blvd Zighout Youssef

Blvd Ben Boulaid

R Asselah Hocine

R Larbi ben M'Hidi

R Aït Hariched

R Ali Hariched

R Said Yousub

R Docteur

R Ibn
Batouta

Chemin
Poulanne

R Emile
Allaux

R Françoise Ceay

Av Gald Malika

Chemin des 7 Merveilles

Chemin Aïn Zeboudja

R Sidi Brahim

R Raïse Salah

Blvd Salah

Blvd Salah Bouakouir

Av-Z Ferradj

Maurice Ravel

R Lafayette

R Benaïche Yaha

R El-Bar

Av Pasteur

Av Didouche Mourad

Blvd Colonel Amirouche

R de Bapaume

R de Beauvais

R de Bézeirs

R de Chatons

R de Compiègne

R Hassiba ben Bouali

R Victor Hugo

R Ahmed Zabana

Bouhila Khalifa

R N Mennan

Blvd Mohammed V

Blvd Mohammed V

Ave Franklin Roosevelt

R
Sfindja

R Pasteur

Sacré
Coeur
Cathédral

Gare
Agha

To Airport; Jardin d'Essai; Makam
Echahid & Musée National du
Moudjahid; Musée des Beaux-Arts;
Palais de la Culture

To Bar Deci; Bardo Museum;
Danish Embassy; Dar Diff;
French Embassy; Hôtel-el-Djazair;
National Museum of Antiquities;
Pasha Nightclub

emperor Napoléon III and his wife, the empress Eugénie, visited in 1860, the area south of the Casbah was laid out as the Ville Nouvelle, with broad boulevards and large buildings. It was, in the words of an old colon (colonial) sifting through his memories, 'one of the most beautiful cities the French ever built'. It also became part of metropolitan France, unlike other French-controlled cities in North Africa, such as Tunis and Casablanca, which were mere colonies.

Algiers' strategic importance was underlined during WWII, when it became the base for Charles de Gaulle's Free French army as well as the headquarters of British and American war planners. Winston Churchill and General Eisenhower were among the power players who spent time in the city from 1943 to the end of the war.

The independence movement's origins stretch way back, but it began in earnest with the end of the war – VE Day celebrations in Constantine, Guelma and especially Sétif became bloody confrontations. Although Algiers was quieter than other northern towns and cities, by the late 1950s it was the epicentre of an increasingly savage struggle to free the country, which culminated in independence in 1962.

Algeria's oil and gas resources have helped turn the former colonial capital into a modern city, although progress was halted in 1992 when the military-backed government annulled an election it had just lost to an Islamist party. The resulting violence, during which corpses were regularly thrown out into the streets, cast a pall of anxiety and suspicion over the city, which is only now, and very slowly, beginning to dissipate.

ORIENTATION

Algiers spreads around a huge crescent bay, hemmed in by steep hills and facing north into the Mediterranean. The city skyline is dominated by two structures, both impossible to miss. To the south of the centre is the 92m-high Makam Eshahid (Martyrs' Memorial), and closer to the city centre, a concrete box rises on pillars above the whitewashed colonial city, the five-star Hôtel Aurassi.

The Casbah, the heart of the old or 'upper' town, fills the hillside above the northern part of the port, and is topped by the citadel. South of the Casbah is the French-built Ville Nouvelle, the 'lower' town. This is the commercial and business centre, where you will find the major shops, banks, hotels and the post office. The train station and *gare maritime* (ferry terminal) are only five minutes' walk north of this area, and the *gare routière* (bus station) 20 minutes to the south.

Algiers is a good city to walk in, especially in the lower town (see the walking tour p97). However, you are advised against walking in parts of the Casbah unless you feel confident about the risks (see p92). Most sites in the centre are within walking distance.

The French adapted a grid system of roads to the curves of Algiers bay. A major highway runs along the edge of the water, passing the train station, port and continuing out to the airport. The city centre is raised above this, with blvd Zirout Youssef serving as a corniche, popular in the evenings as a place to stroll and catch the evening breeze.

A long street, which changes name several times – rues Bab Azzoun, Ali Boumendjel, Larbi ben M'Hidi, Emir Abdelkader, Didouche Mourad – joins the upper and lower towns, running south from the place des Martyrs at the edge of the Casbah, past the elegant place Port Said and the Grande Poste to climb to the residential heights lined with shops, offices and restaurants.

Most embassies are in the suburb of Hydra, 5km south of the centre, or in the suburbs of El-Biar and Bouzaréah, all easily reached by taxi or by bus from place des Martyrs.

Traffic in Algiers has become worse in recent years, as the number of privately owned cars has risen dramatically. The morning and evening rush hours are now a real problem, and it can take hours to make a journey which, at other times, might take half an hour.

Maps

The **Institut National de Cartographie et de Télédétecion** (INCT; ☎ 021 739260; 20 rue Abane Ramdane) is the state mapping agency and produces excellent 1:7500 large-scale sheet maps of the city. You usually have to buy them in sets of six, but Sheet 1.5 covers all of central Algiers, from Bologhine in the north to beyond the transport hubs at Sidi Mohamed in the south (and with a larger-scale inset of the Casbah). The INCT maps may also be available, or can be ordered, in some bookshops.

ALGIERS IN...

Two Days

The obvious place to start the first day would be the citadel, above the Haute Casbah, but as it is closed for the foreseeable future, start with a coffee or mint tea on the terrace of the **Tontonville Café** (p101), watching the crowd and money-changers on place Port Said. Visit the **Palais des Raïs** (p95) and then follow the lower Casbah walk (p97), which takes in the best of the old town. Save the afternoon for museums – the **Bardo Museum** (p96) and the **National Museum of Antiquities** (p96). From here you are well placed for a drink at the **Hôtel el-Djazaïr** (p102), or you could cross town for the spectacular view over the city from the **Cathedral of Notre-Dame d'Afrique** (p95).

Start early the second day, beating the rush hour, and get to **Tipaza** (p104). Spend the morning among the ruins, then have lunch at one of the restaurants beside the park, or move on to **Cherchell** (p106). Drive back to Algiers before nightfall for dinner in town (p100).

Three Days

If you have more time in the city, be sure to check if the **Jardin d'Essai** (p97) has reopened. If not, walk the seafront in the morning and spend the afternoon walking through the Ville Nouvelle or at the **Makam Echahid** (Martyrs' Memorial; p96) and the **Musée National Du Jihad** (p96).

Agir-Plus Edition has used these maps in its pocket-size *Guide et Plans d'Alger* (DA750), also packed with practical information.

INFORMATION
Bookshops

Algiers has several bookshops, but most of them only sell books in French and Arabic. The few English-language titles on sale tend to be either practical or academic.

Librairie des Beaux-Arts (☎ 021 634014; 28 rue Didouche Mourad) A small but excellent shop on one of the main shopping streets, with staff who know books and are happy to help. It has a good selection of books in French about Algeria, including guides, history, fiction and picture books.

Librairie du Tiers Monde (☎ 021 715772; place de l'Emir Abdelkader) A larger store than the Beaux-Arts, it doesn't have much more of a selection when it comes to French or English books. Although it does have a larger French-language fiction selection.

Cultural Centres

Centre Culturel Français (☎ 021 730100; 7 rue Hassani Issad) The most active of the foreign cultural centres, it has a library and theatre-cinema.

Goethe Institut (☎ 021 741959; 165 Chemin de Sfindja) Housed in the German embassy, it stages theatre and screens films around town.

Palais de la Culture (☎ 021 291010; Les Anassers, Kouba) Stages music and literary events.

Emergency

SOS Santé (☎ 115)
SOS Sécurité (☎ 112)

Internet Access

There's no shortage of internet places in the centre, often off the main streets, in a basement or up on the 1st floor. Fees are usually around DA50 to DA80 per hour. These are among the more reliable:

Cyber ADSL (53 rue Larbi ben M'Hidi)
Cybersoli (16 rue Hassiba ben Bouali)
Planète Internet (☎ 021 643196; rue Didouche Mourad; per hr 60B)

Medical Services

For medical emergencies you should call **SOS Santé** (☎ 115), but for something less urgent, French speaking **Dr Maouchi** (☎ 073 341322) has been recommended.

CHU Mustapha Pasha (☎ 021 235555; place du 1 Mai) One of the most central general hospitals.

Pharmacie l'Opéra (☎ 021 731342; 4 rue Abane Ramdane; ☼ 8am-midnight Sat-Thu, 5pm-midnight Fri) This place is particularly helpful.

Money

Algiers is awash with ATMs, but only one is likely to accept foreign cards, the **Crédit Populaire d'Algérie** (☎ 021 635687; blvd Colonel Amirouche), and even that is not to be relied on. Travellers cheques can be cashed at several large banks near the Grande Poste, but it is slow, as is drawing cash on Visa. There are many Western Union branches, the most central at the Grande Poste. Cash can be changed at many banks, hotels and, at the best rate, on the street at place Port Saïd.

Post

The **Grande Poste** (p97; ☎ 021 726072) is on place Grande Poste, a Moorish monolith right at the centre of town; it sells stamps and phone cards. There are several branches in the city, including one at 119 rue Didouche Mourad near the Sacré Coeur.

Telephone

You don't have to walk far in the centre to find a taxiphone (an inexpensive metered phone service), by far the easiest and cheapest way to make local and international calls. Post offices sell prepaid cards for the many orange call boxes scattered across the city. And if you have an unlocked mobile phone, it might be worth buying a SIM card, which usually comes with credit.

Tourist Information

The **Office Nationale de Tourisme** (☎ 021 712981; www.ont.dz; 2 rue Smail Kerrar; ☺ 8am-4.30pm Sat-Wed) was undergoing a face-lift at the time of research, but should have a shiny new office just off blvd Ernesto Guevara and some information on travelling in the country.

Travel Agencies

L'Île de l'Occident (☎ 021 300134; www.iledel occident.com; Lot H, 39 rue El-Achour) The leaders in cultural and adventure tourism, as well as a general travel agency. Highly recommended.

Mili Voyage Algérie (☎ 021 633643; 16 rue Didouche Mourad)

ONAT (☎ 021 742985; www.onat-dz.com; 2 rue Didouche Mourad) The state-owned agency has several branches in the city, but this is the largest and most central for local and international travel.

Touring Voyages Algérie (☎ 021 739516; www.tour ingvoyagesalgerie.dz; 21 rue Abane Ramdane) One of three branches in the capital for this nationwide agency.

DANGERS & ANNOYANCES

Algiers is a big and busy city that has seen more than its fair share of violence over the years, as plaques around the centre commemorate. At times tension bubbles up and there is a visible increase in the number of police in the street and roadblocks on the main arteries. At the end of 2006 bombs went off on the outskirts of the city. Most of this violence is targeted at police, but a bus carrying foreigners was also attacked.

Some parts of the city are more difficult for foreigners to visit than others, the upper

---

ROCKING THE CASBAH

In the 1937 cult French film *Pépé le Moko*, Jean Gabin plays a French gangster who is safe from the police as long as he stays in the Casbah. The days when the police feared to enter the steep, narrow alleys are long gone, though not forgotten, and the Casbah still poses difficulties for travellers: even some of the most experienced have had bags or cameras snatched there. Poverty-fuelled crime is not exclusive to the Casbah, but if foreign governments advise against travelling anywhere in the city, it is here. With care, and following our route (p97), you will find more frequented areas where it is safer to visit, particularly in the lower Casbah. All areas of the Casbah should be avoided after dark unless you know where you are going or are walking with an Algerian known to you.

Casbah being the most obvious example. The greatest risk is of petty theft and, as with big cities throughout the world, you will greatly reduce the risk of being a target if you take care of your valuables and ensure that you are not alone in the busier, and the quietest areas.

Foreigners are also targeted by the city's thieves, whose scams may include an outward show of friendship leading to an invitation to a meal, during which a theft may occur. The majority of theft, however, is opportunistic: if you leave a camera sitting on a table or a bag hanging over the back of a chair, it may not be there for long.

SIGHTS

Algiers, like many other places in the country, is only just beginning to recognise its tourism potential. As a result, some of the city's most popular sights are often closed and in the process of being renovated. The municipal authorities made efforts to speed things up as Algiers celebrates being Arab Cultural Capital in 2007, but many sites remain closed.

Entry into all mosques is officially closed to non-Muslims, but in practice it is possible to visit between the morning and noon prayers (roughly between 9am and noon) if you obtain permission from the mosque's imam and are dressed appropriately, which means no shorts or short sleeves. Women will need to wear a headscarf.

The Casbah & Around
THE CASBAH
The Casbah of Algiers is a unique urban environment, a fact recognised by Unesco when it inscribed the Casbah on the World Heritage list and described it as 'one of the finest coastal sites on the Mediterranean'. The part of the city that sits on the steep hill between the citadel and the seafront, the Casbah was mostly built between the 16th and 18th centuries. It is a tight-knit warren of alleys where whitewashed houses lean so close they cut out the sharp sun for most of the day. Difficult to police and therefore a home to lawlessness for much of its history, the Casbah has changed dramatically over the past few decades. With problems of sanitation and water shortages, many of the old Casbah families who were able to, moved out to more modern accommodation elsewhere in the city. The Casbah has suffered: since independence as many as a thousand houses have been lost. Not all were of architectural beauty, yet part of the wonder of the place is in the sum of its parts. But it is not too late and it seems that things may be changing. The state does provide funds, and there are various organisations devoted to helping save the Casbah. A great deal of restoration work is ongoing and several significant houses have already been restored.

DJEMAA EL-DJEDID
Colonial French town planners cleared many Ottoman buildings when they redesigned the Algiers waterfront and laid out what is now the place des Martyrs, but they left the **Djemaa el-Djedid** (place des Martyrs). Contrary to its name, the New Mosque, sometimes also called the Pêcherie Mosque, was built in 1660 on the site of an earlier Quranic school and paid for by public subscription. The mosque is unusual for Algiers, built in a recognisably Turkish style, with a series of domes and vaults, although the minaret is Andalusian in style. It is also unusual for being designed as a cross: local legend has it that the architect was a Christian, supposedly executed for his trickery. It has two entrances, one on the place and another on the steps of the ramparts, leading down to the port. One of the most popular of the inner city mosques, entry to non-Muslims is periodically banned.

DJEMAA EL-KEBIR
A few steps away, the **Djemaa el-Kebir** (Grand Mosque; rue el-Mourabitine) continues a tradition that goes back to the early history of Algiers. On a rise above the inner port, early Berber and Phoenician inhabitants built places of prayer here, which the Romans turned into a temple; later it was converted into a Christian basilica. One apse of the basilica faced east and was hung with carpets and icons. This was later torn down and replaced, in the 11th century, by the mosque, which has since been much altered and enlarged. Inside the five doors the prayer hall is supported by rows of columns, 72 in all, and contains a cedarwood minbar which carries an inscription stating that the mihrab, the niche indicating the direction of Mecca, was constructed in 490AH (AD 1097). This supports the idea that the mosque was built by Youssef ben Tachfine, the Almoravid ruler of Tlemcen at a time when the Mediterranean was transformed by the First Crusade. The minaret, 15m high, carries an inscription urging us to contemplate its beauty and the magnificent appearance of its crowns.

The mosque's location made it central to Algiers' court life – this was where the bey came for Friday prayers, in procession from his palace by the port or from the citadel. Among the later additions to the structure were a small garden and, after the British bombardment in 1816, an installation for four cannons. Just over a hundred years later, in a ceremony held here in March 1919, the French government officially recognised the sacrifice of the *indigènes* (native North Africans) who died in WWI by awarding the mufti Ben Nacer the Legion of Honour in their name.

DJEMAA ALI BITCHINE
In the rough days of Algerian piracy, when a man might be snatched off a ship in the high sea and given a choice of slavery or conversion, there were many so-called renegades, people around the Mediterranean who changed religion. Ali Bitchine was one. A sailor from Venice, his original name may have been Piccinino. Whoever he had been

in Italy, in Algiers he was a sailor who rose to become a grand admiral of the fleet. In 1622 he built the **Djemma Ali Bitchine** (rue Soualah). The plan is unusual, the domed design clearly influenced by Italian or Byzantine churches. Like several other mosques, this one was used as a church during the French occupation, when it was known as Notre Dame des Victoires. The minaret was destroyed towards the end of the 19th century. The building was reclaimed as a mosque in 1962 and at the time of writing was being restored.

DJEMAA KETCHOUA

Of all the central Algiers mosques the Djemaa Ketchoua has had the most turbulent history. Its exact date of construction is not known, but it is estimated as being some time at the beginning of the 17th century and certainly before the Djemaa el-Djedid. Its name translates as place or plateau of goats, a reminder of the time when this space – between the port and citadel – was open ground. It was remodelled in 1794 by Hassan Pasha, when he built his palace next door (below). The work is commemorated by a long inscription that begins: 'What a beautiful mosque!' Today it seems more unusual than beautiful, with its high steps, three-tierd minarets and parttiled walls.

A plaque to the left of the great doors notes that on 5 July 1830 a cross was placed on top of the mosque, beginning more than 130 years of French occupation. During this time it served as the city's cathedral and one of the centrepieces of the French-held city: French artists and sculptors decorated it, Emperor Napoleon III took Mass here in 1860 and the composer Saint-Saëns played the organ here in 1873. The building was reconsecrated as a mosque on 5 July 1962, 132 years to the day after it was converted to a church and just two days after General de Gaulle recognised independent Algeria.

DAR HASSAN PACHA

The building beside the Ketchoua Mosque was once the city's grandest mansion and carries the name of its original owner, Dar Hassan Pacha. Hassan was the ruler or dey of Algiers, a man with a sense of purpose – in 1795 he concluded a peace treaty with the fledgling United States of America guaranteeing their ships safe passage in Algiers' waters. Before that, around 1791, he began his palace on the edge of the Casbah, but away from the waterside, which was vulnerable and damp in winter. When Algiers fell to the French the house was turned into the governor's winter residence. Its façade was remodelled, and unlike most large houses here the Dar Hassan Pacha was given a European-style front, with rows of large windows and balconies, and a grander entrance. During the occupation it played host to the great and good: the Emperor Napoleon and Empress Eugénie stayed during their 1860 tour. The house has been undergoing a major renovation since 2005 and is closed to the public, but photographs suggest that some of the early decoration has survived, including wall tiles, ornate plasterwork and carved and painted wood ceilings.

DAR AZIZA BENT EL-BEY

Aziza may have been a *bent* (daughter) of the bey of Constantine, who built the sumptuous Dar Aziza for her. In contrast to Dar Hassan Pacha, immediately opposite, its whitewashed façade has smaller windows – a less impressive face to the world. Inside, however, this was one of the most gorgeous of Algiers' grand houses, which was built beside – and perhaps at one time part of – the Jenina, the old palace of the deys, since demolished. Dar Aziza is currently the office of the National Archaeology Agency and is closed to visitors, although there are occasional exhibitions.

MUSEUM OF POPULAR ARTS & TRADITIONS

This **museum** (☎ 021 713414; www.musee-mnatp .art.dz; 9 rue Mohamed Akli Malek, Dar Khedaoudj el-Amia; adult/student DA20/10; ❖ 10am-noon & 1-4.30pm Sun-Thu, 1-4.30pm Sat), is the most accessible of the buildings one can visit in the Casbah. The museum is housed in a fine example of an Ottoman-period town house, the Dar Khedaoudj el-Amia, which follows the classic town house plan, with an entrance leading to an inner hall and a staircase up to the principal rooms. The museum contains a fascinating collection of traditional Algerian arts and crafts.

The ground floor corridor of fluted marble columns leads to rooms showing traditional Berber crafts, including *ikoufan*, huge pots used for storing grain, and *sendouk*, large carved wooden chests for storage of clothes and linen. The upper floor, which still has decoration from the 1860s, has four rooms off a central court, in which are shown leatherwork, the highly skilled craft of embroidery on velvet (much prized here), jewellery and copperware. There is also a mock-up of a traditional room such a mansion would have had.

CITADEL
The city's stronghold, the citadel dominates the Casbah and the port and was, from the 16th century, the guarantor of peace and a safe haven in times of war. Although there was a Berber stronghold here from early times, the present massive structure was begun in 1516 by Aroudj, the brother of Kheireddin Barbarossa. With its walls lined with batteries of canon, 188m above sea level, it dominated the port, the lower town and the surrounding countryside: canons were placed facing inland as well as out to sea, for the ruler of Algiers was never free of threats from Berber and Bedouin tribes. The citadel was little more than military barracks until 1816, when the British bombardment of Algiers persuaded the ruler, Dey Ali, to move up from his palace by the port. It took 76 mules to move his gold and silver up with him. It was here, in 1830, that Dey Hussein slapped the French consul and gave France a pretext for invasion.

The citadel has been closed for some years, while renovation works continue on the palace, the harem, barracks and other buildings in the complex, all of them having suffered during years of occupation and, after independence, of local squatters. So for now, visitors have to make do with a view from the imposing gate, a glimpse into the Mosque of the Invitées (another Ottoman-period structure just beside the gate), and some spectacular views over the city and out to sea.

PALAIS DES RAÏS BASTION 23
So many of Algiers' historic buildings are either derelict, undergoing renovation or newly restored but closed to visitors, that it comes as a relief to find the **Palais des Raïs** (☎ 021 739570; www.palaisdesrais-bastion23.dz; adult/child DA20/10; 10am-noon & 1-4.30pm Sun-Thu, 1-4.30pm Sat) open. The palace is in fact a row of several large waterfront houses, joined up to form a single compound and now home to the Centre des Arts et de la Culture. Palace 18, the main building, was begun in 1750 and completed around 1798 by the Dey Mustapha Pacha, who used it as one of his residences. The French military occupied it for a while, after which it served as the American consulate, a school and a library before becoming the most successful restoration project in the city. The buildings are used as exhibition space for some excellent shows, but much of the pleasure and interest is in seeing inside a grand, Ottoman-period mansion. The rooms are rarely massive, occasionally elaborately decorated with tiles and painted ceilings, but there is a sense of grandeur about the compound and it is still possible to get a sense of the good life that might once have been lived in this place, helped for once by descriptions in English and French.

NOTRE DAME D'AFRIQUE
The Byzantine-inspired **Notre Dame d'Afrique** (11am-12.30pm & 3-5.30pm), known locally as Madame Afrique, sits above the bustle of the city, seemingly impervious to the fact that the people who created it and filled its pews have long gone. The idea for the church is said to have come from two women of Lyon, who missed the shrine that sits above their native city and who placed a statue of the virgin in the hollow of an olive tree on the north of the city. The basilica was finally consecrated in 1872 by Bishop Lavigerie, founder of the White Fathers. Four years later, the statue was crowned 'queen of Africa' with the approval of the Pope in Rome. The date of that event, 30 April, has become the statue's feast day. Sitting 120m above sea level on the plateau of Bouzaréah, the basilica is, above all, a monument to departed French piety; its walls are covered in small memorial plaques, placed by people in need of the Virgin's help. Mass is said daily in French (6pm) and on Friday in English (10am). In November 2006 the EU, French government and city of Algiers agreed to share the cost of restoring the building.

Ville Nouvelle
The Ville Nouvelle (New Town) is not new and nor is it completely French. Early

on, the Ottoman-backed rulers of Algiers and their powerful courtiers were building themselves summer houses and pleasure pavilions up on the heights of the broad crescent of hill that backs the bay of Algiers. Although the entire hillside and much beyond has now been developed to accommodate a growing population, some of the old villas remain, a few of them converted into museums and other public spaces.

BARDO MUSEUM

The **Bardo Museum of Prehistory & Ethnography** (☎ 021 747641; www.musee-bardo.art.dz; 3 rue Franklin Roosevelt; adult/child DA20/10; ☯ 9am-noon & 1-4.30pm Sun-Thu, 1-4.30pm Sat) was built at the end of the 18th century as the country residence of a Tunisian prince exiled in Algiers. Enlarged by a Frenchman during the colonial period, it has been a museum since 1930, displaying the early history and later ethnology of the region. This includes some fabulous fossils, a collection of Neolithic pottery and stones, and particularly impressive rock carvings and paintings of horses and chariots brought from deep in the Sahara in the Tassili N'Ajjer region. Better still is the collection of urban artefacts in the ethnography section. See the elegant copper tea pot, the carved and painted wooden furniture and the grand rooms in which these objects are displayed. Stroll out into the upper courtyard with its cooling central pool and the world in which these objects were created suddenly seems much more familiar. The gardens are a delight. A café

was planned at the time of our visit, but was not yet open.

NATIONAL MUSEUM OF ANTIQUITIES

The richness of Algeria's heritage is brought home in the understated but well chosen collection on display at the **National Museum of Antiquities** (☎ 021 746686; www.musee-antiquites .art.dz; adult/child DA20/10; ☯ 9am-noon & 1-4.30pm Sun-Thu, 1-4.30pm Sat), a short walk from the Bardo Museum. The collection of antiquities is drawn from sites around the city and throughout Algeria. Among the early works are fine ivory carvings and large, totemic Libyan-period warriors on horseback. There is sculpture from Cherchell and mosaics from Tipaza, a room of bronzes including a wonderful fragment of a horse's leg and hoof, and an extraordinary 3rd-century figure of a chubby child holding an eagle to its chest. There is also a collection of Islamic art from across the Maghreb. The museum sits at the top of the Parc de la Liberté, a classic piece of French urban planning at the top of rue Didouche Mourad.

MAKAM ECHAHID & MUSÉE NATIONAL DU MOUDJAHID

One of the most recognisable landmarks in the city, the **Makam Echahid** (Martyr's Memorial; Riadh el-Feth) celebrates the sacrifice of the unknown martyr who fell for his country. The monument, constructed by the Canadians in the early 1980s, is made up of three massive concrete palm fronds that come together and soar 92m into the

---

SHANGHAI BLUE   *Zahia Hafs*

Traditionally the trousers and jackets worn by the fishermen were made of thick blue cotton called 'le bleu de Shanghai' (Shanghai blue). If you walk around Algiers' charming fishing port, near the place des Martyrs, especially at night during Ramadan, you will still see 'the blue men' sitting at small terraces, sipping strong coffee or mint tea, eating pastries and playing dominos. Others hang around smoking their cigarettes with delight on the parapet and the steps leading to the water. This outfit has passed through time with whole generations of men who work the seas wearing the distinctive garments. In the past they also wore white sandals and it was appropriate for unmarried men to have a mint leaf stuck behind their ear allowing girls to know they were single.

If you walk around the Casbah you will also see some elderly men, mainly retired fishermen, wearing this blue costume. However, little by little, the younger generations are dropping this outfit and with it one part of typical Algiers' scenery.

Strangely, across the Mediterranean in Marseille the distinctive two piece outfit is not called 'Shanghai blue' but 'China blue', and back across the seas in Tamanrasset, in the south of Algeria, it is called 'Marseille blue'.

sky; they represent the coming together of agriculture, culture and industry to make independent Algeria great. The nearby Bois des Arcades offers shade and some great views.

The **Musée National du Moudjahid** (☎ 021 743414; Riadh el-Feth, Martyrs' Memorial; adult/child DA20/15; ☒ 9am-5pm Oct-Feb, 9am-7pm Mar-Sep) sits beneath the memorial, its mission to collect, preserve and display objects and memories of the struggle against colonialism. It starts with the story of the French invasion of 1830, but focuses on the glorious struggle from the uprising in Sétif, Constantine and Guelma in 1944 to Independence Day in July 1962. Although information is in Arabic, the meaning of the exhibits is easy to understand, from Abdelkader's pistols to reports of executions of 'terrorists'. The museum's lower floor is a domed sanctuary, a natural shrine of low light and no noise, its walls inscribed with verses from the Quran.

MUSÉE DES BEAUX ARTS

At the edge of the Jardin d'Essai and a short walk from the Martyrs' Memorial, the **Musée des Beaux Arts** (☎ 021 664916; placette Dar es-Salaam, El-Hamma; adult/child DA20/10; ☒ 9am-noon Sun-Thu, 1-5pm Sat) houses the best collection of art in the country. Opened in 1930 and with some 8000 items on the walls and in store, it traces the progress of European and particularly French art from the 16th century, starting with Barnaba di Modena, passing through the neoclassicists such as David and Delacroix, Orientalists including Fromentin and a Renoir painted during the artist's visit in 1882. There is also a sizeable collection of work by Algerian artists and by artists from elsewhere, donated when Algeria won independence.

GRANDE POSTE

A post office might not be high on everyone's list of things to see, but **Grande Poste** (☎ 021 726072; place Grande Poste), completed in 1908 after eight years of construction, is a classic piece of French-inspired hispano-Moorish architecture and is worth a brief visit, even if you don't need stamps or a phone card. One of the world's most elaborate post boxes is near the entrance, while the façade carries the names of Algeria's principal towns and cities.

JARDIN D'ESSAI

Another grand civic project planted by the French, the **Jardin d'Essai** (El-Hamma; www .jardindessai.com) dates to the first years of their occupation. In the early 1830s, as soon as the French were in control of Algiers, land was set aside for a model farm and a garden in which they could try out various plants. The idea was to test what would grow best here, given the soil and climate, in the hope of improving crop yields and greening the landscape. The model farm disappeared, but the Jardin d'Essai flourished and by the end of the 19th century was one of the world's great natural hothouses. It has continued to develop and is currently undergoing improvements. A place of outstanding beauty, when it reopens it will once again be somewhere to escape from the overwhelming whiteness of the city, among the avenues of palms, the stands of exotic trees and the rows of plants.

ACTIVITIES
Golf

As everywhere else in the world, golf is becoming increasingly popular among a certain section of Algerians. If you can't resist the urge to play, **Le Golf Club de Dely Brahim** (☎ 021 375362) has an 18-hole course.

Swimming

Many Algerians are happy to jump into the sea near the port, but the water is far from clean and you need to drive a long way out of the city to find clean water. Swimming pools can be just as difficult to find. The **Complexe Nautique** (☎ 021 924787) has one indoor and two open-air Olympic-sized pools, although you may need to join (and therefore bring a passport) to get into the water. Easier, though more expensive, is the pool of the **Hôtel el-Djazaïr** (☎ 021 230933; www.hoteleldjazair .dz; 24 av Souidani Boujmaa; s/d DA2300/4000).

WALKING TOUR

The Casbah has a reputation as a difficult place for foreigners to walk and not entirely without reason: even experienced travellers have been mugged here recently. This walk is designed to give a take of the safer, lower Casbah, taking in many of the city's most remarkable sights. However, avoid taking this tour at night (for more information see the boxed text, p92).

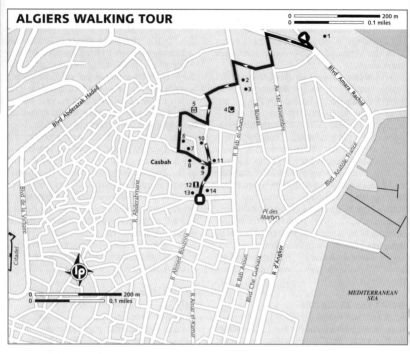

ALGIERS WALKING TOUR

Start at the **Palais des Raïs** (**1**; p95). From its windows (or the road nearby if you don't want to enter), take a look at the admiralty, the bit of land that closes Algiers' inner port, with its lighthouse built by Barbarossa. This was where the legendary figures of the city's history plied their trade and now is a military zone. Cross blvd Amara Rachid and the small place with a fountain of rearing horses. Beyond it, turn left onto av 1 Novembre and then take your first right, crossing rue Bouras. Just before you reach rue Bab el-Oued, you pass (on your left) **Dar el-Hamra** (**2**; closed to visitors). The last dey of Algiers, Hussein, built this fine mansion in 1800, before he reached power. It was rented by the British Consul Robert St-John in the 1820s, although Dey Hussein returned to it for some days in 1830, after the city had fallen to the French.

The **Bab el-Oued** (**3**), the River Gate, was the northern entrance to Algiers, but was not wide enough for carts heading to the port jetty and was dismantled in 1846. One of the pedestrian arches of the gate has survived near Dar el-Hamra. Just beyond it, past the covered market, the **Djemaa Ali Bitchine** (**4**; p93) is being restored, but its outside fountain and tile work can be admired. Take the passage that leads between the mosque and market, the pedestrian rue Prof Mohamed Boualah. As you climb the steps, the Casbah rises above you. Take the first left, rue Hadj Omar. No 2, the École Ahmed Hamouche, is a large Ottoman house currently undergoing some restoration work.

The first right turning off rue Hadj Omar is rue Mohamed Akli Malek. Visit the **Museum of Popular Arts & Traditions** (**5**; p94) at No 9, in the Dar Khedaoudj el-Amia. Continue up the hill from the museum, then take the first left (rue Mohamed et Ahmed Mecheri), which leads to an open space in front of the restored but closed **Dar es-Souf (6)**.

Turn left at the end of the street, onto rue de l'Indépendence. This street is lined with some of the largest houses in the Casbah. No 1, **Dar Zaid Aissa (7)**, has a massive white façade and the sign *monument classé*. At No 7 you can just make out the sign for the *Tribunal de 1er Instance*, one of the old town courts. At a turn in the street, on the right, **Dar Mustapha Pacha (8)** was built, like many of these houses, at the end of the 18th century. It was given to a religious order. Under the French it was turned into a library and still bears an engraved, Bibliothèque Nationale, sign. More impressive is the carved cedarwood canopy above the main entrance. Just before the end of the street on the right is No 2, the **Hammam Sidna (9)**, a classic hammam of 16th-century origin, at one time used by the court. The hammam was working until recently (as recently as the poster of Zidane and his Real Madrid colleagues, which still hangs on the wall). There are plans for it to reopen in the near future.

You are now back on rue Hadj Omar. On your left are another pair of classic Algerian houses: at No 17, a marble entrance and large wooden door announce the **Dar el-Cadi (10)**, while across the road at No 10, a large doorway supported by four pillars is the entrance to **Dar Ahmed Bey (11)**, now the headquarters of the Algerian National Theatre.

Turning right onto rue Hadj Omar, the road comes into an open space. **Dar Hassan Pacha (12**; p94), once the residence of the French Governor of Algeria (under restoration) and **Djemaa Ketchoua (13**; p94) are both on the right. On your left is the whitewashed façade of **Dar Aziza (14**; p94), the headquarters of the Archaeological Agency, and beyond it lies the place des Martyrs, convenient for transport, close to the restaurants of the Pêcherie (p100) and a short walk from the cafés of place Port Said.

TOURS

The travel agencies listed in the Information section (p92) all offer tours of the city and the surrounding sights. Île de l'Occident is particularly recommended for cultural tours.

SLEEPING

Algiers has a large number of hotels, but a shortage of good beds. Many of the places listed here are small, although 'boutique hotel' is a concept that has not yet arrived. The big hotels, with one notable exception, are concrete blocks, some from the tourism boom of the 1960s and 70s. The Minister of Tourism has vowed to improve the situation by encouraging investment, and there are rumours of Saudis and others trying to buy the city's prominent hotels, but none of this has brought the necessary improvements.

Hotels in Algiers tend to be more expensive than elsewhere in Algeria (with the possible exception of Oran). While you can still find a budget room for under DA1000, many will cost up to DA1500, while midrange may cost as much as DA3500 a double.

Budget

Hôtel Marhaba (☎ 021 711666; 4 rue Abdelkader Aoua; s/d DA400/600) Overlooking the Ketchoua Mosque and a busy street, the Marhaba has grubby rooms with basins and worn beds, but no in-house showers. Basic.

Grand Hôtel Tipaza (☎ 021 736515; 4 rue Rachid Kessentini; s/d B&B DA800/1000) This long-standing backpackers favourite is a one-star dive above the noisy square, cafés and shops, right in the centre and a short walk from train and shared taxi connections. It has communal showers.

Hôtel Terminus (☎ 021 737817; 2 rue Rachid Kessentini; s/d B&B from DA900/1500) A noisy former colonial hotel overlooking place Port Said and the sea, it has some rooms (at midrange prices) with air-con. Not ideal for women travelling alone.

Hôtel Arago (☎ 021 739495; rue Haffaf Nafaa; s/d DA975/1545) A survivor from the days when French colonial officials and their families flocked to the city, the Arago has dropped the Grand from its name and offers simple, clean rooms, without air-con, in a more salubrious part of town than the Port Said area, but still near the port and train station.

Grand Hôtel des Étrangers (☎ 021 743359; 1 rue Ali Boumendjel; s/d/tr B&B DA1200/1300/1400) A welcoming hotel in the cheap-hotel area, it's a little less noisy than the others.

Midrange

Central Touring Hôtel (☎ 021 737644; 9 rue Abane Ramdane; s/d DA1638/1930; 🗙) On a busy street in the centre of town, this is another old favourite and a cut above most of the city's budget places. Air-con rooms available.

Hôtel Regina (☎ 021 740035; 27 blvd ben Boulaïd; s/d B&B DA3000/3200; 🟫) The welcome could be warmer, but rooms in this imposing seafront hotel, a short walk from the Grande Poste, are well maintained and a good size, if a little noisy.

Hôtel Samir (☎ 021 630251; www.hotelsamir.com; 74 rue Didouche Mourad; s/d/tr B&B DA3100/3600/4600; 🟫) One of the best midrange hotels in the centre, a very popular place in a 19th century building on a busy shopping street. Reservation recommended.

Hôtel Safir (☎ 021 735040; 2 rue Asseleh Hocine; s/d B&B DA4200/4800; 🟫) You get more than a bed to sleep in at the Safir, a hotel popular with out-of-town officials with business at the local government offices. Under French occupation this was the Aletti, one of the city's chic addresses. The building is grand, the view over the harbour perfect and some of the rooms still vast and decorated with character, but while renovation continues, much of the furnishings and fittings are tired and the plumbing unreliable. Expect to pay more for renovated or seafront rooms.

Top End

our pick **Hôtel Albert 1** (☎ 021 736506/737441; hotelalbert@yahoo.fr; 5 av Pasteur; s/d B&B DA 4100/4700; 🟫) In another city, or in Algiers in another time, the Albert 1 would have taken more advantage of its fabulous wedding-cake building and central location, right on one of the main squares and with views out to sea. As it is, rooms are worn, water is erratic and street noise can be bad, even late at night, but this is still one of the most interesting places to stay in town.

Dar Diaf (☎ 021 361010; Chemin de la Redoute, Cheraga; s/d DA5300/7200; 🅿 🟫) The better of the two hotels of this name (though not nearly so convenient), Dar Diaf is a long drive out of the centre. And while it's rated four star it's still a long way from being a luxury hotel. That said, it does offer clean and comfortable rooms and has a good restaurant.

Hôtel el-Aurassi (☎ 021 748252; 2 blvd Frantz Fanon; s/d from DA10,000/11,000) There's no missing the Aurassi, one of the city's landmarks that people either love (the modernists) or hate

(everyone else). A concrete box perched on a concete plinth, it is due for a much needed overhaul. Views of the city are fabulous as are the gardens.

Hôtel el-Djazaïr (☎ 021 230933; www.hotel eldjazair.dz; 24 av Souidani Boujmaa; s/d 18,000/22,000; 🅿 🟫 🚉) Minor shortcomings with service and upkeep of the rooms are far outweighed by the charm of the place, which has been the city's address of choice for over a century. Famous guests include Rudyard Kipling and André Gide. The Allied Force Headquarters was based in Room 141 while planning the invasion of Sicily, and Churchill and Eisenhower met here in June 1943. They might tut at the modern extensions but would still enjoy the gardens and pool, the elegance and character.

Hilton Algiers Hôtel (☎ 021 219696; www.hilton .com; Pins Maritime; s/d from 27,000/31,000; 🅿 🟫 🚉) A huge curve of concrete out of town near the Exhibition Centre and therefore usually full of delegations (and the British embassy and British council, which has permanent residence here). The Hilton is extremely secure, very comfortable and has just about everything you would expect at this price.

EATING

There is no shortage of places to pick up a quick bite. There are also many restaurants in the centre, often serving French-influenced food.

Budget

Milk Bar (40 rue Larbi ben M'Hidi; snacks DA50-100) A reliable all-day food stop on place Emir Abdelkader, it's good for a coffee and croissant, or a slice of pizza at lunch, and has pavement seating.

Big Blue (1 rue Didouche Mourad; DA60) Omelettes, burgers and fries are served from this stall, just opposite the gates of the university. Extremely popular at lunch and dinner.

Restaurant le Faubourg (rue Pichon; mains DA150-250) Down a flight of steps off place Audin, this restaurant is a simple place that serves straightforward meals of soup and roast chicken on plastic tables, either in the main room (with TV) or *salle familiale* (family room). No alcohol is available.

Le Brussels (☎ 021 633754; 2 rue Didouche Mourad; breakfast & light lunch DA150-300) A cool café that runs all day on a Belgian theme, it serves hot chocolate and *pain au chocolat* (chocolate croissant) for breakfast, sugar and sa-voury crepes for lunch, and good coffee all day to a young crowd, most of whom come from the nearby university.

Le Magelan (☎ 021 710130; 8 Rampe de la Pêch-erie; DA200) There's a line of fish restaurants along the Rampe de la Pêcherie, the pas-sage that leads from beside Djemaa el-Djedid to the port (or used to until the lower gate was blocked during the 1990s). All have the same sort of product and prices: choose a fish from the display and say whether you want it grilled or fried. Le Magelan (formerly the Sirène de Mer) also does a fine fish soup, but no alcohol is available.

Tontonville Café (☎ 021 748661; 7 place Port Said; mains DA200-300) The entrance is on the side street by the theatre. Inside this high-ceilinged canteen, popular at lunchtime, take a tray and choose from a range of dishes – perhaps a tagine, a lamb stew, or a couscous – and have drinks served. Af-terwards, you can go out front and have a coffee on the terrace.

Restaurant Yulmaz (☎ 021 7333301; 8 rue Pichon; mains DA300-500) This small, bright place just off place Audin is a little more expensive than others in the alley, but it is a cut above the rest with good grills and tagines, al-though there's no alcohol.

Midrange

L'Arc en Ciel (☎ 021 738360; 3 rue Col Haouas; mains DA500-800) This place is particularly busy at lunchtime, when the small room fills with people from the town hall and other nearby offices, who look as though they have been coming here for years. Service is fast, food is unfussy and fish, couscous and paella are the specialities.

La Vague Bleu (rue d'Angkor; mains DA500-1000) The owner is a fisherman who sells what-ever he has caught on his boat in this dark little restaurant under the city rampart, across the road from the port. There's not a lot of ambience and no alcohol, but the fish couldn't be fresher and the prices are reasonable for the quality.

La Maison de Couscous (rue Claude Debussy; mains DA600-800) Up by the concrete Sacré Coeur Cathedral, high up rue Didouche Mourad, this local no-frills place serves what its name says: couscous. Algerians don't often go out to eat couscous – it's the sort of dish your wife or mother cooks best – but they come here in numbers. No alcohol is available.

Top End

our pick **Brasserie des Facultés** (☎ 021 6440531 rue Didouche Mourad; meals DA1000-1500) The food side of this popular and often smoky bar fills up early and for good reason. It isn't the cheapest place in town, but it is consistently good, with a well-priced plat du jour. Tables alongside the window are referred to as *front de mer*, overlooking not the beach but the passage along busy rue Didouche Mourad and the entrance to the university.

Le Dauphin (☎ 021 716557; rue d'Angkor; mains DA1000-1500, whole fish per kilogram DA1500-2700) Don't be fooled by the faux Greek exterior or the Muzak inside, this is one of the city's best, where the freshest fish and the best wine is enjoyed by well-heeled locals and oil work-ers. Alcohol is served and it has a terrace.

Dar Lahlou (☎ 021 210807; maisonlahlou@yahoo.fr; Pins Maritimes; dinner DA1000-2000) A relative new-comer, Dar Lahlou is doing the seemingly impossible: serving upmarket couscous. Yet, it works. But then this isn't just any old couscous. The family is from the Kab-ylie where they and women in surrounding villages still make couscous by hand, for which they won the gold medal for the best couscous in the Mediterranean in 2005, a source of national pride. If wheat couscous is hard to digest, try the barley, corn or rice couscous, though Dar Lahlou also serves tagines and roasts in a place that the owners have made look like home.

Auberge du Moulin (☎ 021 361073; 24 rue Abane Ramdane, Cheraga; mains DA1000-2000) Consist-ently rated the best meal in town, the old windmill, set in a beautiful garden, serves fine Franco-Algerian food with great style. There's dining outside when the weather allows.

Self-Catering

There are several large food markets around the centre, excellent for stocking up on fresh food. The most convenient is on rue Amar el-Kama, off place Port Said. There is a larger, covered market off rue Didouche Mourad, near the junction of rue Ahmed Zabana and rue Boukhlfa Khalifa. There are also plenty of food shops and bakeries in the centre, not to mention the ever-present pizza place.

Les Puits d'Amour (☎ 021 237356; 93B rue Didouche Mourad) If you need some serious French baked goods, look no further than this retro patisserie.

Promy Plus (☎ 021 747770; 39 rue Larbi ben M'hidi) This department store has dried foods in its basement.

DRINKING

Considering its image abroad as a hotbed of Islamic fundamentalism, there are a surprising number of places to drink in the city. Most of these will be filled with men out to get drunk and are, therefore, not the sort of place where a foreign girl is going to have a quiet time. The exceptions are hotel bars, where access is often restricted to hotel guests.

Bar Dey (☎ 021 230933; Hôtel el-Djazaïr, 24 av Souidani Boujmaa) This is one of the most relaxing places to drink, especially on a warm day if you can persuade the waiters to serve you in the garden. The bar has an elaborate Moorish interior. Drinks are suitably expensive, up to DA550 for an imported beer, a little less for a half bottle of local wine.

Also recommended:

Alger Bar (1 av Pasteur) Also known as Chez Frères Acherar.

Taverne du Parc (117 rue Didouche Mourad)

ENTERTAINMENT
Cinema & Theatre

The risks associated with going out at night during the 1990s, the lack of spare cash and the advent of the DVD all spelled trouble for Algiers' cinemas. But some are still managing to run decent programmes of films that may be in French or Arabic. Also worth checking is the space in front of the Hôtel Albert 1, off av Pasteur, where free outdoor films are often screened.

Cinéma Algeria (rue Didouche Mourad)

Cinématheque Algérienne (26 rue Larbi ben M'Hidi)

Théâtre National Algérien (☎ 021 717607; place Abdelkader Alloula) Stages regular performances of theatre, music and dance in its grand 19th-century building.

Live Music

Algiers has several live music venues, two of the most popular being the Théatre de Verdure and the Salle Ibn Zeydoun, at **Riadh el-Feth** (☎ 021 670282). Listings are published in papers such as the daily *El-Watan*.

Le Racym's (☎ 021 716883; 8 rue Aouchiche Larbi) The kitchen managed to spoil even the most basic French dishes, but perhaps its claims to serve authentic Vietnamese food are more convincing. Instead, come late for the music, especially on nights when there is a live act, when the place gets packed and the audience begins to move.

Nightclubs

A number of nightclubs go in and out of fashion depending on the season, including the VIP, Veranda and Triangle, all near the Martyr's Memorial. These are currently among the more popular:

Pasha (☎ 021 230933; Hotel el-Djazaïr, 24 av Souidani Boujmaa) The nightclub of the Hôtel el-Djazaïr.

Star Studio (☎ 021 377 7777; Sheraton Club des Pins, Staouelli; P ⌘ ⌘) A long ride out of town, it's worth checking if it is running before making the trip.

GETTING THERE & AWAY
Air

The newly expanded **Houari Boumediène Airport** (☎ 021 506000; www.algiersairport.free.fr) is 19km from the centre and has separate domestic and international terminals.

For details of international airline offices in Algiers, see p208. **Air Algérie** (☎ 021 742428; www.airalgerie.dz; 1 place Maurice Audin) flies to more than 20 destinations within the country. Fares are reasonable and service, although often a little delayed, is reasonably efficient. Return fares are usually twice the price of a one-way ticket, which makes open-jaw tours possible. One way to Tamanrasset, the southernmost airport and furthest from Algiers, costs from DA14,000.

Boat

Algiers is an important port with plenty of traffic and good sea connections to Spain and France.

Algérie Ferries (☎ 021 635388/641864; 6 blvd Khemisti) Also known as the Entreprise Nationale de Transports Maritimes de Voyageurs (ENTMV), Algérie Ferries sails from Algiers to Marseille (19 hours) and Alicante (12 hours).

SNCM-Ferryterranee (☎ 021 718115; blvd Zirout Youcef) Also sails to Marseille and Alicante.

Bus

The Algiers **gare routière** (☎ 021 497151/54; av de l'ALN), unlike most in the country, still functions properly, with information desk, café, shops and departures board. It is several kilometres from the centre, along the road to the airport. From the centre, 200m south of place Audin, catch the bus headed to Tafoura. A taxi from there or the Grande Poste should cost DA250 to DA300.

There are departures to all corners of the country, including Annaba (DA700, nine hours), Oran (day/night DA540/710, seven hours), Biskra (DA470, eight hours) and Ouargla (DA900, 12 hours). To get to Tamarasset and the deep south you need to change at Adrar (DA1500, 12 hours).

Car

Given the number of road incidents in Algeria as a result of dangerous driving and also false roadblocks – one of the favourite techniques of kidnappers – you need to know what you are doing before you rent a car. With some agencies you also need to be over 30. However, it is possible to drive yourself, and several agencies would be delighted to have your business. As well as international agencies, the following local agencies rent cars, from DA3300 per day for a basic car.

Love Tour (☎ 021 509262; Houari Boumediène Airport) It also has a desk at the ONAT office on 2 rue Didouche Mourad.

Rapide Car (☎ 021 509512/506112; www.rapidecar .com; Houari Boumediène Airport) It also has an agency at the Hôtel el-Aurassi.

Taxi

Long-distance communal taxis, which have six places in three rows and are marked 'Inter-Wilaya', leave when they are full, from the Rampe Magenta, which slopes down from near place Port Said to the train station. Taxis leave for destinations across the northern half of the country including Biskra (DA800, six hours), Bou Saada (DA500, four hours), Oran (DA900, six to seven hours), Constantine (DA900, six to seven hours) and Annaba (DA1100, 10 hours).

Train

The Algerian national rail company, **SNTF** (☎ 021 711510) runs services out of two train stations in the capital. **Gare Centrale** (☎ 021 647380/81; rue d'Angkor), beside the *gare maritime*, has services along the eastern line to Bejaia, Constantine and Annaba (1st/2nd class DA1330/945, seven to 10 hours). Trains from the **Gare de l'Agha** (☎ 021 636525; off rue Hassiba ben Bouali) run four times a day

along the western line to Oran (five to six hours), from where there is a daily service to Tlemcen (2½ hours). Since the closure of the Algerian–Moroccan border, the international express has been stopped.

GETTING AROUND
To/From the Airport

A shuttle bus runs to the airport (DA50) from blvd Zirout Youcef, near the Hôtel Safir, during the day and early evening. Departures occur at least once an hour, sometimes every 30 minutes. The journey takes at least 30 minutes, more during rush hours. A taxi will cost up to DA1000 depending on the time of day/night and your ability to haggle.

Car & Motorcycle

Driving in Algiers is a frustrating experience, for much of the day traffic is bumper to bumper. And when you get where you are going, there is always a shortage of parking spaces. Happily this has created work for space minders (official or otherwise), people who will usher you into a space and watch your car, for a fee. However, it is not worth renting a car while staying in the city as there are plenty of taxis and much of the centre is easier to walk than drive around, while the Casbah is mostly pedestrian-only.

Public Transport

Buses serve most parts of the city, leaving from several main points around the centre: place des Martyrs, place Grande Poste, place Audin, Bab el-Oued and place 1 Mai, south of Agha train station. Destinations are marked at each stop, although increasingly these are in Arabic only. Entry is through the back door, where you pay the conductor.

An underground system has been under construction for some years – you could be fooled into thinking there is one already by the subway entrances near the Grande Poste. Work seems to have stalled, but the first line, running near the coast from Bab el-Oued to Hussein Dey (for the Tarfoura *gare routiére*), is due to be completed in 2008.

Taxi

There are plenty of taxis cruising the streets of the centre and although they can be in short supply during rush hours, at other times it is usually possible to hail one in the street. Taxis should be equipped with meters, but especially after dark and when taking a taxi from a hotel, expect to haggle. Local *taxis collectifs* (share taxis) run along some of the main streets of the city, their destination written on a board in the window or on the roof. Flag one down, if it is heading in your direction and get out when you like. DA20 per ride.

If you need to be sure of a service – useful to get around, essential if you are not being met on arrival at the airport – call **Taxi Yacine** (☎ 071 170026) or **Taxis Minutes** ☎ 021 666666).

AROUND ALGIERS

If you want to get out of the city for some hours or a day, then look to the west: you don't have to go far to find beautiful countryside, evocative ruins and sleepy villages alongside the deep blue sea. Tipaza is the must-see sight, an ancient Roman port impressive enough to be inscribed on Unesco's list of World Heritage sites and a delightful place to wander around. Cher-

chell, the other side of the headland and another natural harbour, is its twin, with a particularly rich museum. Between these two towns and the capital, the coast road passes some of the better resorts around Algiers.

Getting There & Away

The road between Algiers and Tipaza is currently being upgraded and, at the time of writing, there was a dual carriageway until 15km before Tipaza. Buses run regularly during the week between Algiers and Cherchell, stopping at Tipaza (1½ hours).

TIPAZA تيبازة

Albert Camus wrote that Tipaza was inhabited by the gods in spring of the sun and silvered sea, blue sky and flower-covered ruins. But Tipaza isn't just beautiful and inspiring in spring. Somehow the gods are still talking if you go in the summer, when the ruins buzz with vibrating cicadas; in autumn ,when the winds blow brine off the sea; even in winter, when the weak sun brings out the honey tones of marble and sandstone.

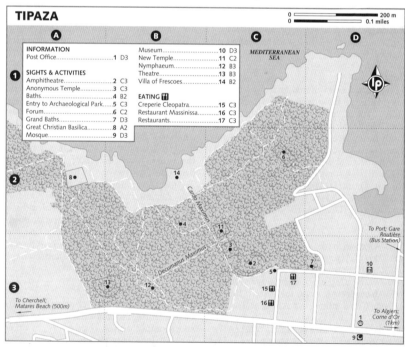

TIPAZA

0 ———— 200 m
0 ———— 0.1 miles

INFORMATION	
Post Office.............................1	D3

SIGHTS & ACTIVITIES	
Amphitheatre.........................2	C3
Anonymous Temple................3	C3
Baths.....................................4	B2
Entry to Archaeological Park.....5	C3
Forum....................................6	C2
Grand Baths...........................7	D3
Great Christian Basilica...........8	A2
Mosque.................................9	D3

Museum.................................10	D3
New Temple...........................11	C2
Nymphaeum...........................12	B3
Theatre..................................13	B3
Villa of Frescoes.....................14	B2

EATING 🍴	
Creperie Cleopatra.................15	C3
Restaurant Massinissa............16	C3
Restaurants...........................17	C3

MEDITERRANEAN SEA

Cardo Maximus

Decumanus Maximus

To Cherchell;
Matares Beach (500m)

To Port; Gare
Routière
(Bus Station)

To Algiers;
Corne d'Or
(1km)

Seventy kilometres along the coast road, Tipaza is a delight at any time.

History

Most settlements along the Algerian coast began as anchorage for early travellers, perhaps Phoenician, perhaps even earlier, as their primitive boats clung to the coast during a journey from Carthage or further east towards the Pillars of Hercules. There are no records of this early period nor of the Numidians who lived here in the early centuries BC, just the clues thrown up by the 5th- or 4th-century BC cemeteries. The first mention of Tipaza is by Pliny the Elder, in the 1st century, by which time it was under Roman control. It was then that the town we can visit took shape.

Tipaza's story is shaped by the same forces and influences as other big towns in the region; it grew by strengthening its ties across the Mediterranean and reaching a peak of wealth and influence under the Severan emperors in Rome, particularly Septimius Severus (AD 193–211), a North African by birth. During this period much wealth was spent on civic projects, including an impressive enclosing wall. Like other towns along the coast, Tipaza embraced Christianity with enthusiasm in the first half of the 3rd century, a time when pagan buildings were neglected and Christian basilicas built. While neighbouring Cherchell (p106) and Icosium, the ancient settlement at Algiers, were sacked by rebel Berbers in AD 371, Tipaza's wall – 2200m long, defended by 37 towers, held, only to give way the following year to the force of the Vandals. There was a brief renaissance under Byzantine rulers, but the end was irresistible, a slow seeping away of power and people, after which many of its stones were carted away to be reused in the building of a new city, El-Djezaïr (Algiers).

Sights

Tipaza was built on a beautiful site and the ruins of this **archaeological park** (9am-noon & 2.30-6.30pm) roll down, through pine and other trees, to the beach, dominated by 900m Djebel Chenoua to the west. It is best to start at the **museum** (021 478938/477543; www.musee -tipaza.art.dz; rue du Musée; 9am-noon & 2-5.30pm) outside the park, which has some fine funerary stele showing warriors on horseback and

a mosaic of captives – the centre depicts parents and their son bound; around the border are heads of various Africans. Here too are finely carved sarcophagi and some exquisite 1st- to 3rd-century AD glass.

The site is divided into two, the main part being to the west of the museum. The entrance leads almost immediately to an **amphitheatre**, which would have been one of the main entertainment centres of the ancient town. There isn't much left of the surrounding structure, but the oval walls of the arena still describe the area where, in the 4th and 5th centuries, gladiator fights and other popular events were held. Just beyond the amphitheatre the path leads to to the central point of the town, where the two main streets, the paved *decumanus* and *cardo maximus*, join. Follow the *decumanus*, to the left, and you will come to the other place of entertainment, the theatre. This is also much ruined, but the props that supported the stage are there, as is the slope that was once covered with seating blocks. North of here – head straight for the sea – there is an area developed by Christians. The religious complex here includes two basilica, tombs and baths, all of which can be easily identified. The grand **basilica** was the largest Christian building in North Africa when it was finished in the 4th century.

Return back along the shoreline, the middle of this cove was devoted to large villas and bath complexes, some of which still have mosaics on the floors. The house at the centre, on the *cardo maximus*, was the Villa of Frescoes, an unusually large house of 1000 sq metres built at the height of Tipaza's prosperity, in the 2nd century AD.

The civic buildings lie to the east of the cardo, on a promontory which formed one of the arms of the port. Beyond the remains of the ancient wall lie the **forum**, a 25m by 50m paved area which originally had porticoes on three sides and the capitol on the fourth. Little remains of this, the town's most important temple, beyond its steps and podium. Here too are the *curie* (municipal assembly), where political matters were settled, and the courthouse, a basilica built at the end of the 2nd century AD.

On the east side of Tipaza, beyond the museum, the old Punic harbour is still in use, protecting the town's boats. Further east, beyond the walls of the ancient town, the remains of two more Christian basilica stand in a cemetery that stretches from the sea and the main road.

Sleeping & Eating

Because most people visit Tipaza as a day trip, accommodation is limited and the choice is between budget and top end.

Auberge de Jeunesse (☎ 024 439752; Route de Tipaza; per person DA100) Has a central location in town.

Corne d'Or (☎ 024 470815; s/d half board DA5050/7070; P X) Just beyond the town limits in the direction of Algiers, this place is an attractive domed compound with its own small harbour, but was for sale at the time of writing and barely functioning.

Just beyond the western limit of the archaeological zone is the **Complexe Touristique de Matarès** (☎ 024 461822; P X), a large whitewashed tourist village with a fortress-like façade above a beautiful beach, and the dilapidated four-star **Hôtel de la Baie** (☎ 024 470822; s/d B&B DA1800/3400; P). These developments remain controversial – you don't have to be an archaeologist to recognise the historical value of the site. You can swim off the beach here.

The pedestrian street that leads from the entrance back to the main road is lined with restaurants. There isn't much to choose between them – they all do simple meals of chicken and lamb and may have some fresh fish. Most have shaded terraces and will serve mint tea or fresh juices. **Restaurant Massinissa** (☎ 042 470216; mains DA230-600) and **Creperie Cleopatra** (☎ 076 740473; mains DA200-650) are among the better ones here.

CHERCHELL شرشال

Unlike Tipaza, where the ruins were exposed before the modern town could infringe too far (although there is always tension between conservation and development), Cherchell (ancient Caesarea) has less to show of its glorious past. The small town is, however, a delightful place to visit: it's slow, a little sleepy, well shaded with great sea views, and its museum ranks as one of the finest in the country.

Remains from a 5th-century BC Punic settlement have been found and Caesarea obviously flourished long before Tipaza, as it is mentioned as a town and port in a *periplus* (nautical guide), written in the 3rd,

perhaps even the 4th century BC. It rose to prominence in the 1st century AD thanks to the Numidian King Juba II. His father, Juba I, resisted the rise of Rome in North Africa and when his army was defeated by Julius Caesar, preferred suicide to the humiliation of being taken in triumph to Rome. His son, Juba II, was taken to Rome, where he was educated in the conqueror's house and after 44 BC, by Caesar's nephew, Octavius Augustus. He showed great intelligence and aptitude and by the end of his studies, wrote a book on Roman archaeology. He was also a warrior and fought alongside Augustus at the Battle of Actium, at which they defeated the combined forces of Mark Antony and Cleopatra. Juba married their daughter Cleopatra Selene and returned to North Africa as King of Mauretania. Caesarea, their capital, flourished in this period – 'most splendid Caesarea' it was referred to at the time – and Juba lived an exceptional life, worshipped as a god by his own people and honoured as far away as Athens, where a statue was raised in his honour. But following Juba's death in 23 BC, Caesarea's story follows that of other settlements along this coast: adopting Christianity (it was visited by St Augustine in AD 418) it was overwhelmed soon after by the Vandals, enjoying a brief resurgence under the Byzantines and then sinking into obscurity. By the 10th century it was described as a town of great antiquity with a port and the debris of ancient buildings, much like today.

The main inland road from Tipaza crosses some beautiful countryside of lush fields and old trees that shade the road. Closer to Cherchell, you will see pieces of ancient columns and capitals along the road, and the remains of the great aqueduct Juba II built to bring water from a source 35km away. At the eastern entrance to the modern town, the remains of the amphitheatre and eastern baths lie just off the main road. This road follows the ancient road to the centre of town and the place des Martyrs, site. The wide plaza, shaded by hundred-year-old fig trees, was one of the ancient forums: this one, from the 3rd century AD, was a later addition. Remains of columns line the modern square and a copy of a monumental Roman fountain crowns its centre. The ancient port, the site's original attraction, is still used by local fishermen. If you need a guide, multilingual Abdelkader

Bensalah (☎ 071 427 426) is a local archaeologist who knows a huge amount about the town's sites and Algeria's antiquities.

Leading off the place des Martyrs, the **museum** (adult/child DA20/10; ⏰ 9am-noon & 2-5pm Sun-Fri) houses some of the finest sculpture in the country, much of it from the reign of Juba II. Among many highlights are marble busts of the royal family, who wear the royal band across their foreheads, and an exceptionally rare portrait of Juba's late mother-in-law, the famous Cleopatra of Egypt. A colossal statue of a Roman emperor, probably Augustus, is wonderfully carved, especially the breast-plate with figures including a deified Julius Caesar. The finest of the sculptures, though, is a statue of a naked Apollo in finest white marble (a copy of a 5th century BC Greek original), believed to be by the master Phidias. The collection of mosaics is equally stunning and includes a scene of Odyssesus and his followers passing the sirens, and a vivid portrayal of agricultural scenes. Cherchell has provided such a rich source of antiquities that, in spite of the export of many pieces before and during the colonial period (now in museums across Europe), there is too much to contain in the original 1908 building. A second, larger museum (same ticket, same opening hours) was opened in 1979 at the mosaic park (left-hand side of the road as you enter from Tipaza) to display mosaics, sculpture and glass from antiquity and the early Islamic period. Marked 'Nouveau Musée', it stands next to military barracks, flanked by Roman columns.

The ancient theatre can be reached by continuing along the main road, away from Tipaza, and taking the third street on the left, rue du Théâtre Romain. The theatre is believed to be another of Juba II's constructions. If it is, then it is one of the earliest surviving Roman theatres. The stage has survived, the capitals of the theatre's columns can be seen in place des Martyrs, some of its statues are in the museum and you can see where seating was arranged for 5000 spectators, although the stones are said to have been taken to be used as pavements by the French.

Return to the main street along rue Youcef Khodja. On the left, at No 25, **Herboristerie ibn Sina** (☎ 077 211323) is a third-generation business where Kamel Djebbour and his son Amine distil essential oils and prepare tisanes, herbs and spices *á l'ancienne*. If the shop is closed feel free to ring the bell – they live above the shop.

Further down the street on the right, are the remains of Caesarea's first forum, now enclosed between buildings behind a railing. The site was discovered by chance in 1977, when a statue was discovered when builders started digging the foundations for a new cultural centre. An Algerian-British team excavated the site over two seasons and, as well as the forum, revealed a church and remains of earlier Punic settlement. Down this street on the right, the family-run **Restaurant Cercle de la Fraternité** (☎ 071 544223) serves the freshest of fish and delicious salads, soups and desserts in a large, bright room, beneath mementoes of members of the Cherchell football team, who died in the independence struggle between 1948 and 1950.

BETWEEN TIPAZA & ALGIERS

The 100km of coast between Cherchell and Algiers has some good beaches, all of which can be busy in summer and full of washed-up refuse at any time. If you are going east to Annaba or Bejaia, or west to Oran, you will find better beaches. Thirty-one kilometres from Tipaza, heading east towards the capital, the highway turns inland, while the N11 hugs the coast, passing the resort village of Zeralda. There are two good, popular beaches – **Les Sables d'Or** and **Palm-Beach Plage** – between here and the next resort, **Sidi Ferdj**. Formerly Sidi Ferruch, the resort has the dubious distinction of being the place where the French landed their army on 14 June 1830, and where the Algerian president now has a villa. There is a range of **accommodation** (☎ 021 376778; www.sidiffredj-hotels.com), built around a pleasure port which has a range of facilities, including port, nightclub, shops and companies running motorboat excursions out to sea (count on at least DA3000 an hour for a boat holding five passengers). Most places like the hotels around Tipaza, are state-owned, run down and up for sale. Among the restaurants, if you can't wait for the city, are **Le Vivier** (⏰ 021 376910; mains DA700-900), a fish restaurant tucked away from the main drag and overlooking the sea, and the more central **Le Corso** (⏰ 021 376910; mains DA500-900), serving Algerian dishes including couscous and *brik*. Both restaurants serve alcohol.

Northeast Algeria

East of Algiers, beyond the soaring hills of the Haute Kabylie, lies a region rich in natural beauty and stirring history. The rugged coast of pine-clad hills and headlands hides a succession of natural harbours and, by Mediterranean terms, unspoiled beaches. Towards the Tunisian border the landscape levels out as meandering rivers irrigate a rolling countryside of rich farmland. It was this combination of good anchorage, reliable water supplies and fertile land, which drew the succession of peoples who shaped the northeast – first Berbers, then Phoenicians, Numidians, Romans, Vandals, Byzantines, Arabs, Spaniards, Ottoman Turks and French. The traces they left behind – especially the Numidian and Roman remains, as at Timgad and Djemila – are the region's big draw.

The northeast is graced with some of Algeria's most interesting towns and cities and some striking landscapes. Constantine, perched high above a river gorge and reached by vertiginous bridges, should not be missed. The coastline around Annaba is one of the highlights, a rugged line of plunging wood-clad hills and hidden coves of fine sand and clear water. In all these places, as in Sétif, Guelma and elsewhere in the northeast, tourism outside the summer rush of returning Algerian expats is a low-key affair – you may have hotels, restaurants and sites to yourself. Until tourism picks up, one of the features of the region, particularly of the towns, will be a sense of abandonment, of financial hardship and broken dreams, glimpsed in the faces of people who walk the streets or sit in cafés and on benches, apparently with nowhere better to go and nothing much to do.

HIGHLIGHTS

- Hang over the edge of Constantine's vertiginous **Mellah Slimane Bridge** (p119), before strolling around the atmospheric old city

- Take in the ancient town of **Djemila** (p132), as close as you can get to stepping back in time

- Walk in St Augustine's footsteps at **Hippo Regius** (p113) before cooling off under the elegant colonial arcades of **Annaba** (p110)

- Admire the **Aïn Fouara** (p131) and the incongruity of this statue of a naked French woman gracing a fountain near the central mosque of Sétif

- Line up with the legionnaires who founded **Timgad** (p126), a perfect example of Roman town planning with its carefully planned grids and many baths

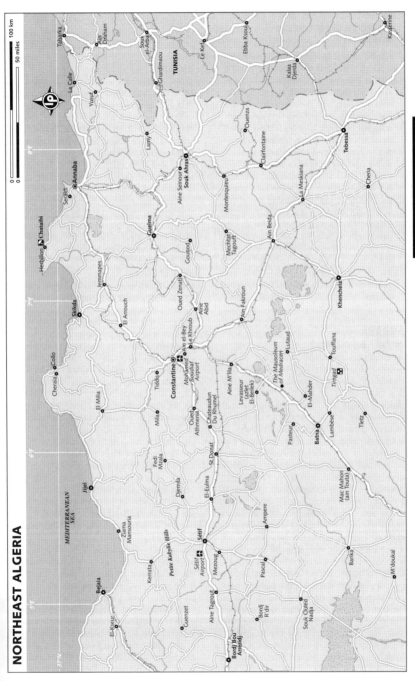

WARNING: SAFETY IN THE NORTHEAST

Northeast Algeria has seen continued violence over the past few years, even as the rest of the country has remained quiet. There are both historical and social reasons for this, and the aftermath of the 2003 earthquake – when the government dragged its feet over providing relief, especially to the militant town of Boumerdes – has not helped. Many foreign governments continue to advise against travelling through parts of the northeast, especially the Haute Kabylie, the recommendation being to fly into Sétif, Annaba or one of the other regional centres if possible. While this may seem extreme, especially when the situation is calm, there is clearly a continuing risk to foreigners travelling in remoter parts of the region as well as in some towns; police were attacked in Tebessa in 2006 and Skikda in early 2007, and four bombs were exploded in Tizi Ouzou in February 2007.

ANNABA عنابة
☎ 038 / pop 352,000

Annaba's excellent natural port and its proximity to fresh water and some very fertile farmland drew the Phoenicians here in the first place and have ensured the city's continuing prosperity. Today, its port handles the majority of the country's considerable mineral exports. But alongside business, Annaba has preserved its sense of history and culture. The city where St Augustine chose to live out his last years, known variously over the centuries as Hippo Regius, Hippone, Annabe, Bône and now Annaba, has a reputation for being a quiet haven, in spite of the fact that in 1992 President Mohamed Boudiaf, recently returned from 28 years in exile to head a reconciliation government, was assassinated here. Annaba saw little of the violence that scarred other cities during the 'black years' of the 1990s and many families moved here from Algiers and the west.

The port, the steel mills and tourism, centred around the stunning remains of nearby Hippo Regius and, in the summer, the beaches, provide the majority of work opportunities. Annaba is Algeria's fourth largest city, with a sizeable university. Ringed by hills, close to some good beaches and with an elegant colonial-period centre, the city makes an excellent start or end point for a tour of the northeast.

History

The Phoenicians settled beside the natural port some 3000 years ago, connecting this part of the country with Carthage (in today's Tunisia) and a string of trading colonies that stretched across the Mediterranean. Since then Numidians, Romans and Vandals, Byzantines and Arabs, Ottomans and French have all fallen for the site, with its natural defences and ready supply of food and fresh water.

The original settlement, Hippo Regius, later known as Hippone, lies a mile south of the present city: in antiquity, there was more of an inlet, since filled in by silt from the Seybouse River. The Numidians developed the settlement, but Hippo Regius flourished most under the Romans, becoming a municipality under Augustus and then elevated to a colony under Hadrian. Its wealth then, as now, rested on its port – Hippo Regius shipped wheat that fed Rome. But of the ancient settlement's many stories, the most poignant is that of St Augustine. Christianity first appeared here in the mid-3rd century – Bishop Theogenes was martyred in 259 – but Augustine was not baptised into Christianity until he was 33. Four years later, in 391, the Christians of Hippo Regius chose him as their priest, and he was soon elevated to bishop. Under Augustine, and particularly after Rome fell to the Visigoths in 410, the city became one of the key centres of Christianity. Shortly after Augustine's death in 430, Hippo Regius fell to the Vandals and began a rapid slide into obscurity.

The settlement was moved to its present site – presumably to escape flooding – in the 11th century and in the 16th century was given its present name by the pirate Kheireddin Barbarossa. When he took the town in the 1520s, he is said to have noticed the abundance of jujube trees, called Annabe in Arabic. Ottoman rule did little to advance the town, when it became subject to Constantine. But after the French invasion of 1832, Annaba – renamed Bône – was developed into a modern city and major port. British and American forces used it as a base during WWII, which led to it being heavily bombed from 1942 to 1943.

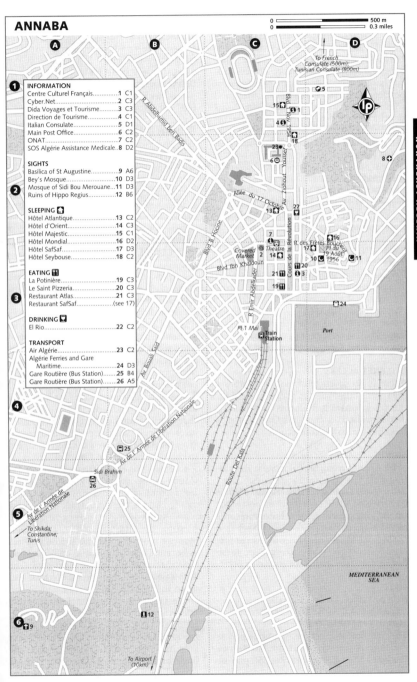

ANNABA

0   500 m
0   0.3 miles

INFORMATION
Centre Culturel Français............1 C1
Cyber.Net.............................2 C3
Dida Voyages et Tourisme........3 C3
Direction de Tourisme...............4 C1
Italian Consulate....................5 D1
Main Post Office.....................6 C2
ONAT..................................7 C2
SOS Algérie Assistance Medicale..8 D2

SIGHTS
Basilica of St Augustine............9 A6
Bey's Mosque.......................10 D3
Mosque of Sidi Bou Merouane....11 D3
Ruins of Hippo Regius..............12 B6

SLEEPING
Hôtel Atlantique....................13 C2
Hôtel d'Orient.......................14 C3
Hôtel Majestic......................15 C1
Hôtel Mondial.......................16 D2
Hôtel SafSaf........................17 D3
Hôtel Seybouse......................18 C2

EATING
La Potinière.........................19 C3
Le Saint Pizzeria....................20 C3
Restaurant Atlas....................21 C3
Restaurant SafSaf................(see 17)

DRINKING
El Rio.................................22 C2

TRANSPORT
Air Algérie...........................23 C2
Algérie Ferries and Gare
    Maritime.........................24 D3
Gare Routière (Bus Station)......25 B4
Gare Routière (Bus Station)......26 A5

To French
Consulate (500m);
Tunisian Consulate (800m)

R Abdelhamid ben Badis

Allée du 17 Octobre

Blvd B. Hocine

Av Zighout Youcef

1956 Blvd

Cours de la Revolution

R des Frères Bouch...

Pl. du
19 Août
1956

Covered
Market

Theatre

Blvd Ibn Khaldoun

R Emir Abdelkader

Pl.1 Mai

Train
Station

Port

Av Bouali Said

Av de l'Armée de Libération Nationale

Route Del Kala

Sidi Brahim

Av de l'Armée de
Libération Nationale

To Skikda;
Constantine;
Tunis

MEDITERRANEAN
SEA

To Airport
(10km)

NORTHEAST ALGERIA

Orientation

The modern city revolves around the Cours de la Révolution, a large open space, covered in trees and lined with grand buildings, leading down to the port. The colonial city has seen much development since independence, and has spread north, west and south of here, while due east of the Cours lies the older Ottoman town. The remains of ancient Hippone and the Basilica of St Augustine lie just over 1.5km southwest of the Cours.

Information

CULTURAL CENTRES

Centre Culturel Français (☎ 038 864540; www.ccf -annaba.com; 8 blvd 1 Nov 1954; ♥ 9.30am-5.30pm Sun-Thu) Has a library and theatre, and shows regular films.

EMERGENCY

Police (☎ 17 or 038 546664)
SOS Algérie Assistance Médicale (☎ 038 860858; 3 Chemin des Caroubiers)

FOREIGN CONSULATES

France (☎ 038 860583; rue Sebti Ghouta)
Italy (☎ 038 868080; 8 rue Khaya Mohamed Tahar)
Tunisia (☎ 038 864568; av du 28 janvier 1957)

INTERNET ACCESS

There is no shortage of places all around the centre, but if you can't see one, head for the small square behind the theatre. **Cyber .Net** (☎ 038 805325; 23 rue Emir Abdelkader; per hr DA60) has the fastest connection.

MONEY

Several banks along the Cours de la Révolution and in the new town will change money and a few, including the **Crédit Populaire Algérie** (No 7) have ATMs, as does the main post office (though none that accepted European cards at the time of our visit). Hotels Seybouse (p114) and Majestic (p114) will change foreign currency, but the best rates are to be had in the street around the covered market.

POST

Main post office (1 av Zighout Youcef)

TOURIST INFORMATION

The Syndicat d'Initiative was not open at the time of our visit, but the **Direction de Tourisme** (☎ 038 863013; 9 blvd 1 Nov 1954) may be able to help.

TRAVEL AGENCIES

Of the many travel agencies in town, the following offer a booking service for shipping (Algérie Ferries, SNCM) and flights (Air Algérie, Aigle Azur).
Dida Voyages et Tourisme (☎ 038 866666; www.dida -voyages.com; 3 Cours de la Révolution)
ONAT (☎ 038 865891/865886; 1 rue Tarek Ibn Ziad)

Dangers & Annoyances

Like any port and like any city with work shortages, you should take extra care of your valuables, carry only the necessary on you and be wise about where you walk. Be particularly careful in the area around the market and the casbah in the daytime, and everywhere at night.

Sights

CITY CENTRE

Bône la Coquette (the Elegant) they used to call it, and the centre of town has retained some of its charms, if a little jaded. The **Cours de la Révolution** was the centrepiece of the French city and remains the bustling heart today. A long, broad street, its lanes separated by a broad, tree-shaded esplanade, it also boasts the city's most elaborate architecture, where, with buildings such as the Amphorae and the Lion & Caryatid, colonial architects vied to outdo each other in the extravagance of their façades. In the middle, palms and giant fig trees provide shade for a number of popular outdoor cafés, where the city's elderly and idle while away the day. Here too is the Hôtel d'Orient (p114), the theatre and town hall.

Rue des Frères Boucherit leads off the Cours, to the place du 19 Aout 1956, the centrepoint of the old town, some of it dating back to the 16th century, when the pirate Kheireddin Barbarossa claimed Annaba for the Ottoman sultan. The streets here are more narrow and the houses less elaborate. There is a small second-hand and food market in the square most days. The **Bey's Mosque**, built soon after Barbarossa had taken the town, looks over the square and is the largest in this part of town. More interesting is the **Mosque of Sidi Bou Merouane**, 250m away, reached via a steep climb up the street. Named after an 11th-century holy man, the mosque is smaller than the Bey's but built using columns and stones from Hippo.

THE CHURCH FATHER

St Augustine was born to a pagan father and Christian mother (later canonised as St Monica) in Tagaste, now Souk Ahras, on 13 November 354. Nothing about his early life suggested what was to follow. A teenager of exceptional intellect, he went to Carthage to finish his studies like other promising Numidian students. As well as furthering his education, Augustine fell for the temptations of the city, kept a mistress and fathered an illegitimate son before he was 18. He lived during the end of the Roman Empire, taught literature in Tagaste and then Carthage before moving to Rome and then, in 384, to Milan, where he was appointed Professor of Rhetoric at the imperial court, one of the most important intellectual posts in the empire. He was just 30 and had the emperor's full attention. In Milan he was won over to Christianity by Bishop Ambrose (later a saint), who baptised Augustine and his son, Adeodatus, on Easter Saturday in 387. The conversion was the end of his court ambitions: Augustine longed for a quiet retreat where he could pray and read scripture. He settled in the town of his birth in 391, but two years later was on a visit to Hippo Regius when the congregation pressed him into being their priest. In 393 he was elected to the bishopric of Hippo, a position he held, and from which he preached and wrote, until his death. Augustine's contribution to Christianity lies in his works, *Confessions* (397), his autobiography and *De Civitate Dei* (413), a reaffirmation of fundamental Christian values at a time when the church was seen as corrupt and in decline. In May 430 Vandals under Genseric besieged Hippo Regius. Augustine died on 28 August, just before the city fell.

HIPPO REGIUS عنابة

The ruins of the ancient city of **Hippo Regius** (adult/child DA20/10; 8.30am-noon &1-4.30pm), also known as Hippone, are among the most evocative in Algeria, stretched across a rolling site, full of flowers, rosemary, olive trees, birds and sheep, and overlooked by the imposing, colonial-era Basilica of St Augustine. You enter from what was the seafront, the water having receded several hundred metres over the millennia. There is a good plan of the site by the entrance. It is worth climbing the small hill to the **museum**, before seeing the ruins. The ground floor contains a good collection of sculpture in the Salle des Bustes, including the Emperor Vespasian found in the forum. The star piece of the museum, the unique 2.5m-high Trophy, is a bronze representation of a post on which is hung a cape and military armour. On the wall is a fine mosaic of four Nereids. There are more mosaics across the hall, the most impressive being a 3rd-century hunting scene, in which lion, leopards and antelope are chased into a trap. Another mosaic, of a fishing scene, includes a view of 3rd-century Hippo.

The ruins are spread over a large area. The district near the entrance and 'seafront' was residential and the remains of several villas can be visited, their courtyards marked by columns, some of the walls and floors still visible. The so-called **Villa of the Labyrinth** and **Villa of the Procurateur** are the most impressive. Here too are the remains of the smaller southern baths.

The path continues to the Christian quarter where the 42m-long outline of the **grand basilica** can still be traced, especially its central apse, which unusually faces north, while its floors are still covered with mosaics. This may well have been the basilica where St Augustine was bishop – the date is right, but there is no other evidence to prove the possibility. A path of massive paving slabs, laid over drains, leads to the market (a central dias reached by three steps and enclosed by four acanthus-capped columns) and then on to the **forum**. It stands 76m by 43m, with some of its 3.6m-high columns still intact. The forum was surrounded by a colonnade, several small shrines, a fountain at the north end and latrines to the south. In the middle stood the ancient capitol and several statues (of which nothing remains), and beyond is an inscription by one of the city's benefactors, C Paccius Africanus, made proconsul in AD 78 by Emperor Vespasien. The great North Baths, beyond the forum, were closed at the time of research.

Towering above the ruins, on its own small hill, the colonial-era **Basilica St Augustine** (9-11.30am & 2.30-4.30pm Mon-Thu, 11-11.30am & 2.30-4.30pm Fri & Sun, closed Sat) was intended as a sign of France's revival of past glory. The first stone was laid in 1881, the basilica completed in 1900. Beneath the soaring nave and huge arches, surrounded by Carrara marble, Grenoble stained glass and local onyx, lies a statue of St Augustine, its right arm containing one of the saint's arm bones.

The 1st-century **theatre** of Hippo, with the largest stage of any antique theatre in North Africa, lies at the foot of the hill. The gate separating the ruins from the basilica can only be opened from the side of the antiquities, so if you want to visit both on foot, you will need to start at the ruins and walk up the winding path to the basilica.

Sleeping

Hôtel Mondial (☎ 038 862946; 9 rue des Frères Boucherit; s/d B&B with shower DA750/1200) A hangover from the groovy 1960s, its bright, simple, spotless rooms all have heating and fan. The halls are lined with photos and plants, the Hertz car-rental sign at reception is now just a souvenir of times past, but the owner is as friendly as ever.

Hôtel Atlantique (☎ 038 862857; 2 rue Bouzbid; s/d B&B DA850/1600) Rooms with shower here are what you would expect at this price, straightforward and functioning, but the cleanliness leaves a lot to be desired. The location is good though.

Hôtel Touring (☎ 038 861449; 3 rue des Volontaires; s/d B&B DA1400/1800; ✖) The calling card says the hotel has been entirely renewed, but, judging by the state of the rooms here, that might have been a while back. The 1930s building is well placed, the reception friendly and the rooms OK, with shower and TV.

Hôtel SafSaf (☎ 038 863435; place 19 Aout 1956; s/tw/d/tr B&B DA1600/2200/2400/2900; ✖) An unexpected find, this modern, midrange hotel on the central square of the old town has been well renovated. It offers comfortable rooms with private bathrooms and a reputedly good restaurant.

Hôtel d'Orient(☎ 038 860364; 13 Cours de la Révolution; s/d B&B DA2500/3000; ✖) The obvious choice for lovers of old hotels, the d'Orient still has some of its colonial splendour, including a piano in the café and plenty of Moorish Orientalist touches. Rooms overlooking the main road can be noisy, but have excellent views.

ourpick Hôtel Majestic (☎ 038 865454; www .hotel-lemajestic.com; 11 blvd 1 Nov 1954; s/d/ste B&B DA5000/5800/7800; P ✖) A plain exterior disguises this extremely well-run hotel. Opened in 2006 at the end of the Cours de la Révolution, the Majestic has large, soundproof rooms with good bathrooms (and baths), an extremely helpful reception and a panoramic restaurant serving typical Algerian dishes. A free shuttle runs to the airport, though you need to contact the hotel in advance to be met.

Hôtel Seybouse (☎ 038 862093; 1 blvd 1 Nov 1954; s/d B&B DA6000/10000; P ✖) The city's only five-star hotel sits right in the centre. It's a 1970s block with smart rooms, a panoramic restaurant, a bar that serves alcohol and, should you feel the need, a disco.

Eating

Le Saint Pizzeria (☎ 037 327715; 9 Cours de la Révolution; mains DA200-300) A popular pizza place right in the centre of things, under the arcades of the Cours. Pick up your pizza and eat under the trees, perfect on a warm evening.

Restaurant SafSaf (☎ 038 863435; place 19 Aout 1956; mains DA300-400) It's hard to fault this simple restaurant, on the 1st floor of Hôtel SafSaf. Clean, air-conditioned and run by a meticulous maître d', it serves simple, well-prepared dishes including lamb shoulder and grilled fish. There is often a good-value lunch menu.

La Potinière (☎ 038 866141; 1 Cours de la Révolution; mains DA400-600) Right at the beginning of the Cours, the Potinière is an Annaba old-timer, serving reliable French-inspired food, a cut above (and a little more expensive) than most of the competition.

Restaurant Atlas (☎ 038 802570; 2 Zenine Larbi; mains DA500-600) A reliable air-conditioned restaurant just off the Cours de la Révolution, it serves grilled steaks and *merguez* (spicy seasoned lamb or goat sausages), calamari rice and fresh fish. It also serves alcohol.

Drinking

Alcohol is hard to find in Annaba outside of the places mentioned above and **El-Rio** (30 Cours de la Révolution), which tends to stay open later than most. If the weather allows, the cafés under the fig trees along the Cours are popular for a tea or ice cream.

Getting There & Away

AIR

Rabah Bitat Airport (☎ 038 520132; www.egsa-constantine.dz) is 12km from the centre and as there is no bus, you'll need to go by taxi (up to DA500). A new terminal building is currently being planned. **Air Algérie** (☎ 038 847333; Rond Point Sidi Brahim ☎ 038 867120; www .airalgerie.dz; Cours de la Révolution) flies to Algiers and Oran, as well as Paris, Lyon, Marseille and Nice (France).

BOAT

Most of the shipping in Annaba's port is industrial, but **Algérie Ferries** (☎ 865557; www .algerieferries.com; Gare Maritime) sails to Marseille (France) and Alicante (Spain).

BUS

The *gare routière* (bus station) is just over 1km from the centre along the av de l'Armée de Libération Nationale at Sidi Brahim, a 20-minute walk or DA100 taxi. Since the buses were nationalised, the upstairs information and booking office has been abandoned and you must ask at the quays for tickets and information. Main services include Algiers (DA700, 10 hours), Sétif (DA350, four to five hours), Constantine (DA150, 1¼ hours) and Guelma (DA70, one hour). For many other destinations, you need to change at Sétif. The Tunis service seems to have been discontinued, though there are still shared taxis.

TAXI

Shared taxis leave from the Sidi Brahim *gare routière*. Destinations include Algiers (DA1200), Sétif (DA500), Constantine (DA250), Biskra (DA600), Tebessa (DA400) and Guelma (DA100).

TRAIN

Annaba's huge mosquelike **station** (☎ 038 863302/855263) with a minaret clock tower is a short walk from the end of the Cours de la Révolution and close to the port. The overnight express to Algiers leaves at 8.20pm (sleeping car 2nd/1st class DA1221/1650, seat DA945; 10 hours). Other destinations include Sidi Amar (DA20) and Souk Ahras (DA95).

Getting Around

Most places you will want to visit in Annaba are within easy walking distance of the Cours de la Révolution, even the ruins at Hippo Regius. A taxi to Hippo should not cost more than DA150, although you will need to negotiate to be picked up. There is no public transport to the airport. A taxi should cost around DA500.

AROUND ANNABA

Beaches

Annaba's inability to exploit beach tourism has long had Algerians gnashing their teeth. In 1995 the municipality drew up a new plan to develop and promote beach tourism in the area, but progress is ultra slow. However, this doesn't mean the beaches will be empty. The huge Al-Hadjar steel works and other industrial plants on the outskirts of the city mean the nearest beaches are not as pristine as they might be, but if you come in July or August you will find the place packed with holiday-makers and locals cashing in on the accommodation shortage by renting out rooms as B&Bs. The coast west of the city is the place to head for, a series of beautiful coves, where the hills fall right into the sea. The best of them start at **Ras el-Hamra**, also known as Cap de Garde and include La Caroube, Toche and Ain Achir. A lighthouse, built by the French in 1850, marks the *ras* (headland) at El-Hamra. Out of season it's given over to mussel and oyster farmers, lovers in need of privacy and pilgrims coming to pay their respects to Sidi Nour. The cave to the left of his white, barrel-vaulted tomb, known as Beit el-Qaïd, is used for religious and family gatherings. The best of the beaches lie between Ras el-Hamra and Chataibi.

SLEEPING & EATING

Hôtel Shams les Bains (☎ 038 882155; rte Cap de Garde; info@shemslesbains.com; ⓟ 🅧 🅡) Algeria's first private resort isn't as fresh as when it first opened in 1984, but in season it still gets lively with Algerian families. There's a cabaret and disco at night.

Hôtel Mountazah (☎ 038 874118; village of Seraïdi; ⓟ 🅧 🅡) Among the hotels the French architect Fernand Pouillon built in Algeria from the 1950s, the Mountazah ranks as one of the most inspired. A white fortress perched on a rock in this hillside village, it has large whitewashed rooms, a restaurant that works well when busy and a curvaceous pool that overlooks magnificent woods and the sea.

Hôtel Rym el-Djamil (☎ 038 882143; rte Cap de Garde; P ⓧ ⓧ) There are no budget hotels along this stretch of coast and only one four-star, the Rym, popular in summer with honeymooners. The hotel is above a small, semiprivate beach.

There are few outstanding restaurants along the coast, the exception being **La Caravelle** (☎ 038 822950/805373; rte de la Corniche; mains DA400-1000), an old-timer with plenty of fresh fish. It's reputedly the best of the lot.

GETTING THERE AND AWAY

It's 50km from Annaba to Chataibi. During the day there are a few departures from the *gare routière* at Sidi Brahim towards Ras el-Hamra and then on to Chataibi. A taxi will save time and aggravation (around DA800 to Chataibi).

Guelma قالمة

☎ 037 / pop 110,000

If you are following the story of ancient Algeria and still have an appetite for ruins, then you will want to stop at Guelma. The small agricultural town, 65km southwest of Annaba, 115km northeast of Constantine, sat near the frontier of ancient Numidia and Proconsul Africa. The town's early history is something of an enigma, but it is known that the Roman army was defeated near here by Jugurtha in 109 BC. By the time of Trajan, Guelma (or Calama as it was known) was a Roman municipality and in AD 283 became a colony. St Augustine's biographer Possidius lived here before the Vandal invasion of 437. In 533 the Byzantines retook the town and made it one of their North African strongholds, but with the arrival of the Arabs in the 7th century Guelma sank into obscurity. When the French army arrived in 1836 it was a ruin.

The modern town is a sleepy, provincial place with little to show for its illustrious past. Walking along the main street, blvd 1 Novembre, you would be forgiven for missing it, while finding most of what a traveller needs in the way of banks, hotels, restaurant and taxiphones. The rue 8 May 1945, just beyond the central Hôtel la Couronne, leads to the **Jardin Archéologique**, where columns and statues have been arranged in a garden that was locked at the

time of our visit. Beyond lies the **theatre and museum** (admission DA20; ⏱ 8am-noon & 2pm-4.30pm Sat-Thu). Most of the ancient theatre was quarried over the centuries, so what stands today – a soaring backdrop, an imposing stage and rows of seating – dates back no further than 1902, when the French archaeologist M Joly began the reconstruction. The site is impressive though, as are the statues of Neptune and Aesclepius on stage, and a mosaic of the triumph of Venus in the right-hand side-chamber. But Guelma's most celebrated sculpture is the so-called 'schoolboy of Madaure', supposedly a representation of St Augustine as a child.

If you need to stay in Guelma en route for Constantine, **Hôtel Mermoura** (☎ 037 262626; av Ali Chorfi; s/d/ste DA2750/3300/12000; P ⓧ), an uninspiring concrete-block three-star hotel, a 10-minute walk from the *gare routière*, is the best option, with comfortable beds and a helpful reception. The restaurant is lacklustre and better food is to be found in the simple restaurants along and just off blvd 1 Nov, where a meal of soup and chicken couscous will cost up to DA300.

Guelma is easily visited en route between Annaba and Constantine. The *gare routière* is at the end of the main street and there are regular buses to Annaba (DA40) and Constantine (DA70). Collective taxis run to Constantine (DA200), Annaba (DA100) and as far afield as Algiers (DA1000), Tebessa (DA300) and M'Sila (DA700).

CONSTANTINE قسنطينة
☎ 031 / pop 485,000

Algeria's third city, Constantine, is one of the grand spectacles of the north, made by nature but embellished by man. Over time, the Oued Rhumel carved out a deep gorge around an outcrop of rock, creating a natural fortress that was already occupied in Neolithic times. Since then Constantine (Cirta as it was known in antiquity, Qacentina as it has also been called) has always been a city of political, cultural and economic significance.

The Numidians made it their capital and after Julius Caesar defeated the army of Juba I at Thapsus, it remained the capital of Roman Numidia. The Romans destroyed the city after a rebellion in AD 311, but the Emperor Constantine then gave orders for it to be rebuilt – and renamed, using his name.

The French writer Alexandre Dumas called it 'a fantastic city, something like Gulliver's flying island'. The sense of fantasy has still not left it, for however much building has gone on around, the heart of Constantine remains on that upland shelf, reached by bridges. It is a cosmopolitan place which, over the centuries, has attracted traders, as well as invaders, from around the Mediterranean including Jews from France and Spain, Ottoman Turks, Genoese and others. From the 16th century, after the Turks conquered much of what is now Algeria, Constantine – Qacentina – became an important, independent beylik, and even after the last bey was chased from his palace by the colonising French, the bey continued the struggle from elsewhere in the region until resistance became impossible, for a while. On 8 May 1945 (a date commemorated in street names across the region) it was here, and in neighbouring Sétif and Guelma, that the independence movement started (see the boxed text, May Day p129).

Constantine today has grown far away from its original fortifications – the new city spreads down across the plain below the old battlements – but it has not lost sight of its origins. There is remarkably little to see, considering how long and interesting a history it boasts, but there is something special about the place, evident in *malouf,* its Arabo-Andalusian music, in its sophisticated embroidery and a dozen other ways that express Constantine's long, proud story.

Information
CULTURAL CENTRES
Centre Cultural Français (☎ 031 912591; www.ccf constantine.com; 1 blvd de l'Indépendence) As active here as elsewhere in Algeria, with a library, theatre and regular film screenings.

EMERGENCY
Hospital Ibn Badis (☎ 031 944966)
Town hall (☎ 031 922900)

INTERNET ACCESS
Constantine is currently not as well-endowed with internet cafés as other northeast towns, such as Annaba and Sétif, but there are several dotted around the centre, including one with good connection across rue Hamlaoui from the Hôtel Central (p120).

MONEY
There are banks and ATMs on place 1 Novembre, though the bureaus may only take cash and the ATMs may not accept foreign cards. Hôtel Cirta (p121) may change foreign cash. There are usually people willing to change money on place 1 Novembre. You will know them by the wads of cash they will be fluttering.

POST
The main post office is one of the large, whitewashed buildings on place 1 Novembre.

TOURIST INFORMATION
Office Locale du Tourisme (☎ 031 943954/932661; 32 rue Abdane Ramdane)

TRAVEL AGENCIES
EGT Est (☎ 031 929235; Hôtel Cirta)
ONAT (☎ 031 941403; 16 rue Didouche Mourad) One of two branches of the nationwide agency, it can book flights and hotels as well as local tours.
Zénith Voyages (☎ 031 620023; 9 rue Larkab SMK)

NORTHEAST ALGERIA

CONSTANTINE

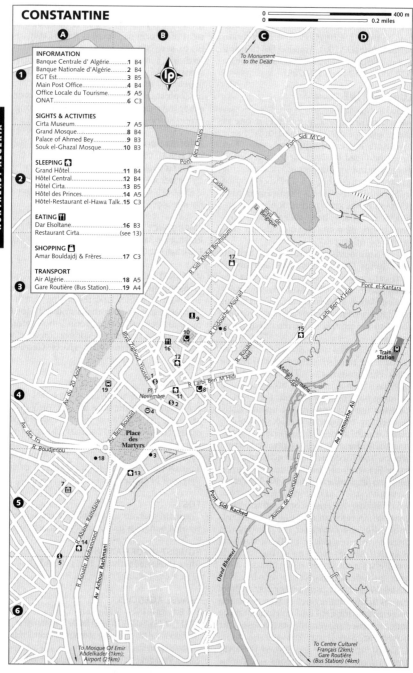

INFORMATION
Banque Centrale d' Algérie............1 B4
Banque Nationale d'Algérie...........2 B4
EGT Est.................................3 B5
Main Post Office.......................4 B4
Office Locale du Tourisme...........5 A5
ONAT...................................6 C3

SIGHTS & ACTIVITIES
Cirta Museum...........................7 A5
Grand Mosque..........................8 B4
Palace of Ahmed Bey.................9 B3
Souk el-Ghazal Mosque............10 B3

SLEEPING
Grand Hôtel............................11 B4
Hôtel Central..........................12 B4
Hôtel Cirta.............................13 B5
Hôtel des Princes.....................14 A5
Hôtel-Restaurant el-Hawa Talk..15 C3

EATING
Dar Elsoltane.........................16 B3
Restaurant Cirta....................(see 13)

SHOPPING
Amar Bouldajdj & Frères............17 C3

TRANSPORT
Air Algérie.............................18 A5
Gare Routière (Bus Station)........19 A4

Sights

SIDI M'CID BRIDGE

The Sidi M'Cid Bridge (also known as the Suspended Bridge) is Constantine's iconic monument, its image defining the city. It is a 164m-long suspension bridge, opened to traffic in April 1912. The bridge links the casbah to the slopes of Sidi M'Cid hill. Views of town and the gorge 175m below you are stunning and, in spite of movement, the bridge is quite safe; 12 of its cables were replaced in 2000. Unfortunately, in recent years this bridge (and the others around town) have become popular for suicides, as it seems that the majority of Constantine's suicides are people jumping off the bridges.

PALACE OF AHMED BEY

Hajj Ahmed became bey or ruler of Constantine in 1826, and started building his new **palace** (place Si-El Haoues; ☺ officially closed at the time of writing) two years later. Progress was slow, partly due to objections of the more powerful dey of Algiers, but Ahmed finally occupied his new home in 1835. Beyond the high white walls lies one of the finest Ottoman-era buildings in the country. With a series of courtyards surrounded by tiled arcades, it is filled with gardens of olive and orange trees, and decorated with Tunisian and French tiles. Ahmed's enjoyment of this wonderful place was short-lived because two years after he moved in, the French chased him out and turned the palace into their headquarters. After independence the Algerian military moved in. The palace has been closed for more than 25 years but was undergoing significant restoration at the time of research. It's a massive project – there are, for instance, some 250 marble columns, acres of tiles and 45 carved cedarwood doors. A completion date was not announced, but it may be possible to visit by contacting the **Agence Nationale d'Archéologie et de Protection des Monuments et Sites** (☎ 031 946831; 2 rue Siaf Med).

MELLAH SLIMANE BRIDGE

Of all the dramatic bridges that cross the Oued Rhumel, none is as exciting to walk across as the Mellah Slimane Bridge, some 100m above the water. Stretching 125m long and a mere 2.5m wide, it joins the train station with the centre of the old town.

Eight years in the making, it was opened in 1925 and is heavily used today, so much so that you will feel it swing and wobble as you cross the centrepoint. Steep steps lead up from the bridge to street level on the city side. A **lift** (DA3; ☺ 7am-6pm Sat-Thu, 9am-12.30pm Fri) will save your legs.

CIRTA MUSEUM

The city doesn't have much to show for its illustrious past, but the colonial-period **museum** (☎ 031 923895; www.cirtamuseum.org.dz; Plateau Coudiat; admission DA20; ☺ 8.30am-4pm Sun-Fri) has proof enough. The collection comes from excavations in the city and nearby Tiddis (see p122) and with the displays being something of a jumble, it appears as an old-style 'cabinet of curiosities'. But there are some stunning pieces, the highlights include a seated terracotta figure from a 2nd-century BC tomb and an exquisite marble bust of a woman known as the 'beauty of Djemila'. Also worth seeing is the beautifully cast bronze sculpture of winged 'Victory of Constantine', found by soldiers while excavating the streets of the casbah in 1855. If you are planning a visit to the Roman site at Tiddis (p122), look out for the collection marked *Vie quotidienne à Tiddis* (Daily Life in Tiddis). The museum also houses a small collection of paintings by Algerian and French Orientalists, including a study of a horse by the French 19th-century romantic Eugène Fromentin.

SOUK EL-GHAZAL MOSQUE

The Souk el-Ghazal Mosque is closed to non-Muslims, but is worth a look on your way to the Bey's palace. Built in 1730 by Abbas ben Alloul Djelloul, a Moroccan, on the orders of the then Bey of Constantine, Hussein Bou Kemia, it reuses Roman-period granite columns. After the French defeated the Bey and took control of the city, the mosque was enlarged, realigned and converted into the cathedral, Notre-Dame-des-Sept-Douleurs in 1838. It was turned back into a mosque after independence.

OTHER MOSQUES

Constantine is graced with several other beautiful mosques, but these, as all others, are only open to Muslims. The oldest, and one of the most visible, is the **Grand Mosque** (rue Larbi ben M'Hidi). Built in the 13th century on the site of a pagan temple, it was intended, as the Friday mosque, to hold most of the city's population. Although it has been rebuilt over the centuries and has a modern façade, the interior has retained some of its original features, including some pillars and Corinthian capitals brought from Hippo Regius. The city's most prominent monument – you will see its twin 107m high minarets as you approach the centre – is the **Mosque of Emir Abdelkader**. The project started in 1968 as a desire to build a mosque capable of accommodating 10,000 in its prayer hall, but when the then president Houari Boumediène became involved, it grew into the current, ambitious building: one of the world's largest mosques and Algeria's first modern Islamic university.

MONUMENT TO THE DEAD
Just beyond the Sidi M'Cid Bridge, on a hill of the same name, stands the Monument to the Dead. It was built specifically for the people of Constantine, from Alfred Abdilla to Jacob Zitoun who died 'Pro Patria', the country being France, not Algeria. The monument is a copy of the arch of Trajan at Timgad (p128). The statue of winged Victory that tops the monument is an enlarged replica of the bronze sculpture in the Cirta Museum (p119).

Walking Tour
With its winding streets, sloping alleys, sudden staircases and dramatic views, central Constantine is perfect for walking. You could rush around the main sights in, say, half a day, and think that you've been there and done that, but you definitely would have missed something important: the essence of the place. This isn't something found in any one sight, instead it is something to be absorbed, glimpsed perhaps in a doorway or up an alley, as you walk about the centre. This tour will take you past most of the main sights and past places with stunning views of the city and gorge.

Begin at the **Cirta Museum (1**; p119), a good place to start, as it gives a comprehensive overview of the hidden history of the city, from prehistoric to the Islamic period. Take the steps down opposite the entrance and, at the bottom, veer left, then turn right onto rue Boudjenou passing the Hanatchi Bookshop on your right and coming into the

place des Martyrs (2). With the white bulk of **Hôtel Cirta (3**; opposite) on your right, continue to place 1 Novembre. Several streets lead out of the north side of the square: take the one straight ahead, rue Didouche Mourad, beside Café el-Andalous. A little way down, steps on your left lead past the **Souk el-Ghazal Mosque (4**; p119) to the small square (currently an unofficial car park) in front of the **Palace of Ahmed Bey (5**; p119). The Café de la Place is a good place for refreshments. Take the small road beside the café and turn right, beside the Banque Extérieure Algérie, and continue up rue Sidi Abdul Bouhroum.

At the top of the hill, opposite the lively Café des Chasseurs and a good embroidery shop, is the 1848 **Porte de la Casbah (6)**, the French-built gate to the fort, now (as always) off-limits to civilians. The road continues down to the spectacular **Sidi M'Cid Bridge (7**; p119). Cross the bridge and take the path on the left, from where there are stunning views of the casbah, gorge and city. Continue to the triumphal **Monument to the Dead (8**; left), with more big views over the plains, and then return to the bridge and follow the road left, beneath the huge, domed, colonial-era hospital. Look out on the right for steps, which lead steeply down into the gorge and end up at an elegant, tiled villa. Turn right, over the railway lines, and staying on the east side of the gorge, follow the busy road past the train station and the statue of Constantine. On your right you will see the old city, up on the hill, and the pedestrian-only **Mellah Slimane Bridge (9**; p119). Cross the bridge (if you don't have a head for heights, you'll want to stay close to the rail) and then take the lift (if it is working) to the street below, the rue Larbi ben M'Hidi. Turn left, past the Grand Mosque, and return to the place des Martyrs and the Hôtel Cirta, perfect for a drink or meal.

Sleeping
Hôtel Central (☎ 031 641321; 19 rue Hamlaoui; s/d with DA450/600) Rooms are basic but it lives up to its name, though it is on an alley that some will find seedy. No breakfast is available but the Café el-Andalous is around the corner.

Grand Hôtel (☎ 031 642201; 2 rue Larbi ben M'Hidi; s/d B&B 615/930) Grand by name but not by nature, this basic hotel, in a colonial-era building just off the central place 1 Novembre,

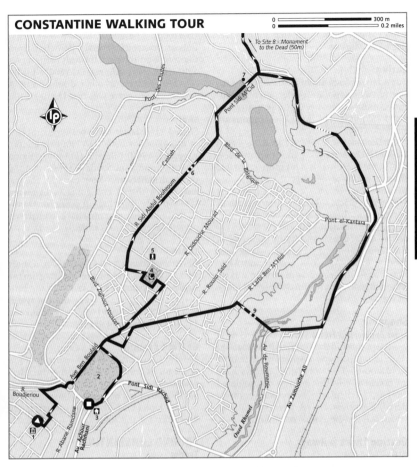

CONSTANTINE WALKING TOUR

WALK FACTS

Start Cirta Museum
Finish Hôtel Cirta
Distance 3km
Duration Two to three hours

has plenty of character and is clean and warm. It doesn't have showers though, and you'll need to cross the road to the passage marked Café des 2 Arcades for that.

our pick Hôtel des Princes (☎ 031 912625; 29 rue Abdane Ramdane; s/d/tr B&B DA1000/1500/4100; 🕸) On the arcaded street that runs down to the main square, the family-run Hôtel des Princes has the city's most elegant reception

and a range of rooms and prices. All rooms are extremely comfortable, equipped with good beds, shower (some with bath) and fridge. Rooms on the street (and mosque) side can be noisy, but that's a small price to pay for quality at this price.

Hôtel-Restaurant el-Hawa Talk (☎ 031 940480; 88 rue Larbi ben M'hidi; s/d/tr B&B with shower DA1130/ 1330/1740) Another budget place on this busy street, but this one's further down the hill, past the mosque and the lift down to the Mellah Slimane Bridge. Rooms are adequate but not always very clean.

Hôtel Cirta (☎ 031 921980; 1 av Rahmani Achour; s DA4300-5600; d DA5200-6000; tr/ste DA5600/8900; 🅿 🕸) Not the city's finest but certainly its most atmospheric, the three-star Cirta is a throwback to colonial days. It's a huge white Moorish building that looms over place des Martyrs.

Eating

For a city of such sophistication, Constantine has a disappointing selection of restaurants, most of them being little more than fast-food joints. The notable exceptions are the following:

Dar Elsoltane (☎ 031 642256; 23 rue Hamlaoui; mains DA300-600) Up a staircase in a narrow alley, the 'Sultan's House' is a lot more reputable than its entrance suggests. It's still nothing to write home about – a good restaurant at reasonable prices – but given the dearth of competition this one stands out.

ourpick Restaurant Cirta (☎ 031 921980; 1 av Rahmani Achour; mains DA500-950) In the hotel of the same name, this is some of the best food in town. A mix of French and Algerian dishes are served with style in a large Moorish hall, accompanied by a good range of wines.

Shopping

Amar Bouldajdj & Frères (☎ 031 947725; 15 rue 19 Juin 1965) Embroidery is valued throughout Algeria, but perhaps nowhere more than in Constantine. The Bouldajdj brothers have an excellent selection of new embroidered clothes, particularly *mejboudi* (embroidered, sleeveless, velvet gowns), some of which sell for thousands of dinars.

Getting There & Away

AIR

Constantine's **Mohamed Boudiaf Airport** (☎ 031 810101; www.egsa-constantine.dz) is 21km from the centre near the village of Ain el-Bey and as there is no public transport you'll need to go by taxi (up to DA400, depending on the time and your negotiating skills). **Air Algérie** (☎ 031 927070; www.airalgerie.dz; 1 place des Martyrs & 36 rue Abdane Ramdane) flies to Algiers, Ouragla, Oran, Tindouf and Tamanrasset and in France to Paris, Lyon, Nice and Marseille. **Aigle Azur** (☎ office 031 810186, reservations 021 642020) flies to Paris, Lyon and Marseille.

BUS

Constantine has suffered with the privatisation of bus services. There are two *gare routière*. SNTV 17 Juin serves destinations to the east, including Skikda, Souk Ahras

and Annaba. There is also a service to Tunis (DA1600). The larger, eastern SNTV station at Boussouf, several kilometres from the centre on the road towards Sétif, serves Sétif (DA130), Algiers (DA600), Biskra (DA270) and many other destinations. A taxi from the centre will cost DA100.

TAXI

Shared taxis leave from beside the SNTV at Boussouf for Sétif (DA200, two hours), Alger (DA900), Bejaia (DA400), Batna (DA200) and Bou Saada (DA600) among other destinations. You can, in theory, also find a shared taxi going to El-Eulma (DA150), the jumping-off point for Djemila, but in reality you may have to charter a private taxi as there is little demand.

TRAIN

The **train station** (☎ 031 641988/948831), a short walk from the end of the Mellah Slimane Bridge and fronted by a statue of the Emperor Constantine, is really only of use if you want the service to Algiers (6.30am and 11pm) or Annaba (4.45pm).

Getting Around

Central Constantine is best visited on foot. Local buses leave from near the train station, on the east side of the gorge, for both SNTV stations. There is a yellow taxi rank outside Hôtel Cirta, but you can often flag down taxis in the street.

AROUND CONSTANTINE

Tiddis تيدس

Although it in no way compares to the splendour of Djemila (p132), the Roman town of **Tiddis** (adult/child DA20/10; ⏱ 8am-4pm) makes a great day trip from Constantine. The guardian will appear at your arrival to sell you a ticket and may want you to pay for guiding services. Drinks and snacks are sometimes available, but you should be sure at least to bring your own water in summer.

There was a settlement on this site from early times, at least since the Neolithic Berbers, but it was the Romans who developed Castellum Tidditanorum, which, as its name suggests, was a *castellum* or fortress, one of a series of fortified villages that surrounded the larger settlement at Constantine (then Cirta) and protected its territory.

Excavations began in 1941 but have not been touched since 1969.

Perhaps it required Roman genius to understand how to develop the site, on the slope of a hill near the gorge of Khreneg, carved by the same Oued Rhumel that moulded the landscape around Constantine. The Romans arrived during the age of Augustus, but built much of what can now be seen in the 3rd century AD, adapting their fundamental rule of town planning – two straight central streets that cross at the heart of the community – to the curves of the site. Tiddis had no water sources, so one of the most interesting features of the houses here are the channels and cisterns. They were designed to preserve the rains that fell, on which the community depended during the long, hot summers.

From the car park you are greeted by rock, striking red earth and the remains of several circular tombs, some of which are pre-Roman. The main entrance to the village is a classic Roman arch made of massive stones. You can still see where the gate hung and was locked, even this far out into the countryside. Much of what lies beyond the gate – houses; sanctuaries to the Roman gods Ceres, Vesta and Mithra; a solar god of Persian origin; olive presses; and later Christian baptisteries – are little more than ruins, but there are still fascinating traces to be seen. The cisterns can still be clearly seen on the upper part of the site: three large basins flowing into each other; between them they could hold some 350,000L of water. On the lower side of the site, the large 'Villa of Mosaics' is marked by the pair of columns flanking its entrance, and here you can make out mosaics, the remains of an olive press, and baths that were later used as a pottery. Above the site, but still on the flank of the hill, there is a cave heated by thermals (which is welcome in winter but you might want to avoid it in summer). The summit of the hill is topped with a sanctuary, originally dedicated to old African gods, rededicated by the Romans to their corn god Saturn, appropriate in a place where agriculture was so important.

The turn-off to Tiddis is signposted off to the left, 27km north of Constantine along the Jijel road. The site is another 7km from the sign, along a narrow road, which should be drivable throughout the year. There is no public transport to the site. You could take a bus or collective taxi from Constantine heading to Jijel, and jump out at the appropriate place, but you are unlikely to find return transport. So if you don't have a vehicle, the surest way is to arrange a private taxi from Constantine. The return trip, including an hour or two at the ruins, is likely to cost around DA1000.

BATNA باتنة

☎ 033 / pop 250,000

It may only be a 100km drive from Constantine, but Batna is a world away. Separated from the coastal northeast by a series of salt flats, Batna is the capital of the Aurès Massif, a continuation of the Moroccan Atlas Mountains. South of the Aurès, the Sahara begins.

There isn't much history here: Batna's beginning was its most significant moment, created by a decree signed by the Emperor Napoleon III on 12 September 1848. The reason for its creation is the reason you might want to visit: it sits at the crossroads of east–west and north–south trade routes and has good transport links, which makes it a useful base for visiting the Roman site at Timgad.

Ville propre, citoyen propre (clean town, clean citizen) is the slogan plastered on billboards around town and it seems to have been a successful campaign in most places, because, at least in its centre, Batna is clean and tidy. Sitting in the middle of a broad valley at 980m above sea level, it also boasts good air, though winters are cold and summers very hot. Batna is going through a massive building boom and the centre is surrounded by a landscape of concrete apartment blocks, among them housing for the more than 30,000 students attending the city's thriving university.

The centre of town is around the junction of the avs de l'Indépendance and de la Révolution.

Information

ONAT (☎ 033 804345; 14 allée ben Boulaïd) The state-owned travel agency for tours and plane tickets.

Timgad Voyages (☎ 033 803888; www.timgad-voyages.com;1 place de la Liberté & the old *gare routière*; ⊙ 8.30am-5pm Sat-Wed, 8.30am-3pm Thu) Arranges guided visits to Timgad. Its office in the old *gare routière* may also be able to change money.

Tourist Office (av de l'Indépendance)

Sleeping

BUDGET

Hôtel es-Salam (☎ 033 556847; 10 av de l'Indépendance; s/d B&B DA500/900) One of several cheap hotels along the avenue, with a black-tile entrance in a white building, the Salam has basic rooms and communal showers.

Hôtel el-Hayat (☎ 033 804601; 18 rue Mohamed Salah Benabbes; s/d B&B DA600/1000) The best of the budgets, in a modern building between the main street and the market, it has rooms with showers and heating.

Hôtel Karim (☎ 033 805181; s/d B&B DA600/1000) Another long-time favourite, the Karim is well kept and has rooms with a choice of shower or bath.

Hôtel el-Mansour (☎ 033 805766; 46 allée ben Boulaïd; s/d/tr B&B DA700/1300/2000) A popular choice up at the top end of the *allée* near av de l'Indépendance, the modern Mansour is well placed for Batna's facilities.

TOP END

Hôtel Chelia (☎ 033 865334; 2 allée ben Boulaïd; s/d/ste B&B DA4200/5100/8000; ℗ 🖭 🖳) It could just be another classic concrete box of past decades, but the four-star Chelia offers a friendly welcome, large well-equipped rooms and a reasonable restaurant. It is also the only top-end hotel in town. Reception can arrange transport for Timgad.

Eating

There doesn't seem to be much call for gastronomy in Batna, but there are a few places where you can eat simply and well. Several places serve good grills and rotisserie chicken along allée ben Boulaïd and around the central market, at the end of rue Mohamed Salah Benabbes.

Pizza Mango Pulp (75 allée ben Boulaïd; pizza around DA190) Of the many pizza places this is one of the smartest and serves the best thin-crust pizzas. No alcohol, of course.

Restaurant Kimel (☎ 033 852803; 56 av de l'Indépendance; mains DA200-500) This is the fanciest place in town (which isn't saying much). It advertises *banquet sur commande* (feast on command) but can usually be relied upon to serve a good steak or roast.

Getting There & Away

AIR

Aéroport Mostafa Benboulaid (☎ 033 868543) is 15km from the centre. **Air Algérie** (☎ 033 870305; www.airalgerie.dz; rue des Frères Maazouzi) flies to Algiers and also direct to Paris, Lyon, Nice and Marseille.

BUS

The old *gare routière* in the centre of town now only handles local buses. The new *gare routière* is several kilometres from the centre (local bus 5 and 15, DA10, or taxi DA80 to DA100), right on the outskirts of the sprawling suburbs. There are regular departures to most cities in Algeria including Algiers (DA600), Annaba (DA250), Constantine (DA100), Sétif (DA100) and Biskra (DA130).

TAXI

Taxis collectifs (shared taxis) leave from the parking beside the new *gare routière* on the outskirts of town. Destinations include Algiers (DA850, eight hours), Annaba (DA450, two to three hours), Constantine (DA200, 1½ hours), Sétif (DA200, two hours) and Biskra (DA200, one hour).

Getting Around

There is a service from the old *gare routière*, in the centre of town, to the airport (but its schedule is uncertain). A taxi from the centre will cost around DA500.

AROUND BATNA

The Mausoleum of Medracen مدغسن

As you approach over the flat farmland, something vast and cone-topped appears over the horizon which you would be forgiven for thinking is a hill. It is, instead, a mausoleum and one of Algeria's many archaeological mysteries.

The mausoleum is 18.5m high and 59m in diameter, and composed of a vast number of cut stones laid over a rubble core. It is an imposing construction, a circular base with a conical roof. It was built out of massive stone blocks, the base decorated with 60 columns topped with Doric capitals. It was obviously intended as a royal burial place: there is a false door and a real, hidden entrance that leads – via steps to a corridor and then a cedarwood door – to the empty burial chamber beyond.

Now for the mystery: it was long assumed this was the burial place of Micipsa, son of the great Numidian king of Massyli, who died around 119 BC. But carbon dating suggests that it was built earlier, perhaps before the 4th century BC, though for whom it is not known. Whenever it was constructed, the mausoleum is evidence of a sophisticated people, influenced by Berbers and Libyans, Carthaginians and Greeks, and who knew how to cut and manipulate massive stones with great accuracy.

The mausoleum lies some 34km northeast of Batna: heading towards El-Khroub and Constantine, the turn-off onto the W165 is on the right. Public transport (either bus or *taxi collectif* running along the Batna–Constantine road) can drop you near the turn-off, but it is a long walk and there is little local traffic. Unless you have your own transport you will need a private taxi (around DA1000 including a little waiting time).

Lambèse-Tazoult تازولت

The road from Batna towards Timgad and Khenchela makes a slight detour around the modern village of Tazoult, infamous as the location of a high-security prison, the latest incarnation of a penitentiary built by the French in 1855. But military presence here goes back much further than the French because all around (and beneath) Tazoult lie the remains of a settlement that once served as the capital of Roman Numidia and was, for a long time, the partner and sometime rival of nearby Timgad. Lambaesis has disappeared from most itineraries and, if seen at all by visitors, it is usually glimpsed from the window of a car or bus as they shuttle between Batna and Timgad.

There was a small army post at Lambaesis around AD 81, manned by detachments from the Third Legion, properly called Legion III Augusta. Although the legion built a colony at nearby Timgad (p126) in AD 100, it built its main military base here in the late 120s, during the reign of the Emperor Hadrian. The legion was the only Roman force stationed in Numidia at the time, made up of some 5000 men, all Roman citizens, and their local support teams. The Emperor Septimus Severus gave the legion the title, 'Faithful Avenger'. The base at Lambaesis had two functions: the legion had responsibility for maintaining the Pax Romana along the Saharan fringe, from Numidia (southern Algeria) across what is now Tunisia and southern Libya, and it was expected to control traffic and collect tax along the important trade route. Lambaesis consisted of a military camp – not unlike a modern military base, with barracks, armoury, hospital and so on – surrounded by a wall and watchtowers, and civilian camps outside the perimeter.

The most visible remains of the camp is the four-sided arch, often called the praetorium, erected in 268. This massive, two-storey limestone structure, which is 23m by 30m, stood in front of the ancient parade ground and is now less than 100m from the prison. The amphitheatre, due east a couple of hundred metres, was built in AD 169 and could hold up to 12,000 spectators. It was quarried by the French to build the prison.

The remains of the town that built up around the military camp are spread over a considerable distance. Northeast of the amphitheatre lies a large cemetery; archaeologists were able to piece together some of the camp's history from the inscriptions they found. South of here, at the edge of the modern village, the remains of an arch dedicated to Septimus Severus mark the beginning of the ancient town. Beyond are the ruins of baths and a temple to Asclepius, the god of healing, of which only some stones and fragments are standing; the temple was yet another victim of quarrying – in the 19th century, the entire façade was intact. The nearby capitol, dedicated as ever to the trinity of Jupiter, Juno and Minerva, is recognisable by its pedestal and surviving sections of walls and columns, with others laid out in front of it.

In the modern village a small **museum** (adult/student DA20/10; ☑ 9am-noon & 1.30-4.30pm Sun-Fri) has a limited but surprisingly rich collection, the highlights of which include mosaics discovered near the arch of Septimus Severus in 1905; the works of sea monsters and of the nymph Cyrene are of very high quality. Statues of the god Asclepius and his daughter Hygieia were found in the temple grounds. If the temple is not open, look for the guardian in the nearby village.

Lambèse-Tazoult is a little over 10km from Batna. Buses run to the village of Tazoult from Batna. The best way to visit is to drive, or arrange a taxi (count on DA1000 to DA1500 for the return ride, depending on how long you spend there), and take in Timgad, taking lunch with you to share with the ghosts of Roman legionnaires.

NORTHEAST ALGERIA

TIMGAD تيمقاد

Nothing in the surrounding area – certainly nothing in concrete-clad Batna, the jumping-off point 40km away – prepares you for the grandeur of **Timgad** (adult/child DA20/10; 8.30am-noon &1.30-5pm Sun-Fri). Even the entrance is deceptive, a large car park, a line of trees, a museum and then… an entire Roman town. At first sight it may seem just a vast field of stones and rubble, but walk around, take the time, inhabit the place, and Timgad will more than repay the effort.

History

Whatever happened at this site before AD 100 is of little consequence: the story of Timgad begins in grand style when the Emperor Trajan decided to build a colony for soldiers and veterans of his Legion III Augusta. The Colonia Marciana Traiana Thamugadi, to give it its full name, is, in the words of the Unesco report that recommended inscribing it on the World Heritage list, 'a consummate example of a Roman military colony'.

Timgad was intended to provide accommodation for 15,000 in all, but it soon outgrew that number and moved beyond the original grid, with new quarters being added to the original ground plan over the next 300 years, leading to a quadrupling of the original camp. During its 2nd- and 3rd-century heyday, Timgad stood as a clear expression of Roman power in Africa – solid, brilliantly conceived and executed, and perfectly located at the head of the Oued el-Abiod and a crucial junction that gave Romans control of one of the main passes through the Aurès Mountains, and therefore of access to and from the Sahara.

There was a Christian presence at Timgad from the mid-3rd century, which grew to such prominence that a Church Council was held here in AD 397. The Vandal invasion of 430 brought an end to any centralised power and at the end of the 5th century the region was so weak that Timgad was sacked by tribes from the nearby Aurès Mountains, the very people the camp had been designed to control.

Timgad was revived in 539 under the Byzantine Emperor Justinian, when a fortress was built outside the original town, reusing many blocks from earlier Roman buildings, but this remote outpost could

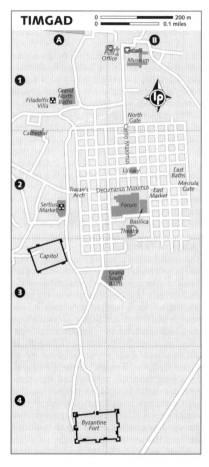

only survive with a strong central power and, with the Arab invasion in the 7th century, the end was at hand. The site was abandoned some time in the 8th century.

Ruins

The entrance leads to the **museum** (closed for renovation at the time of our visit), which contains a particularly impressive collection of more than 200 mosaics. Among the masterpieces here is a large still life (in the first hall) with panels showing various foods, The Triumph of Venus (right-hand room) surrounded by a grand decorative border, and the mosaic of Filadelfis Vita, in which the god Jupiter chases Antiope.

From the museum a path leads northwest to the **Great Baths of the North**, a huge public place of some 40 rooms built outside the original camp walls. The baths were designed symmetrically, with the same latrines, warm and hot rooms on either side of the complex, leading to a central *frigidarium,* the cold room with an icy plunge pool and a room off either end for relaxing after the bath. Just beyond this are the remains of a large private villa, evidence of the wealth Timgad enjoyed. Apart from a number of good-sized rooms, the owner of this desirable residence had his own baths, in the hot room of which once stood the mosaic of Filadelfis (now on show in the museum).

Back towards the museum, the path, which was once the road to Constantine (then Cirta), continues to the town's north gate. The original Roman town was designed as a perfect square, 355m long on each side, with this gate set into the middle of its north wall. From here you'll hit the *cardo maximus,* the main north–south street, a long straight stretch of chariot-rutted paving that runs uphill to the centre of town. Five metres wide and 180m long, it covered one of the main drains and was, in its prime, bordered by colonnaded arcades or porticoes.

The first building on the left inside the gate was another of Timgad's 14 baths or spas, while the house next door, one of at least a hundred that have been excavated here, shows evidence of having been turned into a Christian chapel at a later date. The most interesting building of all along this street lies five *insulae* or blocks in from the north gate, before reaching the centre. Designed in the 4th century reusing an earlier structure, this is one of only two known Roman-period public libraries, the other being at Ephesus. The most easily recognised part of the **public library** is the book shop, a semicircular room which still shows the niches in which the 'books' (actually manuscript pages or parchment rolls) were stored. Just beyond here, the cardo ends at a T-junction with the *decumanus maximus,* the town's main east–west artery. There's a great view of rows of columns west along the street, and, in the distance, Trajan's Arch. Eastwards the paved way leads to the **east baths**, completed in AD 146, and the **Mascula Gate**, which marked the eastern end of town

and the start of the road to what is now Khenchela.

But continue immediately south, across the *decumanus,* to the large open space that was the **forum**. The street side of the forum was taken up with a row of shops and, on your left were the public latrines, a large room with 24 squat holes over an open drain along which, one hopes, water constantly flowed. The forum, 50m by 43m and surrounded by limestone Corinthian columns, statues, temple, municipal offices and, later a large basilica, would have provided some welcome open space in town. It seems also to have inspired an envy-worthy sense of well-being because engraved on the steps is the following slogan, *Venare, lavari, ludere, ridere, occ est vivere* – hunt, bathe, play, laugh, that is life.

Due south of the forum, the **theatre** was one of Timgad's civic joys. It was created in the 160s by cutting into a hillside and had seating in its rows, for as many as 3500 people. French archaeologists reconstructed most of what we see today; the original was quarried by the Emperor Justinian's soldiers when they built the nearby fortress in 539. Whatever went on here in antiquity – and whatever happens here during the summer Timgad festival – the main spectacle for visitors today is the great view of the whole site from the 'gods', the theatre's uppermost seating. From here or from the hill beyond it, you can use our map to identify the major monuments, from museum and baths in the north to the Byzantine fort in the south, the southern baths just below you, Trajan's Arch in the west and, in the distance, the Aurès Mountains.

From the theatre it is worth walking across the pitted path and through the scrub to the **fort**. The Byzantines chose to build outside the original settlement, on the site of an earlier shrine to the guardian divinity of a water source. In contrast to the original camp of Timgad, which was never walled, the fort is a massive military structure, 112m by 67m, its limestone walls 2.5m thick, defended by towers in each corner and at the gate. Inside the fort, officers were quartered on the right, around the basin associated with the water deity, and soldiers on the left. The remains of barracks and many other rooms can be made out among the overgrowth. The land around the fort, like much of Timgad, has yet to be fully excavated.

Returning towards the centre, veer left towards the remains of the **capitol**, easily identified by two vast columns still standing on its raised platform. The capitol was dedicated, like the temple it echoed that stood in the centre Rome, to the gods Jupiter, Juno and Minerva. This was the most sacred place of pagan worship and, when it was completed in AD 160, the most impressive, enclosing a larger space than the forum, reached by a flight of 28 steps. Little remains beyond the two reconstructed, 14m-high columns and some fragments that have fallen nearby. Lack of perspective sometimes makes it difficult to grasp the scale of these buildings, but you can get an idea of scale by standing beside the decorated capitol in front of the pedestal, which is more than man-high.

This outer road continues past the 'new' **Sertius market**, with its slabs where traders laid out their wares, to one of Timgad's major monuments. When it was first built Timgad had a western gate much like the gates at the other cardinal points. But at the beginning of the 3rd century, when the town had already spread westward beyond its original grid and was closed by a new triumphal gate, the original inner gate was replaced by **Trajan's Arch**. The soaring, three-arch pile helps to join the new town to the old and is the most elegant of Timgad's surviving structures. The high central passage was reserved for chariots, their passage smoothed along the bumpy stones by the cutting of guiding grooves. The arches either side were for pedestrians, who passed beneath a pair of tall flanking columns and the gaze of imperial statues.

Sleeping & Eating

There are – or were – two hotels just outside the site, the Hôtel Timgad and the Hôtel el-Kahina, but at the time of our visit both were locked. A small bar, just outside the entrance to the site, serves drinks and some snacks, although the availability of anything more than packets depends on luck and the season – the more visitors, the more likely you are to get fed, assuming they haven't run out. As ever, if you worry about not having anything to eat or drink, come prepared.

Getting There & Away

Several buses and *taxis collectifs* run from Batna along the N88 towards Khenchela and Aïn Beida and pass close to Timgad. The turn-off, on the right, is signposted. The monuments are a short walk from the turn-off. Returning to Batna might be more difficult. Private taxis can be hired for DA500 one way or up to DA1500 return (less if you can haggle), including some hours' waiting time.

SÉTIF سطيف

☎ 036 / pop 215,000

Algerians keep saying that Sétif is more than a convenient stopover en route to the wonders at Djemila: it is a destination in its own right, a pleasant town of broad streets and some elegant buildings. The climate is also a draw: at 1096m above sea level, Sétif manages to stay cooler when the rest of the country bakes in the summer. Algerians also come to remember that this was one of the centres of resistance against French rule.

Like many other towns in the region, Sétif is a Roman creation. Originally known as ancient Sitifis, it was founded around AD 97, during the reign of Roman Emperor Nerva, and was settled with retired Roman soldiers who had seen duty in North Africa. The colony grew thanks to the success of the wheat harvest and in the early 300s, as capital of a region, Mauretania Sitifienne, was considerably expanded, with an amphitheatre and hippodrome. Falling to the Vandals in the 5th century, the town was retaken by the Byzantines in the mid-6th century and enclosed by a high stone wall (p130). The ruins of the ancient town were still largely visible at the time of the French conquest, but have since mostly been buried beneath the urban sprawl.

The French had the same plans for Sétif as the Romans: recognising its strategic value, along the main east–west highway and on a route from the Sahara to the Mediterranean coast, they built up a military town and provincial capital where, in May 1945, the war for independence began (see the boxed text 'May Day' opposite). Today, Sétif is a conservative place with a centre that has retained much of its French-era charm, and around which the 21st-century city has grown. With good hotels and restaurants, it makes an excellent base for Djemila, 45km away.

MAY DAY IN SÉTIF

The date 8 May 1945, also the name given to the main street in town, was a decisive moment in Algerian history as the day the War of Independence began. There had long been unrest in Algeria over French colonial rule, but things came to a head at the end of WWII. Algerians had been encouraged to believe that they would earn independence by supporting the Allied fight against fascism. As the war drew to a close, the Algerians realised they had been fooled – General de Gaulle gave a speech in Brazzaville (the modern-day Republic of the Congo) announcing increased legislative power for Algerians, but it did not go far enough.

Messali Hadj, leader of the Algerian People's Party (PPA), who had been against sacrificing Algerian lives to further French interests abroad, joined with pro-autonomy groups and religious parties to form a new group, Friends of the Manifesto and Freedom (AML). As tension escalated in April 1945, the French deported Messali Hadj to Brazzaville. The AML prepared to march on 8 May to celebrate VE day, for the Allies success in Europe. But in Sétif and Guelma things got out of hand.

In Guelma a hardline deputy head of police encouraged colonists and militia to attack local communities. Hundreds, perhaps thousands, were killed. In Sétif where permission had been given for a march, trouble started when police confiscated the PPA flag (now the Algerian flag) and banners demanding the release of Messali Hadj. French soldiers opened fire on the crowd and then chased protesters through the town, committing a number of atrocities. The violence spread, local tribes rose and the French used artillery and aircraft to bomb the protestors into submission. In the immediate reprisals 102 Europeans are believed to have died. The French authorities, who carried out many investigations and inquiries, never released a definitive figure for the number of dead Algerians, the calculation made more difficult by the fact that many bodies were immediately burned in lime kilns. French historians have cited 1500 dead Algerians. Algerian sources put the number at 45,000. The actual figure is likely to lie between the two.

General Duval, who gave the order to open fire on the Sétif crowd, told his superiors in Paris that he had set the independence movement back 10 years, but that if France did nothing in the meantime the Algerian nationalists would be unstoppable. On 1 November 1954 the nationalists began their campaign of violence.

As part of the 1962 independence agreement, signed at Evian in France, no French soldiers were ever brought to justice for atrocities committed in Sétif and Guelma.

Orientation

The French built their town around a central street, the av 8 Mai 1945, which runs east–west, to Algiers and Constantine. It still holds many of the town's main offices, from the post office and banks to hotels and mosques. One block north lie the remains of the Roman city of Sitifis and modern Sétif's pride and joy, the amusement park and zoo. Two blocks south of the main avenue is the market, liveliest in the morning. Everything in the centre is within walking distance.

Information

INTERNET ACCESS

There are several internet places on the streets between Ahmed Aggoun and rue des Frères Meslem.

MONEY

The most useful banks are to be found along av 8 Mai 1945, including a **Banque**
Extérieure d'Algérie across the road from Air Algérie, but its ATM was not accepting foreign cards at the time of writing. You can change money inside and perhaps also, at worse rates, at the reception of Hôtel el-Rabie. The best rates are to be had on av Ben Boulaïd, where money changers can usually be found fanning wads of cash.

POST

The main post office is a large concrete building on av 1 Novembre, the continuation of av 8 Mai 1945, on the eastern side of the blvd Filistin intersection and the clocktower roundabout.

TOURIST INFORMATION

There is neither a tourist office nor an ONAT, but someone at the Direction de Tourisme on blvd Filistin beyond the museum, may be able to help with information or general inquiries.

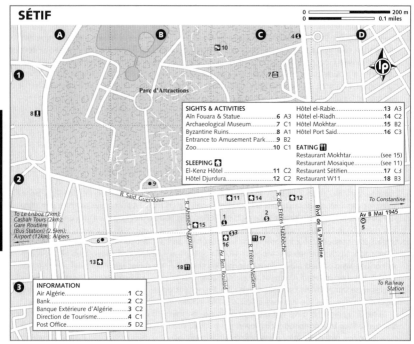

SÉTIF

SIGHTS & ACTIVITIES
Aïn Fouara & Statue.................6 A3
Archaeological Museum.........7 C1
Byzantine Ruins.....................8 A1
Entrance to Amusement Park....9 B2
Zoo.......................................10 C1

SLEEPING
El-Kenz Hôtel.......................11 C2
Hôtel Djurdura.....................12 C2
Hôtel el-Rabie......................13 A3
Hôtel el-Riadh......................14 C2
Hôtel Mokhtar......................15 B2
Hôtel Port Saïd.....................16 C3

EATING
Restaurant Mokhtar.............(see 15)
Restaurant Mosaïque...........(see 11)
Restaurant Sétitien..............17 C3
Restaurant W11....................18 B3

INFORMATION
Air Algérie.............................1 C2
Bank......................................2 C2
Banque Extérieure d'Algérie........3 C2
Direction de Tourisme...............4 C1
Post Office.............................5 D2

TRAVEL AGENCIES
Casbah Tours (☎ 036 845261; 39 rue Saïd Boukhrissa)

Dangers & Annoyances
Sétif is a calm place, but as everywhere, you are advised to take care of your money and valuables.

Sights
An amusement park might not be what you came to Algeria to see (and its attractions are lame by comparison to any European park), but it is worth walking through here, if only to marvel at its existence and at the fact that it is so popular. For while cinemas, bowling alleys and other civic amenities in so many northern towns have remained closed since the end of the black years of sectarian violence, the **Parc d'Attractions** pulls in the pundits. The park is a large open space of gardens, cafés, and booths selling CDs. In the centre, there is a boating lake, dodgem, big wheel and various other amusements, which really come into their own in summer. There is also a **zoo** (adult/child DA20/10; ☺ 9am-5pm), a place where camels,

porcupines, wild boars, foxes, vultures and an ark-full of other animals are crammed into spaces that must contravene international protocols. Most of these creatures were once found in abundance in the wild here, as were the zoo's prize exhibit: a pride of lion. And just to show that survival instinct has withstood captivity, a lioness gave birth to two cubs in October 2006. The staff cannot be faulted for their enthusiasm.

Not far from the zoo, on the east side of the park you can still make out some of the scant remains of the ancient town. The park is still partly enclosed by a stretch of **Byzantine wall**, built when Sétif was retaken from the Vandals and before it fell to the Arabs. There is more history on show at the **Archaeological Museum** (blvd Filistin; admission DA20; ☺ 8.30am-noon & 2-5.30pm Sun-Thu, 2.30-5pm Fri Apr-Aug, 8am-noon & 2-5pm Sun-Thu, 2.30-5pm Fri Sep-Mar) and although locals may not be aware of its existence, it is worth seeking out this bunkerlike building, fronted with canons, because although small, it holds a couple of treasures. As well as cabinets filled with pottery and lamps from Roman Sétif, and a good selection of pieces from the Byzantine and Fatimid periods, the real stars here (and more than enough of a reason to stop in Sétif) are the mosaics in the ground floor central court. One depicts the Triumph of Venus, a 4th- to 5th-century work showing the goddess sitting in a shell, naked but for her jewellery, surrounded by monsters and cherubs. The masterpiece, however, is the Triumph of Dionysos, the theme being a triumphal procession to celebrate the god's conquest of India. All sorts of exotic and bizarre creature are here including tigers, elephants, camels, lion and the only known Roman-period North African portrayal of a giraffe. Another section of the same mosaic, displayed nearby, shows a wild boar hunt. Both have an extraordinary subtlety, a stunning range of skin colour and tone, muscle definition and facial expression.

One attraction all Algerian visitors seem to know about is **Aïn Fouara**, a fountain that sits in an island in the middle of av 8 May 1945. The fountain is a classic piece of French-period urban decoration. The base is a large stone fountain, with spouts on four sides, facing the cardinal points. But the real attraction here is the figure of a naked young girl that sits on top. The nude was carved in 1892 by French artist Francis de St Vidal (1866–1911). Legend has it that he used a young French woman, born in Sétif, as his model. The military governor of Sétif fell for the statue while it was on display in the Louvre and arranged for it to be shipped south. Public nudity seems strange in the middle of modest Sétif, especially some 50m from the Grand Mosque, but the statue has become a local treasure and has acquired a reputation for finding husbands for unmarried women. There was outrage in April 1997 when the fountain was blown up, but the young lady has since been restored to her original glory.

Sleeping

Hôtel Djurdjura (rue des Frères Habbèche; s/d DA600/800) Closed for works at the time of our visit, the long-established Djurdjura, in a side street near the park, provides standard budget rooms, without showers and, for the moment, without a phone.

Hôtel Port Said (☎ 036 843810; 6 av Ben Boulaid, s/d/tr/q DA700/1000/1500/1800; 🔀) Comfort and calm are promised, but the quiet may not

always be guaranteed given the proximity of this 21-room hotel to the mosque. Rooms are basic but acceptable, as are the communal showers (DA60). Some rooms have air-con. Breakfast is served in the café downstairs. It's a reliable budget option.

Hôtel el-Riadh (☎ 036 843832; 2 rue des Frères Meslem; s/d/t/q 900/1200/1600/2000) Rooms have showers and TV, but breakfast is another DA70 per person.

Hôtel el-Rabie (☎ 036 845794; place de 'Indépendance; s/d/t B&B DA2800/3276/3500; P 🔀) Immediately in front of the Aïn Fouara fountain, right in the centre of town, El-Rabie has maintained its popularity in spite of the arrival of two newer, better-equipped rivals. Rooms are large and well kept, but both reception and the restaurant lacked a smile.

Hôtel Mokhtar (☎ 036 843550; 39 av 8 Mai 1945; s/d/t B&B DA3000/3500/4000; P 🔀) Sétif's newest hotel, opened in the summer of 2005, is on the main street, close to the central fountain. It has well-equipped rooms and good views from the upper floors. The restaurant is also recommended.

El-Kenz Hôtel (☎ 036 845454; www.hotel-el kenz.com; 10 rue Saïd Guendouz; s/d B&B DA4000/4500; P 🔀) The Setifis Hôtel, down near the *gare routière*, has more stars, but the newly-built Kenz is currently the best hotel in town. Right opposite the Parc d'Attractions, rooms come in a variety of styles, colours and sizes, some with small balconies, some with bathtubs instead of showers. The restaurant is excellent, the reception helpful and management is keen to maintain high levels of service.

Eating

There has been an explosion of pizza places in Sétif and there are a couple of good ones along rue des Frères Meslem and av Ben Boulaïd, south of av 8 Mai 1945. Some are no more than a counter selling pizzas whole (around DA120) or by the slice (DA20). More than a dozen basic restaurants serve simple grilled meals (up to DA400) on rue Saïd Guendouz, facing the Parc d'Attractions. The restaurants listed below serve more substantial meals. Most will close for Friday lunch, the exception being the smarter hotels.

Restaurant Mokhtar (☎ 036 843550; 39 av 8 Mai 1945; mains DA400-700) A small 1st-floor restaurant with bright lights and little atmosphere, but it has attentive service and some excellent cooking from a diligent chef. Daily specials are announced on a board outside.

Restaurant Sétifien (☎ 036 925066; 8 rue des Frères Meslem; mains DA500-800) On a street of pizza takeaways, the Sétifien serves a range of salads, fish and French-style meat dishes, including kidneys. It also has a licence to serve alcohol.

Restaurant Mosaique (☎ 036 845454; www.hotel -elkenz.com; 10 rue Saïd Guendouz; mains DA600-800) The Mosaique is tucked away in the basement of El-Kenz Hôtel, so it's a good place for lunch on a hot summer, or a cold winter night – it snows here most years. The menu is mostly French and generally comforting, including grilled swordfish and rolled veal. Service is sharp, the TV is usually on and fellow diners tend to be discreet.

Le Lisboa (☎ 036 815630; Cité Hachemi; mains DA600-900) A taxi ride from the centre, the Lisboa is run by an Algerian-Portuguese husband-and-wife team who serve dishes from both countries and can usually be relied upon to have wine.

our pick **Restaurant W11** (☎ 036 820909; 11 rue Ahmed Aggoun; mains DA700-1000) The political complexities of running a restaurant-bar in a town as conservative as Sétif mean that W11 may well be closed by the time you get there. But ring the bell anyway because the staff sometimes locks the door to deter drunks. The smoke-filled upstairs bar is popular with locals in the early evening, while the ground-floor restaurant goes on later, serving Mediterranean cooking with plenty of fresh seafood and grilled meat, prepared with a flair often missing elsewhere in town. The owner is usually there, shaking hands, checking food, suggesting drinks. Music is soft and the range of Algerian wine and foreign spirits more interesting.

Getting There & Away

AIR

Sétif's **airport** (☎ 036 933140) is 12km west of town. The new passenger terminal was opened in 2006 amid some confusion, as domestic and international passengers were being mixed together, with the result that people heading to Algiers found themselves being searched by customs officials.

Air Algérie (☎ 036 919292, reservations 036 936406; 13 av 8 May 1945) flies direct to Algiers and

Paris. **Aigle Azur** (www.aigle-azur.fr) flies to Paris, Marseille and Lyon and, at certain times of year, to Bordeaux and Toulouse. It doesn't have an office in town, but its Algerian reservation number (☎ 021 642020) is open for reservations 8am to 6pm from Saturday to Thursday.

There is no airport bus. A taxi will cost DA250 for the 40-minute ride (could be longer if there is much traffic at the town-limits roadblock).

BUS

The **gare routière** (☎ 036 842140) is a couple of kilometres from the centre, at the end of av Saïd Boukhrissa, in the direction of Algiers. Sétif has good services across the country, with regular departures to Algiers (DA350, six hours), Constantine (DA120), Ghardaia (DA600, 14 hours), Oran (DA700, 15 hours) and elsewhere. There are also several buses a day to El-Eulma, the turn-off for Djemila.

TAXI

When full *taxis collectifs* leave from beside the *gare routière*, on av Said Boukhrissa, for Algiers (DA600), Constantine (DA200), Ghardaia (DA1000), Oran (DA1200) and elsewhere.

TRAIN

The train station is on the east side of town, just walkable from the centre. The SNTF runs to Algiers (2nd class DA520) and Annaba (2nd class DA440). There are usually two departures a day in either direction.

Getting Around

The only local bus you are likely to need runs from the *gare routière* to several places in the centre. There is a taxi rank just off av 8 May 1945, a few metres from the fountain.

DJEMILA جميلة

A highlight of Algeria (and of North Africa for that matter), the remarkable World Heritage site of Djemila is all that remains of the ancient Roman town of Cuicul. Tucked into the strikingly beautiful Petite Kabylie hills, some 40km inland from the Mediterranean, Djemila is one of the most perfect expressions of the meeting of Roman power and African beauty. Here, more than almost anywhere else this side of the Mediterranean, perhaps even more than in the great Libyan sites of Leptis Magna or Sabratha, you can come closer to understanding the Roman aesthetic: the marriage of order and beauty. It is, as the French writer Albert Camus observed, 'a lesson in love and patience'.

History

Djemila's early history is lost, but it was occupied by Berber tribes in the early centuries BC. The surviving town can trace its origins only as far back as the 1st century AD, during the brief reign of the Roman Emperor Nerva (96–98). As well as the new colony at nearby Sétif (p128), Nerva ordered that some veteran soldiers from the Legion III Augustan, the same who were to found Timgad a few years later, be settled at a place then known by its Berber name, Cuicul.

The site had advantages and disadvantages. The biggest advantage was its position, 900m above sea level on a spur of land created by two mountain rivers, the Guergour and Betame, surrounded by rolling hills. The hilly stronghold was easy to defend. The main disadvantage was the irregularity of the spur – the classic Roman townplan was a square, bisected by two broad streets, the *cardo* and *decumanus maximus*, but here it had to be turned into an irregular triangle to fit.

The early years were some of the best: Cuicul took shape under the Antonine emperors – this was when the forum, the *curie* (town hall), market, capitol and other temples and even the theatre were built. Growth continued under the Severan emperors (AD 192–235), themselves of North African origin, and Cuicul outgrew its original enclosure wall – new roads were laid out, the great temple to the Severan family built, the nearby baths plumbed, and a new forum was built outside the original town. But even with these developments, Cuicul was never a grand city: its grandeur lies in the location and in the arrangement of stone buildings in such an unrestricted landscape.

Christianity came to Cuicul in the 3rd century – the first bishop, Pudentianus, is first mentioned in AD 255. By the beginning of the 4th century the town, perhaps now with some 12,000 inhabitants, had spread up the hill and developed what is now known as the Christian quarter, with its chapels, baptistery and basilicas.

The Vandal army reached here in 431 and the town easily fell. The Vandals moved on in 442 and the area was retaken by the Byzantines in the first half of the 6th century, but abandoned on the eve of the Arab invasion of North Africa, after which Cuicul – which the Arabs later called Djemila (beautiful) – sank into obscurity.

Soon after the French conquest of Algeria, attention was turned to the antiquities: the Duc d'Orleans hatched a plan to dismantle Caracalla's monumental Arch and reassemble it in Paris. Although that plan was dropped, some sculptures were shipped to France in the 1840s, intended for an Algerian museum in Paris that never came to fruition.

The site was excavated relatively late; work started in 1909 and immediate progress was made. In the first year the northern part of the House of the Donkey, the temple and the Severan forum were discovered. The main streets were uncovered and mosaics removed from the House of Amphitrite in 1912. The old forum was revealed between 1913 and 1915. In 1917 the grand baths, theatre and cardo were excavated. Work finally stopped in 1957.

But much remains and is in need of attention. The extremely knowledgeable and friendly M Mohand Akli Ikherbande, conservator of the museum, is unequivocal about threats to the site. A brief look around shows up the problems: even the mosaics removed from houses into the museum for safekeeping are falling off the walls. Whether the Algerian authorities will provide necessary funds before these and other treasures are lost remains to be seen. But with Djemila inscribed on Unesco's World Heritage list as 'one of the world's most beautiful Roman ruins', it would be a matter of national shame and international scandal were this to happen.

In August 2006 the president of Algeria was patron of the 2nd International Festival of Djemila, a nine-day celebration of Algerian music held at the site.

Ruins

Djemila (☎ 036 945101; adult/student DA20/10; ☼ 9am-noon & 1.30-5.30pm) is small enough to allow you to walk around the entire site

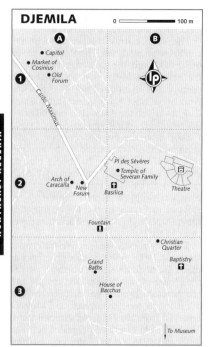

DJEMILA   0 _____ 100 m

- Capitol
- Market of Cosinius
- Old Forum
- Cardo Maximus
- Pl des Sévères
- Temple of Severan Family
- Arch of Caracalla
- New Forum
- Basilica
- Theatre
- Fountain
- Christian Quarter
- Grand Baths
- Baptistry
- House of Bacchus
- To Museum

NORTHEAST ALGERIA

comfortably in half a day. But spend longer here, linger in the temples and markets, stroll through the bath chambers, or just lie down on one of the pavements or in the shade of villa walls (as a number of locals were doing during our visit); the magic will be felt and this unique place will be better understood.

The **museum** is to the left on entering the site and, as ever, is best visited before the ruins. At quiet times, it is kept locked, but will be opened if you ask at the entrance to the site. Outside the museum building there are many tombstones and other funerary sculptures, the outer walls lined with mosaics salvaged from the site, the covered court housing busts of the emperor Septimus Severus and his wife, Julia Domna. The mosaics, which line most of the interior walls, are more impressive. Among the treasures here are a mosaic showing a hunting scene; the 10m-long so-called Mosaic of the Donkey, which shows a huge range of local animals; and the inscription of Bishop Cressonius, a statement of faith lifted from the floor of the South Basilica. The master-

piece – one of the greatest North African mosaics – is of the Legend of Dionysos, brought from the House of Bacchus and now in the third hall. The mosaic shows four scenes in the legend of Dionysos: being nursed by the nymph Nysa; being carried on a tiger; an offering made at a cult festival in winter; and an initiation scene during which a woman turns her head from a phallus. The mosaic's central panel shows another scene from the Dionysos myth in which the nymph Ambrosia is murdered by King Lycurgus. The design and execution suggest the level of sophistication achieved in ancient Djemila. Also in this last room is a 4th- to 5th-century mosaic of men on foot and horse, hunting lion, boar and panther – note the kneeling hunter levelling his spear at a leaping lion. In the cabinets, a range of objects found at the site, including medical instruments, door locks, jewellery and pottery objects, help to give an idea of how life was lived. Also worth taking in here is the scale model of the ruins, which gives a useful overview of what is to come.

From the museum, ignore the path between the trees (which will bring you to the later Christian quarter) and cross the meadow directly to the ruins. This will bring you to the end of the later extension of the *cardo maximus*. This street, which runs north–northwest, crosses the centre of Djemila. Passing a series of houses, after some 50m you will pass on the left the **Grand Baths**, built in AD 183 during the reign of Emperor Commodius. These were designed along a symmetrical plan where a double-sided exercise room leads to two changing rooms and then on to the hot, tepid and cold rooms. The baths are well preserved and below floor level, beyond the hot room, you can see where fires were stoked to provide heat. Water was stored in cisterns along the north side. Immediately to the south of the baths is the **House of Bacchus**, a grand mansion built around the beginning of the 5th century, with two gardens and a pool which served as the household fish tank.

Continuing north past a ruined fountain (on the left), the *cardo* comes into the **place des Sévères** (Square of the Severus family), the centrepiece of the extended town. Immediately to the left is the **Arch of Caracalla**, decorated with columns and Corinthian capitals. Originally it was graced with statues of the emperor and his parents, Septimus Severus and Julia Domna. This was the town's west gate and, at 12.5m high, it made an imposing entrance for people coming from Sétif and beyond. The arch was dismantled by the Duc d'Orleans in 1839, ready to be shipped to Paris, but when the duke died three years later the project was scrapped. The arch was reconstructed in 1922. Immediately to the north of the arch was a fabric market, built in the 360s, and a public latrine. Across the expanse of the square stands the **Temple of the Severan Family**. Reached by a grand staircase, fronted by rows of massive Corinthian columns, this early-3rd-century building is one of Cuicul's most prominent landmarks, just as Septimus Severus would have wanted it. The statues of the emperor and his wife, on display in the museum, were found here.

Across the square, the *cardo maximus* enters the old wall and into the original settlement. A building on the right, marked with a phallus, has often been mistaken as a brothel, an unlikely attribution: brothels would have been placed in less central locations. Rather than being a shop sign, the phallus is more likely to have been a totem, a good-luck charm to bring fertility or wealth. The *cardo* then leads past a row of large houses and through an arch to the **old forum**, a paved area, 48m by 44m. Originally lined with porticoes, it was flanked by three of the town's most important buildings: the *curia*, a basilica that served as town hall; and the capitol, the central temple dedicated to Jupiter, Juno and Minerva. Little remains to distinguish these buildings, although there is a fascinating stone altar with a scene of animal sacrifice carved on its side.

There is more to be seen in the **Market of Cosinius**, which is lined with tables on which traders spread their wares. There is plenty of decorative carving to be spotted as you walk around this delightful enclosure, which makes it easy to imagine how it must have been when the stalls were full of olives, wheat, hunks of meat, fish from across the hills and whatever else Roman Cuicul fancied for dinner. Also here is a carved stone that shows how weights and measures were checked. Immediately below the market, but entered from the *cardo*, there is a subterranean prison, presumably used to hold traders and others found to be cheating. The arches and vaults are impressive and the place is still evocative.

Heading back south across the forum and up towards the place des Sévères, as you leave the original town walls, with the remains of the public granary on your left, take the path to the left of the Temple of the Severan Family. This will lead past a Latin inscription declaring that Julius Crescens and the executor of his will, Caius Julius Didius Crescentianus, built an arch here decorated with statues of Fortune and of Mars, the colony's protecting deity. As the path suddenly drops down towards the deep valley, it leads to the **theatre**, cut into the hillside in the 2nd century. The theatre was placed outside the original walls to avoid jams for the 3000 people who attended plays and other performances.

The **Christian quarter** lies at the southern, upper end of the town, the furthest from the original enclosure walls. At the centre of the Christian community was a group of Episcopal buildings: two basilicas, a baptistery and chapel. The baptistery is the most easily identified beneath a dome constructed by archaeologists to preserve the mosaics that adorn the floors. The building is often locked, but can be visited (you may need to ask at the museum). Beside it are baths, perhaps for religious purification, and the northern basilica, a 6th-century building where services were held immediately after baptisms. This building was linked by a corridor to the larger basilica of Cresconius, named after the bishop whose name was celebrated on a large mosaic, now in the museum. Forty metres long, its central nave lined with elaborately topped columns, its floor covered in mosaics, this basilica seems to have been the last significant structure built in Cuicul, presumably after the Byzantines had re-established themselves in North Africa, a last flourish before the town died.

Sleeping & Eating

The modern village of Djemila has little to detain visitors.

Hôtel Belle Vue (☎ 036 945110/070 920529; s & d B&B DA1500) This very pleasant hotel, just outside the gates of the ancient town, has eight rooms around a vine-covered courtyard, as well as heating, communal showers and toilets. Until tourism picks up, and whether you are staying in the hotel or not, you need to call a day or two ahead if you want to be sure of something to eat. A full meal of salad, meat or chicken and dessert will cost DA800 to DA1500.

You can also buy food in town and picnic among the ruins (being sure to leave no rubbish behind you).

Getting There & Away

Unless you are going to stay at the Hôtel Belle Vue, Djemila is most easily visited as a day trip from Constantine or Sétif.

There is a direct bus from Sétif, but it is infrequent and irregular. The easiest way of getting to Djemila is by changing at El-Eulma. There are regular bus and collective taxi services to El-Eulma along the main Constantine–Sétif road. There is a bus from there to Djemila but you will be spending your time better by continuing by taxi. One way by private taxi over the 30km from El-Eulma to Djemila should cost around DA500. Expect to pay more than double if you want the driver to wait. Returning from El-Eulma, there is more chance of a collective taxi to Sétif than Constantine.

Northwest Algeria

It has rolling hills, fertile farmland, some glorious – and gloriously uncrowded – beaches, big ports, and towns embellished with reminders of the region's glorious past, yet the northwest is the least visited region of northern Algeria.

Oran, the capital of the northwest, is Algeria's most important port and naval base. Home to pirates and princes, fought over by the Spaniards and Ottomans, and rebuilt in grand style by French colonialists, Oran today is a lively Mediterranean city with a distinctive character that sets it apart from Algiers.

The northwest also contains some of Algeria's richest farmland, particularly around Tlemcen, which in part explains why that town became the capital of the Maghreb, this part of northern Africa, in the 14th century. The region has also long been noted for its grapes and it was here that French colonists based their winemaking, a tradition that continues today – the best of Algeria's considerable selection of cuvées come from around Tlemcen and the area south of Oran.

Outside of Oran the pace is slow and the sight of foreign visitors less expected. Tlemcen contains the best of the sights, both in town and on the heights above it. The coast from the Moroccan border to Oran has some of the Mediterranean's most unspoiled beaches, with beautiful coves and large swaths of sand, although significant coastal developments are being planned as Algeria – and the northwest – gears up to attract more visitors.

NORTHWEST ALGERIA

HIGHLIGHTS

- Take in the royal view from the ruined sultan's palace in Tlemcen and then visit the neighbouring tomb of the revered mystic **Sidi Boumediene** (p149)

- Be moved by the beat of rai in the place of its birth – if you can't be there to join the crowds at the August festival, head to one of Oran's nightclubs at **Ain el-Turck** (p145)

- Stretch out on the pristine **beaches** (p142) along the coast west of Oran – the further you head, the more likely you will have the place to yourself

- Have a quiet moment in the **Grand Mosque** (p148) of Tlemcen, one of the Maghreb's most impressive religious buildings

- Stroll around the casbah and old town of **Oran** (p139) for a taste of its pirateering days

★ Oran

★ Tlemcen

NORTHWEST ALGERIA

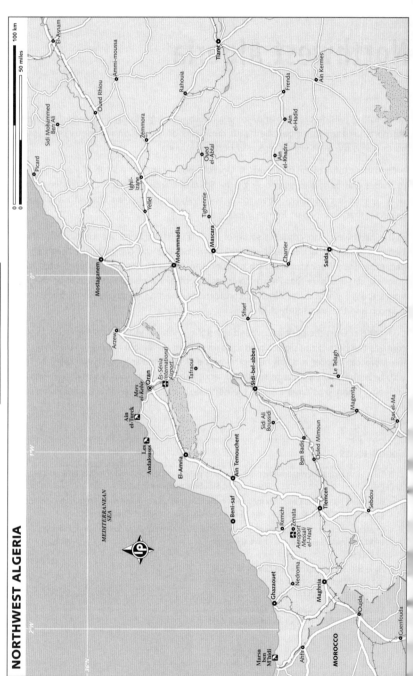

History

There's a strong Moroccan influence in the northwest, which is unsurprising considering its location up against the Moroccan border. Under Roman rule the northwest was farmed intensively, and the region's main town at the time, Pomaria (modern-day Tlemcen), was a stopover along the south Mediterranean coastal road. When Arab armies swept through the region in the 7th century during their conquest of North Africa and Spain, they were merely following the Roman – and pre-Roman – road. A few centuries later Berber armies arrived from the west and left a lasting Moroccan influence that can still be seen in the buildings of Tlemcen. Nineteenth-century French colonists, who had different priorities, recognised that the soil and location were ideal for vines and the area remains Algeria's centre of wine production.

Dangers & Annoyances

Northwest Algeria has seen less violence recently than the northeast. Nevertheless, at the time of writing several foreign governments continued to advise against travelling in the area west of the Massif de Ouarsensis, particularly around Relizane and Mascara, and the area south of Blida, especially near Medea.

ORAN وهران

☎ 041 / pop 1.5 million

Algeria's second city is a lively port with plenty of history and a lot of rhythm. Yet here, more than in Algiers, the consequences of the violence of the 1990s and the subsequent government neglect are plain to see, and every ship that sails north to Europe is watched by hundreds of people. Many of them long to make the journey to what they believe will be a better life, perhaps hoping to emulate Oran's most famous émigré, fashion designer Yves Saint Laurent. Albert Camus, who found the city dull and dusty when he lived here in the 1940s, used it as the setting for his novel *The Plague*. But for all its problems, Oran is still fascinating, a city with a sense of its own history and culture, which has contributed much to the world, not least North Africa's liveliest music movement, rai.

History

Humans settled around the broad sweep of the Mers el-Kebir bay 100,000 years ago, but the story of Algeria's second city really starts when it became the port of Tlemcen. Andalusian traders started using the harbour in the 10th century. Spanish soldiers conquered it in 1509 and held it intermittently until 1792. The Spanish built fortifications that remain some of the city's most prominent landmarks today. The city was fought over by the Spaniards and Ottoman Turks throughout the 18th century and lost much of its importance in the process. Its prospects were made worse in 1790 when it was hit by an earthquake so large that tsunamis battered the Spanish coast. Oran's fortunes revived from 1831, when French colonists began to develop the port and to build a large naval base in the harbour of Mers el-Kebir. Under French control Oran became a *departement* of France and one of France's largest cities, a cosmopolitan place of whitewashed houses, broad avenues and grand civic buildings. At the outbreak of WWII the Mers el-Kebir naval base was home to a significant squadron of French battleships. When France surrendered to the Germans in 1940, British forces attacked the French fleet to stop it falling to the Germans, killing 1300 French sailors in the action. Almost half of Oran's population left after independence.

Orientation

The oldest part of town, the casbah, sits just above the old port, with its back to 400m high Djebel Murdjadjo and the Spanish-built fort of Santa Cruz. With each development the city has spread to the east and south, lining the bay. The colonial French city with its boulevards of whitewashed buildings sits above the more modern, eastern port. To the south of the French city, modern blocks spread far back into the interior. To the east the new Sheraton hotel, built on a rise overlooking the sea, serves as a useful marker. The place du 1 Novembre still serves as a focal point, while the *front de mer* (waterfront), known locally as the balcony, attracts crowds in the evening. The parallel streets of rue Mohamed Khemisti and rue Larbi ben M'hidi are the main shopping streets. Albert Camus lived at 65 rue Larbi ben M'hidi, above what is now Boutique Warda.

NORTHWEST ALGERIA

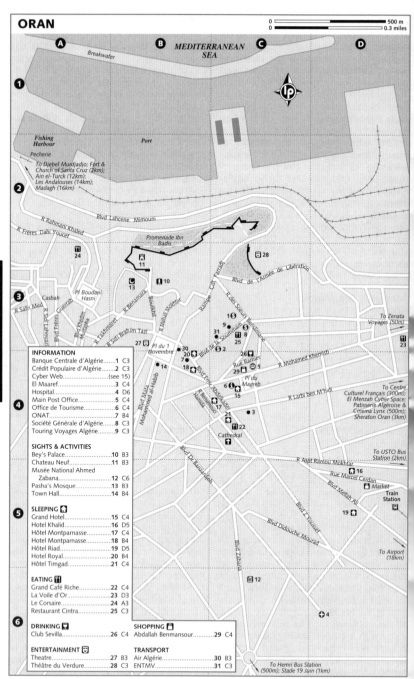

ORAN

| 0 | 500 m |
| 0 | 0.3 miles |

MEDITERRANEAN SEA

Breakwater

Port

Fishing Harbour

Pecherie

To Djebel Murdjadjo; Fort & Church of Santa Cruz (2km); Ain el-Turck (12km); Les Andalouses (14km); Madagh (16km)

Blvd Lahcene Mimouni

R Rahmani Khaled

R Frères Dahi Youcet

Promenade Ibn Badis

Blvd de l'Armée de Libération

To Zenata Voyages (50m)

Casbah

Pl Boudani Hasni

To Centre Culturel Français (300m); El Menzah Cyber Space; Patisserie Algéroise & Cinema Lynx (500m); Sheraton Oran (3km)

Rue Ramier

Pl du Magreb

Cathedral

R Aspt Ramiou Mokhtar

To USTO Bus Station (2km)

Rue Marcel Cerdan

Market

Train Station

To Airport (18km)

To Hemri Bus Station (500m); Stade 19 Juin (1km)

INFORMATION
Banque Centrale d'Algérie......1 C3
Crédit Populaire d'Algérie......2 C3
Cyber Web............................(see 15)
El Maaref...............................3 C4
Hospital.................................4 D6
Main Post Office....................5 C4
Office de Tourisme.................6 C4
ONAT...................................7 B4
Société Générale d'Algérie.....8 C3
Touring Voyages Algérie........9 C3

SIGHTS & ACTIVITIES
Bey's Palace.........................10 B3
Chateau Neuf.......................11 B3
Musée National Ahmed
    Zabana.............................12 C6
Pasha's Mosque....................13 B3
Town Hall.............................14 B4

SLEEPING
Grand Hotel..........................15 C4
Hotel Khalid.........................16 D5
Hôtel Montparnasse..............17 C4
Hôtel Montparnasse..............18 B4
Hôtel Riad............................19 D5
Hotel Royal..........................20 B4
Hôtel Timgad.......................21 C4

EATING
Grand Café Riche..................22 C4
La Voile d'Or........................23 D3
Le Corsaire..........................24 A3
Restaurant Cintra..................25 C3

DRINKING
Club Sevilla..........................26 C4

ENTERTAINMENT
Theatre................................27 B3
Théâtre du Verdure...............28 C3

SHOPPING
Abdallah Benmansour............29 C4

TRANSPORT
Air Algérie............................30 B3
ENTMV................................31 C3

Information

BOOKSHOPS

El-Maaref (☎ 066 640972; 10 rue Larbi ben M'hidi) A helpful bookshop tucked into an arcade along this busy shopping street, which can usually get hold of Institut National de Cartographie maps of Algerian cities within 24 hours.

CULTURAL CENTRES

Centre Culturel Français (CCF; ☎ 041 403541; www .ccf-oran.com; 112 rue Larbi ben M'hidi; ⊙ 9am-noon & 1.30-8pm Sun-Thu) The CCF is particularly active, with a library, a selection of French newspapers and magazines, and regular performances of music and theatre. It also shows films each Monday and Thursday.

Instituto Cervantes (☎ 041 409730; 22 rue Médécin Belhoucine; ⊙ 9am-1pm & 1.30-4.30pm Sat-Wed) Proof of Spain's continuing influence in Oran, the Instituto holds Spanish courses, has a library and organises music, literary and theatrical events.

EMERGENCY

Ambulance (☎ 041 403131)

Police (☎ 17)

INTERNET ACCESS

Internet cafés are opening all over the centre, one of the best being **El-Menzah Cyber Space** (3 rue Pomel; DA60 per hour; ⊙ 9am-2am Sat-Thu, 2pm-2am Fri), with good connection speeds and a nice air-con room near Cinema Lynx. **Cyber Web** (du Magreb place; DA50 per hr; 9am-11pm Sat-Thu, 2pm-11pm Fri), beside the Grand Hôtel, also has fast connections.

MEDICAL SERVICES

Civil Hospital (☎ 041 343311, 343316; 76 blvd Benzerdjeb)

MONEY

There are a growing number of ATMs, but only the **Crédit Populaire d'Algérie** (blvd de la Soummam) accepts foreign bank cards and even that is not guaranteed, although you can also withdraw cash on a Visa card during banking hours. Banque Centrale d'Algérie and Société Générale d'Algérie (both on blvd de la Soummam) change money, the latter also running a Western Union money transfer service. You may be able to change foreign currency on the street near the Main post office on rue Mohamed Khamisti.

POST & TELEPHONE

Main post office (rue Mohamed Khemisti) Sells stamps and also phonecards for public phones.

TOURIST INFORMATION

Association Bel Horizon (☎ 061 210714; www.oran -belhorizon.com) A local organisation promoting the city's history and culture. It publishes books and CD-ROMs about the city.

Office de Tourisme (☎ 06 395130; 4 rue Mohamed Khemisti) Has some city maps (though not necessarily of Oran) and basic tourist information.

TRAVEL AGENCIES

ONAT (☎ 298210, 393106; 10 blvd Emir Abdelkader) This state-run organisation runs tours and can arrange both domestic and international plane tickets.

Touring Voyages Algérie (☎ 041 598078; www .touringvoyagesalgerie.dz; 5 blvd de la Soummam)

Zenata Voyages (☎ 041 391227; www.zenatavoyages .com; 24 Blvd Tripoli) Offer a similar service to ONAT.

Dangers & Annoyances

As well as the usual precautions, care should be taken when walking in the area around the casbah. Oran has a large number of unemployed people and tension does rise in the street. In the summer it can get very crowded – and the noise in the centre of the city can continue late into the night.

Sights

Most of Oran's attractions are to be found within walking distance of each other and part of the pleasure on offer here is the scenes glimpsed as you wander.

PLACE DU 1 NOVEMBRE

Oran's main square, the place du 1 Novembre, is the definitive expression of French rule in Oran. The city's main meeting place (called place Napoleon, place d'Armes and place Maréchal Foch at various times in its history), it has a baroque **theatre** on one side and the **town hall** on the other. In the middle of the square stands an obelisk topped with a Winged Victory, erected by French sculptor Dalou in 1898. The original work commemorated the French soldiers who died at the battle of Sidi-Brahim in 1845. After independence the French sculpture was replaced by busts of the Sufi saint Moulay Abdelkader. The town hall, which Camus thought pretentious, has a magnificent onyx staircase and restored painted ceilings (you can usually walk in if the door is open). It's a short walk from here to the Promenade Ibn Badis, the *front de mer,* created in 1847 with excellent views of the port and old town.

MUSÉE NATIONAL AHMED ZABANA

The main museum is little-visited by foreigners, but the **Musée National Ahmed Zabana** (☎ 041 403781; 19 blvd Zabana; admission adult/student DA20/10; ۝ 8.30am-noon & 1.30-5pm Sat-Thu) is one of the keys to understanding the city, although the collection doesn't always live up to the grandeur of the building. A large 1st-floor room tells the local story of the battle for independence, most moving being the list of local people executed by the French between 1954 and 1962. The extensive, neglected natural history collection includes giant lobsters and calamari and, in the basement among the stuffed animals, a shark, all caught in the bay. More interesting are the ancient sculptures, some good mosaics and terracotta portraits. The paintings are more surprising, being a mix of works by 20th-century Algerian artists, French Orientalists including Eugene Fromentin and some 18th-century studies of mythical subjects.

BEY'S PALACE & PASHA'S MOSQUE

Much of the area around the headland overlooking the port is a military zone, but don't let that stop you visiting the misnamed **Chateau Neuf** (New Castle), which is in fact the old, 14th-century fort of Merinid Sultan Abou Hassan. While some of the complex is closed, the **Bey's Palace** (rue Meftah Kouider; admission adult/student DA20/10; ۝ 9am-4pm Sat-Wed) is open, in spite of closed gates (you may have to shout for the guard). The massive walls were first built in the 1340s by Merinid Sultan Abou Hassan and reinforced by the Spaniards in 1509, by the Ottomans in the 1700s and the French in the 19th century. The location is perfect, above the town, port and sea, and the gateway is impressive, but there is little majesty left in the building, now dominated by the concrete shell of a stalled building project.

The bey, Mohamed el-Kebir, moved his residence into the fort after the Spaniards vacated it in 1792; he was encouraged by the fact that this was one of the few places untouched by the disastrous earthquake of 1790. The main public room, the *diwan,* has a fireplace where the sultan's throne once stood beneath a painted ceiling. In the inner courtyard, on the left is the room of the favourite concubine, a place of pleasure with elaborate stucco walls and painted ceilings, restored in 2002 and already peeling. The two-storey bey's residence is now in danger of collapse. The **Pasha's Mosque** (rue Benamara Boutkhil; ۝ visits to the mosque are possible out of prayer times.), below the western side of the Chateau Neuf, was built in 1797, as its foundation inscription attests, by 'the great, the elevated, the respectable and useful, our master Sidi Hassan Bacha'. In better condition than the palace, it reflects in its elegance and lightness the joy at the city's liberation from foreign rule.

DJEBEL MURDJADJO

Wherever you are in the city, there's no missing Murdjadjo, the wooded hill that dominates the skyline, and the best view of the city is from the plateau. Getting there will be considerably easier when the funicular is working. Until then, taxi is the only way. The most obvious landmark is the **fort of Santa Cruz**, built by Spaniards in the late 16th century and closed for renovation at the time of our visit. The nearby **Church of Santa Cruz** was built to commemorate the end of the 1849 cholera outbreak and is the scene of festivities each Easter. Above the fort, on the plateau, stands a 15th-century **marabout** (monument) to Abdelkader, who died in Baghdad but is still revered here. A café serves the many visitors the site attracts.

Activities

SWIMMING

The sea immediately around the city can be dirty, although the beach at **Ain el-Turck** is very popular in summer. The best beaches – and the best swimming – are found further west and you will need your own transport, or a friendly taxi driver, to get to them. **Les Andalouses** has long been one of the most popular summer beaches, and is increasingly encroached upon. You may find parts of it turned into private **beach clubs** (DA150 to DA350). **Madagh**, an idyllic double cove beyond Les Andalouses, was voted Oran's best beach in 2006. In town the **Sheraton** (☎ 041 590100) welcomes nonguests to its pool for DA1500 per person.

Walking Tour

If the town hall is open at the **place du 1 Novembre** (1; p141), walk inside to admire the onyx staircase and newly restored glass ceiling.

ORAN WALKING TOUR

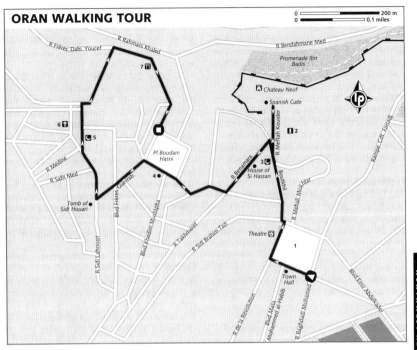

WALK FACTS

Start Place du 1 Novembre
Finish Place Rabah
Distance 2km
Duration Two hours to half a day if you visit the sites

Passing the theatre, leave the square heading due north, down the sloping rue Benamara Boutkhil. Take the first turning right, rue Meftah Kouider, following it to the left, towards a dead end. Above you are the ramparts of the Chateau Neuf and the balcony of the **Bey's Palace** (**2**; opposite; 9am-4pm Sat-Wed). The street ends at the massive Spanish-period gateway to the fort. Inside, on the right, a modern gate leads up to the palace – call out for the guards if they are not on duty and they will let you visit. The views over the city and port from here are wonderful.

Retracing your steps after visiting the palace, rue Benamara Boutkhil curves past the old Armes et Cycles shop and around the **Pasha's Mosque** (**3**; opposite) to the House of Si

Hassan, a tobacco trader who became Bey of Oran in 1812. The house, dating from 1700, was restored in 1900 and is closed to visitors. Continue down the slope until it reaches place Boudali Hasni, also known as place Rabah, an elegant centrepiece to the 'lower town', much of it built in the early 19th century and now derelict. On your left (south), pass the old **Gendarmerie (4)** and head up blvd Frères Guerrab – some houses off this street date back to the Spanish period. Where the boulevard veers left, continue straight uphill along a market street and follow the stalls right, onto rue Sidi Lahaouri.

Sidi el-Houari, Oran's holy man, died here in 1439 and gave his name to the street and the district, the heart of the casbah and home, well into the 1900s, of a largely Spanish-origin population. More recently the king of rai, Cheb Khaled, was born here on 29 February 1960. The **mosque of Sidi el-Houari (5)**, built in Moorish style in 1793, is up the street on the right and is a popular place of pilgrimage for Algerians, as is the saint's tomb, south along the same street. Visits may be possible out of prayer times.

The **Cathedral of St Louis (6)** was built by the French in 1839 on the site of a 1679 Spanish church, destroyed, like much of this part of the casbah, in the 1790 earthquake. The cathedral is now closed and derelict, but if you find the resident guardian you may be allowed to look around.

From here, head northeast to rue Frères Dahl Youcef, then east, passing **Le Corsaire (7**, right)–here the street is also known as pl de la Republique–then south back to place Boudani Hasni, also known as place Rabah. From the square, head back to the upper town.

Festivals & Events

The **Festival National de la Chanson du Rai d'Oran** (www.festival-rai.over-blog.org) is the city's celebration of its home-grown sound. Started in 1985, it takes place in August in the Théâtre de Verdure, the outdoor arena beneath the eastern bastion of Chateau Neuf fort. The festival has long suffered from cash shortages, but the government has promised to increase its support.

Sleeping

Hôtel Riad (☎ 041 403850; 46 blvd Mellah Ali; s/d/tr DA400/700/1000) A very basic option across from the train station (and mosque), for those times when the budget won't stretch to anywhere else. Some rooms come with showers.

Hôtel Khalid (☎ 041 332628; 21 rue Marcel Cerdan; s/d incl breakfast DA1500/1700, s/d with air-con incl breakfast DA1800/2200; 🟦) The best of several budget places along the backstreets close to the centre. More expensive rooms have streetside windows.

Grand Hôtel (☎ 041 391533; 5 place du Magreb; s/d DA2000/3000; 🟦) A reminder of the city's glory days, the Grand is well past its prime, rooms are as tired as reception staff, but there is still plenty of atmosphere and it has a central location.

ourpick Hôtel Residence le Timgad (☎ 041 394797; www.hoteltimgad.com; 22 blvd Emir Abdelkader; s/d incl breakfast DA3400/4150; P 🟦 🖳) An extremely well run and friendly hotel in an uninspiring modern block right in the centre of town. Rooms are large, spotless, double-glazed and well appointed. The ground-floor restaurant is reliable, and the parrot in reception does a great imitation of phones ringing. It may have detailed city maps for sale. Recommended.

Hôtel Montparnasse (☎ 041 395338; 9 rue Bensenouci Hamida; s/d DA3500/4000; 🟦) Don't be put off by the 'back door' on blvd Emir Abdelkader, this is a good, clean, central hotel with shower, fridge and TV.

Sheraton Oran (☎ 041 590100; www.sheraton.com/oran; Route des Falaises Es Seddikia; s/d incl breakfast DA13,300/18,000; P 🟦 🖳 🟦) Currently the best in town, the Sheraton has a curvaceous mirrored wall containing the height of Oranese luxury (at least until the Royal is running). It's a short drive from the centre, with fully equipped rooms and a range of restaurants.

Hôtel Royal (☎ 041 393144; www.sofitel.com;3 blvd de la Soummam) When it reopens in 2007, the Royal will be Oran's most elegant hotel and should live up to its name. At the time of our visit, the gilding was being applied to the ironwork.

Eating

A recent survey found that 60% of men in Oran prefer to eat breakfast in a café rather than at home and, as a result, the city is packed with cafés. Good restaurants are harder to find, and it's harder still to find the local speciality of *brannieh* (a stew of lamb or beef with courgettes and chickpeas).

La Voile d'Or (62 rue Mohamed Khemisti; dishes DA400-500; 🕑 lunch & dinner Sun-Thu) A simple air-conditioned restaurant near a popular public garden, serving fresh fish dishes and alcohol.

Restaurant Cintra (☎ 041 393345; 14 blvd de la Soummam; dishes DA450-1200) An old-timer on one of the grand boulevards with an international menu of Catalan tuna, Spanish crevettes and French sole. Alcohol is served.

Le Corsaire (☎ 041 397620; 6 place de la Republique; dishes DA500-600; 🕑 closed lunch Fri) The restaurants by the Pecherie serve some of Oran's best fish, but none match the Corsaire, its motto *on y est bien en famille* (you are among family here). Chose from the display and have it cooked the way you want. Paella, a speciality, is best ordered in advance. No alcohol.

Grand Café Riche (☎ 041 394797; 22 blvd Emir Abdelkader; dishes DA800-950; 🕑 lunch & dinner) The name is misleading: not a big, bustling café, but the restaurant of Hôtel Residence le Timgad. Food is standard French, the cloths are crisp white, the room curtained and service is friendly and efficient. Alcohol is served.

Drinking

There are plenty of seedy bars in town (look for the Stella signs).

Club Sevilla (5 rue Ramier) is a cut above the rest. It's a small bar with food and music till late.

Entertainment

Oran is the proud birthplace of rai and it won't be long before you hear its distinctive beat. But it can be hard to track down live music, outside of the August festival. The circuit tends to shift by the season and fashion, but in high summer the clubs of Ain el-Turck should all be running. Look out for Le Biarritz (where Khaled first performed), Le Chalet and El-Jawhara. L'Ambiance at the Sheraton also has live music.

The **Centre Culturel Français** (☎ 041 403541; www.ccf-oran.com; 112 rue Larbi ben M'hidi) has regular screenings of French-language films. Something more macho can be found at **Cinema Lynx** (81 Larbi ben M'hidi; films DA69).

213tv (☎ 015 028030; www.213tv.com). A new Franco-Algerian operation with a mission to revitalise Oran's cultural life, stages regular live music events.

Shopping

Rue Larbi ben M'hidi and rue Mohamed Khemisti are the city's main shopping streets, lined with boutiques and sports shops.

Abdallah Benmansour (☎ 041 397882; 5 rue Mohamed Khemisti). Benmansour is one of Algeria's most respected artists; his paintings hang in the shop and are for sale. He also sells stationary and art materials.

Patisserie Algéroise (☎ 041 398759; 81 rue Larbi ben M'hidi).The best *baklava* and local pastries in town are sold at this patisserie.

Getting There & Away

AIR

Es-Sénia International Airport (☎ 041 511153/591031) is 18 km southeast of town, near Tafraoui village.

Air Algérie (☎ 041 427205, 041 427206; www.air algerie.dz; 2 blvd Emir Abdelkader; ☺ 8am-noon & 2-5pm Sat-Wed, 8am-noon Thu) flies direct from Oran to a number of airports around Algeria including Algiers (approximately DA3720), Tindouf, Tamarasset (approximately DA14,200), Adrar and Annaba.

International destinations served by Air Algérie include Paris, Lyon and Marseille. **Aigle Azur** (☎ 041 390940; www.aigle-azur.fr; airport) also operates a daily direct service to Paris.

BOAT

There are regular sailings from Oran to Alicante (Spain; 12 hours) and Marseille (France; 11 hours). Tickets must be bought in advance from one of several agencies in town, **ENTMV** (☎ 041 392166; 9 blvd de la Soummam) being the biggest.

BUS

Oran has several bus stations, which can be confusing for visitors, especially since they are strung out across the city and, since the privatisation of bus services, there is no reliable information.

Agence Castor, off the 2nd blvd Peripherieque, is a relatively new bus station serving northwest Algeria, including Mostaganem (DA80), Mascara (DA90) and Chlef (DA90).

The **Gare Routiere el-Hemri** (Blvd Colonel Lotfi), formerly known as SNTV, was the central bus station until bus services were privatised. Destinations include Algiers (DA470, eight hours), Tindouf (DA2100, 14 hours), Constantine (DA900, 14 hours), Setif (DA700, 12 hours), Ouargla (DA900, 12 hours), Ghardaia (DA700, 10 hours) and other distant places. There is no phone service, but M Boumazair of **Amin Voyages** (☎ 070 122926) at the station can provide information.

Buses leave the **Yaghmourassen station** (rue Yaghmourassen) for Tlemcen (DA200) and the west. **Transport Veolia** (☎ 021 498024) runs a day and night Oran–Algiers service from here (day/night DA720/820, eight hours).

TAXI

Taxis leave round the clock from the car park beside **Stade 19 Juin** (av des Martyrs de la Revolution) for Algiers (DA900, six hours) and from 4am to 8pm to Constantine (DA1600, 12 hours) and eastern Algeria.

Standard *taxis collectifs* (shared taxis) destinations from the **USTO station** (off rue Djemila, near Clinque Nekkache) include Biskra (DA120), Ghardaia (DA1100) and Msila (DA900).

TRAIN

The **train station** (☎ 041 401502, 041 361788; blvd Mellah Ali) is a 10-minute walk from the centre. The service to Morocco stopped when the border closed, but there is a daily service to Sidi Bel Abbes at 4.10pm (one hour, 20 minutes), to Ain Temouchent (one hour) and Tlemcen at 1.30pm, Relizane at 3.45pm (1½ hours) and Algiers at 7.45am (1st/2nd class with 15% reduction on return fares, DA990/705, 4½ hours). There is no left-luggage facility.

Getting Around

TO/FROM THE AIRPORT

EGSA, the airport operators, runs a bus service from the airport to outside a pharmacy on blvd Maatra Mohamed Habib, opposite the town hall. It officially operates from 7am to 7pm, but may not connect with flights. A taxi may cost up to DA500.

BUS

Most places inside Oran are within walking distance, the exception being Santa Cruz and Djebel Murdjadjo, which can only be reached by taxi. Regular buses for Ain el-Turck (DA20) and the beaches to the west leave during the day from rue Benamara Boutkhil, just off place 1 Novembre.

TAXI

Taxis are easy to find (out of rush hour) and cheap enough: few trips in town will cost more than DA200. Make sure the meter is working or that you have fixed, in your mind at least, what the journey is worth. There are *taxis collectifs* to Ain el-Turck during the day (DA50), but at night a private taxi is your only option (at least DA200).

TLEMCEN تلمسان

☎ 043 / pop 150,000

Of all Algerian towns and cities, only Tlemcen boasts Moorish buildings to rival those in Morocco or Andalusia. The Romans recognised its strategic and economic importance and built a stronghold, Pomaria, here during the reign of Septimus Severus, but nothing remains of the classical town. In the 8th century Idriss I built a new town, which he called Agadir. Tlemcen grew in importance

---

SPAIN IN AFRICA

If you detect a hint of Spain, something Andalusian perhaps, about parts of Oran, you're on the right track: for 200 years Oran and its surrounding area was under Spanish control, and even before that there were regular contacts.

Andalusian traders founded Oran in the 10th century with an eye on Tlemcen and the North African interior. The town behind the port took on an even stronger Andalusian feel after Muslims were expelled from Spain in 1492. One of the key figures of the Spanish move against Moors in Spain was Cardinal Cisneros, Archbishop of Toledo and head of the Inquisition. In 1505 he paid for a force to attack Oran, taking control of the port of Mers el-Kebir. Four years later he personally led the Spanish attack on Oran, the beginning of what he hoped would be a crusade in North Africa. Although the city fell in a day, King Ferdinand of Spain had little interest in the cardinal's crusade and with the help of Mujedars (Moorish refugees from Andalusia) the pirate Kheirredin Barbarossa took Oran, eventually holding it for the Ottoman sultan, although not before he lost his elder brother fighting the Spanish inland near Tlemcen in 1510.

The Spanish finally wrested control of Oran in 1732 and immediately fortified it. Buildings such as the fort of Santa Cruz on Djebel Murdjadjo (p142) and some in the centre of the casbah are reminders of Spanish presence. Although control of Oran passed in 1792 to the Ottomans and later to the French, there was still a significant Spanish-origin presence in the city in the early 20th century, with the area around the mosque of Sidi el-Houari (p143) referred to as the 'Spanish town' (as opposed to the area around the Pasha's Mosque, on the opposite side of the valley, known as the Turkish town).

Cardinal Cisneros hoped to make Oran a Christian foothold in North Africa, but his legacy has been more unexpected. Part of it can be seen in the surviving Spanish-era structures and in the reputation the people of Oran have for fun. But most obviously it can be heard in the city's music: the Algerian-Andalusian music that accompanied the most popular singers of the 20th century, such as Reinette el-Wahrania, the Oranaise, as she sang in the Spanish-town nightclubs and in the Ville Nouvelle theatres; and in rai, the sound of new Oran.

TLEMCEN

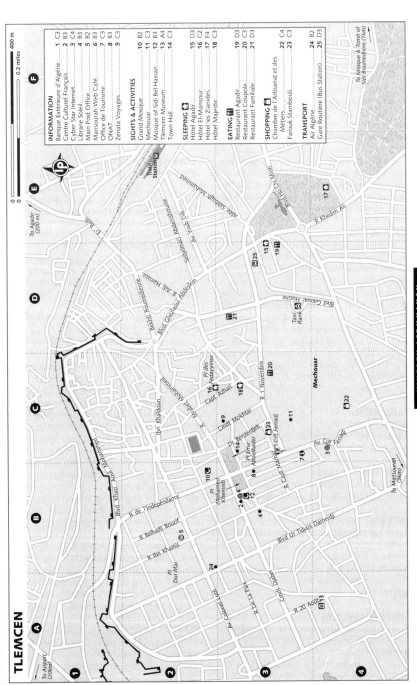

NORTHWEST ALGERIA

under Almoravid ruler Youssef ben Tach-fine, who moved his capital here; for centuries it was one of the centres of power in the Mahgreb. In the first half of the 14th century the Merinid sultan Abou Yacoub besieged the town for so long that his camp, Mansourah, became a town in itself. During the colonial period Tlemcen held off the French for more than 10 years and always had a strong anticolonial movement. Algeria's first independence movement was founded by a Tlemceni in 1924. Today, easy-going Tlemcen, known as 'the town of cherries', is a pleasure to visit. It also has a vision: Algeria's largest university campus is currently being built by a Chinese contractor.

Orientation

The town sits beneath the wooded ridge of Lala Setti, on the edge of the rich farmland of the Henneya and Maghnia plains. It has had several centres over the centuries: the Idrissid one at Agadir, the Almoravid one at Mansourah and the Zianide one around the Mechouar. The Grand Mosque and place Emir Abdelkader are now the town's main hub and most sights and facilities are to be found within a 20-minute walk of here. Mansourah lies to the southwest of the centre, Agadir to the northeast. Both are too far to walk.

Information

BOOKSHOPS

Librairie Soleil (☎ 043 266501; 39 rue Ibn Khamis) Has a good selection of French novels and history.

CULTURAL CENTRES

CCF (☎ 043 261722; www.ccf-tlemcen.com; 1 rue Col Djeber) Has a library, an exhibition space and a cinema.

INTERNET ACCESS

Cyber Star Internet (17 av Cdt Ferradj) Above Café Mechouar, opposite the entrance to the Mechouar. Has fast connections in a nice room.
Mansourah Web Café (Optique Opthalmique Bldg, Place Emir Abdelkader) Near the Grand Mosque; also reliable.

MEDICAL SERVICES

Civil Hospital (☎ 043 261821; 76 blvd Ben Zerdjeb)

MONEY

Don't count on the Tlemcen ATMs accepting your bank cards. Several banks in

the centre will change foreign currency, including **Banque Extérieure d'Algérie** (av Cdt Faradj). Hôtel les Zianides may change a small amount, though at a less favourable rate.

POST & TELEPHONE

As elsewhere in Algeria, you don't have to walk far to find a taxiphone booth.
Main post office (av Colonel Lotfi) Sells stamps and also phonecards for public phones.

TOURIST INFORMATION

Office de Tourisme (☎ 043 263456; 17 rue Cdt Ferradj), run by the very helpful M Boubakar, has maps, information and a library (mostly French). Some information is also available online at www.tlemcen-dz.com.

TRAVEL AGENCIES

ONAT (☎ 043 271660; 15 rue de l'Independence)
Zenata Voyages (☎ 043 277090; www.zenatavoyages .com; 11 rue Cdt Mokhtar) Offers domestic and international travel facilities.

Sights

GRAND MOSQUE

Tlemcen's **Grand Mosque** (place Emir Abdelkader; ⏱ 8-11am Sat-Thu) is one of North Africa's most important Islamic buildings. Begun by the Almoravid leader Youssef ben Tachfine around 1091, it has been substantially rebuilt several times over the centuries but retains some important early features, including the mihrab, elaborately decorated in stucco and carved stone, and a fine cupola with a massive chandelier. More impressive, though, is the atmosphere of reverence that fills the building. There are 133 steps to the top of the minaret, the oldest in this part of the Maghreb and the highest in town. To visit the mosque, you need to observe the instruction that 'women must wear long clothes'.

PLACE EMIR ABDELKADER & PLACE MOHAMED KHEMISTI

Tlemcen revolves around these twin squares, divided by rue de l'Independence. On the south side is the old colonial-era **town hall** (1843), opposite is the Grand Mosque and on the west side is the 12th-century **Mosque of Sidi Bel Hassan**, built in 1297 by the son of the noted local ruler Yaghmorassen and dedicated to a local holy man. The squares are busy throughout the day, particularly after prayers, when the cafés are buzzing and

---

THE GRAPEVINE

The French pride themselves on having created the Algerian wine industry, during the long years of colonisation, but wine-making in the region goes back much further than the mid-19th century.

Ancient Persians are said to have planted vines near the town of Medea several thousand years ago and the Numidians exported wine to Rome, enough of a reason for some, for the Roman conquest. Arabs brought new varieties of grapes, including the Grenache, from Spain, while the Ottomans brought other varieties from the eastern Mediterranean. And in the 1860s French wine-makers looked with envy to their new colony as French vineyards were decimated by Phylloxera, a North American aphid which is calculated to have destroyed 40% of French vines.

The French looked to Algeria for quantity, not quality. Towards the end of the colonial period, Algeria was producing more than 500 million gallons a year, much of it exported to blend with weaker north Mediterranean wine. Current production is around 15 million gallons, set to rise over the next few years to 40 million. But the Algerians now have their sights on quality. They compare their soil type to California, but with more rain.

The northwest is the main wine-growing region, accounting for as much as three quarters of the country's production, with important vineyards around Mascara, Medea and Tlemcen. The Coteaux de Tlemcen and Coteaux de Mascara, both robust, dark ruby wines, best served lightly chilled, are among the best and are widely available in Algeria.

---

men sit under the shade trees. Northwest of here, at the end of rue Docteur ben Zerdjeb, is the lively **Kissaria**, the market area.

MECHOUAR

Very little remains of the early settlement of Agadir, but the camp Youssef ben Tachfine occupied during his siege of Agadir has now become the Mechouar (entrance on av Cdt Ferradj). A citadel was built over the camp in 1145 and has been one of the town's centrepieces ever since. The Zianide ruler Yaghmorassen moved his residence inside the Mechouar walls in the early 14th century and a mosque was built in the 1310s. The Ottoman admiral Barbarossa used it as his stronghold in the 16th century and the French followed suit after the fall of Tlemcen, using it as a barracks and hospital. Today the Mechouar offers a place of peace inside its massive walls and across its broad esplanade. The Moorish mosque, restored in 2003, is currently closed. One of the central buildings houses the **Chambre de l'Artisanat et des Métiers** (☎ 043 263224; ⏱ 8.30am-noon & 1.30-5pm Sat-Thu), where local handicrafts, including embroidered camel saddles and hand-woven covers, are on sale at fixed prices.

TLEMCEN MUSEUM

Given the wealth of history, you would be forgiven for expecting the **museum** (rue 20 Aout;

admission DA20; ⏱ 8.30am-noon, 1.30-5pm Sat-Thu) to be equally rich. It is not. The collection used to be housed in the mosque of Sidi Bel Hassan, on place Mohamed Khemisti, but now occupies a 1905 college building. Arranged over two floors, the collection is basic and the arrangement is confusing, with Almoravid, Merenid and Zianid coins, brass lamps, carved stile and stucco all jumbled together. Among the treasures are 15th-century carved epitaphs from royal tombs. Also worth finding are the 1940s oil paintings by local artist Abdelhalim Hemeche.

SIDI BOUMEDIENE

About 1.6km southeast of the centre, as the crow flies, lies one of Algeria's most beautiful complexes, the **Mosque & Tomb of Sidi Boumediene** (Al Ubbad; ⏱ 9am-4pm Sat-Thu), restored by craftsmen from Fès in 1986. Abu Madyan Shu'ayb ibn al-Husayn al-Ansari, to give him his full name, was born near Seville around 1115 and studied with Islamic mystics in Morocco before settling in Bejaya on the north Algerian coast and creating his own Sufi circle. A mystic, poet and man of great integrity – he was called the Sheikh of Sheikhs and the Nurturer – Abu Madyan, or Sidi Boumediene, as the Algerians call him, died in Tlemcen in 1197, on his way back to Marrakech. His tomb has become a place of pilgrimage and his cult was still sufficiently strong for former Algerian President

Mohamed Boukharouba to have adopted the name Boumediene as his nom de guerre during the independence struggle.

The *sidi's* tomb is down steps on the left as you enter the complex. The tomb is a simple affair, Boumediene on the right, Sidi Abdelsam el-Tonsi on the left. The tiled antechamber houses a worn, marble well, its water believed to bring blessings from the *sidi*. Beside the tomb, a doorway leads to the Dar es-Soltane. Abou el-Hassan, the Merinid ruler of Fès, refused to live in Mansourah, so had this residence constructed beside the saint's tomb. The rooms are ruined – a little carved stucco remains in some corners, enough to suggest vanished grandeur – but there is no mistaking the beauty of the site and the wonderful views over the plain.

Across the way stands the mosque, built by Abou el-Hassan in 1328. The building is both grand and beautiful. A stairway leads to a massive entrance porch and, through massive bronze-clad cedar doors, to the mosque, an open-sided, rectangular prayer space, beautifully proportioned and finely decorated in tiles and carved stucco.

A *madrassa* (Quranic school) was built above the mosque by Abou el-Hassan in 1347. The courtyard is elegant but undecorated, surrounded by 25 cells for students. It was here, soon after it was finished, that the great Arab scholar Ibn Khaldun gave classes.

If the gates of the mosque or *medersa* are locked, look for the guide, Habri Belattar, who runs the last stall on the right as you approach the complex.

MANSOURAH

Just under 3km from the Mechouar, **Mansourah** (⏲ 24hr) – the victorious – never lived up to its name. It started as the camp where Merinid sultan Abou Yacoub settled his army in 1299, when he besieged Tlemcen. The siege lasted eight years, during which the camp became a residence, complete with palace and mosque. Just as the city was about to fall, the sultan was murdered by one of his slaves and the Merinids retreated. Remains of the 12m-high walls that protected the camp stretch across the olive groves far into the distance. The main sight here, though, is the remains of the massive **mosque**, rebuilt by Sultan Abou el-Hassan

of Fès when he came to besiege Tlemcen in 1335. The prayer hall measures 60m by 55m, but most impressive is the 40m minaret, a twin of the Tour Hassan in Rabat and the Giralda in Seville, its inner side having fallen leaving it a vulnerable and evocative shell. The site is open at all times. The lions you might hear roaring as you visit are across the road in the Mansourah Zoo, closed at the time of writing.

Sleeping

Hôtel Majestic (☎ 043 762546; place Cheikh Ibrahimi; s/d without bathroom DA400/800) The welcome is fresher than the rooms in this central budget hotel, where the only washing facilities are a washbasin or the nearby public baths.

OUR PICK Hôtel El-Mansour (043 265678; place des Fedayyines; s/d/tr without bathroom DA450/650/950) The Mansour is run by a very attentive patron, who calls himself a 'sleep trader' and keeps the best budget hotel in town, perhaps even the region. It is secure, as well. Most rooms are arranged around a courtyard, those on the upper floor being brighter, the few that look into a corridor being darker but having less mosque noise. There are no fans, so it can be hot in summer, but there are showers on the ground floor and a sweetwater well in the courtyard.

Hôtel Agadir (☎ 043 271962; 19 rue Khedim Ali; s/d/tr incl breakfast DA1600/2400/3000) A modern hotel beside the bus station, a short walk from the centre. Rooms have showers and TV, but no fans or air-con.

Hôtel les Zianides (☎ 043 277221; 12 rue Khedim Ali; s/d B&B DA3000/5000; P ✕ ❐) The red-brick Zianides, designed by celebrity French architect Fernand Pouillon, was Tlemcen's pride and joy when it opened in 1973. But the state-owned hotel has been neglected, rooms are shabby and dire cooking is served in a restaurant where waiters chase cockroaches. The pool sits in a mature garden.

Eating

Tlemcen doesn't have much to offer by way of culinary delights – the tourist office only recommends a place kilometres out of town. So, with the restaurant of Les Zianides to be avoided, the best food is going to be simple. There are plenty of pizza places and bakeries in and around place Emir Abdelkader.

Restaurant Agadir (☎ 043 271962; 19 rue Khedim Ali; dishes DA300-600) Situated in the hotel of the same name, this restaurant serves a good couscous dinner, though check ahead, because it sometimes closes if the hotel is empty.

Restaurant Familiale (blvd Gouar Hocine; meals DA300-400) On a row of several simple restaurants, this place serves excellent meals of *harira* thick meat, lentil & chickpea soup and rotisserie chicken with vegetables, inside or out on the covered terrace. Recommended. Near Bab Sidi Boumediene

Restaurant Coupole (4 rue 1 Novembre; meals DA300) Across the road from Hôtel Moderne, the Coupole isn't quite up to Familiale's standards, but the simple meals are reliable and the service is friendly.

Shopping

As well as general shopping in the Kissaria and crafts in the **Chambre de l'Artisanat et des Métiers** (☎ 043 263224; inside the Mechouar; ☼ 8.30am-noon & 1.30-5pm Sat-Thu), Tlemcen is noted for its textiles. You can find good-quality burnouses along rue Merabet Mohamed, which runs east of Pl Emir Abdelkader. **Farouk Stambouli** (☎ 043 264783; 8 place Cdt Ferradj) is a long-established merchant who has a range of top-quality, hand-woven rugs and blankets.

Getting There & Away

AIR

Aeroport Messali el-Hadj is 21km out of town, near the village of Zenata. **Air Algérie** (☎ 043 264518; www.airalgerie.dz; rue du Docteur Damardji Tedjini) flies direct from Tlemcen to Algiers (from DA4558, one hour).

BUS

There are regular departures during the day from the station beside Hôtel Agadir on blvd Ghezlaoui Abdeslam to Oran (DA150, five hours), Sidi Bel Abbes (DA80, two hours) and towns en route to Algiers (DA600, 12 hours). Safar Mabrouk Coaches runs an express service to Algiers leaving at 6pm (DA700, 10 hours).

TAXI

Taxis collectifs leave from beside the bus station. The main destinations are Oran (DA250, three hours), Sidi Bel Abbes (DA180, two hours) and Algiers (DA1100, nine to 10 hours)

TRAIN

Since the Oran–Casablanca express was cancelled following the closure of the Moroccan border, the only service running out of Tlemcen station is the 7.30am for Oran.

Getting Around

The centre of Tlemcen is easy to walk around, though there are taxis if you get tired. *Camionettes* (local buses) are unlikely to be of use getting to Mansourah or Sidi Boumediene unless you are leaving from the station. Taxis can be flagged down in the street or call **Taxi ben Ali** (☎ 043 203148/49).

There is no bus to the airport, but a taxi should cost around DA100.

GHAZAOUET غزوات

Algeria's westernmost port sits in a well-protected bay, some 70km from Tlemcen (DA150 in *taxis collectifs*). The road is busy with *halabiyah,* the so-called 'milk run' of vehicles, from trucks to small cars, smuggling cheap Algerian petrol to the Moroccan border.

The Romans called Ghazaouet Ad Fratres (the Two Brothers), after the twin 25m rocks that rise out of the water at the mouth of the harbour. Under the French the port was known as Nemours, after the French aristocrat who governed here, and had a reputation for the quality anchovies and sardines canned in its factory. The centre still has a French feel, with its covered market (1938) and the central church, now a library (1931). The **Pecherie**, at the east end of the port, is a good place to walk and watch the fish being landed off boats as well as locals trying their luck with rod and line.

The best **swimming** is found away from the port. There's a fashionable beach 10km east where, it is said, 'even the rich like to go'. There is also good swimming west, at Marsa ben M'hidi, a 2km stretch of fine sand that is cut through by the Moroccan border. To get there you'll need a car. Some people hitch with the petrol smugglers.

Sleeping & Eating

Hôtel Ziri (☎ 043 323025; www.hotel-ziri.com; P ☒) Ghazaouet's only viable hotel. Perched on the rocks on the eastern end of town, its 34 rooms all have bathrooms and sea view balconies.

NORTHWEST ALGERIA

There are several cheap places to eat near the market in the centre of town, a few minutes from the church, but the best food in town is served at Le Dauphin (closed for refurbishment at the time of writing) in the Pecherie, where the local catch is served grilled or fried. Fish is also on offer at the more basic Etoile de Mer, in a nearby shack.

Getting There & Away

The Spanish ferry company **Trasmediterránea** (www.trasmediterranea.es) operates a ferry service between Ghazaouet and Almeria in Spain. Inland there is an irregular bus service to Tlemcen (DA140, one hour and 40 minutes). *Taxis collectifs* make the journey for DA200 a seat. Otherwise, a private taxi for the day will cost around DA1200.

Ghardaïa & the Grand Ergs غرداية العرق

This vast area of central Algeria is home to some of the country's most beguiling attractions. It is dominated by the Grand Ergs – great oceans of windswept sand rising hundreds of metres high and covering great swaths of the landscape. The Grand Erg Occidental (Great Western Erg) covers some 80,000 sq km, extending from the Atlas Mountains in the north to the Tademait Plateau in the south. To the east, the much larger Grand Erg Oriental (Great Eastern Erg) nudges the centre of the country and then stretches well into Tunisia.

It's not just endless waves of multihued dunes though. The landscape is surprisingly diverse and in between the sand seas you'll see wide scrub-dotted plains framed by Colorado-style flat-top mountains, hectares of perfectly flat bone-white sand, fertile green valleys and black volcanic plateaus.

Few roads pass through the Grand Ergs – the environment is too harsh for life to survive – but they are encircled with ancient towns and emerald oases. At this region's heart, perched on the edge of the Grand Erg Occidental, is the World Heritage site of Ghardaïa, part of a pentapolis of five hilltop cities built almost a thousand years ago by a Muslim Ibadi sect called the Mozabites.

This is an area also known for its high temperatures and in the summer they can rise as high as 50°C. As the towns of the region swelter under an intense heat, some hotels close down and residents traditionally retreat to the cool of the palm groves.

HIGHLIGHTS

- ■ Explore the unique architecture and fascinating history of the five ancient towns in the palm-lined **M'Zab Valley** (p155)

- ■ Wonder at the spiked, ochre buildings and watch the sun descend over the red salt lake in **Timimoun** (p169) 'le rouge'

- ■ Wander the crumbling oasis of **Beni Abbès** (p166); then scramble to the top of the nearest dune for unforgettable vistas over the great western sand sea

- ■ Try your hand at sand skiing and spend the night among ghosts in the 1000-year-old fortified village of **Taghit** (p165)

- ■ Scale the central minaret of **El-Oued** (p172) and gaze over domed rooftops to the dunes beyond

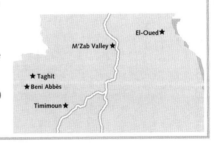

GHARDAÏA & THE GRAND ERGS

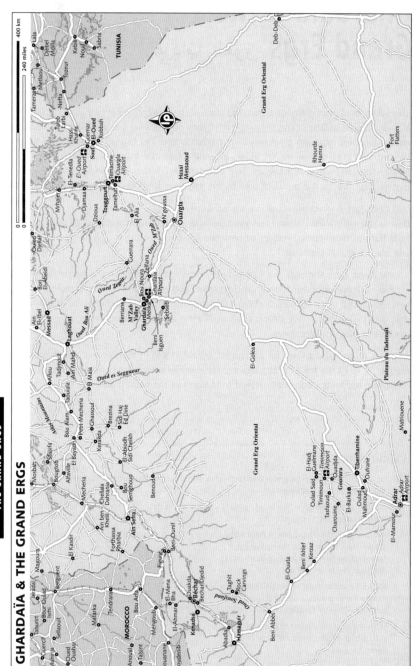

GHARDAÏA & THE M'ZAB غرداية مزاب

Classified as a World Heritage site by Unesco in 1982, the M'Zab is a deep, narrow valley crowned by a pentapolis – five towns rising up sharply from different points along its length. Ghardaïa is the main town and the others, which surround it, are Melika, Beni Isguen, Bou Noura and El-Atteuf; although Ghardaïa is often used to refer to all five. Each town is built on a knoll, its pastel-coloured box like buildings climbing up towards a slim, turreted minaret. The old town centres are riddled with narrow, winding streets and covered alleyways and are excellent places to explore.

The oasis is massive, stretching for some 10km along the valley, which is lined with hectares of palm groves; and fruit trees of all kinds battle each other for room under the shadow of the palms. Traditionally, the cities' inhabitants would escape to these *palmeraie* palm groves in the summer to shelter themselves from the intense heat.

The M'Zab Valley is home to the Mozabites (see boxed text, p160), part of the Ibadi sect (see the boxed text, p48), who broke away from mainstream Islam and built a home in this harsh arid landscape during the 11th century. The Mozabites' culture and religion are fiercely protected and the towns have managed to retain much of their original character and many traditions.

History

The history of the M'Zab is inextricably linked with the Ibadis. Yet nomads also lived here, as did Berber tribes, and archaeologists have found traces of life – in rock engravings and ancient ruined villages – going back for many centuries.

It was with the arrival of the Ibadi in the 11th century, however, that really shook things up. Having broken from mainstream Islam a few hundred years before, they were chased from their North African capitals, including Tahert in the Atlas Mountains and Sedrata near El-Oued. In order to secure a safe future for themselves, they fled to a place where they would be far removed from potential enemies, choosing the harsh territory of the

M'Zab. Here they set about building a series of towns, choosing to build them on hills to enhance their security. Little by little the existing inhabitants of the valley were assimilated into Ibadi culture and religion.

El-Atteuf was the first city to be founded in 1013, followed by Bou Noura in 1065, then Ghardaïa in 1087; two centuries later Beni Isguen (1321) and Bou Noura (1355) followed.

GHARDAÏA غرداية

The first glimpse you catch of Ghardaïa is unforgettable; all main roads leading there skim the edge of the hills offering majestic views of Ghardaïa and its surrounding towns, framed by dense green palm groves and the Oued M'Zab (dry river bed). The sight is even more impressive if you've come to the valley overland, through the barren, stony wasteland that surrounds it.

Ghardaïa is the largest and most important of the five towns and is the commercial and administrative hub of the M'Zab – indeed the commercial hub of the Algerian Sahara – sprawling way beyond its original city centre. It's the only town with proper tourist facilities (apart from a couple of lodges in Beni Isguen), and the place where all long-distance transport pitches up, so it's likely that you'll end up staying here. As well as a number of hotels and restaurants, there are several shops around the town's cobbled market square, selling souvenirs and carpets, a speciality of the area.

Orientation

Ghardaïa's old city, housing the market and the mosque, lies immediately west of the Oued M'Zab. Just south of the old town on rue Emir Abdelkader is where you'll find the main banks, the Office National Algerien du Tourisme (ONAT) and several hotels. Follow this road south as it becomes av du 1er Novembre, and you'll eventually hit Beni Isguen. If arriving by bus you'll be deposited at the main station on rue Ahmed Talbi, on the eastern bank of the Oued M'Zab, a few minutes' walk from the town centre.

Information
INTERNET ACCESS
There are several internet cafés in Ghardaïa. Both **Riad Computer Service** (av du 1 Novembre; per hour DA100; ⊗ 8.30am-9pm) opposite M'Zab

Tours and **Cyber Café** (DA80; ☉ 8am-10pm) just opposite the main bus station have high-speed, reliable connections.

MEDICAL SERVICES

Clinique Aicha Bouker (☎ 029 898815; ☉ 7am-6.30pm) In Beni Isguen; a good place to go for more minor ailments.

Clinique des Oasis (☎ 029 889999; cliniqueoasis@ yahoo.fr; El-Moustadjeb-Bouhraoua) A well-managed private hospital with excellent facilities.

SOS-SUD Ambulance (☎ 029 880447/061, 645193/071, 751535; fax 029 880435; rue Ahmed Talbi) A 24-hour, seven-days-a-week emergency ambulance service which provides a service all over southern Algeria.

MONEY

Banque de Développement Locale (rue Ahmed Talbi; ☉ 8.45am-12:30pm & 1.30-3.30pm Sun-Thu) Changes foreign currency but not travellers cheques. Also has an ATM that didn't accept foreign cards at the time of writing.

Banque Nationale d'Algérie (av du 1er Novembre; ☉ 8.45am-12:30pm & 1.30-3.30pm Sun-Thu) Also changes travellers cheques.

Credit Populaire d'Algérie (rue Emir Abdelkader; ☉ 8.45am-12:30pm & 1.30-3.30pm Sun-Thu) Has a foreign-exchange bureau that changes travellers cheques. It is also possible to get a cash advance on a Visa or MasterCard. You'll need your passport for this and it takes about 30 minutes.

There's a branch of Western Union in the main post office next to the *gare routière* (bus station).

POST & TELEPHONE

The **post office** (☎ 029 643730; 8am-noon & 1-6pm Sat-Thu) is next door to the main bus station just off rue Ahmed Talbi. There are taxi-phone shops all over town.

TOURIST INFORMATION

There's a helpful **ONAT** (☎ 029 881751) office on rue Emir Abdelkader which offers useful information about the region and can organise guides for the town as well as 4WD tours further afield.

TRAVEL AGENCIES

Big Sun Destination (☎ 029 891491; www.bigsun .populus.ch; Cite Ider Est, Beni Isguen) Organises guided tailored trips for tourists and businessmen, cultural visits, car and driver hire and stays in traditional homes.

M'Zab Tours (☎ 029 880002; www.mzabtours.com; av du 1er Novembre) An excellent and well-organised agency offering individually tailored tours from around €50 per person per day depending on the number of people in your party. It can also organise daily guides for Ghardaïa, car hire and border pick-ups. It has a sister agency in Taman-rasset which organises similar excursions in the south, as well as guesthouses in Beni Isguen (see p161), El-Goléa (see p171) and Tamanrasset (see p187).

VEHICLE REPAIR

Rue Ahmed Talbi is like one giant mechanic workshop. Come here for a wide choice of garages, vehicle-repair shops and spare parts.

Dangers & Annoyances

There's not much threat to personal safety for visitors to Ghardaïa. However it still pays to keep a close eye on your valuables, particularly in crowded areas such as the market, and to take care when walking around at night.

Sights & Activities

The entrance to the **old city** is along rue Ibn Rosten, which leads to a pretty cobbled open square in the middle of the old part of the town, where the daily **market** is. You can pick up all manner of things from jewellery, sportswear and nuts to herbal medicines for haemorrhoids. Ghardaïa's most famous souvenirs are its traditional carpets (see p159) and luckily most of the shops that

---

THE STORY OF GHAR DAÏA

An old Berber tale tells the story of a young woman by the name of Daïa who was passing through the M'Zab with a group of wandering nomads when, straying away from her group in search of water one day, she found herself left behind. Scared and alone she made her home in a cave (a 'ghar') and each night would light a fire to ward off danger. The founders of the city, camped up in the hills above, saw lights flickering below and grew more and more curious as to their origin. One day, one of the founders sent his servant to find out the source of these strange lights and the servant returned with the young girl. So taken was he by her beauty that he asked for her hand in marriage and, legend has it, named the city he founded in her name.

GHARDAÏA &
THE GRAND ERGS

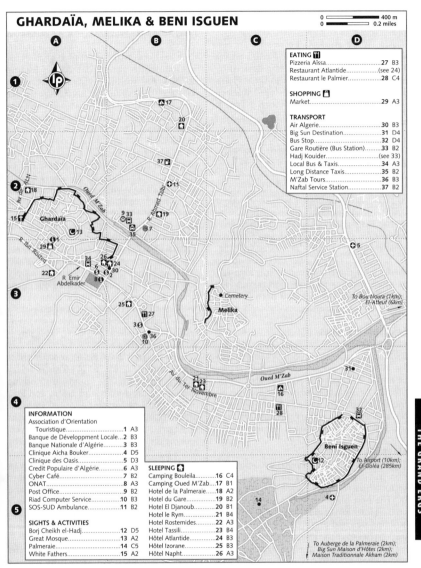

GHARDAÏA, MELIKA & BENI ISGUEN

0	400 m
0	0.2 miles

EATING 🍴
Pizzeria Aïssa............................**27** B3
Restaurant Atlantide.............(see 24)
Restaurant le Palmier..............**28** C4

SHOPPING 🛍
Market......................................**29** A3

TRANSPORT
Air Algerie................................**30** B3
Big Sun Destination..................**31** D4
Bus Stop...................................**32** D4
Gare Routière (Bus Station).......**33** B2
Hadj Kouider..........................(see 33)
Local Bus & Taxis.....................**34** A3
Long Distance Taxis..................**35** B2
M'Zab Tours.............................**36** B3
Naftal Service Station...............**37** B2

INFORMATION
Association d'Orientation
  Touristique................................**1** A3
Banque de Développment Locale..**2** B3
Banque Nationale d'Algérie.........**3** B3
Clinique Aicha Bouker..................**4** D5
Clinique des Oasis.......................**5** D3
Credit Populaire d'Algérie............**6** A3
Cyber Café..................................**7** B2
ONAT..**8** A3
Post Office...................................**9** B2
Riad Computer Service................**10** B3
SOS-SUD Ambulance...................**11** B2

SIGHTS & ACTIVITIES
Borj Cheikh el-Hadj....................**12** D5
Great Mosque.............................**13** A2
Palmeraie...................................**14** C5
White Fathers.............................**15** A2

SLEEPING 🛏
Camping Bouleila.......................**16** C4
Camping Oued M'Zab.................**17** B1
Hotel de la Palmeraie..................**18** A2
Hotel du Gare............................**19** B2
Hotel El Djanoub........................**20** B1
Hotel le Rym..............................**21** B4
Hotel Rostemides........................**22** A3
Hotel Tassili...............................**23** B4
Hôtel Atlantide..........................**24** B3
Hôtel Izorane.............................**25** A3
Hôtel Napht...............................**26** A3

To Bou Noura (1km);
El-Atteuf (6km)

Cemetery

Melika

Beni Isguen

To Airport (10km);
El-Goléa (285km)

To Auberge de la Palmeraie (2km);
Big Sun Maison d'Hôtes (2km);
Maison Traditionnale Akham (2km)

GHARDAÏA & THE GRAND ERGS

---

line the main square are in the carpet-selling business. Unlike in some parts of the country, you can get away with bargaining here and it's all part of the fun; you might well be invited to take tea with the shop owner while you peruse the stock room.

To venture further into the old city you'll need to be accompanied by a guide. For this you should visit the Guides Office at the **Association d'Orientation Touristique** (☎ 029 882699; 🕒 8am-noon & 2-6pm; guides available) on rue Cheikh Ammi Saïd, signposted just off the market square. Guides cost DA250.

Walking up rue Cheikh Ammi Saïd you'll come to the **Great Mosque**. It has a fortresslike appearance; its main feature is the unadorned, pyramidal minaret, typical of the mosques of the M'zab.

Also of interest is the town's ancient **water distribution system** in the palm groves northwest of town, which was devised by the Mozabites as a solution to the region's arid climate. Rainwater is stored in deep wells and then dispersed though a system of underground channels, which divide the flow so that it is fairly distributed among separate palm gardens.

You could also pay a visit to the **Pères Blancs** (White Fathers; p50) at their hermitage near the old city. If it's a convenient time they will be happy to chat and to show you their library with its excellent collection of books about the Sahara. The White Fathers were founded in the 1860s by the then Archbishop of Algiers, Cardinal Charles Lavigerie, and have been in Algeria since the 1870s. Today there are orders throughout the country; they are involved in inter-religious relations and taking care of local Christians and also participate in their local communities.

Festivals & Events
FÊTE DU TAPIS

In March/April every year, a carpet festival takes place in Ghardaïa, in celebration of the local carpet-making industry. More than 200 people take part, representing almost 30 different *wilaya* (provinces) and it's a chance for vendors to show off their wares as well as take part in competitions.

Sleeping

There's a good range of hotel accommodation in Ghardaïa, mostly in the midrange sector with a couple of budget places thrown in. The best place to stay in town used to be the Hotel Rostemides, a sprawling white building perched on top of a hill with fantastic views over the town. Out of action for several years, at the time of writing it was undergoing extensive renovations and due to reopen in 2007. There are two campsites in Ghardaïa: Camping Bouleila about 1km southeast of the town centre on the El-Goléa road and Camping Oued M'zab, on the route out of town to the north. Although the sites were still reasonably well equipped they were closed at the time of writing due to lack of custom. Check locally to see if the situation has changed.

BUDGET

Hôtel Atlantide (☎ 029 882536; av Ahmed Talbi; s & d DA500) This place has bland rooms (nicer, quieter ones with air-con available for DA1000) with shared bathrooms leading off blue and white mosaic-tiled corridors. The best thing about this hotel is the restaurant downstairs which serves some of the best roast chicken in town (see opposite).

Hôtel Napht (☎ 029 890832; place Andalouse; s/d with fan from DA500/800) A good choice for those on a budget and is well located, right next to the old town and the taxi ranks. The 12 rooms are very basic and the owner's fondness for red light bulbs makes some of them feel a little seedy. There's a small terrace overlooking the rooftops, where you can sleep in the summer if it gets too hot, but the view isn't up to much.

Hotel de la Palmeraie (☎ 029 882312; av de ALN (Rte l'Oasis); s/d/tr without bathroom DA600/900/1000; **P**) The rather grubby exterior on a busy road doesn't look very promising but inside it is a different story. Simple, clean rooms with spotless shared showers open onto a lovely (despite the bright-pink walls) central courtyard filled with cacti, bougainvillea and palm trees.

Hotel le Rym (☎ 029 893202; av du 1er Novembre; d/tr/from DA1200/1800; **P** **✖**) This is a very welcoming place. The rooms are nothing special but are roomy and clean, and lead off a bright airy corridor adorned with traditional carpets, paintings and photographs of Algeria. There's also a big terrace overlooking the av du 1er Novembre and nearby Melika.

Hotel Tassili (☎ 029 885583; fax 073 1182 80; av 1er Novembre; d/tr/apt DA1200/1800/2200; **P**) Another good choice with mosaic-tiled hallways and stairs, clean simple rooms and a groovy three-bed apartment with proper bath (mosaic-tiled of course) and little private roof terrace.

Hotel du Gare (☎ 029 964315; rue Ahmed Talbi; s & d DA1400) A hop and a skip away from the *gare routière* this place is convenient and reasonably priced, with a selection of airy double rooms and very welcoming management. There's hot water in the winter.

MIDRANGE

Hôtel Izorane (☎ /fax 029 889238; carrefour Wilaya de Ghardaïa; s/d 1200/1600; **✖**) This small and very friendly place is a good choice with a cosier feel than most. Rooms are clean and comfortable with televisions, fridges and air-con and there's a small terrace with a nice selection of cacti overlooking the main street.

TOP END

Hotel El-Djanoub (☎ 029 885631/888987; fax 029 886 881; s/d DA3070/3886; P 🖵 🏊) This is the only top-end hotel in Ghardaïa but it doesn't really deserve that distinction. While it has facilities such as swimming pool, air-con and satellite TV, the immense lobby and endless gloomy corridors reek of good times passed and the rooms are as bland as can be.

Eating

Pizzeria Aïssa (☎ 029 882486; av du 1er Novembre; pizzas DA200; 🕒 9.30am-9.30pm) This is a very lively place – you can order takeaway pizzas at the front or sit in the back room. It costs DA100 to DA350 for a tasty thin-based pizza, and there's also a separate family-friendly room if you want to get away from the all-male atmosphere.

Restaurant Atlantide (☎ 029 882536; av Ahmed Talbi; meals DA300; 🕒 lunch & dinner) Owned by the same people as the hotel upstairs, this place is clean and very friendly, drawing people in from the street with a lip-smacking window display of grilled chickens and platters of herb-covered chips. It also does excellent *chorba* (vegetable soup with noodles and meat), very fresh salads and zesty tagines.

Restaurant le Palmier (☎ 029 899038; av du 1er Novembre) This is the best and most established restaurant in town. It has a very chic dining room – bright white walls with traditional arts and crafts on display – and the welcome is warm. There's a three-course menu from DA950 as well as an à la carte mix of European and Algerian food. Dishes include *bourek* (beef-stuffed pastry rolls), and tagines. It's also one of the few places in Ghardaïa that serves alcohol.

Shopping

The greatest concentration of shops in Ghardaïa is around the market square where you'll find all manner of things from electronic goods and bootleg CDs to tourist-oriented jewellery and crafts. There are also a few souvenir shops along rue Emir Abdelkader. If you are interested in buying any of the beautifully colourful rugs here, many of which contain symbols representing the different towns of the M'Zab, check the quality closely as they can vary enormously; the better ones have more knots per square centimetre. You can pick up a cheap synthetic carpet here for as little as €10 but for a good-quality rug expect to pay upwards of €50.

Getting There & Away

AIR

Air Algérie (☎ 029 884663; fax 029 887280) is in the town centre on rue Ahmed Talbi. The **airport** is 10km south of town on the road to El-Goléa. There are three flights a week to Algiers (DA4600, 1½ hours), one to Tamanrasset (DA9800, two hours 20 minutes) and one to Illizi (DA7300, two hours 10 minutes).

BUS

The main *gare routière* is on rue Ahmed Talbi, just across the Oued M'Zab and only five minutes' walk from the town centre. It is the departure point for long-distance taxis and the national TVSE buses as well as several long-distance, private bus companies. It's best to make reservations in advance.

The main destinations are Adrar (DA1000, 11 hours), Algiers (DA650, seven to eight hours), Annaba (DA920, 14 hours), Constantine (DA770, 10 hours), El-Goléa (DA400, three hours), In Salah (DA800, eight to nine hours), Ouargla (DA200, two hours) and Timimoun (DA970, 10 hours) and Tamanrasset (DA1500, 19 to 20 hours). There are also several private bus companies with offices around the main bus station, which tend to be more expensive. For example **Hadj Kouider** (☎ 072 092038/072, 290944) at the main bus station charges DA2000 to Tamanrasset.

TAXI

Share taxis leave from a stand next to the main *gare routière* and cover the same main destinations including Algiers (DA1000, seven hours), Tamanrasset (DA1500, 18 to 20 hours) and Ouargla (DA500, two hours).

Getting Around

TO/FROM THE AIRPORT

The airport is 10km out of town on the El-Goléa road. The only way to get into town from the airport is by taxi, which costs from DA100 per person to the centre of town.

GHARDAÏA &
THE GRAND ERGS

BUS

The station for the local buses is on rue Emir Abdelkader just by the entrance to the old city. There are buses for Beni Isguen, Bou Noura and El-Atteuf and journeys should cost around DA20.

TAXI

You can also pick up local taxis at the local bus station. Short journeys around town should cost around DA50. Alternatively it is also possible to hire taxis by the hour for around DA400 to DA500.

BENI ISGUEN بنى ازقن

The town is built on the slope of the hill, 2.5km southeast of Ghardaïa. This is the most important religious town in the M'Zab and also has an excellent reputation for science and education. Constructed in the 14th century, it's also known for its ramparts, which are 2.5km long and 3m high. The people here hang on very firmly to their traditional ways, and the amount of outside influence is kept to an absolute minimum.

The town's narrow streets are entered from the main Ghardaïa road. It is compulsory for all tourists entering the town

to have a guide, and you can pick one up at this entry point. At the entrance to the town is a sign reminding tourists that photography and smoking are forbidden in the town, and modest dress is compulsory (no shorts or bare shoulders). However, you will normally be permitted to take photos as long as there are no women passing.

Sights & Activities

A guide costs DA200 and you can pick one up at the entrance to the town. The guide will show you all the interesting bits and pieces in Beni Isguen. The highlight is the Turkish tower, **Borj Cheikh el-Hadj** (also known as Borj Boleila), in the western corner of Beni Isguen, which you can climb up for stunning views over the town and beyond. Your guide will probably leave you at the **marketplace**, which has a few shops nearby selling the colourful local rugs. The best time for a visit is in the late afternoon, when the market square comes alive with the daily auction – the **Marché à la Criée**. The square is lined with stone benches where tourists and locals alike can sit to observe the action. Those taking part yell out the price of their item until someone buys it, or the price is brought down.

THE MOZABITES

Mozabites are a close-knit group that practises a form of Islam known as Ibadi Islam (see the boxed text, p48). The Ibadis arrived in the M'Zab Valley in the 11th century after being driven from their homes in the north; they chose the harshest and least accessible region they could in order to protect their community. The Ibadis of this region came to be known as the Mozabites.

They're a very traditional people who have managed to cling on to their unique lifestyle, clothing, traditions and beliefs over the centuries. They have a strong network of community support, tend not to marry outside their religious group, and have special councils and assemblies to preside over their affairs. Traditionally, women stayed in the towns of the M'Zab even when their men left for the north to make their fortunes in business. This was to ensure that Mozabite men retained close ties with their towns and that their children were brought up within the M'Zab. Mozabite women would contribute to the economy by weaving carpets and wool garments to send to their men to sell.

Today, Mozabites are still well known for being astute merchants; many of them have migrated to Algiers and now own businesses there, in France and further afield. Even while abroad they retain close ties with Ghardaïa and continue to contribute to the life of their community, returning regularly to the M'Zab Valley from wherever they are in the world.

Those who have remained in the M'Zab are still fairly conservative, particularly the older generation. Traditions are strong here, and many of the people (especially the women) still wear traditional dress. For men that means white tunic, baggy pants and white hat, but the effect of the women's outfits is altogether more ghostly, and one of the first things you'll notice about a visit to this region. Walk around the streets of the M'Zab, particularly in Beni Isguen, and you'll see women shrouded from head to toe in white fabric, revealing nothing but a single eye.

It is interesting to watch: as there are no cafés in the town, it becomes the social event of the day.

At the entrance to the town is the **museum**, which the guide will probably show you at the end of your tour. It is constructed in the style of a typical Mozabite home complete with examples of a kitchen, traditional refrigeration system, and marriage bedroom, as well as some interesting carpet weaving paraphernalia.

The **palmeraie** at Beni Isguen is probably the best in the M'Zab. It stretches for a couple of kilometres behind the town. The gardens here are green havens, veritable gardens of Eden. They are difficult to see properly, however, as they are mostly behind high walls. Once behind the wall, the contrast is vivid – you'll find every kind of fruit here, from grapes and figs to bananas and dates.

Sleeping

There are no hotels in Beni Isguen itself, as foreigners are not allowed to stay within the walls of the city. However a number of guesthouses have sprung up over the past few years in the *palmeraie*. They are based in traditional-style houses with simple rooms and shared bathrooms. Those mentioned below are all within a five-minute walk of each other. To get to the *palmeraie* just continue on the road past the entrance to Beni Isguen, where it winds around to the back of the *palmeraie*. Or you could get a bus to the *palmeraie* from outside the entrance to the old city of Beni Isguen. The guesthouses are difficult to find though, and not well signposted so if you don't have a car it's best to arrange to be picked up from the bus station or airport. In any case, they all ask that you make reservations in advance.

Big Sun Maison d'Hôtes (☎ 029 887616; s/d B&B from DA1500/2000) This is owned by Big Sun Destination (see p156). It is a smaller and more intimate place than the Caravansérail (but just as pretty) with a laid-back atmosphere; the owner encourages you to strip yourself of your watch and mobile phone and the emphasis here is on generating an understanding of Mozabite culture. At the time of writing Big Sun was in the process of building a traditional Bedouin camp complete with organic fruit and veg garden, a camel, goats and a tradition

well system. Reservations must be made in advance.

Caravansérail Ghardaïa (☎ 029 899702; www .mzabtours.com; B&B/half/full board per person from DA1500/2500/3200; ▣) Owned by the proprietor of M'Zab Tours (see p156) this is an enchanting guesthouse in the heart of the *palmeraie*. It's based around a centuries-old traditional house and is a veritable warren of curved, low-ceilinged, white-walled rooms and terraces, constructed to be cool in summer and warm in winter. Meals are taken around low tables in a large dining room scattered with traditional carpets and artefacts, or, in fine weather, outdoors under the stars. There's also a swimming pool, for use during the summer months. Full board is encouraged and in high season half-board is obligatory. It can also arrange guides for visits to Ghardaïa and the surrounding towns.

Maison Traditionnale Akham (☎ 029 873127, 071 774820; takbout_said@yahoo.fr; half/full board DA2400/ 3000) This place is larger than its neighbours and has an airier feel about it with multi-levelled pretty terraces, skylights and a trellis-covered shady terrace and swimming pool. In the evenings the gardens are lit up with twinkling lights – built into the stairs and strung up between the trees – and there's an outdoor fireplace around which to congregate. It also has some less charming rooms with fridges and bathrooms for those who want greater privacy.

Getting There & Away

Local buses leave Ghardaïa from the local bus station outside the entrance to the old city and cost DA15. They drop you outside the gates to Beni Isguen. Alternatively, it's a half-hour walk.

MELIKA مليكة

It is from Melika that you get the best overall views of the Oued M'Zab and Ghardaïa itself. The town is about a kilometre to the southeast of Ghardaïa, high above the *oued*. The main point of interest is the curious **cemetery** on the northern side of the town where Sidi Aïssa and his family are buried. It's a series of eerie white tombs with conical structures, almost like turrets, pointing towards the sky.

As the story goes, Sidi Aïssa was a Malakite Muslim who converted to Ibadism after a dream in which he saw three cemeteries. The first was surrounded by flames and smoke and, he believed, was that of the Jews; the second was a Malakite cemetery which emitted groans of pain; and the third cemetery, which he believed was the cemetery of the Ibadis, was bathed in a serene light. After an argument with Melika's chief, Sidi Aïssa shut himself away, refusing to receive guests, until his death. After his death, the people of Melika, who were very fond of him, decided to build a magnificent tomb.

Getting There & Away

The easiest way up to Melika is on foot from Ghardaïa. It takes about 30 minutes to make the climb, and the best route is the road which leads south opposite the main *gare routière*. It is also possible to cross the *oued* anywhere and just scramble up the side of the hill.

EL-ATTEUF العطف

El-Atteuf is the oldest city of the M'Zab and it costs DA200 for a guide, who you can pick up at the office of the Association Tadjnint pour le Tourisme at **l'Artisanat El-Atteuf Ghardaïa** (☎ 029 875038; tadjnint@caramail .com). The main reason to come to El-Atteuf is to see the **mosque of Sidi Brahim**. Some 700 years old, it's a simple white building complete with curved walls, arches and inclined pillars made from palm trunks. It contains the remains of Sidi Brahim, a Muslim scholar, and is said to have inspired the French architect Le Corbusier to build a church in a similar fashion in France: the Chapel Notre-Dame-du-Haut in Ronchamp.

Getting There & away

El-Atteuf is 9km away from Ghardaïa so is a bit of a walk. Take bus 30 from the local bus station outside the old town in Ghardaïa. It costs DA15 and takes about 10 to 15 minutes.

BOU NOURA بونورة

Four kilometres away from Ghardaïa, Bou Noura is less interesting than and not as well maintained as the other towns. Its main point of interest is its construction. The walls of the city seem to rise out of the rocks on which they were built. To get here take a bus from the local outside the old town of Ghardaïa.

GRAND ERG OCCIDENTAL
العرق الغربي الكبير

One of the two great sand seas, the Grand Erg Occidental occupies an enormous area south of the Saharan Atlas Mountains in the west of Algeria. Anywhere else this would constitute a sizeable desert in its own right, but in the Sahara things are a bit different. Some of the most beautiful oases in the country are to be found here. What's more, the excellent sealed roads make them very accessible; given a week or more you could drive (or bus) around and visit a diverse selection of these desert towns.

Unlike what you might expect, not all oases are the same – highlights of this region include the mud-red fortress of Taghit, dwarfed by the looming dunes behind it; the white crumbling buildings and laid-back charm of Beni Abbès; and Timimoun – nicknamed 'the red' after its vast red salt lake and ochre buildings – with its strangely shaped, porcupine-spiked constructions.

The real stars of the show, though, are the sands themselves. You could trek through them (with camel or without), ski down them, spend the night out under the stars using the nearest dune as a pillow or simply gaze out in awe at their changing colours and seemingly never-ending expanse.

AÏN SEFRA عين سفرة

This town at the foot of the Saharan Atlas Mountains is the gateway to the desert from the northwest and is about as far north as you will find sand dunes on this side of the country.

As you approach the town from the north, it looks like a big, dusty building site and the multicoloured apartment blocks by the side of the road must rate as some of the worst eyesores in the country. Turning into the town itself, however, you see that it is a likeable little place with wide, tree-lined streets and a convivial atmosphere.

Perhaps the most famous thing about Aïn Sefra is that it was here that the young writer and adventurer Isabelle Eberhardt was drowned 1904, when a flash flood swept away houses and their occupants. See the boxed text, opposite, for further information.

ISABELLE EBERHARDT

It almost sounds too strange too be true: Isabelle Eberhardt was the cross-dressing, hard-drinking, illegitimate child of the widow of a Russian general and her Armenian-born lover, who travelled solo through Algeria on horseback and drowned in the middle of the desert.

She was born in Switzerland in 1877. Her mother had moved from Russia to Geneva four years previously – along with her children and the children's tutor, anarchist ex-priest Alexandre Trophimowsky – for a period of convalescence, a few months after which her husband, the Russian General Pavel de Moerder, died of a heart attack. When Isabelle arrived, she was registered as illegitimate, her mother never admitting to her family, or to Isabelle herself, that Trophimowsky was in fact her father.

Isabelle was given a diverse education, Trophimowsky teaching her Arabic and several other languages, as well as metaphysics and chemistry. Even at this early age, her rebellious streak was apparent and she would sometimes dress as a boy to see what freedoms this would allow her.

In 1897, Isabelle went to Algeria for the first time, along with her mother, to visit her brother who had been stationed there. They were both seduced by the local culture and religion and ended up converting to Islam.

Isabelle's mother died suddenly and Isabelle returned temporarily to Europe but was soon pulled back to Algeria. She had a particularly good understanding of Arab culture and politics, and could speak and write the language fluently, helped by the unconventional education given her by Trophimowsky. She adopted the persona of an Arab man, calling herself 'Si Mahmoud Essadi', and travelled alone all over the Sahara on horseback, even ending up working for a time as a journalist covering military campaigns around Béchar.

It was well known that she was a woman – she was sexually adventurous and had a whole host of lovers – yet she was accepted as a man by the local Algerians. In El-Oued in 1900 she fell in love with Slimene Ehnni, a young soldier, whom she would go on to marry a year later. He put up with her affairs as well as her bouts of drunkenness and fondness for hashish.

In 1904, after seeking hospital treatment for malaria in Aïn Sefra, on the edges of the Sahara Desert, Isabelle's short life came to an end when she was drowned in a freak flash flood. Her body was found two days later, stuck under a wooden beam. She is buried in the town's Muslim cemetery.

Isabelle wrote about her travels in many books (see p15) and French newspapers, and her diaries also make interesting reading.

Information

Roads into town from both the south and the north lead directly to the town centre, situated around the dry riverbed. There are several cafés, groceries and taxiphone bureaus as well as a Banque Nationale d'Algérie and a Banque de l'Agriculture et du Développement Rural. Buses drop you off at the *gare routière* near the northern entrance of Aïn Sefra from where it's a short walk into town. The main post office is over the river from the town centre on the road heading up to the Hotel el-Mekhter.

Sights

The Muslim cemetery where Isabelle Eberhardt is buried is located on the outskirts of the western side of town. The cemetery has a wild, romantic feel about it, its swaying grasses framed by the rising dunes and mountains behind. The best way to get here is by car or on foot; ask locally for directions. There's normally a caretaker there and he'll be happy to show you her grave.

Sleeping

Hotel el-Hidab (☎ 049 761722/061, 260123; s/d/tr DA600/700/1000) In the centre of town, close to the river. It has clean simple rooms with sinks, and friendly service. There are toilets in the corridor but to take a shower you'll have to use the public showers on the floor below, which cost DA50 a pop.

Hotel el-Mekhter (☎ 049 771771; fax 762897; s & d DA2050; 🖳 🖳)The only tourist-class accommodation is around 1.5km out of town, across the river from the town centre and signposted past the military barracks. The place is rather rough around the edges and has obviously seen better days. It is nicely situated, however, backed up against a sand dune on the edge of town, and the multi-levelled, wood-beamed rooms, though ramshackle, are quite appealing. They look out onto the dunes behind or open out onto terraces overlooking the swimming pool and courtyard. There's a restaurant, but it doesn't open if there aren't enough guests; breakfast, which is always available, is included in the price of the room.

Getting There & Away

There are buses north to Algiers (DA650, eight to nine hours), Oran (DA500, four to five hours) and Tlemcen (DA400, three to four hours), and south to Béchar (DA400, three hours).

BENI OUNIF بني ونيف

This totally unremarkable little border town used to give travellers coming from Morocco their first glimpse of Algeria, but since the closure of the border, it sees much less trade. The town is small – only about half a kilometre from one end to the other, centred on one long main street – so there's no difficulty in finding things.

There are two banks here, a Banque Nationale d'Algérie and a Banque de l'Agriculture et du Développement Rural, both off the main drag, but neither exchange travellers cheques. There's also a petrol station.

The road between here and Béchar still bears some of the few remaining signs of the battle for Algerian independence. Right along this border, some distance in from the actual line, the French built a continuous barrier of barbed wire some 5m wide. The whole section was patrolled by soldiers stationed at forts, each built in sight of the next, and the line was more than 1000km long on this side of the country. The idea, largely successful, was to isolate the Algerian nationalists from any support from Morocco. Most of the forts are still there today; so is much of the barbed wire.

Sleeping

Hôtel Afrique (☎ 049 842090/074 821328; rue FLN Route No 06; s/d DA300/600) This is the only place to stay in town and although nondescript it is clean and welcoming. There are 11 simple and airy rooms overlooking the main street, and a decent restaurant. The next closest accommodation is at Béchar, 114km to the south.

Getting There & Away
TO/FROM MOROCCO

The road to Morocco leaves the main road south of town and the (currently closed) border post is about 1.5km away through the gap in the mountains.

From here, it's another few hundred metres to the Moroccan side – from where it's a further few kilometres to Figuig. If the border reopens the whole crossing should take about half a day.

BUS

There is no bus station here; all the buses just stop outside the Hôtel Afrique. You have to be lucky to get a seat at times.

TRAIN

The train station is just near the shops in the centre of the town. There are currently no passenger trains stopping at Beni Ounif, although an option will become available when the new Oran–Béchar service opens in 2007/2008.

BÉCHAR بشار

This is a modern, sprawling administrative town and capital of the Saoura region (as this corner of the Sahara is known). It has not much to recommend it, but you will probably find yourself stopping for a night here on the way through.

From Béchar, the road heads southwest for 100km before curving around the western corner of the Grand Erg Occidental. The N50 heads west from here for the 800km journey to Tindouf in the far west of the country. This route into Mauritania has been closed due to the war in the Western Sahara. Tindouf is the main base for the Polisario fighters, who are actively supported by Algeria. It is out of bounds to foreigners.

Information

There's a Banque Nationale d'Algérie and a Banque de l'Agriculture et du Développement Rural here, and this is the last major town in which you can stock up on things for the route south. The **Air Algérie** (☎ 049 830060) office is on the Aïn Sefra side of place de la République on av de 05 Juillet. The central market has a fair selection of fruit, vegetables and meat. It's next to the mosque with the large minaret on av Colonel Lotfi.

Sleeping & Eating

Béchar Hostel (☎ 049 810844; Cite Riadi; dm DA150) Signposted off the Taghit road. Looks fine from the outside but is run down and spartan with rather cramped dorms and the showers aren't the cleanest.

Hotel Maghreb Arabe (☎ 049 815535; 5 Hai Es-Salem; s & d DA2000, without shower DA1500; ☎) Opposite the new bus station on the Taghit road, this is a large three-story place with a good restaurant, air-con, spotless rooms and a very friendly patron who is happy to dole out advice about worthwhile sights in the region.

Hotel Antar (☎ 049 817161/63; antarhotel@egtouest .com; s/d from DA2100/2500, ste DA10,000; ☎) Signposted just off the main road 1km towards Beni Abbès, this place has air-con rooms looking out onto an interior garden but it feels soulless and neglected. The one up side is the spacious and deliciously kitsch suite, complete with 70s-style patterned sofas, a plastic tree, fake miniature stalactites descending from the ceiling and a scary-looking horse mural.

L'Oscar Restaurant Familial (☎ 040 851009; 151 av de 05 Juillet; mains DA700-1200) One of the most popular places in town, known for its fish specialities – it serves excellent grilled king prawns and paella, as well as French meat dishes such as steak au poivre (black pepper steak).

Getting There & Away

AIR

The airport is 7km north of town and local buses make the trip out there. There are weekly flights to Algiers (DA7200, 1½ hours) and Oran (DA4700, two hours).

BUS

The spanking new gare routière is about 1.5km north of town on the Taghit road, just after the turning for the airport. Timetables are displayed, and there's a restaurant, bank, newsstand, taxiphone shop and pharmacy. Most of the buses heading north travel in the late afternoon and evening because this is one of the hottest areas in the country.

The main destinations are Adrar (DA550, six hours), Algiers (DA1000, 11 hours), Beni Abbès (DA350, three hours), Taghit (DA150, one hour), Timimoun (DA550, six hours) and Tlemcen (DA600, 6½ hours).

TRAIN

There were no passenger trains to Béchar at the time of writing.

TAXI

There's a large taxi brousse (shared taxi) station in an area called Cité Kharassa at the southern end of town. Destinations include Algiers (DA1200, 10 hours), Oran (DA1000, eight hours) and Timimoun (DA700, five to six hours).

TAGHIT تغيت

Pronounced 'Ta-rit', this small oasis village 90km south of Béchar has some of the most spectacular scenery in the Grand Erg Occidental. The dunes tower over the eastern edge of the town, and the view as you come over the hill from the west, of the old ksar (fortified stronghold), tiny against this great theatrical backdrop, is magnificent.

The old mud-brick part of the village is dominated by the ksar, which is currently being restored – this section of the village is a real maze of winding lanes, and the red mud architecture is typical of this part of the Sahara.

Orientation & Information

There is only one entrance to the town and as you arrive you'll see the town spread out before you on the hill against the dunes. On entering the town, continue straight ahead to reach the main square, the place des Martyrs. If arriving by bus you'll be deposited here. Around the square you'll find the post office and the Hôtel Taghit. The road to the left leads to the camp site and youth hostel as well as a few general stores and cheap cafés. There's a Naftal service station at the entrance to the town but Taghit has no bank.

Sights & Activities

The 30-minute climb up the **dunes** to experience the jaw-dropping view is a must. The sand sea stretches out to the east, while the oasis, its river and palm groves are spread out before you to the west. Take a lead from the local kids and have a slide down a dune on a piece of tin or cardboard.

A walk among the winding streets, covered alleyways and cool houses of the **old ksar** is another highlight. Built around a central mosque, this ancient town was constructued in around the 9th century from mud, stone and palm trunks.

If you've got a car, there are some **rock engravings** nearby, a 15-minute drive out of town. Take the road south out past the camp site and youth hostel and keep following the road past the *palmeraie*. The paved road ends abruptly in front of a rock face where you'll find some good examples of rock carvings – mostly antelope and cattle – in front of you. On the drive there, look to your right and you'll see the crumbling remains of 15th-century towns built into the hillside.

For visits to the local rock carvings, nights bivouacking on the dunes, camel treks and even skiing (yes, with proper skis!) on the dunes contact **Abdelkader Sahli** (☎ 040 853711/090 504352), self-titled 'director general' of the desert. Guides can also be arranged at the Hôtel Taghit.

Sleeping & Eating

Camping Taghit (DA150) Close to the centre of town, on the road heading south, right up against the sand dunes. There are basic toilets and showers, a kitchen, and plans to construct some *zeribas* (palm huts).

Youth hostel (☎ 049 863131; dm DA100) Next to the camp site, the town's *auberge de jeunesse* is a simple place with four-bed dorms and a nice central courtyard, and all rooms have balconies with view of the dunes.

Hôtel Taghit (☎ 049 863183; taghithotel@egtouest .com; s/d DA1500/2000) You can't miss the Hôtel Taghit, as it's the only big building in the village. The outside looks like a palatial villa and the communal spaces, including a garden and a bright mosaic-tiled lobby, are lovely, but the rooms are a different story – with malfunctioning TVs, lumpy mattresses and run-down bathrooms. Unfortunately, it's the only hotel in town.

Association du Vieux Ksar (☎ 040 853683; brahimo20@hotmail.com; r from DA1900) For a different and very atmospheric experience you could rent a room in a house, or indeed a whole house in the old *ksar* – these are beautiful and simple traditional houses dating back as far as the 9th century. Facilities are basic, but sitting out on an ancient roof terrace watching the sunset over the dunes and communing with the ghosts of the past is an experience you won't forget in a hurry.

Getting There & Away

There are two buses daily to Beni Abbès (DA250, two hours), two to Béchar (DA150, one hour) and one to Timimoun (DA450, four to five hours). There's not much traffic in either direction, although both roads are sealed. Buses leave from the place des Martyrs in the town centre.

BENI ABBÈS بني عباس

Another beautiful oasis town, Beni Abbès is built on the edge of an escarpment, so it looks down on the *palmeraie* and the *oued,* and like Taghit it's framed with a chain of impossibly high dunes. It has a romantic air about it with faded crumbling white turret-topped buildings, streets lined with peeling white arches, and a vibrant green ribbon of palm groves below. There's not much in the way of formal attractions here, but there's a nice old *ksar* to wander around and an interesting museum. Beni Abbès was also the site where Charles de Foucauld (p189) chose to build his first hermitage, which still exists today.

Orientation & Information

On entering the town across the *oued,* the track to the right just before the shops leads to the *palmeraie,* which has an ancient *ksar* and an excellent swimming pool.

To the left, the road leads to the little museum, the Musée Saharien, owned by the Centre National de Recherches Sahariennes.

The road straight ahead leads up the escarpment past a small row of shops, and then forks. Up to the right lies the market, several cheap, nondescript cafés, bus station, post office and defunct Hôtel Grand Erg, while to the left is the Hôtel Rym, a Banque d'Agriculture et du Développement Rural and the dunes.

Sights

The track into the *palmeraie* leads past the old mud-brick **ksar** off to the right. This dates from the last century and is now gradually returning to the earth.

Beyond the *ksar* and beneath the stone water tower on the edge of the escarpment is a small swimming pool, known as **La Source**. It is a cool, green retreat from the blinding desert all around. A few trees and bougainvillea give shade to the pool, which is filled by beautifully clear spring water and is in a paved enclosure.

The other obvious sight is the **dunes**. Take a scramble up them in the late afternoon when the light is at its best.

The **museum** is about 100m along the track to the left from the main road along the *oued,* and then up the first street on the right. It has an interesting selection of desert fauna and flora, and a display of traditional life in the region.

Sleeping

There's a small palm-shaded camp site next to La Source, which was undergoing renovations at the time of writing.

Hôtel Rym (☎ 049 824203; rymhotel@egtouest.com; s/d from DA1700/2200; P ✕ ⚑) This hotel sits at the foot of the dunes. It's a multilevelled behemoth, beautifully situated with many rooms looking out onto the dunes. At its peak it must have been splendid but sadly it's been very neglected and much of it is in a state of disrepair.

Getting There & Away

The bus station is up by the market. There are twice-daily departures to Béchar (DA350, three hours), and buses leave once a day for Adrar (DA350, three hours) and Timimoun (DA400, three to four hours). All these buses pass through Beni Abbès en route from somewhere else, so seats are not guaranteed.

There is also a bus to Taghit every morning (DA250, two hours).

ADRAR ادرار

Adrar is a major regional capital 120km south of the road which rings the Grand Erg Occidental. There isn't much of interest here, and the only reason you'd pass through would be on your way to the Malian border or In Salah. Its uniform brick-red colour is interesting though and its central square is notable too, if only for its gargantuan size. Because the square is so big, the midday sun here is blinding, and you need to follow the local example and retreat somewhere cooler. The town is virtually deserted in the afternoon.

On the way into the town from the north, keep an eye out for signs of the *fouggara* (underground water channels), identifiable above ground by the lines of small wells

on the surface. This system of channels, now superseded by more modern methods, once stretched for more than 2000km in this area.

Orientation & Information

The centre of town is an absolutely enormous main square, the place des Martyrs – you could just about land a plane on it! Around it are the main buildings: the banks, post office, **Air Algérie** (☎ 049 969365) and the main hotel, the Hôtel Touat. Inside the hotel you'll find **AHNET Voyages** (☎ 049 964026; ahnetvoyages@hotmail.com) which organises tours in the region and beyond. The local tourist office seems to serve primarily as a craft shop and can't provide any useful information about Adrar or travel in the region. There's an internet café in the Maison de la Culture on the main square, and a hospital to the east of the square.

Sights

Adrar doesn't hold a great deal for tourists, however it's worth wandering through the **place des Martyrs**, if only to appreciate its size and interesting architecture. The buildings that encircle it include an impressive mosque, and four large red mud archways, studded with wooden spikes, marking the main entrance points to the square.

Sleeping & Eating

Auberge de Jeunesse (☎ 049 964250; fax 969212; dm DA100) Well located just opposite the bus station, this hostel has a large garden, a friendly atmosphere and four-bed dorms opening out onto a central courtyard.

Hôtel Timmi (☎ 049 960617; s/d from DA410/700) One block from the main square these rooms are simple, clean and friendly but nothing to write home about. The reception is full of photos and maps of Adrar and its surrounds, and the staff can advise you on further travel. You can pay extra for TV and air-conditioning.

Complexe Touristique Mraguen (☎ 049 967 625/29; www.ctm-adrar.com; s/d from DA1500/2000; P ✕ ⚑) Ten kilometres out of town on the road north of Adrar, this is a sprawling complex with bamboo-covered walkways, mini waterfall, a traditional area for music displays, a small 'zoo' with several gazelles and some sorry-looking chickens and turkeys, and rooms decorated with

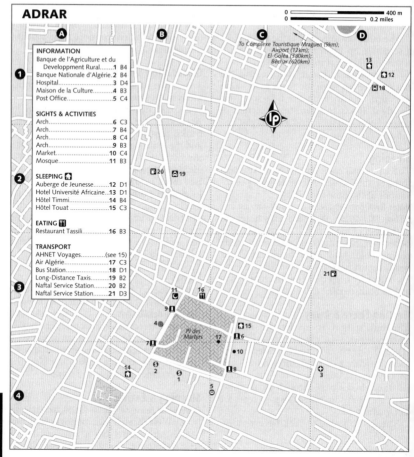

ADRAR

INFORMATION
Banque de l'Agriculture et du
Developpment Rural.......1 B4
Banque Nationale d'Algérie.2 B4
Hospital................................3 D4
Maison de la Culture..........4 B3
Post Office..........................5 C4

SIGHTS & ACTIVITIES
Arch.....................................6 C3
Arch.....................................7 B4
Arch.....................................8 C4
Arch.....................................9 B3
Market................................10 C4
Mosque..............................11 B3

SLEEPING
Auberge de Jeunesse........12 D1
Hotel Université Africaine..13 D1
Hôtel Timmi.......................14 B4
Hôtel Touat 15 C3

EATING
Restaurant Tassili..............16 B3

TRANSPORT
AHNET Voyages.............(see 15)
Air Algérie..........................17 C3
Bus Station........................18 D1
Long-Distance Taxis..........19 B2
Naftal Service Station........20 B2
Naftal Service Station........21 D3

To Complexe Touristique Araguen (9km);
Airport (12km);
El-Goléa (380km);
Béchar (620km)

Pl des Martyrs

bright traditional fabrics. Unfortunately the place is desolate – you can practically see the tumbleweed rolling down the empty corridors.

Hotel Université Africaine (☎ 049 968825/31; fax 049 968894; s/d DA1800/2300; P ☒) The newest hotel in Adrar has mosaic-tastic corridors and reception, and the large rooms come complete with fridge, TV and natty tiger-motif velour bedspreads. There's also enough parking for a monster truck convention.

Hôtel Touat (☎ 049 960425/969933; hoteltouat 2002@yahoo.fr; place des Martyrs; s/d from DA2621/3234; P ☒) Located on the place des Martyrs, this place has large, spotless rooms with an unfortunate choice of clashing décor and a good restaurant. The best (or worst, de-

pending on how you look at it) thing about this hotel is the large courtyard, which fills with hundreds of twittering, swooping birds at dawn and dusk.

Restaurant Tassili (place des Martyrs; ☺ 11am-8pm) One of several identikit restaurants in the town centre selling grills, stews and couscous. At least this place has the advantage of opening out onto the main square, making it a good place for coffee and people-watching.

Getting There & Away
AIR
The airport is 13km north of the town centre and a taxi is the only way to get out there.

Being a fairly important regional town, Adrar is well served by plane. There are four departures a week to Algiers (DA9700, three hours), two to Oran (DA8000, two hours 20 minutes) and one a week to Borj Mokhtar (DA9000, two hours) and Ouargla (DA6600, two hours).

BUS
The bus station is about 1km north of the main square. The large depot is also the graveyard for quite a few broken-down Mercedes trucks and buses.

As all the departures originate here, it is possible (and advisable) to book tickets the day before you plan to leave. Main destinations include Béchar (DA550, six hours), Reggane (DA300, two hours), Ghardaïa (DA1000, 11 hours) and In Salah (DA600, six to seven hours).

If the bus to In Salah is not running, it is possible to get there by taking the daily bus to Reggane and changing there.

There is no direct bus to Borj Mokhtar, on the Malian border, and crossing the border here was inadvisable at the time of writing.

TAXI
Shared taxis run regularly to Timimoun (DA400, two hours) from beneath the tree close to the Naftal service station near the truck park, 10 minutes' walk from the centre of town.

TIMIMOUN تيميمون
If you can stop at only one of the oases around the Grand Erg Occidental, make it Timimoun. It's an enchanting place, full of distinctive red mud buildings studded with wooden spikes, and surrounded by ancient villages. The residents are very friendly and it's one of the nicest places in the Sahara.

Perhaps the best thing about Timimoun is its location – the town is built on the edge of an escarpment, and there are fantastic views out over an ancient salt lake to the sand dunes in the distance; on a bright, moonlit night the effect is magical.

The population of the town and the surrounding area is a real mix: the Haratine (non-Negroid Blacks), the Zénète Berbers, the Chaamba Arabs (originally from the east) and the Black Africans (descendants of Malian slaves). The predominant language

of the region is Zénète, a Berber dialect similar to those of the Kabylie and the M'Zab.

Orientation
The town is small and easily negotiated. There is one long main street, the av du 1er Novembre, around which banks, the tourist office and shops are located. If you arrive by bus or taxi you will be dropped off here. West of the av du 1er Novembre is the old *ksar,* the *palmeraie* and the dunes.

Information
MONEY
There is a branch of the Banque Nationale d'Algérie opposite the post office and a Banque de Développement Local about halfway along the main street.

POST
The post office is close to the roundabout, on the road that connects the main street with the main road from Adrar to El-Goléa.

TRAVEL AGENCIES
The tourist office is in the municipality building, near the roundabout on the main street. It can organise guides from DA1000 per day. It also has a small exhibition room and may be able to provide a map of the Sebkha Circuit.

Agence Mer de Sable (☎ 049 902595; www.agence -merdesable.com) is owned by the same people that run the camp site (see p170) and arranges tours in Timimoun and beyond.

Sights & Activities
The town lends itself well to photography; just walking up and down the main street you'll see plenty of possibilities, with the red buildings and the *koubba* (domed tomb) in the middle of the road, and wandering round the main avenue you catch glimpses of the salt lake and dunes though the gaps in between the buildings.

The **Hôtel de l'Oasis Rouge** (av du 1er Novembre; admission free; ☼ 8am-noon & 3-7pm, closed Friday), originally constructed by colonial missionaries in the early 1900s, is a fine old building and it is worth a wander around inside to see the arched hallways, the courtyard and the walls, which are decorated with traditional designs. It also contains a one-room museum with a small collection of local fabrics, paintings, pottery and basket weaving, most of which is for sale. Another fine example of Timimoun's architecture is the ornate **Porte du Soudan**, also constructed during colonial times and oriented towards the south.

A stroll round the daily **market** is also a good way to pass the time if only for the intoxicating smell of wonderfully fresh herbs and spices.

Down towards the **palmeraie**, along the road to the camp site, the old section of town is a maze of dusty alleys and ochre houses. The *palmeraie* itself is cool and shady, and the individual plots are divided by mud-brick walls. Enter by the road which leads from the main roundabout down past the high school to the camp site and Hôtel Gourara.

SEBKHA CIRCUIT

If you have access to a vehicle, the Circuit de Sebkha, also known as the Gourara Circuit, is an absolute must. This is a 75km loop to the north of Timimoun, skimming the flat red salt lake and taking in some mighty fine scenery; you'll see clusters of little oasis villages and ruined *ksar* clinging to rock faces. Highlights of this circuit include the deep red caves where the locals still come for siestas during the blinding heat of summer, the old ruined town of **Tindjillet** balanced on the edge of an escarpment, and **Tasfaoud**, a small oasis with a 13th-century castle.

Festivals & Events
S'BOU DE TIMIMOUN

For seven days and seven nights the residents of the Gourara region hold celebrations marking the birth of the prophet Mohammed. The S'bou Festival marks the seventh day of the celebrations. During this time the inhabitants of the Gourara region as well as thousands of worshippers from around the country descend on Timimoun. During the day the streets are deserted but at night they're full to the brim as people come to spend the night in prayer.

Its origins lie five centuries ago when Sidi el-Hadj Belkacem, a local marabout (holy man), had a dream in which the Prophet asked him to celebrate his date of birth in a fitting manner. The pinnacle of this festival occurs when the flags of the different brotherhoods of the Gourara are unfurled near Sidi el-Hadj Belhadj's tomb.

Sleeping
BUDGET

Camping la Palmeraie (☎ 049 900956, 074 239617; DA250 per person; **P**) Centrally located next to the Hôtel Gourara with clean ablutions, hot water, a dining hut and a kitchen. The owner can organise camel rides, hiking, traditional folk evenings and the like.

Youth hostel (☎ /fax 049 902581; dm DA100) Ten minutes' walk north of town along av du 1er Novembre this hostel has spartan four- to six-bed dorms, a café, a lounge with table football, and terrace with fine views over the dunes on which one can sleep in fine weather. The bathrooms could be cleaner though.

Hotel Moulay el-Houcine (☎ 049 902083; fax 900897; s/d from DA600/1000) Just off the main road, opposite the Hôtel de l'Oasis Rouge, this place has pretty dull rooms but makes up for it with the warm welcome and the great big roof terrace with views over the town centre and the market.

MIDRANGE

Hôtel Gourara (☎ 049 902627; gourarahotel@etouest .com; s/d from DA1000/1500) Built by Fernand Pouillon in the 1950s the Gourara is slightly dilapidated these days, but what it lacks in up-to-date comforts in makes up for in romantic atmosphere. Slap bang on the edge of the escarpment, many of the rooms have dramatic views over the salt lake and dunes (be sure to ask) and the wide semicircular terrace is a great place to nurse a cold drink and watch the sun go down.

Camping Roses de Sable (☎ 049 902595; www .agence-merdesable.com; huts per person DA2500, r with/ without bathroom per person DA3000/2800; ⊗ closed May-Oct) This is a lovely place set in a large garden where you can sleep in a *zeriba* under the shade of a palm tree or in a room (each one named after an oasis in the region) in the pretty bungalow at the back. Delicious meals are served up daily by the wife and daughters of the owner (prices quoted here include full board), and there's a fantastic multi-levelled terrace with awesome 360-degree views of the surrounding landscape. Even better is the location; walk out of the front gate and it's all there on your doorstep – a long stretch of red sand meets a veritable ocean of dunes as far as the eye can see. To get here follow the road signposted by the entrance to Hôtel Gourara; it's about 2.5km (not 1.5km as the sign claims!). Alternatively it's a 30-minute walk along a footpath which leads from av du 1er Novembre (near the mosque) to the back of the camp site. Be sure to reserve in advance.

Eating

There are a few cafés and restaurants along the main road. You could try Restaurant E Rahma, opposite the Hôtel de l'Oasis Rouge, for rotisserie chicken and chips, as well as local specialities. Restaurant Djudjura, also on the main road, has plenty of outside tables from which to soak up the atmosphere of the streets.

Shopping

As well as the market, there are a few tourist shops along the main street and both the tourist office and the Hôtel de l'Oasis Rouge have items for sale. Be sure to look out for *roses de sable,* which you'll see here. They're natural rock sculptures in the shape of roses, exactly as found in the sand.

Getting There & Away

AIR

The **Air Algérie** (☎ 049 904555) office is on the main square. The airport is 8km to the southeast of town and a taxi costs DA50 per person. There are flights to Algiers and Oran.

BUS

Buses leave from the main street, almost opposite the mosque. It is possible to book in advance on only some of the services, as most are just passing through and don't originate in Timimoun.

There are daily services from Timimoun to Adrar (DA250, two hours), Béchar (DA550, six hours) and Ghardaïa (DA970, 10 hours).

TAXI

Taxis brousse leave from just next to the bus station. The main destination is Adrar (DA400, two hours).

EL-GOLÉA القليعه

The most easterly oasis of the Grand Erg Occidental, El-Goléa is also one of the biggest and a major stop on the route south.

The oasis itself is very lush and, apart from palms, supports a large variety of fruit trees,

including plum, peach, apricot, cherry, orange and fig. The market here has the last decent produce on the southward route, so stock up.

Orientation & Information

The road in from Timimoun will lead you to the main square – known as place Centre Ville – which contains a bank, post office, local taxi and bus stops and several cafés. South of the square is the town's main market behind which you'll find Place Mohammed V where long-distance buses and taxis pull up. There's an **internet café** (per hr DA80; ⏰ 10am–noon & 4-8pm, closed Friday) on av 1er Novembre off place Centre Ville.

Sights & Activities

The town is dominated by the old **ksar**, El-Menia, built on a rocky knoll in the east of town. It was built by Zénète Berbers in the 10th century and is now being restored. It's well worth the scramble up the hill to soak up its atmosphere and get grand views of the town and surrounding oasis.

The other sight worth seeing is the remote **Eglise Saint-Joseph**, some 3km north of El-Goléa; a dreamy looking cream and white church, set among sand and waving palms, next to which you'll find the tomb of Charles de Foucauld where his body was buried in 1929 (see the boxed text, p189, for further details).

Back towards the town centre, the well-maintained **Musée Communale** (☎ 029 913122/ 076 383125; ⏰ 9am–noon & 3-6pm) opposite the Hotel el-Boustane is dedicated to the palaeontology and geology of the region, and has an interesting collection of fossils and ancient pottery and stone tools, as well as written information on prehistory and mineralogy.

Sleeping

Hôtel Vieux Ksar (☎ 029 814310; s/d without bathroom from DA500/800; Ⓟ) On the road south of El-Goléa, 30 minutes' walk from the centre of town, this place has quiet well-kept rooms off a network of bright corridors and a nice garden at the back – all green trellises and fruit trees. Good food can be prepared with advance notice. This is an excellent-value place – only the location is against it.

Auberge Caravanserail (B&B per person from DA1200, camping DA500; Ⓟ) This hotel was in the last stages of renovation at the time of writing but was shaping up to be a great little place. Rooms are housed in a cool white building located just off the **place Centre Ville** and there's space for camping, a big shady garden bursting with palms and fruit trees, and an outdoor fireplace around which to congregate on chilly nights. Reserve in advance through M'Zab Tours (p156) in Ghardaïa.

Hôtel El-Boustan (☎ 029 816050; fax 816402; d from DA1800; P ☒) East of the centre of town on the road to the *ksar,* the state-run El-Boustan is El-Goléa's main hotel but certainly not the nicest. Like so many other state-run hotels, it has bog-standard rooms that are rather overpriced and a complete lack of atmosphere.

Getting There & Away
AIR
Air Algérie (☎ 029 816100) has an office in the centre of town between place Mohammed V and place Centre Ville. The airport is 3km to the west of town and there are weekly flights to Algiers.

BUS
The bus station is nothing more than an office right in the centre of town on place Mohammed V. There are daily departures for Adrar (DA550, five hours), Ghardaïa (DA400, three hours), In Salah (DA750, eight hours) and Timimoun (DA500, four hours).

TAXI
The long-distance taxis leave from an area just a few minutes' walk to the southwest of the centre. The main destination is Ghardaïa, but they also run to Timimoun.

GRAND ERG ORIENTAL
العرق الشرقى الكبير

The Grand Erg Oriental is much larger than its western counterpart, and shares its mass of rolling dunes with neighbouring Tunisia. The main draw of this region is the town of El-Oued, an oasis close to its northern edge. Its domed-roofed splendour is at the heart of the Souf region – a series of oases dotted throughout a small triangular area and one of the hottest regions of the Sa-

hara. The people of the Souf region have an ingenious way of growing dates and other fruits in the desert, digging pits deep in the sand and planting date palms and other fruit trees at the bottom from where their roots can reach the subterranean water. It is not uncommon to see just the tip of a palm tree sticking out of the top of one of these pits. Many of the women of this region sport garments similar to those you see in Ghardaïa – a single robe that covers everything except for one eye.

Touggourt is another oasis town, right on the western edge of the erg, south of El-Oued. The road that connects the two towns passes through some magnificent sand-dune country where it's a constant struggle to prevent the dunes from swallowing the road.

Further south again is the centre of Algeria's oil industry, the source of most of Algeria's export income. The beating heart of this area is Hassi Messaoud, although Ouargla on the edge of the erg is as close as most people need to go, unless they are heading for the Route du Tassili and Djanet.

EL-OUED الواد
El-Oued has been dubbed 'the town of a thousand domes' and it doesn't take long to work out why: the great majority of buildings come crowned with vaults and domes, initially conceived as a way of dealing with the intense summer heat. Temperatures have been known to rise as high as 50°C here and can reach 45°C for days on end. From the correct vantage point, the view out over the shimmering curved roofs to the encroaching sands beyond can be dazzling. El-Oued is also one of the busiest towns of the region and its streets are dirty, chaotic and full of life, especially around the large market where donkey carts vie for space on the streets with cars and pedestrians.

The town is also famous for its carpets, many of which bear the brown Cross of the Souf motif on a white background and you can find these on sale all over the country.

Information
INTERNET ACCESS
There's an **internet café** (per hr DA100 ☒ 8am-1am;) opposite the Hotel du Souf. There's more

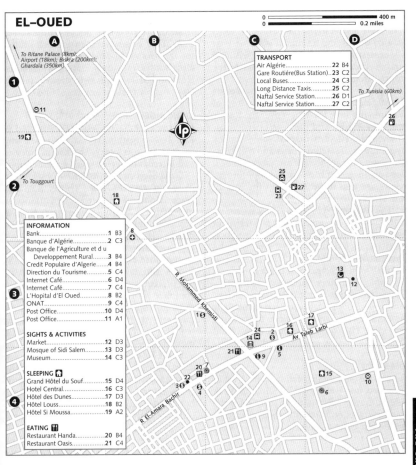

EL-OUED

0   400 m
0   0.2 miles

To Ritane Palace (8km);
Airport (18km); Biskra (200km);
Ghardaïa (350km)

To Tunisia (60km)

To Touggourt

TRANSPORT

Air Algérie	22 B4
Gare Routiére(Bus Station)	23 C2
Local Buses	24 C3
Long Distance Taxis	25 C2
Naftal Service Station	26 D1
Naftal Service Station	27 C2

R Mohammed Khemisti

Av Taleb Larbi

R El-Amara Bachir

INFORMATION

Bank	1 B3
Banque d'Algérie	2 C3
Banque de l'Agriculture et d u Developpement Rural	3 B4
Credit Populaire d'Algerie	4 B4
Direction du Tourisme	5 C4
Internet Café	6 D4
Internet Café	7 C4
L'Hopital d'El Oued	8 B2
ONAT	9 C4
Post Office	10 D4
Post Office	11 A1

SIGHTS & ACTIVITIES

Market	12 D3
Mosque of Sidi Salem	13 D3
Museum	14 C3

SLEEPING

Grand Hôtel du Souf	15 D4
Hotel Central	16 C3
Hôtel des Dunes	17 D3
Hôtel Louss	18 B2
Hôtel Si Moussa	19 A2

EATING

Restaurant Handa	20 B4
Restaurant Oasis	21 C4

internet access (per hr DA70; ☺ 7am-5pm) next to the Restaurant Oasis but the connection is not as fast.

MEDICAL SERVICES

L'Hopital d'El Oued (☎ 032 218891/8041) On rue Mohammed Khemisti near the town's main roundabout.

MONEY

On av Taleb Larbi there's a **Banque d'Algérie** (☺ 9am-2pm, closed Fri & Sat) which changes travellers cheques, gives cash advances on Visa cards and can change Tunisian money. There's also a Credit Populaire Algérie and a Banque d'Agriculture et du Développement Rural on rue El-Amara Bachir. It is also possible to change money at the Hôtel du Souf, and there is a bank at the Tunisian border, although it is not always open.

POST & TELEPHONE

The post office is just down the road from the Hotel de Souf and it has an ATM and phone booths.

TOURIST INFORMATION

The tourist office is in the Direction du Tourisme on av Taleb Larbi near the corner of rue Mohammed Khemisti, and has information on local sights as well as a map of El-Oued. There's an ONAT office on the same road but it serves mostly as a booking agent for flights to other North African countries and can't offer useful advice on El-Oued.

Sights

The daily **market** in the old part of the town is a colourful and animated affair. It is at its busiest on Friday. Most stalls sell food and everyday items, but a few cater to the tourist trade.

In the centre of the market is the **Mosque of Sidi Salem**. You can climb to the top of the minaret here for a view over the town's domed rooftops and the desert beyond, although the effect is marred somewhat by the number of satellite dishes and construction sites. Just ask for the caretaker and he'll let you in to walk up to the top. Similar views are also to be had from the roof of the Hôtel du Souf.

The **museum** (🕭 8.30am-noon & 3-6pm, closed Thu & Fri) opposite the tourist offices consists of just one room. However, it has some good displays, including old aerial photos of the area, a collection of the various insects and animals of the region, and some good *roses de sable* and other geological curiosities. There are also a couple of traditional rugs, and a pair of special wool-and-camel-hair soles which are used to walk on the burning hot sand. The whole thing is a bit dusty and moth-eaten but is worth a quick look.

Sleeping

The range of accommodation is not great in El-Oued, and while there's a fair amount in the midrange section, there is little for the budget traveller. What little budget accommodation there is tends to be below par.

BUDGET

Hôtel des Dunes (☎ 032 246795; av Taleb Larbi; s/d DA250/500) The most central lodgings in El-Oued are housed in a traditional domed building on av Taleb Larbi. It has basic rooms with bars on the windows and the facilities only include toilets, so you'll have to go to the public showers nearby.

Hotel Central (av Taleb Larbi; s & d DA600) Next door to the Hôtel des Dunes this is also a seriously budget place. It has very basic doubles with balcony, sink and fan and like the Hôtel des Dunes, there are toilets but no bathrooms so you'll have to use one of the many public showers in the vicinity.

Hôtel Si Moussa (☎ 032 272838; rue Mohammed Khemisti; d DA800; P ⊠) It's on rue Mohammed Khemisti near the fancy roundabout, complete with pavilion, at the intersection with

the Touggourt road. It is a 15-minute walk from the town centre but is a little closer than some other hotels to the bus station for early-morning departures, and there are also shuttles from town. Hôtel Si Moussa has clean and basic rooms with shower, and it's also possible to sleep on the roof here.

MIDRANGE

Hôtel Louss (☎ 032 210079/99; fax 218755; s/d DA1500/2000; P ⊠) 'Nothing special' is the best way to describe this hotel. The rooms, service and international restaurant are acceptable.

Grand Hôtel du Souf (☎ 032 247320; s/d/ste from DA1500/2000/4700; P ⊠ ⊠) This is the nicest place to stay in El-Oued. The entrance is impressive – full of arched hallways and domed ceilings covered in green-and-white mosaic. The rooms are pretty nondescript but there are some swish suites that come with padded faux leather doors, huge bathrooms and domed ceilings done out in the prerequisite mosaic. The hotel comes complete with its own tower; and the views from the top match those from the town's minaret. At time of writing a traditional tented area for taking tea and traditional meals was being constructed.

Ritane Palace (☎ 032 201539/201885; Daira d'El-Oued; s/d DA2553/2957) Ten kilometres from the city centre, it's only worth staying here if you want to be near the airport. It's a large hotel that wants to be the ritziest in the area (and certainly charges as if it were) and it does try hard – it has very attentive staff and plusher-than-average rooms, and the communal areas are embellished with bold displays of art – yet, because of its isolation, it lacks customers.

Eating

Food is expensive in El-Oued and there isn't a great deal to choose from. For something other than the usual couscous or chicken and chips you'll have to try one of the hotel restaurants, all of which have more varied menus with European as well as Algerian specialities and rather more upmarket surrounding.

Restaurant Oasis (rue El-Amara Bachir; 🕭 11am-9pm) This is a good choice although it has pretty bland surroundings it has a good selection of grills and stews.

Restaurant Handa (rue El-Amara Bachir; ☎ 10am-9pm) Some 100m further west on the same road as Restaurant Oasis, Handa is very similar.

Getting There & Away

AIR
The **Air Algérie** (☎ 032 248686; 🕑 8am-noon & 1-2.30pm Fri-Wed, 8am-noon Thu) office is on rue El-Amara Bachir in the centre of town. The airport is at Guemar, 19km to the north, and can be reached by local bus. There are three flights a week to Algiers (DA4800, one hour 20 minutes).

BUS
The main bus station is about 1.5km north of the town centre – a 20-minute walk; or there are local minibuses which take you to or from the centre of town.

There are departures to Algiers (DA950, 10 hours), Annaba (DA520, six hours), Constantine (DA470, five hours), Ghardaïa (DA520, six hours) and Ouargla (DA300, three hours).

TAXI
Yellow long-distance taxis leave when full from opposite the main bus station to Touggourt (DA400, 1½ hours), Ouargla (DA600, three hours) and towns in the Souf area.

Getting Around
Local bus and taxi services for the town and surrounding villages leave from next to the museum. Short journeys cost DA15.

TOUGGOURT توقرت
A totally unremarkable oasis town, Touggourt is perhaps most famous as the starting point of the first motorised crossing of the Sahara. The Citroën half-track vehicles of the Haardt and Audouin-Dubreuil expedition set off from here in 1922 for Timbuktu via Tamanrasset. The event is marked by a simple pillar in the town square. The town was also once a key stop on the trans-Saharan trading route, and the seat of a dynasty of kings called the Ouled Djellab.

Today the town is a regional administrative centre. There are a couple of banks, a post office and an Air Algérie office. If you have a day to spare you could do worse than spend it here, but don't lose any sleep if you miss it.

Shared taxis also travel to the Tunisian border (DA400, 1½ hours) when full. There's a

4km walk between the two border posts but some people find a car to take them.

Orientation
From the main square, the road to the right curves past the cinema to the marketplace, taxi and bus station. The road straight ahead leads past the old hotel on the left to the Hôtel Oasis and Temacine.

Information
There's a Banque Nationale d'Algérie and a Banque d'Agriculture et du Développement Rural in the town centre. There's an internet café in the town centre opposite the Banque d'Agriculture et du Développement Rural building.

Sights
There's a large **palmeraie** outside town and a couple of old, vaguely interesting **mud-brick villages** to the south.

Market day is Friday; in winter especially, the town is full of itinerant merchants who have come for the market. The marketplace is just off the road to El-Oued, near the taxi station.

Sleeping
Touggourt is seriously lacking in good accommodation options. At the time of writing a new tourist-class hotel was under construction next to the bus station. It will be called the Hôtel el-Nakhil.

BUDGET
Hôtel Essaada (☎ 029 674545; s/d/tr/q DA300/500/600/800) This place overlooks the market and has very basic rooms and shared facilities. There's a *hammam* (bathhouse) underneath that's open from 7am to 9pm.

Hôtel de la Paix (s/d/t/q DA700/900/1400/1800) Between the market and the main street is this is a simple little place with average rooms and shared bathrooms. It's rather dark and noisy though and we got a frosty reception. The only advantage is its central location.

MIDRANGE
Hôtel Oasis (☎ 029 681050/5050; fax 029 682645; s/d DA1500/1950) Located about 500m south of the town centre this is without a doubt the best place to stay in town. It has good rooms, the usual mosaic hallways and a

palm-surrounded pool. In the lobby is a useful (although rather old) sketch map of Touggourt as well as some information on stuff to do in the vicinity.

Eating

There are a few very basic restaurants between the taxi station and the market as well as around the main square, but we didn't find anything great here.

Getting There & Away

BUS

There's a bus station right on the western edge of town, on the route to Biskra, and one in the centre of town next to the large main market place. Both have buses to long-distance destinations.

Daily bus services include Algiers (DA950, 10 hours), Biskra (DA350, three hours), Constantine (DA480, five hours), El-Oued (DA200, two hours) and Hassi Messaoud (DA300, three hours).

SHARED TAXI

The shared-taxi station is next to the marketplace just off the main El-Oued road, five minutes' walk from the town centre.

There are departures for Biskra (DA500, three hours), El-Oued (DA300, 1½ hours) and Ouargla (DA650, four hours), but very little happens after about 1pm.

TRAIN

The train station is close to the centre of town but is currently only served by goods trains.

Getting Around

Local buses for Tamelhat and Temacine leave from a stop just outside the main bus station, next to the market.

AROUND TOUGGOURT

Temacine تماسين

On the edge of the *palmeraie* about 10km from Touggourt is Temacine. At its centre are the remains of a traditional mud-brick village built around a ksar at the top of a small hill. Rains destroyed the village in the early 1990s, and its inhabitants had to move to the new housing which now surrounds the village. Even though the houses are no longer intact, it's still nice to wander round and the ruins exude a romantic air.

The mosque and minaret partly survived and have now been rebuilt.

If you can find the caretaker, it's possible to climb up to the top of the minaret for a view over the ruined village, the nearby salt lake and the *palmeraie*. Next to Temacine is the 'sea', a small salt lake, which holds little interest itself, but has some good ruins – those of **Boha Mar**, a thousand-year-old village, and the **mausoleum** which stands next to it. Coming from Touggourt, take the Ouargla road past the Hôtel Oasis. After about 10km you'll find Temacine on your right.

Tamelhat تاملحات

A couple of kilometres further on is Tamelhat, which was also destroyed by the rains in the early 1990s. There are large open spaces where buildings have collapsed completely and now the town is made up mostly of new buildings.

In the centre of the town is the mosque and mausoleum of **Sidi el-Hadj Ali**; the cupola above the mausoleum is decorated with coloured tiles and stucco.

Getting There & Away

There are local buses from the main bus station in the centre of Touggourt and these will drop you directly in the centre of Temacine or Tamelhat.

OUARGLA ورقلة

The town of Ouargla has slightly more to offer than Touggourt. It has a better range of accommodation, an interesting museum and a nice old town. It's not worth making a special trip here, but if you're passing through it's not a bad place to spend a day. The town's origins lie in the 10th century at Sedrata, about 15km south of Ouargla's present-day location. Sedrata was once a capital for the Ibadis before the city was razed in 1072 and they were forced to flee further south to the M'Zab Valley (see p160).

Orientation

The town's main street is rue 1 Novembre where you'll find the main banks, restaurants and hotels. Another good reference point is *quatre chemins*, the crossroads at rue 1 Novembre and the rte de Rouissat, which many locals will use when giving directions.

Information

There are several banks and an **Air Algérie** (☎ 029 761195) office along rue de 1 Novembre and there's a post office opposite the casbah. To use the internet try the youth hostel on rue 1 Novembre.

Sights & Activities

A few hundred metres south of *quatre chemins* you'll find the old **casbah**. There's nothing of particular significance here but it's nice to wander the narrow, sandy streets with their pretty beige- and rose-coloured buildings. There's also a mosque and circular central market place selling fruit and vegetables as well as deliciously fragrant baskets of fresh herbs.

In between the *quatre chemins* and the casbah is the **Musée du Sahara** (☺ 9am-noon & 2-4pm Sun-Wed), which has interesting information on the geology and plant and animal life of the Sahara and has some prehistoric artefacts and stuffed animals on display.

Sleeping
BUDGET

Youth hostel (☎ 029 713301; rue 1 Novembre; dm DA100; ☐) Located on the Ghardaïa road about 300m from *quatre chemins*, this is a good clean hostel, one of the nicest in the south, and has a cafeteria, internet café and clean bathrooms.

MIDRANGE

Hotel El-Boustane (☎/fax 029 713591; rte de Rouissat; s/d/apt from DA900/1200/2600; ℗ ✄) About 700m past the Hotel El-Anssar also on the right, this place is a multicoloured explosion; the lobby, with its swirly patterned sofas, clashing carpets and giant fish tank, leads to an orange-floored hallway off which there are smallish rooms with thick maroon carpeting and faux-wood-panelled walls.

Hotel le Tassili (☎ 029 763004; fax 761361; Quartier Résidentiel d'IFRI; s/d DA2450/3300; ℗ ✄ ✆) Look for the blue neon signs opposite the Mosque de Ifri just east of the town centre. This is an old hotel dating from the colonial era. It has good rooms with fridges and big mirrors and there's a large, fully equipped suite in a grass hut at the bottom of the garden. There are some nice areas to hang out too – there's a lively terrace where the locals come for a cold drink in the evening; a romantic fabric-swathed, tented area for drinking mint tea, and a cosy lobby with cave-painting reproductions on the walls and a nook with comfy sofas and a big fireplace for chilly winter nights. The car park has a hole-in-the-wall bottle shop and alcohol is served in the bar.

Grand Hotel Touristique el-Anssar (☎ 029 763 745; s/d DA1500/2600; rte de Rouissat; ℗ ✄) Rooms here are large with balconies but feel rather dark; thankfully they are enlivened by such delights as giant glossy waterfall posters and plastic flowers. There's a restaurant, *salon de thé* (tea room) and parking. It's about 200m north of *quatre chemins* on the right-hand side.

TOP END

Hotel Lynatel (☎ 029 714242; lynatel@hotmail.com; rue 1 Novembre; s/d from 3400/3800; ℗ ✄ ✆) On rue 1 Novembre between *quatre chemins* and the SNTV bus station. This is a sparklingly clean place and the swishest digs in Ouargla. The large rooms have high ceilings, plenty of light and seriously comfortable beds. Suites are equipped with computers which will soon be connected to high-speed internet. There's a massive roof terrace with views over town where parties are held in good weather, and there's even a resident pastry chef to knock up goodies for breakfast.

Eating

You'll find plenty of basic restaurants serving chicken and chips along the rue 1 Novembre. Other than those your best bet is the hotels. The excellent **Hotel Lynatel restaurant** (☺ noon-2.30pm & 7-11pm) serves top-quality North African and European food and scrummy desserts. There's a **salon de thé** at the Hotel El-Anssar, where you can get a nice variety of herbal teas, good coffee and fresh pastries; and the Hotel le Tassili restaurant specialises in French cuisine.

Getting There & Away
BUS

The bus station is at the eastern end of town on the Ghardaïa road, about 1.5km from the town centre, and is where the private bus companies are based. There are buses to Algiers (DA920, 12 hours), Constantine (DA620), Illizi (DA950), the Libyan border (DA1450, 14 hours) and Oran (DA1000, 14 hours).

GHARDAÏA & THE GRAND ERGS

The SNTV (state-run) buses operate out of an office across the street from the main bus station. Destinations include Ghardaïa (DA200, two hours), Algiers (DA800, 12 hours), Oran (DA915, 14 hours) and In Amenas (DA1300, 12 hours).

TAXI

Long-distance taxis wait 400m east of the bus station on the Ghardaïa road. They go to Ghardaïa (DA500, two hours), El-Oued (DA600, three hours) and other places.

There are five taxi services a week to Algiers (DA5500, one hour 20 minutes), two to Oran (DA6600, two to five hours), and weekly services to In Amenas (DA5500, 1½ hours), Adrar (DA6500, two hours), Djanet (DA8600, 1½ hours), Illizi (DA6000, one hour) and Tamanrasset (DA9200, four hours).

The airport is on the Touggourt road about 8km out of town on the right.

HASSI MESSAOUD حسي مسعود

Situated 85km southeast of Ouargla, this is solely a service town for surrounding oil operations – there are about 800 oil wells within a 25km radius of the town. There is absolutely nothing of interest, but you will find yourself coming through on the way south on the Route du Tassili N'Ajjer. Driving in the region at night, you're sure to notice a strange orange glow in the night sky – these are the burn-off flames from the oil refineries which can be seen from many kilometres away.

Sleeping

The only decent accommodation in town is 3km from the centre at the northern end of town, and it's expensive at DA2000 for a single.

Getting There & Away

There are regular buses between here and Ouargla, and a daily service to In Amenas, although you'll need luck to get a seat on it as it comes from Ouargla and is likely to be full.

There are 10 flights a week to Algiers (DA6000, one hour) as well as direct international flights to Paris and London.

Tamanrasset, Djanet & the Sahara

تامنراست، جانت، الصحراء

If you thought that the Sahara was all about sand and camels then you'd better think again. While you'll get your fix of unwieldy dromedaries and undulating dunes, this part of the Sahara is also home to an alien landscape of twisted stone forests, stark volcanic mountain ranges, endless black gravel plains and deep dark canyons. It's the trump card of Algerian tourism and, now that the security situation has stabilised, thousands of visitors are heading back to marvel at its eye-popping natural beauty.

Stretching from In Salah right down to the Mali and Niger borders is the Ahaggar (Hoggar) National Park. Created in 1987 to safeguard the considerable riches of this part of the country, it's one of the largest protected areas in the world. At its heart is the laid-back town of Tamanrasset, resting at the foot of the brooding Hoggar massif.

The craggy plateau that surrounds the sleepy oasis of Djanet is known as the Tassili N'Ajjer. Also one of Algeria's protected areas, its caves and canyons hide an abundance of engravings and paintings illustrating the once-blooming plant and animal life of the Sahara.

This is the Algerian heartland of the Tuareg, traditionally a nomadic people, who have roamed the desert regions of Algeria and its neighbouring countries for many centuries. You'll see beautiful women swathed in brightly coloured fabrics and refined silver jewellery and plenty of veiled 'blue men' (as Tuareg men are sometimes called, after the traditional colour of their robes) zipping through the streets of Tamanrasset and Djanet in burly jeeps.

HIGHLIGHTS

- Hike up steep escarpments and through shadowy canyons to reach the treasure trove of prehistoric art at **Tassili N'Ajjer National Park** (p194)

- Climb deep into the Hoggar Mountains for one of the most spectacular sunrises on earth at **Assekrem** (p188)

- Gaze up at great stone castles and bizarre, deformed mountains on the otherworldly plateau of the **Tassili du Hoggar** (p189)

- Evoke the ancient salt caravans by saddling up on a dromedary to experience the majesty of the Sahara near **Djanet** (p191)

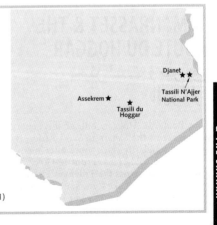

Djanet ★★

Tassili N'Ajjer National Park

Assekrem ★   ★
Tassili du Hoggar

TAMANRASSET, DJANET & THE SAHARA

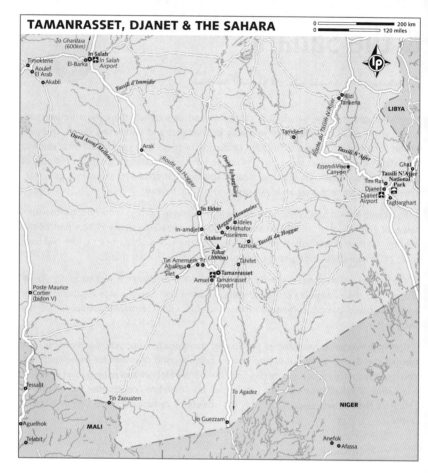

TAMANRASSET, DJANET & THE SAHARA

TAMANRASSET & THE ROUTE DU HOGGAR

تامنراست وطريق الهوقار

The Route du Hoggar, one of the major routes across the Sahara to West Africa, is gaining popularity once more after many years in the wilderness. From El-Goléa, it extends south across the Tademait Plateau, which stretches on like some sunburnt pancake; the largest thing in sight might be a rock the size of a tennis ball. It then passes through In Salah, a town famed for its salty water, past the canyons and mountains of the Tassili d'Immidir (tassili means plateau in the language of the local Tuareg), through the steep gorges of Arak and then on to this region's hub – the Tuareg 'capital' of Tamanrasset. From Tamanrasset, the road continues for another punishing 410km to In Guezzam, which sits near the border crossing into Niger.

Much of the area covered in this section is protected territory and part of the Ahaggar National Park.

'Tam', as it is affectionately known, is the jumping-off point for exploring the attractions of the Hoggar Mountains, the highlight of which is Assekrem, which at

---

SUN, SAND & SAFETY

In February 2003 the dangers of desert driving were dramatically illustrated when no fewer than 32 people disappeared in the Sahara. Several separate expeditions, mostly German and Swiss, vanished in different parts of southeast Algeria. Speculation was rife about their fate: one Algerian source even claimed the travellers were being held illegally in a military facility and search attempts made by the Algerian government were a show put on for the benefit of the media. By March, however, it had become apparent that the travellers were in the hands of an extreme Islamist group, the Salafist Group for Call and Combat (GSPC).

In May, 17 of the hostages were released unharmed and eventually the remaining party was tracked down to Mali after they had crossed the southern Saharan border. Most were successfully rescued after long negotiations; one tourist died in captivity.

In the light of these events, travel in the desert areas south of Ghardaïa must be undertaken with a professional guide. If driving yourself from Mali, you must arrange to be met at the Algerian border by a guide. Several travel agencies in Tamanrasset, Djanet and Adrar can arrange this for you. If you ignore these regulations you will be found out – there are checkpoints throughout the desert.

---

some 2800m is one of the Hoggar's highest peaks. From here you can watch the sun rise over a carpet of peaks from the hermitage of Charles de Foucauld. South of Tamanrasset is the Tassili du Hoggar – a mystical plateau full of mushroom-shaped rocks and saffron sand.

IN SALAH عين صالح

Built in the red Sudanese style, In Salah would be a very pleasant place to stay were it not for the problem that gives the town its name: salty water. The water is disgusting, so bring as much water with you as you can from Tamanrasset or El-Goléa. Even the local soft drinks are made from it and bottled water is often unavailable.

The most interesting feature of the town is the presence of a creeping sand dune on the western edge by the Aoulef road. Behind the mosque you can see how the dune is gradually encroaching on the town. From the top of the dune it becomes apparent that In Salah has actually been cut in two.

The dune moves at the rate of about 1m every five years. The amount of sand on the move actually remains fairly constant, so while it is swallowing up a building on its leading edge, it is uncovering one behind it which may have been under the sand for a generation or two. Once the ruins of a house have been uncovered, it is established who it used to belong to and then that person's relatives rebuild the place and move in.

The view from the top of the dune is great at sunset. To the west of town along the Aoulef road is the *palmeraie*, with some 250,000 trees. Formerly a trading town dealing in gold, ivory and slaves from the south in exchange for European goods from the north, the town's major occupation is now date-growing.

Information

There is a bank in the main street, and the post office is one block to the north. There is a big hospital out in the east of town near the Hôtel Tidikelt.

TRAVEL AGENCIES

Ahnet Voyages (☎ 029 390223; fax 29360999; ahnetvoyages@hotmail.com/ahnet_voyages@yahoo.fr; In Salah) This agency has been organising trips into the Tassili d'Immidir since the late 1980s. It also runs good trips in the Hoggar as well as trips further afield to the M'zab.

Tanezrouft Voyages (☎ 029 360646; www.tanezrouft .com; Ksar el-Arab, In Salah) Offers trekking, camel and 4WD expeditions into the Tassili d'Immidir and Ahnet regions.

Sleeping

Camping Tidikelt (per person DA500) At the end of the main street near the centre of town, this the better of the two camping alternatives. There is a reasonable amount of shade and you can sleep in the tiny palm-frond huts if you want some privacy. It costs DA180 to sleep in the huts.

The only hotel is this three-star place **Hôtel Tidikelt** (☎ 029 370393; fax 029 340799) on the outskirts of town, 10 minutes' walk from the centre. It's a two-story mud-red building with a (mostly empty) swimming

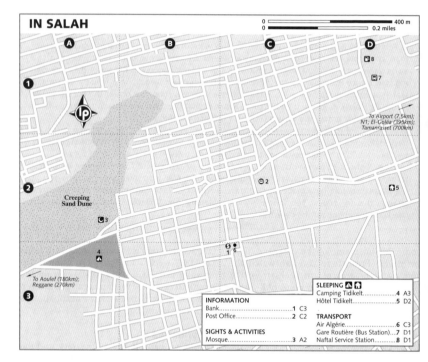

IN SALAH

Creeping
Sand Dune

To Aoulef (180km);
Reggane (270km)

To Airport (7.5km);
N1; El-Goléa (395km);
Tamanrasset (700km)

INFORMATION	
Bank	1 C3
Post Office	2 C2
SIGHTS & ACTIVITIES	
Mosque	3 A2

SLEEPING	
Camping Tidikelt	4 A3
Hôtel Tidikelt	5 D2
TRANSPORT	
Air Algérie	6 C3
Gare Routière (Bus Station)	7 D1
Naftal Service Station	8 D1

pool. Rooms are air-conditioned and in the grand traditional of state-run hotels in Algeria, rather run down. There's a half-decent restaurant and an airport shuttle for those who need it.

Eating

There are several basic cafés in the town where you can get cheap, filling meals for around DA300. For something a bit more upmarket, you'll have to try the fancy restaurant at the Hôtel Tidikelt.

Getting There & Away

AIR

The **Air Algérie** (☎ 029 360239) office is on the main street, next to a bank. The airport is 8km to the northeast, to the right of the El-Goléa road.

There is a weekly flight to Algiers (DA9800, three hours) and one to Tamanrasset (DA5400, one hour).

BUS

The *gare routière* is out in the east on the main Tamanrasset to El-Goléa road, about 20 minutes' walk from the centre. It is actually just a shopping centre (most of it unoccupied), and the bus office is inside towards the back.

There are buses to Adrar, Ghardaïa and Tamanrasset. The Ghardaïa buses leave at 4pm every day and it is essential that you book in advance as the buses come up from Tamanrasset. There are stops along the way (including a meal at Arak), but basically you need to be prepared with a bit of food and water.

TAXI

There are 4WD taxis between In Salah and Tamanrasset costing DA2130. Taxis run regularly from In Salah to Reggane (DA600, three hours), 270km west along the road to Adrar, and from there you can catch a daily bus to Adrar.

AROUND IN SALAH

Tassili d'Immidir

Part of the Ahaggar National Park, the Tassili d'Immidir is one of the least-explored areas of this region, despite its beauty and

TAMANRASSET, DJANET
& THE SAHARA

archaeological riches. Perhaps this is because of its relative isolation – it has to be accessed on foot and even then this is not a straightforward task – but the difficulty in getting here adds to its appeal. The landscape is wild and mysterious and the *gueltas* – pools of water found in the bottom of canyons – produce sufficient vegetation to support a range of animal life: gazelles, mountain sheep, jackals and even leopard can be found here. The Tassili d'Immidir is also rich in archaeological findings – arrowheads, shards of pottery and hundreds of ancient rock paintings all attest to a human presence from Neolithic times.

There is no way of getting here independently so you'll have to join a tour. There are several companies in Tamanrasset and in In Salah that organise tours here.

ARAK عراق

Although the gorges around Arak are quite spectacular, the little settlement itself is very humble. It doesn't have the altitude of Tamanrasset, and subsequently is as hot as all hell.

There is a camp site with *zeribas* (palm huts), a restaurant where you can get a reasonable meal and a fuel station.

If you are on the bus, it will stop here for a meal break.

TAMANRASSET تامنراست

As the last town on the route south to Niger, Tam, with a current population of around 120,000, has long been a vital rest stop for ancient caravans and desert traders and, as a major centre for Algeria's Saharan tourism, is still is a busy crossroads today. It's one of those places where virtually all trans-Saharan travellers stop for a few days to rest up and make repairs to equipment. Tamanrasset is also the place from which to arrange trips up into the Hoggar Mountains, something that should not be missed on any account.

If you arrive by plane, as many tourists do, you will be treated to a spectacular preview of things to come – endless twisted peaks of red and brown are spread out below you and volcanic craters blister the ground like the surface of some far off planet.

With an altitude of nearly 1400m, Tamanrasset has a climate which stays relatively moderate all year round. Even in midsummer the temperature rarely gets above 35°C. There's not a great deal to do here but it's an appealing place in which to while away a couple of days – there's a good market, some nice cafés and a friendly atmosphere. It's also a place where you can get things done – there are banks, one of which can change travellers cheques, several internet cafés and Malian and Nigerien consulates for arranging ongoing visas.

History

The Tuareg were the first settlers in this region, which they called Tamenghest, but when Charles de Foucauld (see the boxed text, p189) arrived in 1905, Tamanrasset was just a dusty cluster of *zeribas*.

From the 1920s onwards, when the French colonial administration settled here because of the town's strategic location, Tamanrasset's growth accelerated. It became a *préfecture* in the 1950s and, after independence, the regional capital of the *wilaya* (province). Access routes were improved and more and more Algerians came to make their home here. In the '80s the explosion of tourism to the Algerian Sahara brought with it economic prosperity and urban planners.

The 1990s were lean years for Tamanrasset, as the town that had come to depend greatly on tourists saw its source of income dry up, due to the country's bitter civil war. The slow improvements brought on by the end of the troubles were dashed again when a group of tourists was kidnapped in the desert regions near the town in 2003, but at the time of writing the safety situation in the region had greatly improved and visitors to the town were on the increase once more.

Orientation

There's one main street in Tamanrasset that leads all the way from the airport through the town itself and out to Mt Adriane, a large peak that dominates the town. The bus station is at the northeastern end of this street, about 1km walk away from the town centre. South of the main street is the Oued Tamanrasset, a large dried riverbed that sometimes also serves as a truck park and camel market. On the south bank of this river you'll find the Marché Africaine

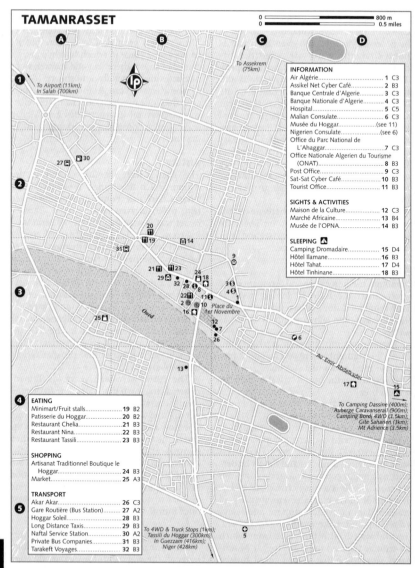

TAMANRASSET

0 _____ 800 m
0 _____ 0.5 miles

INFORMATION
Air Algérie................................	**1** C3
Assikel Net Cyber Café...............	**2** B3
Banque Centrale d'Algerie..........	**3** C3
Banque Nationale d'Algerie.........	**4** C3
Hospital...................................	**5** C5
Malian Consulate......................	**6** C3
Musée du Hoggar......................	(see 11)
Nigerien Consulate....................	(see 6)
Office du Parc National de	
L'Ahaggar............................	**7** C3
Office Nationale Algerien du Tourisme	
(ONAT)................................	**8** B3
Post Office..............................	**9** C3
Sat-Sat Cyber Café....................	**10** B3
Tourist Office..........................	**11** B3

SIGHTS & ACTIVITIES
Maison de la Culture.................	**12** C3
Marché Africaine......................	**13** B4
Musée de l'OPNA.....................	**14** B3

SLEEPING
Camping Dromadaire................	**15** D4
Hôtel Ilamane.........................	**16** B3
Hôtel Tahat............................	**17** D4
Hôtel Tinhinane.......................	**18** B3

To Assekrem (75km)

To Airport (11km);
In Salah (700km)

Oued

Place du 1er Novembre

Av Emir Abdelkader

To Camping Dassine (400m);
Auberge Caravanserail (900m);
Camping Bordj 4WD (1.5km);
Gîte Sahanen (3km);
Mt Adrience (3.5km)

EATING
Minimart/Fruit stalls..................	**19** B2
Patisserie du Hoggar..................	**20** B2
Restaurant Chelia.....................	**21** B3
Restaurant Nina.......................	**22** B3
Restaurant Tassili.....................	**23** B3

SHOPPING
Artisanat Traditionnel Boutique le	
Hoggar................................	**24** B3
Market....................................	**25** A3

TRANSPORT
Akar Akar...............................	**26** C3
Gare Routière (Bus Station)........	**27** A2
Hoggar Soleil..........................	**28** B3
Long Distance Taxis...................	**29** B3
Naftal Service Station................	**30** A2
Private Bus Companies...............	**31** B3
Tarakeft Voyages......................	**32** B3

To 4WD & Truck Stops (1km);
Tassili du Hoggar (300km);
In Guezzam (416km);
Niger (428km)

and the road towards Niger. Tam's best accommodation is located south of town on the route d'Adriane.

Information
FOREIGN CONSULATES
Both Mali and Niger have consulates here. They are next door to each other on av Emir Abdelkader, about 500m from the centre of town.

Malian Consulate (☎ 029 341578; av Emir Abdelkader; ☼ 9am-3pm Sun-Thu) Operates a same-day service for visas. A one-month visa costs €15 for French citizens and €10 for people of other nationalities.

Nigerien Consulate (☎ 029 344122; av Emir Abdelkader; ☼ 9am-2.30pm Sun-Thu) Also operates a same-day service – come first thing in the morning and pick up your visa in the afternoon. Visas costs €50 for one month.

INTERNET ACCESS

Assikel Net (per hr DA100; ☻ 8am-midnight) On a small side road off av Emir Abdelkader. Offers reasonable-speed internet access.

Sat-Sat Cyber Café (per hr DA100; ☻ 8am-9pm) Next to the Hotel Ilamane. The connection is slightly slow.

MEDICAL SERVICES

The main hospital is on the ring road between av Emir Abdelkader and the In Guezzam road.

MONEY

Neither bank can offer cash advances on credit cards.

Banque Centrale d'Algérie (☻ 9am-noon & 2-4pm, closed Fri & Sat) The only bank in town that accepts travellers cheques. You need to have the original receipt as proof of purchase and even then it can be a long process. The foreign-exchange division sometimes shuts earlier in the afternoon so it's best to go in the morning if you want to change travellers cheques.

Banque Nationale d'Algérie (☻ 9am-noon & 2-4pm, closed Fri & Sat) Next to Banque Centrale d'Algérie. Changes cash but not travellers cheques.

POST & TELEPHONE

The post office is northeast of the main street. It has a telephone office where it's possible to make international calls, although with the number of taxiphone offices in town it's not really worth the bother.

TOURIST INFORMATION

Office du Parc Nationale de l'Ahaggar (L'OPNA; ☎ 029 734117; place du 1er Novembre) Office of the national park; sometimes has interesting exhibitions on the life of the park.

Office National Algerien du Tourisme (ONAT; ☎ 029 346717; fax 029 344191; ☻ 8am-noon & 2-5pm) Has very helpful staff and can provide useful information on the local area as well as organising tours in the vicinity from €50 per person per day.

TRAVEL AGENCIES

Most of these agencies deal with bookings from foreign agencies. However, if contacted in advance they should be able to work something out for independent travellers. Prices range from €50 to €80 a day including food and equipment, depending on how many people there are in your party. You won't usually be permitted to join an already existing group and will almost certainly have to arrange an individually tailored tour. If you haven't arranged a tour in advance your best bet is to contact ONAT when you arrive in Tamanrasset.

Many of the agencies have home-based offices so you'll have to make contact in advance by telephone. There are a couple of agency offices in the town centre, but these appear to be closed a lot of the time, so it's still best to phone in advance.

Akar Akar (☎ 029 344638; www.akar-akar.com) One of the oldest and biggest agencies in Tamanrasset and one of the few to have a functioning office in the town centre. Guests are housed in red-walled bungalows or authentic Tuareg tents at their gîte not far from the airport.

Hoggar Soleil (☎ 029 346972; www.hoggarsoleil.com; BP 341 Tamanrasset) A well-established agency created in 1986. It offers treks from four to 14 days in the Tamanrasset environs as well as tours around Djanet and the Tassili N'Ajjer.

Immidir Voyages (☎ 029 344468/2484; www .immidir-voyages.com; BP777 Mouflon, Tamanrasset) Excellent and established agency providing 4WD treks and tours around the Tam region, with great tours into the Immidir, about which the owner is particularly enthusiastic and interested.

Tarakeft Voyages (☎ 029 342007; www.tarakeft.com) Runs 4WD and trekking tours in the region around Tamanrasset as well as tours into Mali and the Dogon country.

Walene Voyages (☎ 029 344229/037 2413004; www .walene-voyages.com; BP 439 Tamanrasset) Circuits include trips to Mali and Niger as well as a special camel trip in the footsteps of Foucauld.

Sights & Activities

There is a daily **market** held in the late afternoon held on the far side of the *oued* (dry river bed) away from the centre of town. As well as fruit, vegetables and grain there are several shoe and clothing stalls as well as tailors' booths.

Also on the far side of the *oued* is the gargantuan **Marché Africaine**, another daily market selling all manner of produce, from spices and traditional clothing to huge metal cooking pots, velour carpets and dodgy cologne (*Tuareg pour Homme* anyone?). To see the market at its liveliest, it's best to come in the morning. The **Musée du l'OPNA** (admission free; ☻ 9am-noon & 1.30-5pm Sun-Thu, 3-5pm Fri) provides interesting information on the history, geography and environment of the Hoggar region. The irregularly opening

Musée du Hoggar (☺ 9am-noon & 2-5pm Sun-Thu) has displays of Tuareg clothing, swords and daggers. You could also check out the **Maison de la Culture** on place du 1er Novembre, which has regular exhibitions about the landscape and animal life of the region as well as good second-hand-book sales.

Festivals & Events

LE TAFSIT

One of the most important festivals in Southern Algeria, this event takes place at the end of April in celebration of spring. Every springtime, different Tuareg tribes from all over the central Sahara have always met in Tamanrasset for a grand celebration of brotherhood, culminating in a camel race. This was formalised in the early '90s and it became known as **Le Tafsit** or the Spring Festival. It lasts for a minimum of three days and much of it takes place in the *'chameaudrome'* 3km from Tamanrasset. As well as the famous camel race, there are exhibitions, music, singing, and street processions.

Sleeping

There are several nice places to stay in Tamanrasset, mostly located a few kilometres out of town. There are a couple of hotels located in the town centre, but these aren't nearly as nice so if you don't mind the walk (it's a pleasant one), you're better off staying away from the action. Places to stay in Tamanrasset are often called *campings*. These aren't camp sites, but are normally gîtes with bungalow or hut accommodation, with plenty of space on the side for pitching tents. All of the *campings* can organise tours up to Assekrem and beyond.

BUDGET

Hôtel Ilamane (☎ 029 345716; s/d/tr DA500/1000/1400) Just south of av Emir Abdelkader, this is the cheapest place to stay in the town centre. It has basic but very spacious rooms with friendly if somewhat confused service. It's nothing special though and unless you're desperate to stay in the centre of town it's best to stay somewhere a little further out.

Hôtel Tinhinane (☎ 029734385; av Emir Abdelkader; s/d DA600/1100) Bang in the centre of town. It is not as cheap as the Hotel Ilamane though and we found the rooms, with shared bathroom, disappointing. At the time of writing

renovations were about to get underway – rooms were being improved and a number of new en suite rooms were planned.

Camping Bordj 4WD (☎ 029 342258; route de l'Adriane; per person without bathroom from DA800, camping per person DA500; ⓟ) Large two-storey pink building providing comfortable accommodation in simple single and double rooms or camping in its lovely gardens.

MIDRANGE

Camping Dromadaire (☎ 029 348252/061 648069; www.dromadaire-tourisme.com; rte de l'Adriane; s/d/tr DA850/1700/2450, dm DA850, camping per person DA400; ⓟ) Nice, spacious place featuring double and triple red circular chalets with palm roofs, a 10-bed dorm, a large garden with plenty of room for pitching tents, a small boutique and plenty of cane-chaired chill-out areas. Meals are available if ordered in advance and dinner costs DA350. It also has a travel agency running tours around the Hoggar.

Camping Dassine (☎ 063 675837; s/d from DA900/1800, camping per person DA500; ⓟ) About 500m further on from Camping Dromadaire, this is a large rambling place with tons of camping space, and clean, cool rooms in bungalows or thatch rondavels with spotless shared facilities. There's a traditional tented area for taking meals and tea or just shooting the breeze, and an outdoor fireplace. Meals are available, aided by a nice salad and herb garden at the back of the plot. To make it even better, there are lovely views of the hills all around.

Gite Saharien (☎ 029 345452/020 812307; info@taghant.com; s&d, from around DA1400 B&B per person) Backed up against Mt Adriane with stunning views from all around the gîte, this is the nicest place to stay in town. It has wonderfully relaxing cool, calm rooms (including larger suites with seating and eating areas) set in red-mud chalets, with rustic beds and tables made from palm trees. There are plenty of areas in which to relax and take in the view, and an inviting lounge with a big fireplace for colder evenings. The huge garden is full of fruit trees and plants, and there are ducks, a goat pen and even a resident monkey. Step outside and the desert is on your doorstep. The gîte is also home to the Taghant Agency which as well as the usual 4WD trips organises simple camel treks in the vicinity of the gîte.

Auberge Caravanserail (☎ 029 345557; B&B per person DA1500, half board DA2300, full boardDA3200; P) Owned by M'zab Tours, who have similar set-ups in Ghardaïa and El-Goléa, this is another good choice. It has simple white bungalows with spotless shared ablutions and a bright courtyard filled with bougainvillea. It costs DA1500 per day for guides and the agency organises tailored trips throughout the Hoggar; there's even a conference room.

Hôtel Tahat (☎ 029 344475; fax 029 344325; av Emir Abdelkader; s/d DA2900/3400) As state-run hotels go this one is quite nice. Rooms are very comfortable and things actually seem to work. There are some nice communal areas including a pretty curtain-swathed, pillow-strewn lounge, plus it has a tour agency and it's one of the few places that you can get an alcoholic drink.

Eating

The restaurant scene in Tamanrasset is hardly pulsating. However there are a few places on the main road that are decent and there are several places to buy fresh fruit, veg and other supplies.

Restaurant Chelia (av Emir Abdelkader; meals around DA300; ☽ lunch & dinner) Just across the street from Restaurant Tassili this place serves tasty grilled kebabs to eat in or take away.

Restaurant Tassili (av Emir Abdelkader; meals DA350; ☽ lunch & dinner) This place has tables outside as well as an interesting dining room decorated with carpets, Tuareg swords, mini deer heads and even a pair of skis. It serves roast chicken, chips, *harissa* (red-chilli paste)and the like.

Restaurant Nina (meals DA400; ☽ lunch & dinner) Round the corner from the Hôtel Ilamane, this is a very popular place whose outside tables fill up at lunchtime. It serves a tasty range of Algerian dishes including *kefta* (meatballs made from seasoned, minced lamb), tagines, grilled camel and home-made *harissa*.

Patisserie du Hoggar has nice a nice selection of cakes and pastries as well as a few tables at which to sit and scoff them. For self-caterers there's a minimart and several fruit stalls near the roundabout at the top of av Emir Abdelkader.

Shopping

There are plenty of souvenir shops along av Emir Abdelkader offering a good selec-tion of Tuareg jewellery and crafts. Things to look out for include heavy silver crosses and agate pendants, Tuareg swords, leather bags and camel saddles and the obligatory *taguelmoust* (Tuareg veil) to shield you from the desert wind. A good shop to try is the Artisanat Traditionnel Boutique le Hoggar, which has a selection of jewellery and tradi-tional clothing and a very friendly owner.

Getting There & Away

AIR

The **Air Algérie** (☎ 029-344499; place Emir Abdelkader) office is in the town centre near the two main banks. The airport is 12km north of town, off to the left of the main road.

There are six direct services a week to Al-giers (DA1400, two hours), and one weekly service to Djanet (DA4100, 50 minutes), Ghardaïa (DA9800, two hours 20 minutes), In Salah (DA5499, one hour 40 minutes) and Ouargla (DA9300, one hour 45 min-utes). There are also direct international flights to Paris and Marseille (France).

BUS

The *gare routière* (bus station) is in the northwestern part of town, a 15-minute walk from the centre. If you arrive late at night, or are heading out early in the morn-ing, it is standard practice to doss down at the station. The bus schedule is displayed on a board inside the building and there are daily departures to In Salah (DA900, 11 hours), Ghardaïa (DA1500, 19 to 20 hours) and Ouargla (DA1600, 22 hours). Make sure you reserve your ticket the day before departure.

There are also a number of private bus companies whose offices are mostly centred on the northwestern end of the town centre. Most of the buses are 30-seater Toyota mini-buses. You can reserve a seat in advance, and the buses tend to leave in the evening or early morning. Destination include In Salah (DA1000, 11 hours) and Ghardaïa (DA2000, 19 to 20 hours).

4WD

About 2.5km from the centre of town on the In Guezzam road there's a 4WD stop with share 4WD taxis heading for In Guezzam and beyond. They leave on a fill-up-and-go basis or if there's a group of you it's possible to hire the whole vehicle. It costs DA1500

TAMANRASSET, DJANET & THE SAHARA

per seat to In Guezzam or DA15,000 to hire the whole car. It is also possible to hire an entire car to go straight through to Agadez in Niger. The price is negotiable but it should cost about DA40,000 for the trip.

TAXI
Long-distance taxis depart from the town centre on av Emir Abdelkader just down from the Hotel Tinhanane. They depart on a leave-when-full basis and it's best to get here very early in the morning. Destinations include In Salah (DA1000, nine to 10 hours), Ghardaïa (DA2000, 17 hours), Arak (DA600, five hours) and Ouargla (DA1200, 19 hours).

TRUCK
Opposite the 4WD station on the In Guezzam road is a truck stop where large goods trucks and heavy vehicles heading for Niger pitch up. Travellers sometimes hitch rides on one of these for a price, although it's likely they don't end up with a seat in the cab but rather on top of the truck. The price for this is negotiable but the cost for a ride to In Guezzam or Niger should be a few hundred dinars.

AROUND TAMANRASSET
Tamanrasset is situated in the mountainous region of black volcanic rock known as the Hoggar Mountains, home to Tahat (3000m) and Assekrem (2800m), and agencies can arrange all manner of trips in the Hoggar and beyond.

Assekrem أسيكرم
Immediately north of Tamanrasset, and part of the Ahaggar National Park, is the plateau of **Atakor**, a Tolkein-esque land of dry earth and dark peaks, at the heart of which is Assekrem, 73km from Tamanrasset, where Charles de Foucauld (see the boxed text, opposite) built his hermitage in 1911. Without your own transport, getting out to the Atakor plateau can be difficult, but it's worth making the effort to get up to Assekrem.

The route up to Assekrem is long and bumpy but the spectacular landscape more than makes up for it. You drive through a warped landscape where strange mountains rise up from the rocky black plateau – many of them deeply scored as if they have been mauled by some mythical beast –

eventually reaching the heights of Assekrem where you'll be greeted with outstanding vistas over the sea of mountains below. Assekrem means 'the End of the World' in the language of the Tuareg and it's easy to see why; standing up here it feels like you're as far away from civilization as can be.

SIGHTS & ACTIVITIES
It takes about five hours to reach the *refuge* (mountain hut) at Assekrem – a collection of stone walled bungalows and a camp site, where visitors stay the night. From here it's obligatory to visit the hermitage of Charles de Foucauld, a monk who came to live in the Hoggar in early last century. He chose to build a simple stone hermitage up on Assekrem (see the boxed text, opposite, for further details). The hermitage is on top of the Assekrem plateau and can only be reached on foot, which takes about 30 minutes from the *refuge*. A few monks from Foucauld's order live up at the hermitage and say mass every morning in the small simple chapel; guests are welcome to join in.

You can't come to Assekrem and not get up for the sunrise. The view from the *refuge* itself is stunning enough and in the cooler months, the slopes surrounding it are peppered with wildflowers, which the sunrise infuses with a dusky pink glow. The best way to experience the sunrise, though, is to climb the hundred or so metres up to the hermitage. This involves getting up at about 5am (the folks at the *refuge* will oblige you by giving you a wake-up knock) and you won't regret it. Watching the light slowly creep across the wild and tortured mountains spread out beneath you is a sight you're unlikely to forget.

SLEEPING
The only place to stay at Assekrem is the **refuge** (B&B per person DA1200) whose price also includes dinner. The refuge consists of a simple stone-walled building containing a couple of dormitories, as well as a few twin rooms in bungalows away from the main building and basic squat toilets away from the sleeping and eating areas. Guides and guests alike reunite for meals and tea in a homely living room, kept warm by a large fireplace. Dinners are taken *en famille* (all together) and are a good opportunity to

CHARLES DE FOUCAULD

Playboy adventurer turned Saharan priest, Père de Foucauld (1858–1916) was born Vicomte Charles Eugene de Foucauld to a wealthy aristocratic family in Strasbourg, France. There was no early indication of the path his life would take; Foucauld was fond of the good life and loved nothing better than to splash the cash on parties, champagne, foie gras and the ladies. He was also short on self-discipline and, while stationed with the French Army in North Africa, got into trouble because of his unruly behaviour. In a twist befitting a Shakespeare play, he turned his back on the army, disguised himself as a rabbi and headed off to explore the hill country of Morocco.

As the story goes, Foucauld found himself deeply touched by the faith of the Muslim people and returned to France a new man, entering a Trappist order at the age of 31. After several years of monastic pilgrimages he was ordained as a priest in 1901 and headed for the Sahara, first to Beni Abbès and then to Tamanrasset, where he discovered a passion for the desert and concocted the idea of a superabstemious religious order that would spend the majority of the day in prayer and live on a paltry diet of dates and barley. No surprises then that this didn't catch on and that the order had a membership of one (himself) during his lifetime. Christianity didn't exactly set the fires burning in the desert either and he only converted one person during his time in Tamanrasset.

Foucauld spent much of his days in the desert striving to get closer to the Tuareg, studying their culture and language and translating the gospels into Tamashek. He also developed the first ever French/Tamashek dictionary. In 1911, he chose the wild and remote Assekrem as the place to construct his hermitage and spent much of his time there before his death. He was assassinated in 1916 by a group of rebels who were resisting French attempts to infiltrate the Algerian Sahara. His body is buried in the cemetery in El-Goléa.

Charles de Foucauld was beatified in Rome in November 2006. His religious order still exists and today many people come on pilgrimages to Assekrem to walk in his footsteps and feel his spirit.

---

chat with the other guests. The food is good and plentiful – you'll usually get salads, couscous, meat stews and fruit. It is freezing at night so make sure you bring plenty of warm clothes as well as a torch (flashlight) in case the (rather unreliable) lights go out. There is also space for camping.

If you're not on a prearranged tour, you can reserve a room at the *refuge* through **Tim Missaw Tours** (☎ 029 347516/061, 649221; tim -missaw@hotmail.com), whose owner also runs the *refuge*. The organisation can also bring you up here; it costs DA7000 per person for a return transfer from Tamanrasset.

GETTING THERE & AWAY

The only way to get up to Assekrem is to hire a 4WD and driver from one of the agencies in Tamanrasset. It is not possible to hire a vehicle without a driver. It will cost from €80 per person per day including food and accommodation. You definitely can't walk there, although the Tamanrasset-based agencies can organise trips with camels from Tamanrasset if you want to do it this way.

TASSILI DU HOGGAR تسيلي الهوڨار

Traversed for many centuries by nomad camel caravans bearing cloth, salt and spices, the Tassili du Hoggar, part of the Ahaggar National Park, is a set of sedimentary rock plateaus that begins approximately 300km south of Tamanrasset and extends to the Niger border. The plateau is characterised by some of the most haunting landscapes imaginable, presenting a mind-boggling series of photo opportunities. Whale-back boulders and craggy mountains share billing space with enormous figures of sculpted rock; squat round hulks stand alone like giant solitary mushrooms; and sharp pinnacles shoot to breathtaking heights, clinging together in clusters to form bizarre city skylines. Great swaths of creamy sand fill the spaces in between.

Information

The only way to get to the Tassili du Hoggar is on a tour, and it is included on many of the longer itineraries, often as part of a trip from Tamanrasset to Djanet. All of the travel agencies in Tamanrasset and Djanet will be able to arrange a trip out here for you. If you're driving your own car through the Algerian Sahara you'll need to be accompanied by a guide anyway.

Despite what you might imagine there's plenty of animal life in the Sahara, although you're not likely to encounter a great deal. If you're lucky, in the Tassili du Hoggar you might see gazelle, tiny, big-eared desert mice, or fennec – a desert fox. If you're unlucky, you might come across a viper or a scorpion. This is not usually a problem in the cooler winter months but be aware that scorpions like to hide in rock crevasses and sometimes shoes; and vipers have been known to hide just beneath the surface of the sand, so don't run around with bare feet.

Sights & Activities

Most trips to this part of the country are by 4WD and you'll normally drive a few hours a day, in between which you'll stop for walks, to climb up dunes, to look at rock paintings or to gather wood for that evening's fire.

You'll be assaulted by jaw-dropping beauty on a daily basis in the Tassili du Hoggar, making it difficult to pick favourites. But possible highlights of a trip here include **El-Ghessant**, whose rock formations look from a distance like a medieval fortress, and **Tin Tarabine**, with its cracked earth and impressive examples of rock engravings. Perhaps the most beautiful sight of all is **Tinakachaker**, which is dominated by a great stone cathedral. All around it are gnarled and twisted stone fingers forming a series of valleys and corridors; and there are massive dunes from whose heights you'll appreciate the dreamlike splendour of the landscape to the full. At night it takes on a different character; the wind murmurs through the valleys and dark stone figures loom from above like the monsters of childhood nightmares.

Sleeping & Eating

There are no camp sites or huts in the Tassili du Hoggar, and on any trip here you'll almost certainly be bivouacking out in the open, but lying out in your sleeping bag under a starry sky is all part of the fun. If you're on a trip with a travel agency, you'll be accompanied by a cook as well as a guide, who'll concoct three meals a day and provide plenty of tea breaks. If you're lucky they might make a traditional Tuareg

bread made from semolina and then baked beneath hot coals in the sand.

IN GUEZZAM إن قزام

This town is 416km south of Tamanrasset and is the last place in Algeria before you cross into Niger. The Algerian border post is 10km south of In Guezzam, so there's no need to stop here long. There's not much to do anyway; there's no bank and one restaurant. Border formalities happen here.

Sleeping & Eating

There is only one restaurant in In Guezzam which has OK food and also allows you to stay overnight for a couple of hundred dinars. In theory it's open 24 hours although this is rarely the case in practice. If you have a tent it is possible to find places to pitch it and free-camp in the environs of town.

Getting There & Away

Daily 4WD shared taxis go between Tamanrasset and In Guezzam on a fill-up-and-go basis every morning at DA1500 a seat. Some people hitch a ride in a goods truck for a couple of hundred dinars. But if you're going to Niger, you are far better off getting a group together in Tamanrasset and hiring a 4WD. From Tamanrasset it's also possible to arrange a lift in a truck to Arlit or Agadez in Niger. Stock up with as much fuel as possible in Tamanrasset as there have been reports of fuel shortages in In Guezzam.

DJANET & THE ROUTE DU TASSILI N'AJJER
جنت وطريق التاسيلي الناجر

This route heads south from Hassi Messaoud along the Gassi Touil, a large *oued* between two sections of the Grand Erg Oriental, to In Amenas, 730km to the southeast and very close to the Libyan border through Illizi and on to Djanet and the Tassili N'Ajjer National Park. There is little traffic along this route and unless you have your own car it's difficult to traverse.

Djanet is a sleepy little oasis with whitewashed buildings, a large *palmeraie* and a relaxed air. It is also the starting point for tours into the Tassili N'Ajjer National Park, and during the high season, plane-loads of tourists from Europe arrive in the town each week. The Tassili N'Ajjer National Park has one of the most important collections of prehistoric cave art in the world. It holds more than 15,000 drawings and engravings which, like an open-air history lesson, tell the story of thousands of years of human evolution and environmental change within this area of the Sahara.

ILLIZI إليزى
Nearly 300km south of In Amenas, Illizi is the main settlement between there and Djanet. For a long time Illizi was called 'Fort Polignac' and was a military post created in 1904 by colonialists in order to keep an eye on the Libyan border.

The town boasts a fuel station, hospital, basic shop, customs post and a hotel. There are some interesting rock sites near here and a travel agency.

If you really get stranded here there are two flights a week to Algiers (DA1100, three hours) and one a week to Ghardaïa (DA7300, two hours 10 minutes). The airport is 5km north of town. The only hotel here is the **Hotel Tahleb Larbi** (☎ 029 421733; fax 029 421181; s/d DA1100/1600) and there's also a camp site.

Mezrirene Aventure (☎ in France 49 30 32 70 37 70; fax 029 422323; www.mezrirene.com) can organise a variety of short excursions to sites around Illizi as well as longer expeditions from Illizi to Djanet. Tours cost from around €50 per person per day on foot and from €70 for tours in 4WDs. It also runs an auberge and camp site for people on their tours.

AROUND ILLIZI
Sights of interest near the town include **Tankena**, which has a notable collection of early stone tools, and **Tamdjert**, which has good examples of Neolithic paintings, including wonderfully fluid pictures of horse-drawn chariots, hunters and dromedaries, as well some writing in Tifinagh – some of the most ancient characters in the world. For more on rock art, see p80.

DJANET جانت
The main town of the Tassili, Djanet is a pretty place with its own colour scheme: whitewashed buildings with blue doors line the main streets, set off by dark blue and gold lampposts that would look more at home in an English seaside town. The setting is charming too – the town is built on the edge of a *palmeraie* so feels quite lush and it is dwarfed by the mountains that surround it. The town centre is tiny with a post office, bank, basic restaurants and shops, although there's no internet café.

Quiet during the week, the town suddenly bursts into life come the weekend when dozens of package tourists arrive on flights from Paris and Marseille (France). They are all here for the main attraction – the stunning collection of rock paintings in the nearby Tassili N'Ajjer National Park.

Orientation
Central Djanet is tiny so it's impossible to get lost. Whether you enter the town from the north or the south you'll end up on the main street which has a collection of cafés, a couple of banks, a post office, a hospital and the Camping Zeriba. West of the main street is a large covered market and the town's *palmeraie*.

Information
There's as large hospital in Ifri, 7km out of town, as well as a smaller hospital in the town centre. The Office National du Parc Tassili (OPTN) is next to the museum and issues permits to visit the Tassili N'Ajjer National Park for DA100 per person, although your travel agency will usually organise this. There's also a Banque Nationale d'Algérie and a Banque de l'Agriculture et du Développement Rural on the main street. Both are open Sunday to Thursday 9am to 3pm and both offer foreign exchange although neither changes travellers cheques. There's also an **ONAT office** (☎ 029 475361; place du Marché).

TRAVEL AGENCIES
There are several travel agencies in Djanet, all of whom offer excursions to the Tassili N'Ajjer. Most of them work in collaboration with European tour agencies and in the high season it can sometimes be difficult to arrange a last-minute tour. Most agencies don't have offices in the centre of town, and those that do exist aren't always open. In addition, you won't usually be permitted to join a group and will have to arrange an individually tailored tour. If you haven't

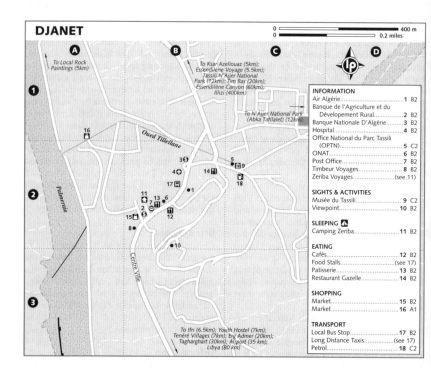

DJANET

0 — 400 m
0 — 0.2 miles

INFORMATION
Air Algérie...1 B2
Banque de l'Agriculture et du
  Dévelopement Rural........................2 B2
Banque Nationale D'Algérie...............3 B2
Hospital..4 B2
Office National du Parc Tassili
  (OPTN)...5 C2
ONAT...6 B2
Post Office...7 B2
Timbeur Voyages...............................8 B2
Zeriba Voyages..........................(see 11)

SIGHTS & ACTIVITIES
Musée du Tassili................................9 C2
Viewpoint...10 B2

SLEEPING
Camping Zeriba.................................11 B2

EATING
Cafés..12 B2
Food Stalls.................................(see 17)
Patisserie..13 B2
Restaurant Gazelle............................14 B2

SHOPPING
Market..15 B2
Market..16 A1

TRANSPORT
Local Bus Stop..................................17 B2
Long Distance Taxis...................(see 17)
Petrol...18 C2

---

arranged a tour in advance your best bet is to contact Zeriba Voyages, whose office is usually open and able to organise excursions at short notice, or ONAT. Prices range from €50 to €80 a day including food and equipment, depending on how many people there are in your party.

Essendilène Voyages (☎ 029 475295; www.essend ilene-voyages.com) This outfit organises trips all over southern Algeria and down into the Ténéré and Aïr regions of Niger. If asked well in advance it can also organise a number of specialised trips into the desert including yoga and trekking, art therapy and family trips for children over the age of two or three. They are also involved in projects that help the local community benefit from tourism.

Rêves et Nature (☎ 029 475860; www.voyages-tim beur.com) As well as camel and 4WD group and individu- ally tailored tours, Rêves et Nature offers assisted 4WD and motorbike tours through the desert, where you drive your own vehicle and are accompanied by an experienced guide. If you're going to arrive in Djanet on your own, it can help put you in touch with like-minded travellers so you can share the expenses of a trip.

Timbeur Voyages (☎ 029 75270; www.voyages-tim beur.com) With offices next to the market this is one of Djan- et's most established agencies. It offers short expeditions

such as trips to Erg Admer and Tagharght as well as longer expeditions to the Tassili N'Ajjer and the Tassili du Hoggar. These cost from about €50 per person per day including airport transfers, taxes, guide, cook and all food.

Timtar Expeditions (☎ 029 346038; www.timtar.com) Has camel, trekking and 4WD expeditions as well as interesting alternatives to the usual treks such as family circuits. Between October and May it also offers week-long and group lessons on how to drive in the desert.

Zeriba Voyage (☎ 061 382853/346924; www.zeriba voyage.com) Based at the hotel of the same name, Zeriba Voyage can organise a variety of excursions, the most popular being trips to Tassili N'Ajjer and longer trips from Djanet to Tamanrasset. This organisation is a good bet if you arrive in Djanet without a pre-arranged tour. Tours cost from around €60 per person per day for a trek into the Tassili N'Ajjer with pack animals.

Sights & Activities

For magnificent **views** over town walk up to the top of the hill just behind the town centre, taking the steps opposite the market. The **Musée du Tassili** (☽ 8am-5pm, closed Thu & Fri) has a small collection of exhibits detailing the history and environment of the region. One room concentrates on the formation of

Tassili N'Ajjer plateau and on its animal and plant life and has some gazelle and sheep skulls, ostrich eggs and ceramics. Another room contains a beautiful photographic exhibition of the rock paintings of the region. The best exhibition contains reproductions of nomad life, including a life-sized *zeriba* and Tuareg jewellery, weaponry and musical instruments.

About 30 minutes' walk out of the town centre to the north is the **Ksar Azellouaz**, the remains of one of the oldest original settlements in this area. It looks quite romantic from the outside and you can wander round the old streets and hollow, crumbling building but the romance is ruined by all of the scattered tin cans and animal skulls and bones. Further afield, about an hour's walk north of town, there are some **rock paintings** including elephant, cattle and giraffe. Walk out past the covered market; turn north and continue past the *palmeraie,* and after about an hour you'll hit the sealed road. Turn left – the paintings are hidden in the rocks about 50m in front of you. It's best to ask in town first before you head out there. If you're staying at Zeriba staff will probably give you a lift.

Festivals & Events
The biggest festival in Djanet is the **Sebiba**. Tuareg from around the Tassili N'Ajjer region meet in Djanet to remember and to reconstruct an ancient peace agreement that ended a long conflict between two warring Tuareg tribes – the El-Mihane and the Azellouaz. The event lasts for 10 days leading up to the reconstruction, all in traditional costume, of the last battle between the two tribes. Women in their most beautiful jewellery cheer on the men.

Sleeping
There's not much choice in Djanet. If you don't have a vehicle the only viable option is Camping Zeriba on the central drag. With a car you could stay at the youth hostel or the hotel called Ténéré Villages, both about 7km out of town. At the time of research Timbeur Voyages was constructing a new 20-room lodge on the outskirts of Djanet.

Youth hostel (☎ 029 470261; dm DA200) Djanet's youth hostel is located 7km from the town centre off the airport road and has 30 beds in three- and four-bed dorms. The rooms

are rather cramped and the showers could be cleaner but it's the cheapest option in Djanet. There's an airy courtyard and a TV room, and meals are available on demand.

Ténéré Villages (☎ 029 470049; www.tenerevoyages .com; s/d/t DA2500/2800/4000) Seven and a half kilometres from Djanet in Ifri, on the way out to the airport. This place has bright airy doubles in rondavels or bungalows, decorated with imitation rock paintings. The best thing about this place is its restaurant framed with a big old balcony giving splendid views out onto the dunes, mountains and the Tassili Plateau. There's also a great traditional tented area where you can take snacks and drinks bang on the side of the dunes. The only down side is the distance from town – it's only worth staying here if you have a car.

Camping Zeriba (☎ 065 594472, 062 067719, ☎ / fax 029 475546; www.zeribavoyage.com; r with/without bathroom DA3200/1500, camping DA400) This is the only place to stay in the centre of Djanet and it's located right on the main street. It's a large friendly place with a variety of rooms; the rooms with bathrooms also have TVs. The place is not in great nick but at the time of writing was undergoing renovations. There's a large area for camping, a *zeriba* in which to take tea and a restaurant. There's no menu and meals normally consist of soup followed by couscous and meat then fruit. Zeriba also has a tour agency.

Eating
There are a few small restaurants around the town centre serving the usual chicken, chips, couscous and stews. They're all pretty similar but you could try Restaurant Gazelle for tasty stews and couscous, or there's a nice large café opposite the bus station which is full of locals and a good place for coffee and people-watching. There are also several snack stalls selling eggs, peanuts and tea behind the bus stops. A great little patisserie next to ONAT sells a selection of French and Algerian pastries. In the evenings it does good pizzas to take away or you can cram in at the counter with the locals. You can pick up fruit, vegetables and meat at a small market just off the main road.

Shopping
The main drag contains quite a few tourist-oriented shops selling jewellery, handicrafts,

postcards and the like. They can be quite expensive though and you're best off heading to the market for cheaper prices. There's a market just off the main road containing fruit and veg stalls, a couple of tourist stalls and several butchers – you may even see severed camel heads on display. There's a much bigger, mostly covered market between the *oued* and the *palmeraie* selling clothing, shoes, cooking pots, electronics, and even spare parts. This is also where you can find the best-value jewellery and crafts. There are a couple of stalls on the outskirts of the market on the *palmeraie* side where you can see the artists at work.

Getting There & Away

AIR

There is an **Air Algérie** (☎ 029 475032; ☿ 8am-noon & 1-4pm, closed Thu afternoon & Fri) office in the town centre. The airstrip is 35km from town. Air Algérie flies twice a week to Algiers (DA13,500, two to three hours), and once a week to Ouargla (DA9000, 1½ hours) and Tamanrasset (DA4000, 50 minutes). **Aigle Azur** (www.aigle-azur.fr) operates direct international fights to Paris and Marseille (France).

BUS

There are no long-distance buses to and from Djanet. Minibuses leave from the town centre to go to the surrounding villages and cost around DA15 per ride.

TAXI

Shared taxis leave for Illizi from the town centre at around 6am daily. The journey takes around six hours and costs DA1000. Taxis also head for the Libyan border at Tin Alkoum but it is currently closed to foreigners.

AROUND DJANET

The reason most people come to this part of the world is to trek in the Tassili N'Ajjer and see its famous rock paintings; but this area has a great deal more on offer. About half an hour's drive out of Djanet, off the road to the airport, is **Tagharghart**. Hidden among the rock faces and the sand dunes is one of the most famous engravings in this area, called **La Vache qui Pleure**, or Crying Cows. It features three graceful, long-horned cattle and is so called because of the teardrops falling from their eyes. It is thought to date

from around 6000 years ago. Near the engravings is a fantastic camping spot, where you can bivouac at the top of the dunes with superb views over the mountains and the Tassili plateau itself.

Also worth a look is **Erg Admer**. About 20km west of Djanet, this is the place to come for a trek through those stereotypical sculpted dunes or to have mint tea at sunset. For the more adventurous, many tour companies in Djanet can arrange for a few hours of dune skiing.

About 30km north of Djanet off the road towards Illizi is **Tim Ras**, where wide sandy planes dotted with jagged mountains give way to broad boulevards of pockmarked rocks, towering like huge deformed beehives – a magical place to spend the night.

More than 60km north of Djanet is the **Essendilène Canyon**, known for its incredible biodiversity. Inside you'll find palm trees, acacias and cool green pools of water.

TASSILI N'AJJER NATIONAL PARK

تاسيلي الناجر الحوض الوصني

This Unesco World Heritage site covers an area of about 80,000 sq km. Tassili N'Ajjer means 'Plateau of Chasms'; and the chasms, canyons and stone forests of this strange, prehistoric landscape, formed by thousand of years of volcanic activity and erosion, are home to a dramatic open-air art exhibition. Imprinted in hidden caves and on rock faces are some 15,000 rock paintings that tell the story of the evolution of human and animal life in this part of the Sahara. They recall times when the Sahara was green and fertile; when men hunted in the valleys and lion, elephant, antelope and buffalo roamed the plains. They also attest to the more 'recent' history of the Sahara and you'll see illustrations of horses, chariots and dromedaries. It's thought that the first human beings settled here more than two million years ago and that the Tassili rock paintings date back as far as 7000 and 6000 BC. For in-depth information on Algeria's rock art, see p80.

The existence of such paintings would be reason enough to visit, but the surrounding landscape makes a stay here even more incredible. The majority of the paintings are up on a plateau, some 600m above Djanet, and can only be reached on foot – it's a four-hour climb to the top, scrambling up rock faces and through narrow, shady canyons.

Information

You are not allowed to enter the area without an official guide. Treks up to the Tassili N'Ajjer plateau are the mainstay of the travel agencies in Djanet so once there it should be possible to arrange a trip heading out within days, for which you'll usually be accompanied by a guide, a herder, and several pack animals to carry your bags, food, water and cooking equipment.

The Tassili N'Ajjer plateau is accessed via one of two very steep passes, which can only be traversed on foot. The most common starting point for trips onto the plateau is Akba Tafilalet, 12km east of Djanet. You're likely to be driven out at an ungodly hour of the morning to this pass where you'll be met by your pack animals. From here, the climb to the top of the plateau, through a series of steep slopes and gorges, takes two to three hours, and once you reach the top it's another two hours to Tamrit, the first camping spot.

The best time to go to the park is November to April as this is the coolest time of year. From May to September the daytime temperatures can prove to be uncomfortably hot and can get as high as 40°C. Bear in mind that during the winter it can be freezing up on the plateau at night. Take plenty of warm clothes and a suitable sleeping bag.

This is not a national park in the traditional sense; you won't come across park wardens and there is no official entry gate but it is a nationally protected area and you must act accordingly. The rock paintings are very fragile. Don't use a flash when photographing them and never wet the paintings in order to get a brighter picture.

Sights & Activities

Tamrit is the first sight you'll see when you reach the top of the plateau – a vast mass of weathered, sand-covered stone and conical towers. It's also home to the **Valley of the Cypresses**. The trees are thousands of years old and you'll find a handful of these knotted giants spread out along a surprisingly green valley. Tamrit has plenty of good camping spots and is usually the base for the first day or so of exploration on the plateau.

There are a number of sights of interest here. About one hour's walk north of Tamrit is **Tan Zoumaitek** – the highlight of which is a large fresco painted in ochre and white

featuring a number of beautifully fluid scenes. You'll see distinctive, round-headed figures, including a mother and child, and a couple of jewel-draped, tattooed women who appear to be on the point of dancing; also interesting are a long-horned mouflon and a curious circular creature that's reminiscent of a jellyfish. An hour's walk to the east from Tamrit is **Timenzouzine** – where you'll find an impressive elephant, engraved on a flat slab on the ground, complete with stepladder for getting a better view.

The next major site on from Tamrit is **Sefar**, some 12km or about a four-hour walk away. It's a tough but spectacular hike through avenues of stone pillars. Sefar has some of the most famous paintings in the park, representing a number of different periods. You'll see battle scenes, archers, antelope, giraffes, masks and, most famously, the Great God of Sefar – a devilish-looking horned figure, rising high above the others.

A good two days' walk 30km south of Sefar is **Jabbaren**, perhaps the most famous sight of all, which features thousands of paintings carried out by successive civilisations, including graceful cattle, horned goddesses, hippopotamuses, dancers and round-headed figures.

In three days you could go up the Akba Tafilalet pass and get to see Tamrit, Tan Zoumaitek and Timenzouzine; four or five days and you could make it to Sefar and back. To reach Jabbaren you would need to do a circular seven-day trek – taking in the aforementioned sights, walking another serious two days to Jabbaren, then descending at **Akba Aghoum pass**, south of the entry point at Akba Tafilalet. Jabbaren can also be reached via the Aghoum Pass, on a back-breaking one-day tour involving a steep and punishing climb starting at the break of dawn to see the paintings and descending again before dark.

Getting There & Away

The only way to get to the Tassili N'Ajjer is on a guided tour. There are a number of different options offered by the agencies in Djanet ranging from a one-day trip to Jabbaren to a comprehensive seven-day circuit. Prices start from €50 to €60 a day depending on the number of people in your party. For further details on Djanet's travel agencies, see p191.

Directory

CONTENTS

ACCOMMODATION

In this guide 'budget' refers to establishments that charge under DA1500 a night for a double room; 'midrange' refers to establishments that charge between DA1500 and DA3500; and 'top end' refers to all establishments that charge over DA3500 for a double room for the night.

Outside of the large northern cities or the tourist towns of the south, really good hotel facilities are few and far between. Single rooms are rare but you'll normally be charged a slightly reduced 'single' price to stay in a twin or double room. Prices tend to stay the same all year although you can often get discounts during the low season.

PRACTICALITIES

- Newspapers and magazines – The major French-language dailies are *Le Quotidien d'Oran*, *El-Watan*, and *Le Soir d'Algérie*. The most popular Arabic-language paper is *El Khabar*.

- Radio and TV – There are three main state-owned radio stations. Channel 1 is in Arabic, Channel 2 in Berber and Channel 3 in French. There are also around 20 local radio stations. The main state-run TV station is called ENTV.

- Electricity – Algeria uses the 220V system. Outlets take European-style two-pin round plugs.

- Weights and Measures – Algeria uses the metric system.

The high tourist season runs from November to March in the south when temperatures are cooler; and the warmer summer months of June to September in the north. At any time of year it pays to make reservations well in advance for accommodation in Algiers; the lack of availability there is notorious. It's also advisable to make reservations for resorts along the Mediterranean coast. In the south you can usually find a room without a problem but the nicest establishments might be full with tour groups during the high season. Some camp sites and guesthouses in the south close during the hotter summer months of May to September, when the weather is uncomfortably hot and there are fewer tourists.

Auberges

A much nicer alternative to hotels are locally run auberges, also known as a gîte or *chambres d'hôtes*. In the south these are often called *campings* and although their purpose is not as a camp site in the traditional sense, they often have space where you can put up your tent and have access to shower facilities and meals. Normally oriented towards the tourist trade, these places tend to have more character than hotels, with rooms in bungalows, traditional-style houses or rondavels and plenty of local artwork and fabrics on display. Rooms tend to be simple, often with shared facilities, but are always spotless. At the majority of auberges you pay per person on a half- or full-board basis. Meals are usually taken with the other guests and the emphasis is on providing good quality regional cooking. Many of these places will also organise activities and tours.

Camping

There are a number of camp sites in the country, particularly along the tourist trail in the Sahara. In the north the sites are limited to a few low-key resorts along the coast. However, due to years of neglect during the '90s, many camp sites are closed or open only sporadically. Those that are open often lack decent facilities. Camp sites cost between DA200 and DA500 per person, and there is usually an additional charge of about DA200 if you have a car. It's not usually possible to hire camping equipment.

You will also come across guesthouses (called, rather confusingly *campings*), which cater to foreign tourists. Many have camp sites attached or space to pitch a tent. These are more expensive than ordinary camp sites but tend to be clean and well managed with excellent shared facilities and good food.

Hostels

There is a system of YHA (Youth Hostel Association) hostels throughout the country offering dorm beds for DA100 to DA150. The standard is normally basic with spartan dorms and shared facilities. There's usually also some sort of common room with a TV or games, as well as a basic café serving snacks. The major drawback is that they are often inconveniently located; and they are not like the backpackers hostels you'll find in Southern Africa. You're unlikely to meet other travellers there, they aren't all that secure and they aren't really suitable for single women – as there are so few women travellers in Algeria, you're liable to end up in a dorm all on your own.

Hotels

At the budget end you can expect a basic double room with sink, shared facilities and sometimes a fan. At the lowest end of the scale, hotels only have toilets, not bathroom facilities and you will need to use a neighbouring *hammam* (bathroom) or public showers. The standard of cleanliness varies greatly from the spic and span to the downright filthy, with some cheap hotels seeming to double up as brothels. Always ask to see the room first.

Midrange hotels differ greatly. Many are state run and tend to be run down, with indifferent service and shabby interiors; but they are often the only viable choice and are normally well located. You'll also find more modern, private places oriented at tourists and businessmen. At the midrange level you'll normally get satellite TV, airconditioning and hot water. Most hotels at this price range include breakfast in the room rate, which usually consists of coffee, bread and jam, and if you're lucky a yogurt or some pastries. The majority of hotels in this price range have their own restaurant and many in the south have swimming pools. In this category you'll find many establishments with bars selling alcohol.

In the north many of the hotel buildings date back to the colonial days and still have the original fittings and furnishings: window shutters, washbasin, bidet, wardrobe and a bed which may be so old it wouldn't be out of place in a museum.

At the luxury end of the scale, accommodation is in fairly short supply in most Algerian towns, and plush international-class hotels tend to be limited to Algiers and the big northern cities. Hotels at the top end of the scale often accept credit cards, many will change foreign currency and some have wireless internet access. They will usually have a choice of good quality restaurants and a bar.

ACTIVITIES
Cycling

Cycling isn't a common way to visit Algeria, but there are a small number of travellers who visit the country by bicycle. As long as you have sufficient time and are willing to rough it, cycling can be a fun way to see the country. There are no specific cycleways, but the roads are in good condition. You'll certainly be an oddity cycling on the main highways and will have to pay strict attention – Algerian drivers are careless at the best of times.

Cycling in southern Algeria can present a problem, however. Due to current restrictions you'll need to be accompanied, which means getting a guide in a car to follow you. The best time to cycle in the Sahara is the cooler, drier period from November to March.

A highly recommended contact is **Bicycle Africa** (☎ /fax 1-206-767 0848; www.ibike.org/bikeafrica; 4887 Columbia Drive South, Seattle, WA98108-1919, USA). Alternatively, **Sablé0** (☎ 33 06 79 95 78 44; www.sableo.com; 1 Lot Jules Comes 66720 Tautavel, France) offers regular cycling trips to the Hoggar Mountains.

Desert Trekking

There are numerous trekking options in Algeria, the most popular being the Hoggar, the Tassili N'Ajjer and the Grand Ergs. Options include walking, 4WD tours, camel treks and even motorbike tours. In the deep south treks are normally organised for small groups, and you must be accompanied by a qualified guide before undertaking such a trek (see p66).

Dune Skiing

A fun way to explore the dunes of the Grand Ergs or Erg Admer is on a pair of skis. This is not often on official itineraries but many companies can arrange this for you. It's literally a question of hauling yourself up the nearest dune, strapping on a pair of real skis and bombing down again with a trail of sand flying behind you. Agencies that can arrange this include Zeriba Voyages (p192) in Djanet.

Rock-Climbing

The area around Tamanrasset in the Hoggar Mountains is the best place for rock-climbing in Algeria, and its spectacular rock formations attract a small but serious number of rock climbers from Europe. Most of the tour companies in Tamanrasset will arrange rock-climbing tours given advance notice. For further information you could also check out *Escalade au Sahara* published by DP Editions, which gives detailed illustrations and instructions of the different routes you can take (complete with advice on equipment and timescale) and includes plenty of beautiful colour photos of the Hoggar Mountains.

Watersports

There are many ways to enjoy Algeria's stunning coastline other than just swimming or sunbathing. Sailing boats, snorkelling and windsurfing equipment can often be hired in the major tourist spots and during the summer season it's possible to arrange scuba trips and fishing excursions.

BUSINESS HOURS

Banks are usually open from around 8.30am in the morning till 3.30pm in the afternoon, often with a one-hour break for lunch around noon. Shops and businesses will usually close a couple of hours later at around 5.30pm. Most cafés are open all day from around 9am to 9pm. Restaurants are open from around noon to 2pm for lunch and 7pm to 10pm for dinner.

The Algerian weekend is Thursday and Friday but several banks and offices open till around noon on Thursday.

During the holy month of Ramadan, most restaurants are closed and many businesses and shops will close early. Business hours will not be listed in this book unless they differ from the above.

CHILDREN

Algeria has few formal children's attractions or childcare facilities, however the strange landscapes of Southern Algeria are bound to make a profound impression on them. Algerians are family-oriented people who tend to be very friendly towards children and travelling with children can sometimes help to break the ice. Having said that, it can be difficult to travel independently with children in Algeria. Road journeys are long and uncomfortable and outside of Algiers it can be difficult to find canned baby food, wipes, disposable nappies or reliable medical facilities.

The best way to travel with children in Algeria is to organise things in advance. Indeed many tourist agencies in the south have developed special family- or child-friendly trips with a gentler pace. **Essendiléne Voyages** (☎ 029 475295; www.essendilene-voyages.com) in Djanet can organise special *voyages familiaux* for families with toddlers and up. **Terres d'Aventure** (☎ 33 08 25 84 78 00; www.terday.com) organises week-long trips in Algeria for kids as young as six.

CLIMATE CHARTS

In the north summers are hot and humid, and the winters mild and wet. In the Sahara summer is ferociously hot with daytime temperatures seldom below 25°C, but the nights can be very cold, particularly in the Hoggar region. Rainfall ranges from more than 1000mm per year in the northern mountains to zero in the Sahara. Some places go decades without a drop.

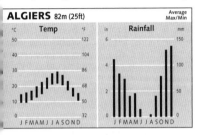

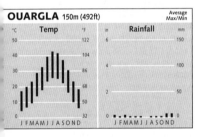

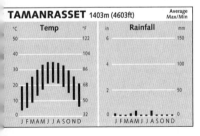

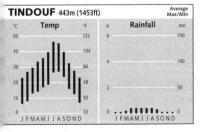

For further information on the best time to travel in Algeria see p14.

CUSTOMS

There's no longer any limit on importing bank notes or travellers cheques into the country. However, on entering the country you'll have to fill in a currency declaration form. On it you must list all the foreign currency that you're bringing into Algeria in both cash and travellers cheques as well as declare any valuables that you might be bringing into the country. This includes cameras, video equipment, jewellery and electrical goods. The form has space on which to record all official transactions you make during your stay; in theory this will be checked by customs when you leave the country and if it doesn't tally up you'll be fined. In reality this form is rarely checked and even it is, it will only be given a cursory glance.

You're allowed to bring in 200 cigarettes, 50g of perfume and 1L of liquor or 2L of wine. It is illegal to import weapons, handcuffs, body armour and binoculars. Algerian dinar must be exchanged before leaving the country.

You should also heed the restriction on taking artefacts out of the country. Over the years souvenir hunters and archaeological expeditions have targeted areas such as the Tassili N'Ajjer and the Hoggar. The penalties for doing so are severe and you could have to pay a large fine or might even end up in prison.

DANGERS & ANNOYANCES
Crime

Petty crime in Algeria has increased over the past few years, particularly in large urban centres of the north. Theft, mugging, carjacking, bag snatching and assault happen as well, especially in urban areas. Don't carry around large amounts of cash and keep an eye on your valuables, particularly when entering the Casbah in Algiers. The far south of the country tends to be safer when it comes to crime, but still watch out for pickpockets operating in the markets of large towns and in crowds. Also, don't leave valuables on display in the car and look for guarded overnight parking places wherever possible.

You might be less likely to get hassled by vendors or hustlers or ripped off in Algeria that you might be in other countries in the region however. There are relatively few tourists in Algeria and people have yet to become adept at taking them for a ride.

Earthquakes

Northern Algeria is a seismic zone. In 2003 an earthquake hit the area east of Algiers destroying houses, killing more than 2000 people and injuring 10,000 others. If you find yourself in an earthquake when you're inside, stay away from windows and exterior walls and stand in a doorway. If you are outside, find an open space away from buildings, trees and electric masts. If you're driving park on the side of the road and wait for the vibrations to end.

Road Safety

Algeria has some of the craziest drivers around so take extra care while driving in the country. Driving in the south presents a whole host of other problems from sand storms to camels crossing. Overland travel between major cities is not advised after dark, particularly in the mountainous region of the north. You should also watch out for false roadblocks in the north, particularly in the Kabylie region, which often leads to kidnapping. For further advice on travel on the roads see p76.

Security

Although safety in the region has increased, particularly in the south, travellers must still take precautions while travelling here and be aware of the risk of terrorism. Foreigners are not usually targets of violence, and mostly it is the security forces that are targeted, but the indiscriminate nature of bomb attacks on public places (such as markets and bus and train stations) makes caution extremely advisable.

This is particularly a problem in the north of the country and advice at the time of writing was that particular caution should be exercised around Algiers and in the northwest of the country. In 2004 the terrorist group GSPC – the Salafist Group for Call and Combat – identified foreigners as a legitimate target and in September 2006 it reiterated its terrorist agenda and links with Al-Qaeda; in 2007 it changed its name to Al-Qaeda. In 2006 there were a series of bomb attacks carried out in Algeria, one

of which involved a number of expatriate workers. The GSPC was also responsible for the kidnapping of more than 30 foreign tourists in 2003 in the desert and mountainous regions of southeastern Algeria, and the group has claimed responsibility for a number of small-scale attacks in Algeria and in neighbouring countries throughout 2006. A serious attack in April 2007, for which Al-Qaeda claims responsibility, killed dozens and injured more than 100 people.

Expeditions into the Sahara pose a whole host of other problems, from fuel shortages to sandstorms and bandits, and independent travel in the desert regions south of Ghardaïa is currently forbidden by the Algerian government (see the boxed text, p181). Before you undertake any expedition in Algeria, check out the security situation thoroughly.

EMBASSIES & CONSULATES
Algerian Embassies & Consulates

Australia (☎ 02-6286 7355; www.algeriaemb.org.au; 9 Terrigal Crescent, O'Malley, ACT 2606)

Canada (☎ 613-789-8505; www.ambassadeAlgérie.ca; 500 Wilbord Street, Ottowa, Ontario K1n 6N2)

France consulate (☎ 01 41 50 48 48; www.consulat-Algérie-bobigny.org; 17 rue Hector Berlioz, 93000 Bobigny); embassy (☎ 01 53 93 20 20; ambassadeAlgérie@free.fr; 50 Rue de Lisbonne, 75008 Paris)

Germany (☎ 49-30-437370; www.algerische-botschaft .de; Görschstraße 45-46, D-13187 Berlin)

Libya (☎ 21821 3610877; 12 rue de Kairouran, Tripoli)

Mali (☎ 220 45 72; BP 2 Daoudabougou, Bamako)

Mauritania (☎ 525 40 07; BP 625 Nouakchott)

Morocco Casablanca (☎ 212 2804175; 159, blvd Moulay Idriss 1er, Casablanca); Oujda (☎ 212 55710452; 12, rue d'Azrou, Oujda)

Niger (☎ 20 72 35 83; BP 142, Niamey)

Netherlands (☎ 070 352 29 54; www.embalgeria.nl; Van Stolklaan 1, 2585 JS, The Hague)

Tunisia (☎ 216 71 846740; www.consalg.com.tn; 83 av Jugurtha, Tunis)

UK & Ireland consulate (☎ 020-7589 6885; www.algerianconsulate.org.uk; 6 Hyde Park Gate, London SW7 5EW); embassy (☎ 020-7221 7800; www.algerianembassy.org .uk; 54 Holland Park W11 3RS)

USA (☎ 202-265-2800; www.algeria-us.org; 2118 Kalorama Rd NW, Washington SCN 20008)

Embassies & Consulates in Algeria

Australia Australia does not have an embassy or consulate in Algeria. Consular assistance for Australian citizens is provided by the Canadian embassy.

GOVERNMENT TRAVEL ADVICE

The following government websites offer travel advisories and information on current hot spots.

Australian Department of Foreign Affairs (☎ 1300 139 281; www.smarttraveller.gov.au)
British Foreign Office (☎ 0845-850-2829; www.fco.gov.uk/countryadvice)
Canadian Department of Foreign Affairs (☎ 800-267-6788; www.dfait-maeci.gc.ca)
French Ministry of Foreign Affairs (www.diplomatie.gouv.fr/fr/conseils-aux-voyageurs_909/index.html)
German Federal Foreign Office (☎ 49 30 50 00 0; www.auswaertiges-amt.de)
Japanese Ministry of Foreign Affairs (☎ 81 3-3580-3311; www.mofa.go.jp)
New Zealand Ministry of Foreign Affairs and Trade (☎ 644-439 8000; www.safetravel.govt.nz)
US State Department (☎ 888-407-4747; http://travel.state.gov)

Canada (☎ 021 914951; www.dfait-maeci.gc.ca/world /embassies/algeria; 18 rue Mustapha Khalef, Ben Aknoun, Algiers)
Denmark (☎ 021 548228; www. ambalgier.um.dk/da; 12 av Emilie Marquis, Hydra, Algiers)
France (☎ 021 692488; www.ambafrance-dz.org; 25 Chemin A Gadouche, Hydra, Algiers)
Germany (Map pp88–9; ☎ 021 741941; www.algier.diplo .de/Vertretung/algier/de/Startseite.html; 165 Chemin Sfindja, Algiers)
Libya (☎ 021 921502; 15 Chemin Cheikh Bachir el-Ibrahimi, El-Biar)
Mali (☎ 021 691351; Cité DNC/ANP, Villa No 15, Hydra)
Mauritania (☎ 021 937106; 30 rue du Vercors)
Morocco (☎ 021 607408; 8 rue des Cédres, Parc de la Reine)
Niger (☎ 021 788921; 54 rue du Vercors)
Tunisia (☎ 021 691388; 11 rue du Bois de Bologne)
UK (Map pp88–9; ☎ 021 230068; www.britishembassy.gov .uk/algeria; 7th fl, Hilton International Hotel, Pins Maritimes, Algiers)
USA (☎ 021 691255; http://algiers.usembassy.gov; 4 Chemin Cheikh Bachir el-Ibrahimi, El-Biar)

FESTIVALS & EVENTS
Religious Holidays

During the most important Islamic holidays much commercial life grinds to a halt in Algeria. The Islamic calendar is based on 12 lunar months totalling 354 or 355 days, so the following holidays always occur about 11 days earlier than they did the previous year. The exact dates are based on the moon and only announced shortly before the event.

Ramadan (begins September 2007/August 2008) The ninth month of the Muslim calendar is the annual fasting month when Muslims do not eat or drink during daylight hours, but break their fast after sundown. Throughout Ramadan offices start to wind down early in the day. Most restaurants are closed during this period.

Aïd el-Fitr This major Islamic holiday marks the end of Ramadan.
Aïd el-Kébir (December 2007/November 2008) Celebrates Abraham's readiness to sacrifice his son to God on his command, and the last-ditch substitution of a ram. It also coincides with the end of the pilgrimage to Mecca and is marked by great feasts with roasted sheep and a two-day public holiday.
Eid a-Moulid (March 2008/February 2009) Celebrates the birth of the Prophet Mohammed and takes place three months after Aïd el-Kébir.

Other Events
Yennayer (January) Celebrated across the country, this annual festival celebrates the start of the Berber new year.

FOOD & DRINK

Outside the major cities you won't find much choice when it comes to eating out. Most 'restaurants' are in reality identikit cafés, with limited menus (they all seem to specialise in chicken and chips) and an all-male clientele. In most towns in Algeria the only place to get an alcoholic drink is in the more upmarket or state-run hotels.

Stalls selling street food aren't widespread in Algeria and what you do find is quite basic. At most you'll see stalls selling boiled eggs, peanuts and tea, all of which you can get a serving of for around DA10. Occasionally you'll see stalls selling kebabs (although these are usually outside cafés or restaurants), which go for around DA100 a pop. Most of the stalls selling street food are to be found near marketplaces or bus stations (*gares routières*).

Budget restaurants (as listed in this guide) are places where you can get a meal for DA500 and under. At the budget end of the scale you'll find no-frills local cafés and restaurants with a small choice of menu items, such as omelette with vegetables or chips, couscous and meat, grilled kebabs, or chicken and chips. You won't be given a menu, they'll normally just come up and tell you what they have; a basket of bread is always included in the price.

The midrange restaurants (in which you might actually be handed a physical menu!) tend to have more comfortable surroundings, but you can still eat for between DA500 and DA1000. You'll get more choice at this price range.

'Top end' refers to establishments that cost DA1000 and over where you can get top-class Algerian cooking as well as a good range of French and international food; most top-end restaurants also serve alcohol. There are few top-end restaurants outside of Algiers and the north. For further information on food in Algeria, see p59.

GAY & LESBIAN TRAVELLERS

Homosexual sex is illegal for both men and women in Algeria, and incurs a maximum penalty of three years in jail and a stiff fine. You're unlikely to have any problems as a tourist, but discretion is advisable.

HOLIDAYS

In Southern Algeria the main tourist season is from November to March, and the best hotels and guesthouses are often full. On the Mediterranean coast the busiest time of year is the summer, from May to September, and at this time hotel rooms are at a premium.

As well as the following national holidays, Algeria also observes Islamic holidays (see p201).

Labour Day 1 May
Revolutionary Readjustment (1965) 19 June
Independence Day 5 July
National Day (Revolution Day) 1 November

INSURANCE

A travel-insurance policy to cover theft, loss and medical problems is essential. Some policies specifically exclude dangerous activities, which can include motorcycling, camel trekking and even trekking and travel across the Sahara. Check that the policy covers an emergency flight home and choose one that covers a large sum towards medical expenses in case you need to be evacuated from the Sahara; this can be very expensive. You might prefer a policy that pays doctors or hospitals on the spot rather than having to pay up and claim later.

For more advice about health insurance policies, see p218. For information about motor insurance, see p215. Worldwide travel insurance is available at www.lonely planet.com/travel_services. You can buy, extend and claim online anytime – even if you're already on the road.

INTERNET ACCESS

Most travellers make constant use of internet cafés and free web-based email such as Yahoo (www.yahoo.com) or Hotmail (www .hotmail.com).

If you're travelling with a notebook or hand-held computer, be aware that your modem may not work once you leave your home country. The safest option is to buy a reputable 'global' modem before you leave home, or buy a local PC-card modem if you're spending an extended time in any one country. For more information on travelling with a portable computer, see www .teleadapt.com.

Internet access is usually available in major towns and tourist areas (with the notable exceptions of Djanet and Timimoun) and connections are normally good. It should cost between DA80 and DA150 an hour to surf. Other than the large and

ISLAMIC HOLIDAYS

Holiday	2007	2008	2009	2010
Ramadan begins	13 Sep	2 Sep	22 Aug	11 Aug
Eid al-Fitr	14 Oct	3 Oct	20 Sep	9 Sep
Tabaski	19 Dec	8 Dec	28 Nov	17 Nov
Moulid an-Nabi	31 Mar	20 Mar	9 Mar	27 Feb
New Year begins	21 Jan (1428)	10 Jan (1429)	31 Dec (1430)	20 Dec (1431)
Eid al-Adha	21 Dec	10 Dec	30 Nov	19 Nov

expensive hotels chains in Algiers, you're unlikely to find hotels with wireless internet connections. Where they can be found we have used the internet symbol (🖳) to denote this.

LEGAL MATTERS

When you are in Algeria make sure to respect local laws and penalties, including those that seem overly harsh; they do apply to you. Your government will certainly try to help you if you get arrested or end up in prison, but it can't get you off the hook. The possession, use and trafficking of controlled substances are all serious criminal offences in Algeria, which carry custodial sentences, and the Algerian authorities have recently announced new measures to crack down harder on drug trafficking. Serious crime, such as murder, may attract punishment by the death penalty.

The photography of military or sensitive sites, including military or security personnel, may lead to arrest and detention. Also remember that there are restrictions on taking artefacts (such as stone tools) out of the country – if you're caught this can lead to a fine or even time in prison.

When driving in Algeria you're bound to come across police and military checkpoint on major roads inside and on the outskirts of Algiers and other large cities, as well as on major highways. You should fully cooperate with and show relevant documentation to the security personnel at these checkpoints.

MAPS

It can be difficult to find accurate maps of Algeria's cities and towns and most of the time they're nonexistent. If you need a country map it's a better idea to buy one before you go. The Michelin Map 741 *Africa: North and West* is an accurate and readable choice. Also worth a look is the Insight Travel Map, *North Africa 2003*. Gizi's *Algeria* map is slightly more detailed and also has names in Arabic.

MONEY

The currency of Algeria is called the dinar. Dinar banknotes are issued in the following denominations: 100, 200, 500, and 1000 dinars. See the Quick Reference section on the inside cover for exchange rates and see p14 for information on the costs involved in travelling in Algeria.

ATMs

You won't have much luck getting money out of ATMs in Algeria. In fact, you will be lucky if you even see an ATM. They are practically unheard of in Southern Algeria and those that you do find tend not to accept foreign cards. Rumour has it, though, that the ATMs belonging to the Credit Populaire d'Algérie *do* accept European ATM cards.

Black Market

A so-called 'black market' does still exist in Algeria, although it is not as widespread as it once was. Money can still be changed on the street should you so choose, and if you ask around discreetly you're sure to find someone to help you out. Moneychangers might also approach you in the street, particularly near border crossings and you may even be offered an exchange by your taxi driver on the way in from the airport. However, you should only change money on the street when it's absolutely necessary. While you'll get a slightly better rate of exchange it really isn't worth the risk. You run the risk of being ripped off or worse. Bear in mind that you're officially supposed to show all your transactions on your currency declaration form. Although it's rarely checked you don't want to be caught out.

Cash

The best foreign currencies to carry are euros, followed by UK pounds. Some Algerians, especially in rural areas, might give prices in centimes rather than dinars (100 centimes equals DA1). To confuse matters further, they might also drop the thousands, so a quote of '130' means 130,000 centimes, ie DA1300. You'll need dinars for day-to-day expenses, although tourist-oriented businesses (hotels, airlines, tour companies and even tourist shops) might accept euros.

Credit Cards

Credit-card facilities are not widespread in Algeria. You'll be able to use them to pay for some top-end hotels and restaurants, some larger travel agencies, car-rental agencies and at some Air Algérie offices in major cities although a commission of around 5% is usually charged for this. In Southern Algeria even the more expensive hotels and agencies don't accept credit cards. The most useful card is Visa, with MasterCard also accepted in a minority of places. It is possible to get cash advances from Visa and MasterCard credit cards in bank branches in major cities, although this can sometimes prove to be a long and drawn-out process. Authorisation can take anything from half an hour to half a day.

Moneychangers

The best place to change money is in one of the national banks, although it is also possible at many of the upmarket hotels. Tour companies will sometimes change money for you and many tourist-oriented shops will let you pay in euros and then give you dinar as change.

Travellers Cheques

Travellers cheques aren't that much use in Algeria and many banks won't exchange them, especially outside of the larger cities. In the south, facilities for changing travellers cheques are practically unheard of and even when you do find such facilities your travellers cheques will be scrutinised and discussed in great detail before they are approved. In order to change travellers cheques you will need your original receipt.

PHOTOGRAPHY & VIDEO

Print and slide film, batteries and a limited range of camera accessories, including memory sticks for digital cameras are available in major towns. Processing a roll of 36 exposures costs around DA600. In most major towns it is also possible to transfer digital images onto a CD, or to print out photographs from a memory stick. Whatever camera you bring, a dust-proof bag and a cleaning kit is essential. The sunlight in Algeria is very intense, so most people find 100 ISO to be sufficient, with possibly 200 ISO or 400 ISO for long-lens shots, or in the coastal regions of the north.

Do not take photographs of airports, ports, government buildings or anything that looks as if it may be police or military property. Always ask permission before taking a photograph of people and don't snap a photo if permission is denied. When taking photographs of rock paintings and carvings flash photography is forbidden.

The best times to take photographs in Algeria, especially in the Sahara are in the early morning, just after sunrise, and the hour or so before sunset; the low sun will enhance the colours in your photographs. Filters (eg ultraviolet, polarising or 'skylight') can also help produce good results; ask for advice in a good camera shop.

For the most comprehensive guide to travel photography, get a copy of Lonely Planet's *Travel Photography: A guide to Taking Better Pictures* by internationally renowned photographer Richard I'Anson.

POST

Post offices are widespread throughout the country and are indicated by a yellow sign. The postal system is quite slow and it's possible that you'll arrive home before your postcards do. A letter to Europe should cost DA30. Cards and letters to the USA and Australia cost DA45. Postcards are slightly cheaper. Many post offices also have branches of Western Union.

SHOPPING

You'll find plenty of souvenirs of your trip, including fantastic jewellery; the traditional Berber pieces are beautiful, especially those from the Kabylie region which are made from different combinations of silver, coloured enamel, semiprecious stones and coral. You will also find plenty of magnificent jewellery in the south – made by Tuareg silversmiths, many of whom are from Niger. You'll find intricately carved silver and agate pendants, strangely shaped crosses – look for the famous 'Croix d'Agadez' – heavy earrings and traditional bangles. You could also pick up a traditional Tuareg sword or a *taguelmoust* (Tuareg veil) to shield you from the elements.

Leather goods are of particularly good quality around Tlemcen, which produces leather belts, shoes, bags and poufs. In the Hoggar many Tuareg artisans specialise in leatherwear. You'll see leather sandals in bright shades of red and green, pouches, Tuareg 'wallets' that you wear round your neck to store your valuables, and you may come across intricately decorated camel saddles.

Carpets are made all over Algeria, the designs – traditional and geometric – vary in colour and style from place to place and a lower quality one can be picked up for as little as €10. Good places to buy traditional carpets include Ghardaïa and the Souf region.

The Tipaza region is famous for its pottery, where you can get exquisitely decorated bowls, plates and couscousiers.

When you're in the desert look out for *roses de sable* – natural rock sculptures in the shape of roses, exactly as they are found in the sand.

Even though it's a Muslim country, Algeria is also a wine producer, continuing to maintain vineyards from the colonial era. All of these vineyards are located in the north and, in particular, produce some good-quality red wines. These can usually be bought in specialised shops in the bigger towns, or in souvenir shops at the airport.

Unlike some other countries in the region, bargaining isn't really done in most of Algeria and most shops have fixed prices. Offence can sometime be taken if you try to haggle, too. Once you head further south, to Ghardaïa, Djanet and Tamanrasset, bargaining is more acceptable, although you're unlikely to walk away with huge discounts.

SOLO TRAVELLERS

Solo travel in southern Algeria can be expensive. If driving through the south you have to arrange to be met by a reputable guide who will accompany you in your car, which can costs anything from €80 a day and up, depending on the season.

Hardly any hotels have single rooms and although they'll usually charge you a reduced rate to stay in a double the reduction is not often significant. The same goes for organised tours. Unless you've organised something in advance, most travel agents will not let you just join in on a group tour, so unless you can find someone to share the costs you'll end up having to arrange a very expensive itinerary for yourself.

The upside is that you may get to interact more with locals. Speaking Arabic or French will make a huge difference to your travels in Algeria. If you are travelling independently, a grasp of at least the basics will help you communicate more effectively –

existing on a diet of broken conversation can prove very frustrating. Algerians are hospitable and you might well be invited for tea or dinner in somebody's home. The down side is that it can be quite isolating – there are not many independent travellers in Algeria, so it could be a good idea to sort out travelling companions before you go. You're unlikely to meet many people to travel with or to share lifts with once you're on the road.

It is possible for solo travellers to get around on public transport, and bus services are relatively frequent, covering all the major destinations of interest. At the time of writing, getting around on public transport in the south could be problematic as you were required to have an invitation from a travel agency as well as a detailed itinerary to account for your time, before being granted a visa. You can get around this (for example, by joining a tour for a short time) and there have been reports of people travelling solo in the south on public transport. However, if you're leaving the south via Tamanrasset or Djanet airports you'll be asked which travel agency you're with and will be in for some hassle if you don't have an answer.

Women travelling solo in Algeria will attract a lot of attention, as even the local women don't tend to travel on their own. You're likely to receive a lot of curious glances and it can be intimidating. Cafés and restaurants away from the big towns of the north are generally all-male establishments and local men may pester you. See p207 for more information on women travellers.

TELEPHONE

Mobile phone usage has seen an explosion in Algeria and use is widespread. Mobile phones are often the only way to get in touch with people, as most Algerians do not have a land line.

Mobile Phones

Mobile phone numbers begin with ☎ 06 or ☎ 07. There are four main mobile networks in Algeria: Djezzy, Mobilis, Nedjma and Allo, out of which Djezzy has the most comprehensive coverage. SIM cards are widely available from mobile phone shops, internet cafés or local stores, and

DIRECTORY

cost around DA80. Calls cost from around DA13 to DA18 a minute for national calls and around DA5 to DA8 for the same network; it's certainly cheaper than using your foreign phone here.

Phone Codes

The country code for Algeria is ☎ 213. To call out of Algeria dial ☎ 00 before the country code.

Phonecards

Post offices and general stores sell phonecards. The most convenient way to phone abroad, however, is by Taxiphone. See below for further details.

Taxiphone

No, not the place to go to call a taxi, a taxiphone is the best way to make a phone call abroad. Taxiphones are essentially small offices with a number of screened-off cabins where you make your call first and then pay later. Expect a five-minute call to Europe to cost about DA300 and a similar call to the USA to cost DA350.

TIME

Algeria is one hour ahead of Greenwich Mean Time (GMT). There is no daylight saving time. The 24-hour clock is usually used.

TOILETS

Public facilities are not very common in Algeria. Facilities range from squat toilets to Western-style toilets in the more upmarket hotels and restaurants. If you're going to be travelling in more remote areas, carry some toilet paper for when you feel the call of nature.

TOURIST INFORMATION

The best place to find tourist information is the **Office National Algérien du Tourisme** (ONAT; ☎ 021 744448; www.onat-dz.com; 126 bus, rue Didouche-Mourad, Algiers) – Algeria's national tourist office. Its services vary greatly according to its location. Some can help out with local information, organise tours around the country or assist you with a map or a daily guide. Others seem to exist as booking agents for Algerians wanting to go elsewhere. The **Touring Club d'Algérie** (☎ 021 541313; www.algeria touring.dz; 30 rue Hassene-Benâmane, Algiers) is also a useful source of information.

ONAT has several helpful regional offices including the following:

Constantine (☎ /fax 031 642257; 16 rue Didouche-Mourad)

Ghardaïa (Map p157; ☎ 029 881751; fax 029 884323; 1 blvd Emir-Abdelkader)

Oran (☎ 041 393106, 041 393889; fax 041 390320; 10bis, rue Emir-Abdelkader)

Tamanrasset (☎ 029 334117; fax 029 344191; blvd Emir-Abdelkader)

TRAVELLERS WITH DISABILITIES

Facilities for disabled travellers in Algeria are practically nonexistent. Only the most expensive hotels have lifts, while streets are not always in great condition and ramps and other things to ease access are nowhere to be seen. Bathroom access in most hotels in Algeria can be difficult and most long-distance public transport is not accessible for wheelchairs. There are no tourist facilities in Algeria aimed specifically at the blind or the deaf.

VISAS

All visitors to Algeria except the nationals of Libya, Malaysia, the Maldives, Mali, Mauritania, Morocco, the Seychelles, Syria, Tunisia, Western Sahara and Yemen need a visa to enter Algeria. All visas must be arranged in advance at an Algerian embassy or consulate; you cannot get a visa on entry to the country. In general you should get a visa before leaving your home country, although if travelling up to Algeria through West Africa, it might be possible to get a transit visa en route in Agadez, Niger. Visas are valid for either one month or three months from the date of entry, but it can be difficult to obtain a three-month visa as you'll have to provide an itinerary and account for all the time that you'll be there.

To get a visa you fill out two application forms, provide two photographs and, if visiting friends or relatives, a stamped *certificat d'hebergement* (certificate of lodging) signed by your host in Algeria and authenticated by the local authorities in your host's hometown. Otherwise you'll need a confirmed hotel booking or an invitation from a travel agency; for a visit to the south you'll need an invitation from a travel agency and a detailed itinerary for your stay. Travel agencies arrange your invitation and can usually fax the embassy a signed and stamped copy.

Visas cost €35 for one month and €100 for three months for Europeans. Visas for citizens of the USA and Canada cost around €50. Multiple-entry visas cost a few euros more. Transit visas are valid for seven days and you'll have to prove you have adequate financial resources and a valid visa for your country of destination. For visa extensions visit the **Department des Etrangers** (blvd Youssef 19A, Algiers).

Visas for Onward Travel

Visas for the following countries are available from embassies in Algiers (see p200) or consuls in Tamanrasset.

Mali One-month visas cost €10 or €15 for French citizens and are usually issued in 24 hours. You'll need two photos.
Niger One-month visas are issued the same day, costing €50. Three photos and three application forms are required.

WOMEN TRAVELLERS

While it's not exactly dangerous to travel as a woman on your own in Algeria, it can prove to be tiresome. It is not common to see women travelling on their own in many parts of the country and consequently you should prepare yourself for the amount of attention you'll receive. In the more laid-back towns of Tamanrasset or Djanet, for example, it will just be curious stares from both men or women. In other places you'll be subjected to a constant barrage of cat-calls and advances.

Travel as a solo woman in Algeria can sometimes be intimidating. Outside of the big cities and the tourist trail, cafés and restaurants are the preserve of men and you'll receive stares and sometimes outright hostility if you enter.

Inventing a husband and wearing a wedding band is always a good strategy and you should also refer to boyfriends as husbands to gain greater legitimacy for your relationship as, unfortunately, many men in Algeria seem to be under the impression that if an unmarried woman is travelling alone then she's 'available'.

It is essential to dress modestly. This is the most successful strategy for minimising attention. Tucking your hair under a hat or tying it back sometimes helps. Although on the streets of Algiers you can get away with bare arms and tight jeans the rest of the country is a different story. Upper arms, legs, shoulders and cleavage should be covered – you don't want to call unnecessary attention to yourself. It's also a good idea to avoid eye contact with local men.

Avoid going out in the evening, particularly on foot, and avoid isolated areas, roadways and beaches. Hitching is not recommended. If staying in hotels alone it's worth paying a bit more money to stay in a place that's secure. It's not unheard of for a man to come knocking on your door in the middle of the night once it's clear you're a foreign woman staying on your own.

Don't let these concerns ruin your trip however. Most of the attention you'll receive, while annoying, is rarely threatening.

Transport

TRANSPORT

GETTING THERE & AWAY

Algeria is easily reached by air or sea from Continental Europe and the UK and there are also frequent flights to and from the Middle East, North and West Africa. From all other areas you'll have to change in Europe. Flights, tours and rail tickets can be booked online at www.lonelyplanet.com /travel_services.

ENTERING THE COUNTRY

Getting into Algeria is fairly straightforward and immigration officials tend to just check your visa before letting you go on your way. You will have to fill in a landing card before entering, but this is pretty simple and it's printed in Arabic, French and English. You also need to fill in a customs declaration form (p199) stating how much currency and valuables you are bringing into the country. This is supposed to be stamped on entry, and may or may not be checked by customs on your way in. Visas are not issued on arrival and you must arrange a visa in advance before entering the country. See p206 for more information about visa requirements.

Passport

Nationals of Israel are not allowed into the country; if you have a stamp in your passport from here your application might be rejected. For visa information, see p206.

AIR
Airports & Airlines

There are direct International flights from Europe to Algiers, Annaba, Bejaia, Constantine, Djanet, Oran, Hassi Messaoud, Tamanrasset and Tlemcen; as well as direct flights from West Africa and the Middle East to Algiers. There are no direct flights to Algeria from North or South America, Asia or Australasia.

Air Algérie is the national carrier and, at the time of writing, the only airline offering internal flights to tourists. Air France, Aigle Azur and British Airways are the main airlines linking Algeria with Europe.

Air Algérie has a fairly decent safety record. Its only fatal air crash was in March 2003, 102 people were killed when a plane lost control shortly after taking off in Tamanrasset. Additionally, a group of unarmed men tried to hijack a domestic Air Algérie flight in January 2003.

The following airlines fly to/from Algeria:

Aigle Azur (ZI; ☎ 21 64 14 52; www.aigle-azur.fr)
Air Algérie (AH; ☎ 21 65 33 40; www.airAlgérie.dz)
Air France (AF; ☎ 21 98 04 04; www.airfrance.com)
Alitalia (AZ; ☎ 21 72 73 56; www.alitalia.com)
British Airways (BA; ☎ 21 67 09 18; www.ba.com)
Egypt Air (MS; ☎ 21 63 39 74; www.egyptair.com)
JetAir (☎ 1293 566000; www.jetair.co.uk)

THINGS CHANGE...

The information in this chapter is particularly vulnerable to change. Check directly with the airline or a travel agent to make sure you understand how a fare (and any ticket you may buy) works and be aware of the security requirements for international travel. Shop carefully. The details given in this chapter should be regarded as pointers and are not a substitute for your own careful, up-to-date research.

CLIMATE CHANGE & TRAVEL

Climate change is a serious threat to the ecosystems that humans rely upon, and air travel is the fastest-growing contributor to the problem. Lonely Planet regards travel, overall, as a global benefit, but believes we all have a responsibility to limit our personal impact on global warming.

Flying & climate change

Pretty much every form of motorised travel generates CO_2 (the main cause of human-induced climate change) but planes are far and away the worst offenders, not just because of the sheer distances they allow us to travel, but because they release greenhouse gases high into the atmosphere. The statistics are frightening: two people taking a return flight between Europe and the USA will contribute as much to climate change as an average household's gas and electricity consumption over a whole year.

Carbon offset schemes

Climatecare.org and other websites use 'carbon calculators' that allow travellers to offset the level of greenhouse gases they are responsible for with financial contributions to sustainable travel schemes that reduce global warming – including projects in India, Honduras, Kazakhstan and Uganda.

    Lonely Planet, together with Rough Guides and other concerned partners in the travel industry, support the carbon offset scheme run by climatecare.org. Lonely Planet offsets all of its staff and author travel.

    For more information check out our website: www.lonelyplanet.com.

Libyan Arab Airlines (LN; ☎ 21 72 51 39; www.libyan arabairline.com)

Lufthansa (LH; ☎ 583 8426; www.lufthansa.com)

Qatar Airways (QR; ☎ 21 67 99 99; www.qatarairways .com)

Royal Air Maroc (AT; ☎ 21 74 45 20/21; www.royal airmaroc.com)

Saudi Arabian Airlines (SV; ☎ 21 68 22 74; www .saudiairlines.com)

Syn-Air (RB; ☎ 21 73 01 02; www.syn-air.com)

Syrian Air (RB; ☎ 21 73 01 02; www.syriaair.com)

Turkish Airlines (TK; ☎ 21 44 68 66; www.thy.com)

Tickets

Since there is so little competition, there are few specials for travel to Algeria. Air Algérie and Air France have daily direct flights from Paris, and British Airways flies to Algiers direct every day except Thursday. Booking online is usually possible and good online agencies include **Opodo** (www.opodo.co.uk) and **Expedia** (www.expedia.com). The best deals to Algeria are from France; **Aigle Azur** (☎ 33 (0) 810 797 997; www.aigle-azur.fr) has regular flights to a number of the more popular tourist destinations in Algeria. **Point Afrique** (www.point-afrique .com) arranges charter flights to Algeria from Paris and Marseilles, and if you're going to Tamanrasset or Djanet it's a better option than changing planes in Algiers.

Africa

Algeria is well connected with North and West Africa, and there are regular direct flights from Libya, Morocco and Egypt to Algiers. Air Algérie flies direct to Niamey (Niger), Ouagadougou (Burkino Faso), Abidjan (Côte d'Ivoire), Bamako (Mali), Dakar (Senegal) and Nouakchot (Mauritania). There are Air Algérie offices in **Mali** (☎ 233 223159; av Modibo Keita, Bamako), **Egypt** (☎ 202 5740 688; El-Nasr Bldg, El-Nil St, Cairo), **Morocco** (☎ 212 222 5681; 1, rue Elamraoui Brahim, Casablanca), **Senegal** (☎ 221 823 55 48; 2 place de l'Independence, Dakar), **Niger** (☎ 227 7338 98; Arcades Rivoli, Niamey), **Mauritania** (☎ 222 525 2059; av Gamel Abdelnasser, Nouakchot) and **Burkina Faso** (☎ 312 102; 398 av Kwame Nkrumah, Ouagadougou). Buying cheap tickets in West and North Africa isn't easy. Usually the best deal you can get is the airline's official excursion fare.

    Flights from East Africa tend to go via the Middle East, eg from Nairobi to Istanbul to Algiers. Flying from Southern Africa the best way to get to Algeria is to fly via Egypt.

Australia & New Zealand

Again, there are no direct flights from Australia or New Zealand to Algeria. The best way to get there is via London on British Airways or Paris with Air France. A return ticket from Sydney to Algiers via London or Paris should cost around A$1800 and should take about 30 hours. Or you could fly with Egypt Air via Cairo, from where there are onward connections to Algiers.

Both **STA Travel** (☎ 1300 733 035; www.statravel .com.au) and **Flight Centre** (☎ 133 133; www.flightcen tre.com.au) have offices throughout Australia. For online bookings try www.travel.com.au.

In New Zealand both **Flight Centre** (☎ 0800 243 544; www.flightcentre.co.nz) and **STA Travel** (☎ 0508 782872; www.statravel.co.nz) have branches throughout the country. The site www.travel .co.nz is recommended for online bookings.

Continental Europe

Lufthansa, Alitalia and Air France all have daily connections from their respective countries to Algiers, and Air Algérie also has good connections with Continental Europe. From Spain there are Air Algérie flights three times a week from Barcelona to Algiers, twice a week from Madrid to Algiers, and two a week from Alicante to Oran. From Italy there are three flights a week from Rome to Algiers. From Switzerland there are two flights a week from Geneva to Algiers and one a week from Basel to Constantine. Air Algérie also flies twice a week from Frankfurt and Brussels, and once a week from Moscow. From other European countries the best bet is to connect in Paris. Return fares from Continental Europe range from between €300 and €500.

The following are a list of recommended travel agencies:

Air Fair (☎ 020 620 5121; www.airfair.nl in Dutch) Well-respected Dutch travel agent.

Barcelo Viajes (☎ 902 116 226; www.barceloviajes .com; Spain)

Connections (☎ 02-550 01 00; www.connections.be; Belgium) Has offices throughout the country.

CTS Viaggi (☎ 06 462 0431; www.cts.it; Italy)

Expedia (www.expedia.de; Germany)

STA Travel (☎ 01805 456 422; www.statravel.de; Germany)

TUI (☎ 0848 121 221; www.tui.ch; Switzerland)

For a return flight from Berlin to Algiers prices start at around €400; from Rome prices start at around €350.

France

Air France has daily flights to Algiers from €300 return. Air Algérie operates daily scheduled flights between Paris and Algiers,

and several flights a week between Paris and the international airports at Annaba, Constantine, Oran, Batna and Tlemcen.

In addition there are direct weekly flights from Bordeaux, Lille, Lyon, Marseille, Toulouse, Nancy and Nice to Algiers.

You can fly from Lyon to Annaba, Constantine and Oran; from Marseille to Batna, Constantine and Oran; and from Toulouse to Oran. For other destinations in Algeria you'll need to connect in Algiers.

Aigle Azur specialises in flights between France and North Africa and has a variety of different flights from French cities to Algeria. For example, from Paris you can get to Algiers, Annaba, Batna, Constantine, Djanet, Hassi Messaoud, Oran, Tamanrasset and Tlemcen. Flights to Algiers also depart from Lille, Lyon and Toulouse. From Marseilles you can get to Annaba, Constantine, Oran and Tlemcen. The airports at Lyon and Toulouse also have flights to Oran.

Point Afrique is an excellent company that organises tours and flights to countries around North and West Africa. It flies from Paris and Marseille to Djanet and Tamanrasset, the advantage being that for the same price as a straight return you can mix and match – you could fly from Paris to Djanet and then return from Tamanrasset, or even from another country in the region. One-way fares to southern Algeria start from around €300.

However, bear in mind that because it operates lowly charter flights, Point Afrique is further down the pecking order when it comes to airport berths, which means that it is sometimes unable to confirm your exact flight details until not long before your departure. Also bear in mind that airport tax is not included in the flight price. This is normally an additional €65.

Recommended booking agencies in France include the following:

Nouvelles Frontiéres (☎ 0825 000 747; www.nouv elles-frontieres.fr)

OTU Voyages (☎ 0825 004 027;www.out.fr) Has branches across France.

Voyageurs du Monde (☎ 0892 688 363; www.vdm.com)

Middle East

There are good connections between Algeria and the Middle East, and the national airlines of Libya, Qatar, Saudi Arabia, Syria and Turkey all have regular direct flights to

Algiers. In addition, Air Algérie flies once a week to Amman (Jordan), twice a week to Jeddah (Saudi Arabia), Damascus (Syria) and Beirut (Lebanon), and three times a week to Dubai (United Arab Emirates) and Istanbul (Turkey).

UK & Ireland

British Airways flies direct from London every day except Thursday. Prices start from around UK£300 return to Algiers. Twice a week British Airways flies direct to Hassi Messaoud from London Gatwick for around UK£400 return. JetAir, a private charter airline, has return scheduled flights to Hassi Messaoud three times a week.

From Ireland the quickest way to get to Algeria is to fly from Dublin with British Airways via London. It's also worth checking the weekend travel ads in newspapers and travel magazines or in *Time Out.* During popular periods such as peak tourist seasons or at the end of Ramadan, prices may rise by another UK£100 or so on scheduled airlines.

The following travel agents are a good place to start to look for deals.

Africa Travel Centre (☎ 0845 450 1520; www.travel africa.co.uk; 21 Leigh St London WC1H 9EW)

North South Travel (☎ 01245 608291; www.north southtravel.co.uk; Moulsham Mill Centre, Parkway, Chelmsford CM2 7PX) Excellent small travel agency whose profits are put into development projects in Africa, Asia and Latin America.

STA Travel (☎ 020-7361 6142/7581/4132; www.sta travel.co.uk) Has offices throughout the country.

Trailfinders (☎ 020-7938 3939; www.trailfinders.co.uk) Has offices all over the UK.

USA & Canada

Currently there are no direct flights from the USA or Canada to Algeria, but a new service is being planned from Montreal to Algiers on Air Algerie from June 2007. The best way to get there would be to take a flight to London or Paris and change there. From New York this would take about 14 hours. The full economy fare from New York to Algiers is about US$1000. The economy fare from Toronto to Algiers is about C$1500.

The following are recommended travel agencies in the USA.

STA Travel (☎ 800-777 0112; www.statravel.com) Has offices in many major US cities; call the toll-free 800 number for office locations or visit its website.

Pan Express Travel (☎ 212 719-9292; www.panex presstravel.com) Also worth trying.

Recommended Canadian travel agencies include the following:

Travel CUTs (☎ 800-667 2887; www.travelcuts.com) is Canada's national student travel agency and has offices in all major cities.

Flight Centre (☎ 1877 967 5302; www.flightcentre.ca) Has offices all over Canada.

In addition to the internet, good places to search include travel magazines. The weekend editions of major newspapers are also useful. You could try the *New York Times* on the east coast, the *Los Angeles Times* or *San Francisco Examiner-Chronicle* on the west coast, and in Canada the *Toronto Star*, *Vancouver Sun* or *Globe & Mail.*

LAND

Algeria has land borders with Tunisia, Libya, Niger, Mali, Mauritania and Morocco. At the time of writing many of Algeria's borders were closed to tourists and the only possible crossings were at Taleb Larbi and Souq Ahras with Tunisia, In Guezzam with Niger and Deb Deb with Libya. On arriving at the border you will normally fill out an immigration card and a currency declaration form and get a passport stamp. If you're driving you'll also fill out a registration form for your vehicle and buy motor insurance.

With any of the following overland routes, you'll need a thorough update on the security situation before setting off. Anybody planning Saharan travel should check out the excellent website www.sahara-overland .com put together by Chris Scott.

Libya

There are two main overland routes you can take from Algeria to Libya: from Djanet on the Algerian side to Ghat on the Libyan side, or from Deb Deb on the Algerian side to Ghadames in Libya. At the time of writing it was not possible to cross into Libya via Ghat. However, if the border reopens anytime soon, shared taxis leave from Djanet's main street to the border at the crack of dawn every day. At the time of research it was possible to cross into Libya from Deb Deb to Ghadames.

An invitation from a tour operator is necessary to obtain a visa for Libya and at the time of writing it was compulsory to travel with a guide if driving in the south. It is not possible to cross the border using public transport. If driving you'll need to get your passport stamped, rent number plates and buy a Libyan carnet and motor insurance.

Mali

The Malian border crossing is on the Route de Tanezrouft, running through Algeria and Mali, via Adrar and the border at Bordj–Mokhtar, ending in Gao. The security situation in northern Mali has been unstable for some time, meaning that the Tanzerouft trans-Saharan route has been effectively closed to travellers. The situation has improved somewhat recently, but the route is still considered dangerous and cannot be recommended. If you must undertake this route, you'll need to be accompanied to the border by an Algerian guide from a reputable tour company.

To get to Mali overland from Algeria your best bet is to go via Niger, crossing the border at Labbénganza, southeast of Gao. You can pick up a visa for Mali in Tamanrasset, but it is also possible to pick one up at the border for CFA15,000.

Mauritania

Crossing from Algeria into Mauritania is currently not advised due to safety concerns in that corner of the country.

Morocco

All borders between Morocco and Algeria were closed at the time of writing.

Niger

The only viable border post between the two countries at the time of writing was between In Guezzam (Algeria) and Assammaka (Niger), a bit more than 400km south of Tamanrasset. If driving you will need an Algerian guide to accompany you to the border (or pick you up), as it is currently illegal for tourists to drive cars unaccompanied in the Algerian Sahara.

Formalities are carried out at the Algerian border post from where it's another 18km or so to the Nigerian authorities at Assamaka. To enter this region of Niger you'll need a licensed guide and a *feuille de route* (official itinerary), which you'll need to arrange through a Nigerian travel agency.

It is not recommended that you use public transport to cross the border into Niger. However, should the situation improve, getting to In Guezzam from Tamanrasset is reasonably straightforward. There are 4WD taxis that leave on a daily basis and it'll cost you DA1500 for a seat. There's not much point doing this though as you'll then have to find a ride to the border post and then onwards to the Nigerian border post at Assamaka and from there to Arlit. From Arlit south, things are very straightforward though and buses run south to Agadez, Zinder, and Niamey. If there's a group of you its possible to hire a 4WD taxi in Tamanrasset to take you all the way to Arlit for around DA40,000.

Tunisia

Most overland travellers enter Algeria via Tunisia. Take the ferry from Tunis and then go overland from Nefta in Tunisia to El-Oued in Algeria via the border at Taleb Larbi. If coming by public transport, you can get a shared taxi from Nefta to the border post at Hazoua. It's a few kilometres between the Tunisian and Algeria border posts, but you should be able to get a lift across. After completing formalities at the Algerian side, there are shared taxis that go on to El-Oued. You can sometimes change money at the border, if not you'll be able to at Debila, the first main town after the border.

The other main border point with Tunisia is between Souq Ahras on the Algerian side and Ghardimao in Tunisia. On both sides the journey can usually be made by *taxis collectifs* (shared taxis), or there are direct air-conditioned buses between Tunis and Annaba or Constantine.

SEA

Algérie Ferries (☎ 021 424650; www.algerieferries .com) and the French company **SNCM** (☎ 33 825 88 80 88; www.sncm.fr) operate regular ferry services between Marseille in France and Oran, Algiers, Bejaia, Skikda and Annaba in Algeria; and between Alicante in Spain and Algiers and Oran.

France

Basic fares cost from around €280 per adult one way and €330 return plus an extra €120 for a cabin. Cars costs from €110 one way; motorbikes from €78.

The following table has information on ferry services from Marseille.

Destination	Frequency (weekly)	Duration (hours)
Algiers	3	22
Annaba	1-2	20
Bejaia	1	21
Oran	3	25
Skikda	2	22

Spain

Basic adult fares cost from €180 one way and €206 return, plus an extra €70 extra for a cabin. Bringing a car costs from €100 one way. It costs from €63 one way to bring a motorcycle and €15 one way for a bike.

From Alicante to Algiers there are two crossings (13 hours) a week. There is a weekly crossing (13 to 15 hours) from Alicante to Oran.

TOURS

Because of the current security situation and the relative difficulty for independent travellers, most people go to Algeria on organised tours. Most of these tours are inclusive and cover your international flight, transport around the country, food, accommodation and guide etc. Most tours to Algeria concentrate on the Sahara; the bulk of them in the desert regions around Tamanrasset and Djanet and some to the Grand Ergs and the M'Zab. Tours are usually conducted in small groups of around eight to 15 people and will either travel by 4WD, trekking on foot with pack animals, or on camels; sometimes it's a combination of all these things. Overland tours used to cross through the Algerian Sahara on trans-Africa expeditions, but since the troubles of the 1990s they have stayed away. Several companies are listed below, but the list is not exhaustive. For tour companies based inside the country, see p217.

Continental Europe

Hommes et Montagnes (☎ 4 3886 6919; www.hommes-et-montagnes.fr) Well-established and extremely professional, this company provides a huge range of trekking options from eight to 22 days. Tours are rated from easy to difficult.

La Route du Sahara (www.laroutedusahara.com) Provides a variety of trekking options in the Sahara as well as cultural tours to the S'biba festival in Djanet and a 'spiritual trek' following in the footsteps of Charles de Foucauld.

Les Matins du Monde (☎ 4 37 24 90 30; www.lesmatinsdumonde.com) Offers hikes, camel treks and 4WD treks in the Sahara, as well as more specialised tours such as rock-climbing.

Point Afrique (☎ 4 75 97 20 40; www.point-afrique.com) This company doesn't just do flights, it also organises personally tailored and group tours. As well as tours in the Sahara it has have treks in the Kabylie Mountains and discovery tours of Northern Algeria's ancient Roman sites.

Terres d'Aventure (☎ 825 847 800; www.terdav.com) Has 10 different desert tours including three family-friendly trips in Algeria for kids as young as six.

Via Nostra (www.vianostra.fr) Offers cultural tours to Northern Algeria.

UK & Ireland

Explore Worldwide (☎ 0870 333 4001; www.explore.co.uk) Has recently launched a small group tour to Algeria, travelling by 4WD, minibus and plane, which takes in Algiers, Tipaza, Ghardaïa, the Tassili N'Ajjer and the Hoggar Mountains.

Sahara Travel (☎ 1 496 8844; www.saharatravel.co.uk) An Ireland-based company that offers 4WD trips in the Algerian Sahara, including self-drive 4WD expeditions where you will be accompanied by a tour leader but drive your own 4WD. Includes channel crossing and ferry crossing from Marseille.

USA & Canada

Adventures Abroad (☎ 1-800 665 3998; www.adventures-abroad.com) Has 12-day small-group tours taking in the ancient sites of the north as well as Tassili N'Ajjer National Park.

Lost Frontiers (☎ 888 508-2454; www.lostfrontiers.com) California-based company offering a three-week tour to the Tassili N'Ajjer and the Hoggar Mountains.

Journeys International (☎ 800 255 8735; www.journeys-intl.com) Offers a North Africa tour that takes in the northern regions of Algeria.

GETTING AROUND

AIR

Because of the huge distances involved in travelling in Algeria, flying can be a good way to get around and there's an excellent network of regional airports. For the more popular and less frequent routes, such as Tamanrasset or Djanet to Algiers, it pays to book well in advance (if you can!). When you've walked through customs to board an internal flight, you'll notice that all of the passengers' baggage is lying on the tarmac. You have to identify your bag to the ground staff before they put it on the plane. If you don't, it'll get left behind.

Airlines in Algeria

Air Algérie (☎ 021 653340; www.airalgere.dz) is the national carrier of Algeria and the only airline currently offering internal flights after Khalifa Airways folded in 2003. There are a couple of smaller airlines in operation such as JetAir Sahara but these mainly serve as charter airlines for workers in the oil and gas industries.

Distances are long in Algeria and if travelling independently you'll probably use internal flights at some point. Although it's quicker to get around by air, tickets are expensive and Air Algérie's customer service can be ridiculously inefficient. In theory it's possible to book internal flights before arriving in the country through the website or international Air Algérié offices, but this can be a nightmare. The schedules are often incorrect and many flights unbookable. It is often the case that a flight will appear on the website or timetable but cannot be booked as seats have not been released yet; sometimes they are not released until a few days before the flight.

On the ground there are often delays, cancellations or time changes with little warning. At local Air Algérie offices you will almost certainly have to pay in cash, but this can usually be done in euros as well as dinars.

BUS

Intercity buses are run by the national company SNTV, sometimes known in the south as TVSE. It serves all major tourist destinations in Algeria. Bus trips are reasonably priced, but vary greatly in comfort level, from old, slow, hot dinosaurs to more modern air-conditioned vehicles. Buses also vary in size and are either full-size buses or 30-seater minibuses.

SNTV covers most major destinations in Algeria going as far south as Tamanrasset, although it is less widespread in the south; Djanet, for example is only served by shared taxis. There are also a number of private companies that usually operate from and have small offices in the main city bus terminals. These tend to be more expensive than the national SNTV buses, but are generally more comfortable, modern and air-conditioned. Most long-distance services leave either very early in the morning or at night to escape travelling in the peak heat. Make sure to arrive at the *gare routière* bus station at least half an hour before the departure time. It's also a good idea to make reservations in advance for more popular or long-distance journeys.

Buses are a reasonably priced way of getting around. For example, a journey from Algiers to Ghardaïa costs DA650, and a journey from Ghardaïa to Tamanrasset costs DA1500.

CAR & MOTORCYCLE

The major route across the Algerian Sahara is the Route du Hoggar, which goes from Ghardaïa to Tamanrasset, and then on to In Guezzam and the Niger frontier. The road is tar all the way to Tamanrasset, although it's patchy after In Salah. Other less-used routes include the Route du Tanezrouft, which runs from Adrar to Borj Mokhtar near the Malian border and includes sections of piste.

There is no longer a need to drive in convoy in Southern Algeria; however, at the time of writing all independent travellers in the south needed to be accompanied by a guide. The guide will meet you at the border and either join you in your own car or, if you are in a motorcycle or bicycle, will follow you in their own car. A guide in your car costs from around €80 a day and must be arranged in advance. Tourist offices in Tamamrasset and Djanet can take care of this.

Algerians aren't exactly known for their careful driving skills; basic road rules are rarely respected and the number of fatal road accidents rises year after year. You'll find plenty of police and army roadblocks on the road, especially in the south. Slow down on approach and wait to be waved through. If you are stopped you'll be asked for papers, passport, visa and perhaps other personal details, such as your home address and the duration of your stay. This can sometimes be a lengthy process but be cooperative.

For further information about driving in the Sahara, see p76. It's also worth consulting the excellent *Sahara Overland* by Chris Scott.

Bring Your Own Vehicle

Anyone planning to bring their vehicle with them to Algeria needs to check in advance what spare parts and petrol are likely to be available. When bringing your car into the country, you'll need vehicle registration documents and it's essential that the details on this document must match those on your vehicle. Unlike some of the neighbouring countries, you don't need a carnet to drive your car into Algeria. Instead you'll be issued with a *passage de conduire* (driving licence) by customs and you'll also have to fill out police and customs declarations forms. European Green Card insurance is not recognised so you'll have to buy car insurance at the border, normally around DA5000 for 30 days for a car and DA2000 for a motorcycle.

If coming from Europe, there are a number of ferry crossings from Marseille in France and Alicante in Spain to several destinations in Algeria. A one-way crossing for a car costs from €386 (including an adult fare). Alternatively, you could come via Tunisia, driving overland to the crossing at Nefta.

Driving Licence

You'll need an International Driving Permit (IDP) as well as your home licence if you wish to drive your own car or hire a car in Algeria. IDPs are easy and cheap to get in your home country and are normally issued by major motoring associations, such as the AA in Britain.

Fuel & Spare Parts

Petrol is relatively cheap in Algeria. At the time of writing petrol cost about DA20 per litre and diesel cost DA14 per litre. Availability of petrol is normally good, with even the smaller towns having at least one petrol pump. In the south the situation is a little different, and with the long distances between towns you should bear in mind that there can be distances of several hundred kilometres between fuel stops. At the time of writing there were also reports of fuel shortages in In Guezzam.

Spare parts will usually be available in all major towns. However, if you have a very recent model it could be a good idea to bring your own spare parts or check with your manufacturer for a list of accredited parts suppliers.

Hire

There are numerous car-hire offices in the major airports in the north and in town centres. They will ask for a piece of identitfication, an IDL and a deposit; check your contract carefully to see what is included in the insurance; you have to be 24 or over to hire a car in Algeria and have to have had a licence for at least two years, but this varies according to the agent. In the south you will have to hire a car with a driver, and most travel agencies mentioned in this guide provide such a service. A 4WD with driver should cost from €100 to €150 a day depending on the season.

Love Tour Algiers (☎ 021 637111); Hassi Messaoud (☎ 029 754994); Oran (☎ 41 394136); Tlemcen (☎ 43 2246521; www.lovetouralgerie.com); . You must be 30 and over to rent a car from these guys. Cars cost from DA2500 a day.

Magi Car (☎ 021 549393; www.magi-car.com) Has two offices in Algiers and one at the airport. From DA2900 a day for the most basic car, usually a Peugeot 206. A car with driver costs from DA6500 a day.

Rapide Car Algiers international airport (☎ 021 509512; www.rapidecar.com); Bejaïa (☎ 034 201048) Rental costs from DA3300 a day and you must be over the age of 26.

Insurance

Fully comprehensive insurance for Algeria is strongly advised, given the number of road accidents that occur here. Make sure you're covered for off-piste travel and if you're planning any cross-border travel, that you're fully insured to do so. In the event of an accident make sure you give your insurance company the accident report as soon as possible.

Third party insurance can be bought at the border from around €50 a month. Green Card insurance is not valid in Algeria.

Road Conditions

Road conditions in Algeria are generally good and most major highways have smooth sealed roads. Notable exceptions are the stretch between In Salah and In Guezzam, which is patchy, and from Reggane to the Malian border at Bordj Mokhtar. Driving off piste is a whole other matter. See p76 for details on driving in the Sahara.

Road Hazards

Some of the biggest road hazards in Algeria are careless drivers – the rules of the road aren't respected here so always be on your guard. Avoid driving at night – the roads are not well lit, and the highways aren't lit at all. Many cars drive on the road at night without lights, and in rural areas animals wander onto the roads.

In the desert keep an eye out for camels, which are sometimes camouflaged against the sand. After sandstorms watch out for build-up on the road, especially at night; sometimes entire sections of the road can be engulfed with sand. For more specific advice on desert hazards, see p76.

Road Rules

Algerians drive on the right-hand side of the road. If a car is fitted with seatbelts, they must be worn, even for passengers sitting in the back. The use of mobile telephones while driving is forbidden.

Because help can take so long to arrive, Algerians generally try to flag down another car in the event of a breakdown, and there is a lot of camaraderie on the roads.

HITCHING

Hitching is never entirely safe in any country and we don't recommend it. People who do choose to hitch will be safer if they do it in pairs and let someone know where they are planning to go.

The Sahara has long been a popular region for adventurers in their own vehicles, so backpackers have traditionally hitched rides. At the time of writing there were very few tourists driving though Algeria so chances of picking up a lift were slim. If you're very lucky you might meet a loner who's happy to offer a spare seat in return for help digging when the car gets stuck

in the sand, and possibly a contribution towards fuel – but don't count on it.

LOCAL TRANSPORT
Bus

Local buses are large, old and can be unreliable but they're reasonably priced and in the larger cities 10-journey carnets and daily, weekly or longer duration passes are available. If you're only around for a short time, it's often faster to use the minibuses that go around the major towns, such as Algiers and Oran, and work on a fill-up-and-go basis.

Metro

An underground system has been planned for many years in Algiers and construction recently began. The first section of the metro is due to be completed in 2008.

Taxi

Taxis are plentiful in most cities and major towns, though they're busy during the early evening as many people use them to return home after work and the practice of sharing a taxi is widespread. If your taxi doesn't have a meter agree on a price before setting off. Short journeys within town should cost around DA50.

SHARED TAXI

Called *taxis collectifs, louanges* or *taxis brousse,* these are normally yellow Peugeots and are a good way of getting around the country. They usually leave from (or near to) the town's main bus station or, in smaller towns, from the local bus/taxi ranks or the main town square.

They tend to be faster then the buses, as they don't have to make so many stops; the

---

LES TAXIEURS *Zahia Hafs*

'Taxieur' is the common expression for a taxi driver. The people in Algiers point out that it takes less time to say 'taxieur' than 'chauffeur de taxi' (taxi driver).

Getting a cab in the city is quite easy and very cheap. Some are yellow cabs while others look more like ordinary cars, but with taxi a sign on top. The *taxieur* usually has a meter but it will not always be on, and the driver will most likely say that it does not work (as is the case in many parts of the world). You can insist, but meters rarely work, and if you are in a hurry you must negotiate a price before heading off to your destination.

At rush hour, which is basically all day long, don't be surprised if a *taxieur* picks up other passengers. It is perfectly normal and you will often find that it is actually a good way to meet people. They love to know where you come from and what you think of Algeria. The likelihood is that you will end up chatting and joking with everybody in the car.

only down side being that there's not as much space for luggage. Shared taxis plough all the main routes in Algeria, from Algiers right down to Tamanrasset. They leave on a fill-up-and-go basis so you'll have to be at the station very early in the morning to get the best chance of catching a ride. They usually take up to six passengers with bags. They are a little more expensive than buses but the journeys are more comfortable and you're more likely to strike up a conversation with your fellow travellers.

From Tamanrasset to the border with Niger and from Adrar to Reggane the routes are covered by 4WD taxis, which cost a little more.

TOURS
Algeria's many tour operators offer 4WD circuits, camel treks, hiking tours, wine-tasting trips and cultural and historic tours. Following is a list of some reliable companies based around the country. For details about foreign travel agencies, see p213.

Club d'Aventure Africaine (☎ 021 697922; www
.caa-dz.com; 7 rue des Fréres Oughlis, Algiers) Offers tours to the Sahara.

Immidir Voyages (☎ 029344468/2484; www.immidir
-voyages.com; Tamanrasset) Excellent and established agency providing 4WD treks and tours around the Tam region, with particularly interesting tours into the Immidir region. The owner is particularly enthusiastic and interested in this area of the country.

Mer de Sable (☎ 049 902595; www.agence-merdesa
ble.com; rue Abd el-Kader Ziadi, Timimoun) Has excellent trips in camel caravans, as well as 4WD tours throughout the region.

Misserghin Tours (☎ 041 458075; www.misserghin
-tours.com; 9 ave de Sidi Chami, Oran) Organises visits to villages around Oran and Tlemcen, themed tours such as Oran under the Ottoman Empire and sporting activities such as hunting and fishing.

M'Zab Tours (☎ 029 880002; mzabtours@hotmail.com; av du 1er Novembre, Ghardaïa) An excellent and well-organised agency, it offers individually tailored tours around the M'Zab Valley and the Grand Ergs. It has a sister agency in Tamanrassset.

Timbeur Voyages (☎ 029475270; www.voyages-tim
beur.com; Djanet) This is one of Djanet's most established agencies. It has offices next to the market and offers short expeditions, such as trips to Erg Admer and Tagharghart to La Vache Qui Pleure, as well as one-day trips to Jabbaren.

Zenata Voyages (☎ 041 391227; 24 rue de Tripoli, Oran) Offers a number of trips based around the culture and history of Oran and Tlemcen, as well as wine-tasting trips. It also organises hotel reservations and car hire.

TRAIN
Algerian railways are run by the **Société Nationale des Transports Ferroviaires** (SNTF; ☎ 021 711510; www.sntf.dz). The train network consists of some 4500km of tracks in the north of the country and hasn't changed much since colonial times. The tracks go as far as Touggourt in the southeast of the country and Béchar in the southwest. At the time of writing the only trains going as far as Touggourt or Béchar were goods trains, but lines were set to resume to Béchar in late 2007 or early 2008. The Algerian government has also launched a scheme to modernise the tracks and trains and to extend its southeastern lines all the way to Hassi Messaoud.

Trains go from Algiers to Annaba, Constantine, Bejaia, Oran and Skikda. Many of the trains are quite old and slow but they are reasonably reliable. There are 1st- and 2nd-class compartments, family cars, couchettes for overnight journeys and air-conditioning on long journeys. Prices for train travel in Algeria are very reasonable. For example, a 1st-class ticket on the overnight sleeper from Algiers to Annaba costs DA1650.

TRANSPORT

Health

CONTENTS

As long as you stay up to date with your vaccinations and take some basic preventive measures, you'd have to be pretty unlucky to succumb to most of the health hazards covered in this chapter. Africa certainly has an impressive selection of diseases on offer, but most of these are extremely rare in Algeria and you're much more likely to get a bout of diarrhoea (in fact, you should bank on it), a cold or an infected mosquito bite than an exotic disease. When it comes to injuries (as opposed to illness), the most likely reason for needing medical help in Algeria is as a result of road accidents – vehicles are rarely well maintained, the roads are potholed and poorly lit, and drink driving is common.

BEFORE YOU GO

A little planning before departure, particularly for pre-existing illnesses, will save you a lot of trouble later. Before a long trip get a check-up from your dentist and from your doctor if you have any regular medication or chronic illness, eg high blood pressure and asthma. You should also organise spare contact lenses and glasses (and take your optical prescription with you); get a first-aid and medical kit together; and arrange necessary vaccinations.

It's tempting to leave it all to the last minute – don't! Many vaccines don't take effect until two weeks after you've been immunised, so visit a doctor four to eight weeks before departure. Ask your doctor for an International Certificate of Vaccination (otherwise known as the yellow booklet), which will list all the vaccinations you've received. This is mandatory for the African countries that require proof of yellow fever vaccination upon entry, but it's a good idea to carry it anyway wherever you travel.

Travellers can register with the **International Association for Medical Advice to Travellers** (IMAT; www.iamat.org). Its website can help travellers to find a doctor who has recognised training. Those heading off to very remote areas might like to do a first-aid course (contact the Red Cross or St John's Ambulance) or attend a remote medicine first-aid course, such as that offered by the **Royal Geographical Society** (www.wildernessmedical training.co.uk).

If you are bringing medications with you, carry them in their original containers, clearly labelled. A signed and dated letter from your physician describing all medical conditions and medications, including generic names, is also a good idea. If carrying syringes or needles be sure to have a physician's letter documenting their medical necessity.

How do you go about getting the best possible medical help? It's difficult to say – it really depends on the severity of your illness or injury and the availability of local help. If malaria is suspected, seek medical help as soon as possible or begin self-medicating if you are off the beaten track (see p222).

INSURANCE

Find out in advance whether your insurance plan will make payments directly to providers or will reimburse you later for overseas health expenditures (in many countries doctors expect payment in cash).

It's vital to ensure that your travel insurance will cover the emergency transport required to get you to a hospital in a major city, to better medical facilities elsewhere beyond Algeria, or all the way home, by air and with a medical attendant if necessary. Not all insurance covers this, so check the contract carefully. If you need medical help, your insurance company might be able to help locate the nearest hospital or clinic, or you can ask at your hotel. In an emergency contact your embassy or consulate.

RECOMMENDED VACCINATIONS

The **World Health Organization** (WHO; www.who.int/en/) recommends all travellers be covered for diphtheria, tetanus, measles, mumps, rubella and polio, as well as for hepatitis B, regardless of their destination. Planning to travel is a great time to ensure that all routine vaccination cover is complete. The consequences of these diseases can be severe, and outbreaks of them do occur.

According to the **Centers for Disease Control & Prevention** (www.cdc.gov), the following vaccinations are recommended for all parts of Africa: hepatitis A, hepatitis B, meningococcal meningitis, rabies and typhoid, and boosters for tetanus, diphtheria and measles. Yellow fever is not necessarily required for Algeria unless you are arriving from elsewhere in sub-Saharan Africa, in which case you may need to show the certificate upon entering Algeria or obtaining your visa.

MEDICAL CHECKLIST

It is a very good idea to carry a medical and first-aid kit with you, to help yourself in the case of minor illness or injury. Following is a list of items you should consider packing.

- acetaminophen (paracetamol) or aspirin
- acetazolamide (Diamox) for treating altitude sickness (prescription only)
- adhesive or paper tape
- antibacterial ointment (eg Bactroban) for cuts and abrasions (prescription only)
- antibiotics (prescription only) such as ciprofloxacin (Ciproxin) or norfloxacin (Utinor)
- antidiarrhoeal drugs (eg loperamide)
- antihistamines (for hayfever and allergic reactions)
- anti-inflammatory drugs (eg ibuprofen)
- antimalaria pills

- bandages, gauze, gauze rolls
- DEET-containing insect repellent for use on the skin
- iodine tablets (for water purification)
- oral rehydration salts
- permethrin-containing insect spray for clothing, tents, and bed nets
- pocket knife
- scissors, safety pins, tweezers
- sterile needles, syringes and fluids if travelling to remote areas
- steroid cream or hydrocortisone cream (for allergic rashes)
- sunblock
- syringes and sterile needles
- thermometer

If you are travelling through a malarial area – particularly an area in which falciparum malaria predominates – consider taking a self-diagnostic kit that can identify malaria in the blood from a finger prick.

INTERNET RESOURCES

There is a wealth of travel health advice on the internet. For further information, the Lonely Planet website at www.lonelyplanet.com is a good place to start. The WHO publishes a superb book called *International Travel and Health,* which is revised annually and is available online at no cost at www.who.int/ith/. Other websites of general interest to travellers include **MD Travel Health** (www.mdtravelhealth.com), which provides complete travel health recommendations for every country, updated daily, also at no cost; the **Centers for Disease Control & Prevention** (www.cdc.gov); and **Fit for Travel** (www.fitfortravel.scot.nhs.uk), which features up-to-date information about outbreaks and is very user-friendly.

It's also a good idea to consult your government's travel health website before departure, if one is available:

Australia (www.dfat.gov.au/travel/)
Canada (www.hc-sc.gc.ca/english/index.html)
UK (www.dh.gov.uk/en/index.htm)
USA (www.cdc.gov/travel/)

FURTHER READING

- *A Comprehensive Guide to Wilderness and Travel Medicine* by Eric A Weiss (1998)
- *Healthy Travel* by Jane Wilson-Howarth (1999)

HEALTH

- *Healthy Travel Africa* by Isabelle Young (2000)
- *How to Stay Healthy Abroad* by Richard Dawood (2002)
- *Travel in Health* by Graham Fry (1994)
- *Travel with Children* by Cathy Lanigan (2004)

IN TRANSIT

DEEP VEIN THROMBOSIS (DVT)

Blood clots can form in the legs during flights, chiefly because of prolonged immobility. This formation of clots is known as deep vein thrombosis (DVT), and the longer the flight, the greater the risk. Although most blood clots are reabsorbed uneventfully, some might break off and travel through the blood vessels to the lungs, where they could cause life-threatening complications.

The chief symptom of DVT is swelling or pain of the foot, ankle or calf, usually but not always on just one side. When a blood clot travels to the lungs, it could cause chest pain and breathing difficulty. Travellers who are experiencing any of these symptoms should immediately seek medical attention.

To prevent the development of DVT on long flights you should walk about the cabin, perform isometric compressions of the leg muscles (ie contract the leg muscles while sitting), drink plenty of fluids and avoid alcohol.

JET LAG & MOTION SICKNESS

If you're crossing more than five time zones you could suffer jet lag, resulting in insomnia, fatigue, malaise or nausea. To avoid jet lag try drinking plenty of fluids (nonalcoholic) and eating light meals. Upon arrival get exposure to natural sunlight and readjust your schedule (for meals, sleep etc) as soon as possible.

Antihistamines such as dimenhydrinate (Dramamine) and also meclizine (Antivert, Bonine) are usually the first choice for treating motion sickness. The main side effect people find when they take these drugs is drowsiness. A herbal alternative is ginger (in the form of ginger tea, biscuits or crystallized ginger), which works like a charm for some people.

IN ALGERIA

AVAILABILITY & COST OF HEALTH CARE

Health care in Algeria is varied: it can be excellent in the major cities, which generally have well-trained doctors and nurses, but it is often patchy off the beaten track. Medicine and even sterile dressings and intravenous fluids might need to be purchased from a local pharmacy by patients or their relatives. The standard of dental care is equally variable, and there is an increased risk of hepatitis B and HIV transmission via poorly sterilised equipment. By and large, public hospitals in Algeria offer the cheapest service, but will have the least up-to-date equipment and medications; mission hospitals (where donations are the usual form of payment) often have more reasonable facilities; and private hospitals and clinics are more expensive but tend to have more advanced drugs and equipment, and better trained medical staff.

Most drugs can be purchased over the counter in Algeria without a prescription. Many drugs for sale might be ineffective: they might be counterfeit or might not have been stored under the right conditions. The most common examples of counterfeit drugs are malaria tablets and expensive antibiotics, such as ciprofloxacin. Most drugs are available in capital cities, but remote villages will be lucky to have a couple of paracetamol tablets. It is strongly recommended that all drugs for chronic diseases be brought from home. Also, the availability and efficacy of condoms cannot be relied upon – bring all the contraception you'll need. Condoms bought in Algeria might not be of the same quality as in Europe or Australia, and they might have been incorrectly stored.

There is a risk of contracting HIV from infected blood if you receive a blood transfusion in Algeria. **The BloodCare Foundation** (www.bloodcare.org.uk) is a useful source of safe, screened blood, which can be transported to any part of the world within 24 hours.

The cost of health care might seem very cheap compared with developed countries, but good care and drugs might not be available. Evacuation to good medical care (within Algeria or to your own country) can be very expensive indeed.

INFECTIOUS DISEASES

It's a formidable list but, as we say, a few precautions go a long way…

Cholera

Cholera is usually only a problem during natural or artificial disasters, eg war, floods or earthquakes, although small outbreaks can also occur at other times. Travellers are rarely affected. It is caused by a bacteria and spread via contaminated drinking water. The main symptom is profuse watery diarrhoea, which causes debilitation if fluids are not replaced quickly. An oral cholera vaccine is available in the USA, but it is not particularly effective. Most cases of cholera could be avoided by close attention to good drinking water and by avoiding potentially contaminated food. Treatment is by fluid replacement (orally or via a drip), but sometimes antibiotics are needed. Attempting self-treatment is not advised.

Diphtheria

Diphtheria is spread through close respiratory contact. It usually causes a temperature and a severe sore throat. Sometimes a membrane forms across the throat, and a tracheostomy is needed to prevent suffocation. Vaccination is recommended for those likely to be in close contact with the local population in infected areas, and is more important for long stays than for short-term trips. The vaccine is given as an injection alone or with tetanus, and lasts 10 years.

Hepatitis A

Hepatitis A is spread through contaminated food (particularly shellfish) and water. It causes jaundice and, although it is rarely fatal, it can cause prolonged lethargy and delayed recovery. If you've had hepatitis A, you shouldn't drink alcohol for up to six months afterwards, but once you've recovered, there won't be any long-term problems. The first symptoms include dark urine and a yellow colour to the whites of the eyes. Sometimes a fever and abdominal pain might be present. Hepatitis A vaccine (avaxim, VAQTA, havrix) is given as an injection: a single dose will give protection for up to a year, and a booster after a year gives 10-year protection. Hepatitis A and typhoid vaccines can also be given as a single dose vaccine, hepatyrix or viatim.

Hepatitis B

Hepatitis B is passed on through infected blood, contaminated needles and sexual intercourse. It can also be spread from an infected mother to the baby during childbirth. It affects the liver, causing jaundice and occasionally liver failure. Most people recover completely, but some people might be chronic carriers of the virus, which could eventually lead to cirrhosis or liver cancer. Those visiting high-risk areas for long periods or those with increased social or occupational risk should be immunised. Many countries now routinely give hepatitis B as part of the routine childhood vaccination. It is given singly or can be given at the same time as hepatitis A (hepatyrix).

A course will give protection for at least five years. It can be given over four weeks or six months.

HIV

Human Immunodeficiency Virus (HIV), the virus that causes Acquired Immune Deficiency Syndrome (AIDS), is spread through infected blood and also blood products, by sexual intercourse with an infected partner and from an infected mother to her baby during childbirth and breastfeeding. It can be spread through 'blood to blood' contacts, such as with contaminated instruments during medical, dental, acupuncture and other body-piercing procedures, and through sharing used intravenous needles. At present there is no cure; medication that might keep the disease under control is available, but these drugs are not readily available for travellers either. If you think you might have been infected with HIV a blood test is necessary; a three-month gap after exposure and before testing is required to allow antibodies to appear in the blood.

Leishmaniasis

This is spread through the bite of an infected sandfly. It can cause a slowly growing skin lump or ulcer (the cutaneous form) and sometimes a life-threatening fever with anaemia and weight loss. Dogs can also be carriers of the infection. Sandfly bites should be avoided whenever possible.

Leptospirosis

Leptospirosis is spread through the excreta of infected rodents, especially rats. It can cause hepatitis and renal failure, which might be fatal. It's unusual for travellers to be affected unless living in poor sanitary conditions. It causes a fever and sometimes jaundice.

Malaria

There is only a slight risk of malaria in Algeria. One million children die annually from malaria in Africa. The risk of malarial transmission at altitudes higher than 2000m is rare. The disease is caused by a parasite in the bloodstream spread via the bite of the female Anopheles mosquito. There are several types of malaria; falciparum malaria being the most dangerous type and the predominant form in Africa. Infection rates vary with season and climate, so check out the situation before departure. Unlike most other diseases regularly encountered by travellers, there is no vaccination against malaria (yet). However, several different drugs are used to prevent malaria and new ones are in the pipeline. Up-to-date advice from a travel health clinic is essential as some medication is more suitable for some travellers than others. The pattern of drug-resistant malaria is changing rapidly, so what was advised several years ago might no longer be used.

Malaria can present in several ways. The early stages include headaches, fevers, generalised aches and pains, and malaise, which could be mistaken for flu. Other symptoms can include abdominal pain, diarrhoea and a cough. Anyone who develops a fever in a malarial area should assume malarial infection until a blood test proves negative, even if you have been taking antimalarial medication. If not treated the next stage could develop within 24 hours, particularly if falciparum malaria is the parasite: jaundice, then reduced consciousness and coma (also known as cerebral malaria) followed by death. Treatment in hospital is essential, and the death rate might still be as high as 10% even in the best intensive-care facilities.

Many travellers are under the impression that malaria is a mild illness, that treatment is always easy and successful, and that taking antimalarial drugs causes more illness through side effects than actually getting malaria. In Africa this is unfortunately not true. Side effects of the medication depend on the drug being taken. Doxycycline can cause heartburn and indigestion; mefloquine (Larium) can bring on anxiety attacks, insomnia and nightmares, and (rarely) severe psychiatric disorders; chloroquine can cause nausea and hair loss; and proguanil can cause mouth ulcers. These side effects are not universal and can be minimized by taking medication correctly, eg with food. Also, some people should not take a particular antimalarial drug, eg people with epilepsy should avoid mefloquine, and doxycycline should not be taken by pregnant women or children younger than 12.

If you decide that you really do not wish to take antimalarial drugs, you must understand the risks and be obsessive about avoiding mosquito bites. Use nets and insect repellent, and report any fever or flulike symptoms to a doctor as soon as possible. Some people advocate homeopathic preparations against malaria, such as Demal200, but as yet there is no conclusive evidence that this is effective, and many homeopaths do not recommend their use.

People of all ages can contract malaria, and falciparum causes the most severe illness. Repeated infections might result eventually in less serious illness. Malaria in pregnancy frequently results in miscarriage

---

THE ANTIMALARIAL A TO D

A: Awareness of the risk No medication is totally effective, but protection of up to 95% is achievable with most drugs, as long as other measures have been taken.

B: Bites Avoid being bitten at all costs. Sleep in a screened room, use a mosquito spray or coils, and sleep under a permethrin-impregnated net at night. Cover up at night with long trousers and long sleeves, preferably with permethrin-treated clothing. Apply appropriate repellent to all areas of exposed skin in the evenings.

C: Chemical prevention Antimalarial drugs are usually needed in malarial areas. Expert advice is needed as resistance patterns can change and new drugs are in development. Not all antimalarial drugs are suitable for everyone. Most antimalarial drugs need to be started at least a week in advance and continued for four weeks after the last possible exposure to malaria.

D: Diagnosis If you have a fever or flulike illness within a year of travel to a malarial area, malaria is a possibility and immediate medical attention is necessary.

or premature labour. Adults who have survived childhood malaria have developed immunity and usually only develop mild cases of malaria; most Western travellers have no immunity at all. Immunity wanes after 18 months of nonexposure, so even if you have had malaria in the past and used to live in a malaria-prone area, you might no longer be immune.

If you are planning a journey through a malarial area, particularly where falciparum malaria predominates, consider taking standby treatment. Emergency standby treatment should be seen as emergency treatment aimed at saving the patient's life and not as routine self-medication. It should be used only if you will be far from medical facilities and have been advised about the symptoms of malaria and how to use the medication. Medical advice should be sought as soon as possible to confirm whether the treatment has been successful. The type of standby treatment used will depend on local conditions, such as drug resistance, and on what antimalarial drugs were being used before standby treatment. This is worthwhile because you want to avoid contracting a particularly serious form such as cerebral malaria, which affects the brain and central nervous system and can be fatal in 24 hours. Self-diagnostic kits (see p219), which can identify malaria in the blood from a finger prick, are also available in the West.

The risks from malaria to both mother and foetus during pregnancy are considerable. Unless good medical care can be guaranteed, travel throughout Algeria when pregnant – particularly to malarial areas – should be discouraged unless essential. Use emergency standby treatment if you are more than 24 hours away from medical help.

Poliomyelitis

Generally spread through contaminated food and water, one of the vaccines is given in childhood and should be boosted every 10 years, either orally (a drop on the tongue) or as an injection. Polio can be carried asymptomatically (ie showing no symptoms) and could cause a transient fever. In rare cases it causes weakness or paralysis of one or more muscles, which might be permanent.

Rabies

Rabies is spread by receiving the bites or licks of an infected animal on broken skin. It is always fatal once the clinical symptoms start (which might be up to several months after an infected bite), so postbite vaccination should be given as soon as possible. Postbite vaccination (whether or not you've been vaccinated before the bite) prevents the virus from spreading to the central nervous system. Animal handlers should be vaccinated, as should those travelling to remote areas where a reliable source of postbite vaccine is not available within 24 hours. Three preventive injections are needed over a month. If you have not been vaccinated you will need a course of five injections starting 24 hours or as soon as possible after the injury. If you have been vaccinated you will need fewer postbite injections and have more time to seek medical help.

Tuberculosis

Tuberculosis (TB) is passed on through close respiratory contact and occasionally through infected milk or milk products. BCG vaccination is recommended for those likely to be mixing closely with the local population, although it gives only moderate protection against TB. It is more important for long stays than for short-term stays. Inoculation with the BCG vaccine is not available in all countries. It is given routinely to many children in developing countries. The vaccination causes a small permanent scar at the site of injection, and is usually given in a specialised chest clinic. It is a live vaccine and should not be given to pregnant women or immunocompromised individuals.

TB can be asymptomatic, only being picked up on a routine chest X-ray. Alternatively, it can cause a cough, weight loss or fever, sometimes months or even years after exposure.

Typhoid

This is spread through food or water contaminated by infected human faeces. The first symptom is usually a fever or a pink rash on the abdomen. Sometimes septicaemia (blood poisoning) can occur. A typhoid vaccine (typhim Vi, typherix) will give protection for three years. In some

HEALTH

MANDATORY YELLOW FEVER VACCINATION

- North Africa – Not mandatory for any areas of North Africa, but Algeria, Libya and Tunisia require evidence of yellow fever vaccination if entering from an infected country. It is recommended for travellers to Sudan, and might be given to unvaccinated travellers leaving the country.

- Central Africa – Mandatory in Central African Republic (CAR), Congo, Congo (Zaïre), Equatorial Guinea and Gabon, and recommended in Chad.

- West Africa – Mandatory in Benin, Burkina Faso, Cameroon, Côte d'Ivoire, Ghana, Liberia, Mali, Niger, Sao Tome & Principe and Togo, and recommended for The Gambia, Guinea, Guinea-Bissau, Mauritania, Nigeria, Senegal and Sierra Leone.

- East Africa – Mandatory in Rwanda; it is advised for Burundi, Ethiopia, Kenya, Somalia, Tanzania and Uganda.

- Southern Africa – Not mandatory for entry into any countries of Southern Africa, although it is necessary if entering from an infected country.

---

countries the oral vaccine Vivotif is also available. Antibiotics are usually given as treatment and death is rare unless septicaemia occurs.

Yellow Fever

Travellers should carry a certificate as evidence of vaccination if they have recently been in an infected country, to avoid any possible difficulties with immigration. For a full list of these countries visit the website of the **WHO** (www.who.int/wer/) or the **Centers for Disease Control & Prevention** (www.cdc.gov/travel/blusheet.htm). There is always the possibility that a traveller without a legally required, up-to-date certificate will be vaccinated and detained in isolation at the port of arrival for up to 10 days or possibly repatriated.

Yellow fever is spread by infected mosquitoes. Symptoms range from a flulike illness to severe hepatitis (liver inflammation), jaundice and death. The yellow fever vaccination must be given at a designated clinic and is valid for 10 years. It is a live vaccine and must not be given to immuno-compromised or pregnant travellers.

TRAVELLERS' DIARRHOEA

Although it's not inevitable that you will get diarrhoea while travelling in Algeria, it's certainly possible. Diarrhoea is the most common travel-related illness – figures suggest that at least half of travellers to Africa will get diarrhoea at some stage. Sometimes dietary changes, such as increased spices or oils, are the cause. To help prevent diarrhoea, avoid tap water unless you're sure it's safe to drink (see p226). You should also only eat fresh fruits or vegetables if cooked or peeled, and be wary of dairy products that might contain unpasteurised milk. Although freshly cooked food can often be a safe option, plates or serving utensils might be dirty, so you should be highly selective when eating food from street vendors (make sure that cooked food is piping hot all the way through). If you develop diarrhoea, be sure to drink plenty of fluids, preferably an oral rehydration solution containing water (lots), and some salt and sugar. A few loose stools don't require treatment, but if you start having more than four or five stools a day you should start taking an antibiotic

Yellow Fever Risk in Africa

Areas with no Yellow Fever

Endemic Zones

(usually a quinoline drug, such as cipro-floxacin or norfloxacin) and an antidiar-rhoeal agent (such as loperamide) if you are not within easy reach of a toilet. If diarrhoea is bloody, persists for more than 72 hours or is accompanied by fever, shaking chills or severe abdominal pain, you should seek medical attention.

Amoebic Dysentery
Contracted by eating contaminated food and water, amoebic dysentery causes blood and mucus in the faeces. It can be relatively mild and tends to come on gradually, but seek medical advice if you think you have the illness as it won't clear up without treatment (which is with specific antibiotics).

Giardiasis
This, like amoebic dysentery, is also caused by ingesting contaminated food or water. The illness usually appears a week or more after you have been exposed to the offending parasite. Giardiasis might cause only a short-lived bout of typical travellers' diarrhoea, but it can also cause persistent diarrhoea. Ideally, seek medical advice if you suspect you have giardiasis, but if you are in a remote area you could start a course of antibiotics.

ENVIRONMENTAL HAZARDS
Heat Exhaustion
This condition can occur following heavy sweating and excessive fluid loss with inadequate replacement of fluids and salt, and is particularly common in hot climates when taking unaccustomed exercise before full acclimatisation. Symptoms include headache, dizziness and tiredness. Dehydration is already happening by the time you feel thirsty – aim to drink sufficient water to produce pale, diluted urine. Self-treatment: fluid replacement with water and/or fruit juice, and cooling by cold water and fans. The treatment of the salt-loss component consists of consuming salty fluids as in soup, and adding a little more table salt to foods than usual.

Heatstroke
Heat exhaustion is a precursor to the much more serious condition of heatstroke. In this case there is damage to the sweating mechanism, with an excessive rise in body temperature, irrational and hyperactive behaviour, and eventually loss of consciousness and death. Rapid cooling by spraying the body with water and fanning is ideal. Emergency fluid and electrolyte replacement is usually required by intravenous drip.

Insect Bites & Stings
Mosquitoes might not always carry malaria or dengue fever, but they (and other insects) can cause irritation and infected bites. To avoid this, take the same precautions as you would for avoiding malaria (see p222). Use DEET-based insect repellents. Excellent clothing treatments are also available; mosquitoes that land on treated clothing will die.

Bee and wasp stings cause real problems only to those who have a severe allergy to the stings (anaphylaxis.) If you are one of these people, carry an 'epipen' – an adrenaline (epinephrine) injection, which you can give yourself. This could save your life.

Sandflies are found around the Mediterranean beaches. They usually only cause a nasty itchy bite but can carry a rare skin disorder called cutaneous leishmaniasis (see p221). Prevention of bites with DEET-based repellents is sensible.

Scorpions are frequently found in arid or dry climates. They can cause a painful bite that is sometimes life-threatening. If bitten by a scorpion take a painkiller. Medical treatment should be sought if collapse occurs.

Bed bugs are often found in hostels and cheap hotels. They lead to very itchy, lumpy bites. Spraying the mattress with crawling insect killer after changing bedding will get rid of them.

Scabies is also frequently found in cheap accommodation. These tiny mites live in the skin, particularly between the fingers. They cause an intensely itchy rash. The itch is easily treated with malathion and permethrin lotion from a pharmacy; other members of the household also need treating to avoid spreading scabies, even if they do not show any symptoms.

Snake Bites
Basically, avoid getting bitten! Do not walk barefoot, or stick your hand into holes or cracks. However, 50% of those bitten by venomous snakes are not actually injected

HEALTH

with poison (envenomed). If bitten by a snake do not panic. Immobilise the bitten limb with a splint (such as a stick) and apply a bandage over the site, with firm pressure – similar to bandaging a sprain. Do not apply a tourniquet, or cut or suck the bite. Get medical help as soon as possible so anti-venom can be given if needed.

Water

Never drink tap water unless it has been boiled, filtered or chemically disinfected (such as with iodine tablets). Never drink from streams, rivers and lakes. It's also best to avoid drinking from pumps and wells – some do bring pure water to the surface, but the presence of animals can still contaminate supplies.

WOMEN'S HEALTH

Emotional stress, exhaustion and travelling across time zones can all contribute to an upset in the menstrual pattern. Some antibiotics, diarrhoea and vomiting can interfere with the effectiveness of oral contraceptives and lead to the risk of pregnancy – remember to take condoms just in case. Time zones, gastrointestinal upsets and antibiotics do not affect injectable contraception.

Travelling during pregnancy is usually possible but always consult your doctor before planning your trip. The most risky times for travel are during the first 12 weeks of pregnancy and after 30 weeks.

Tampons are available in pharmacies and supermarkets in the major cities of Algeria. Further afield choice is limited to pads and even they can be difficult to find. It's best to take supplies from home or stock up in the major towns.

TRADITIONAL MEDICINE

At least 80% of the African population relies on traditional medicine, often because conventional Western-style medicine is too expensive, because of prevailing cultural attitudes and beliefs, or simply because in some cases it works.

Although some African remedies seem to work on malaria, sickle cell anaemia, high blood pressure and some AIDS symptoms, most African healers learn their art by apprenticeship, so education (and consequently application of knowledge) is inconsistent and unregulated. Conventionally trained physicians in South Africa, for example, angrily describe how their AIDS patients die of kidney failure because a *sangoma* (traditional healer) has given them an enema containing an essence made from powerful roots. Likewise, when traditional healers administer 'injections' with porcupine quills, knives or dirty razor blades, diseases are often spread or created rather than cured.

Rather than attempting to stamp out traditional practices, or simply pretend they aren't happening, a positive first step taken by some African countries is the regulation of traditional medicine by creating healers' associations and offering courses on such topics as sanitary practices. It remains unlikely in the short term that even a basic level of conventional Western-style medicine will be made available to all the people of Africa (even though the cost of doing so is less than the annual military budget of some Western countries). Traditional medicine, on the other hand, will almost certainly continue to be practised widely throughout the continent.

Language

Arabic is the official language of Algeria and Berber is afforded 'national' language status. While standard Arabic (MSA) is used in both written and spoken form in the media and government, it differs significantly from the language – known as Algerian Arabic – that the vast majority of people speak in daily life. In Saharan regions, a number of other Arabic dialects are spoken. Several varieties of Berber are spoken, the most common dialect being *kabyle*, which is spoken around Kabylie. French (see p233) is still taught as a second language in schools and many Algerians still speak it, particularly in urban areas. English is now taught in secondary schools, but speakers of any fluency will be very few and far between.

Algerian Arabic will undoubtedly be the most useful language for everyday communication, and any attempts on your part to speak it will be rewarded manifold through the warm reception and encouragement shown by those you practise on.

If you'd like to delve more deeply into the regional dialects of Arabic, including that spoken in Algeria and neighbouring countries, get a copy of Lonely Planet's *Middle East Phrasebook*. Lonely Planet's *French Phrasebook* will also prove very useful in these destinations.

ALGERIAN ARABIC

Algerian Arabic is from the group of Arabic dialects known as the Western *(Maghreb)* dialects, which also includes Moroccan and Tunisian Arabic. It's basically a dialect of the standard language, but so different in many respects as to be virtually another language. As with most dialects, it's the everyday language that differs the most from that of Algeria's other Arabic-speaking neighbours. More specialised or educated language tends to be pretty much the same across the Arab world, although pronunciation may vary considerably. An Arab from, say, Jordan or Iraq will have no problem having a chat about politics or literature with an Algerian, but might have more trouble making themselves understood in a market in Algiers.

There is no official written form of the Algerian Arabic dialect, although there is no practical reason for this; the alphabet is phonetically based and it would therefore be possible to devise a way to transfer spoken language to written language. For some reason though, foreigners who specifically want to learn Algerian Arabic instead of MSA are told that it can't be written in script, and are then presented with one system or other of transliteration, none of which are totally satisfactory. This will give

THE STANDARD ARABIC ALPHABET

Final	Medial	Initial	Alone	Transliteration	Pronunciation
ـا			ا	ā/aa	as in 'father'/as the long 'a' sound in 'air'
ـب	ـبـ	بـ	ب	b	as in 'bet'
ـت	ـتـ	تـ	ت	t	as in 'ten'
ـث	ـثـ	ثـ	ث	th	as in 'thin'
ـج	ـجـ	جـ	ج	j	as in 'jet'
ـح	ـحـ	حـ	ح	H	a strongly whispered 'h', like a sigh of relief
ـخ	ـخـ	خـ	خ	kh	as the 'ch' in Scottish loch
ـد			د	d	as in 'dim'
ـذ			ذ	dh	as the 'th' in 'this'; also as **d** or **z**
ـر			ر	r	a rolled 'r', as in the Spanish word caro
ـز			ز	z	as in 'zip'
ـس	ـسـ	سـ	س	s	as in 'so', never as in 'wisdom'
ـش	ـشـ	شـ	ش	sh	as in 'ship'
ـص	ـصـ	صـ	ص		emphatic 's' (see below)
ـض	ـضـ	ضـ	ض		emphatic 'd' (see below)
ـط	ـطـ	طـ	ط		emphatic 't' (see below)
ـظ	ـظـ	ظـ	ظ		emphatic 'dh' (see below)
ـع	ـعـ	عـ	ع	'	the Arabic letter 'ayn; pronounce as a glottal stop – like the closing of the throat before saying 'Oh-oh!' (see Other Sounds on p229)
ـغ	ـغـ	غـ	غ	gh	a guttural sound like Parisian 'r'
ـف	ـفـ	فـ	ف	f	as in 'far'
ـق	ـقـ	قـ	ق	q	a strongly guttural 'k' sound; also often pronounced as a glottal stop
ـك	ـكـ	كـ	ك	k	as in 'king'
ـل	ـلـ	لـ	ل	l	as in 'lamb'
ـم	ـمـ	مـ	م	m	as in 'me'
ـن	ـنـ	نـ	ن	n	as in 'name'
ـه	ـهـ	هـ	ه	h	as in 'ham'
ـو			و	w	as in 'wet'; or
				oo	long, as in 'food'; or
				ow	as in 'how'
ـي	ـيـ	يـ	ي	y	as in 'yes'; or
				ee	as in 'beer', only softer; or
				ai/ay	as in 'aisle'/as the 'ay' in 'day'

Vowels Not all Arabic vowel sounds are represented in the alphabet. For more information on the vowel sounds used in this language guide, see Pronunciation on p229.

Emphatic Consonants To simplify the transliteration system used in this book, the emphatic consonants have not been differentiated from their non-emphatic counterparts.

you some idea of why few non-Arabs and non-Muslims embark on the study of the language.

Nevertheless, if you take the time to learn even a handful of words and phrases, you'll discover and experience much more while travelling through the country.

TRANSLITERATION

The whole business of transliteration is fraught with pitfalls, and the reality is that it simply isn't possible to devise a truly 'correct' system. The locals themselves can only guess at how to make the conversion – and the result is often amusing. The fact that French has had a big influence in Algeria has also led to many interesting ideas on transliteration. Don't be taken aback if you start noticing half a dozen different spellings for the same thing.

For this book, an attempt has been made to standardise some spellings of place names and the like. There is only one article in Arabic: *al* (the). It's also sometimes written as 'il' or 'el', occasionally contracted to 'l' and sometimes modified to reflect the first consonant of the following noun, eg in Saladin's name, Salah ad-Din (righteousness of the faith), the 'al' has been modified to 'ad' before the 'd' of 'Din'. The article *el* is used only in a few instances in this book, such as well-known places (El-Oued and El-Goléa) or where locals have used it in restaurant and hotel names.

PRONUNCIATION

Pronunciation of Arabic can be somewhat tongue-tying for those unfamiliar with the intonation and combination of sounds. The following guide should help, but it isn't complete because the myriad rules governing pronunciation and vowel use are too extensive to be covered here.

Vowels & Diphthongs

a	as in 'had' (sometimes very short)
aa	like the long 'a' sound in 'air'
e	as in 'bet' (sometimes very short)
ee	as in 'beer', only softer
i	as in 'hit'
o	as in 'hot'
oo	as in 'food'
u	as in 'put'
ow	as in 'how'
ai	as in 'aisle'
ay	as in 'day'

Consonants

Pronunciation of Arabic consonants is covered in the alphabet table (p228). Note that when double consonants occur in transliterations, each consonant is pronounced. For example, *il-Hammaam*, (bathroom), is pronounced 'il-ham-maam'.

Other Sounds

Arabic has two sounds that are very tricky for non-Arabs to produce, the *'ayn* and the glottal stop. The letter *'ayn* represents a sound with no English equivalent that comes even close – it is similar to the glottal stop (which is not actually represented in the alphabet) but the muscles at the back of the throat are gagged more forcefully and air is allowed to escape, creating a sound that has been described as reminiscent of someone being strangled! In many transliteration systems *'ayn* is represented by an opening quotation mark, and the glottal stop by a closing quotation mark. To make the transliterations in this language guide (and throughout the rest of the book) easier to use, we have not distinguished between the glottal stop and the *'ayn*, using the closing quotation mark to represent both sounds. Even though your pronunciation may be a little wide of the mark, you'll find that people will still understand you.

ACCOMMODATION

I'm looking for a ...	*ana inHawwas 'ala ...*
hotel	*oteel*
youth hostel	*daar ash-shabaab*
Where can I find a cheap hotel?	*ween kayin oteel rakhees?*
What is the address?	*waash l-adrees?*
Could you write the address, please?	*mumkin tiktibshee l-adrees?*
Do you have rooms available?	*'andkumshee shambra faarigha?*
I'd like a ...	*ana baghee ...*
I'd like to book a ...	*ana baghee n'erben ...*
bed	*sreer*
single room	*shambra li waaHid*
double room	*shambra doobal*
room with two beds	*shambra ma' sareerayn*
room with a bathroom	*shambra fee-ha beet ham-maam*
room with air-con/ fan	*shambra ma' mirwaha*

LANGUAGE

How much is it ...?	*aash Haal ...?*
per night	*aash Haal il-leela?*
per person	*kul shakhs*
Do you have any	*'andkumshee shambra arkhas?*
cheaper rooms?	
May I see it?	*mumkin inshoof-ha?*
Where is the	*ween beet Ham-maam?*
bathroom?	
(I'm leaving/We're	*(ana nimshi/aHna nimsheeoo)*
leaving) today.	*il-yoom*

Making a Reservation

in the name of ...	*bi 'ism ...*
date	*taareekh*
from (date) **to** (date)	*min inhaar (...) lin-haar (...)*
credit card ...	*kart kredee ...*
number	*noomroo*
expiry date	*taareekh al-'intihaa*

CONVERSATION & ESSENTIALS

Hello.	*salaam*
(response)	*salaam*
Hello/Welcome.	*marHaba beek* (to one person)
	marHaba beekum (to a group)
(response)	*oo beek/beekum*
Good morning.	*sbaaH al-kheer*
(response)	*sbaaH al-kheer*
Good evening.	*masa' al-kheer*
(response)	*masa' al-kheer*
Good night.	*leela sa'eeda*
(response)	*leela sa'eeda*
Goodbye.	*bi-slaama*
(response)	*tibqa 'ala kheer*
Yes.	*waaH* (or *na'am* - more formal)
No.	*la*
Please.	*min fadlek* (when asking for
	something in a shop)
	tfaddel/tfaddelee/tfaddloo (to
	man/woman/group; when
	offering/inviting)
	itfaddel/itfaddelee/itfaddloo (to
	man/woman/group; similar to
	tfaddel, etc)
Thank you.	*saHHa/'ayshek*
(response)	*yeselmek*
Excuse me.	*smaaH lee* (to one person)
That's fine/You're	*blaa imzeeya*
welcome.	
Sorry/Apologies.	*smaaH*
What's your name?	*waash asmek?*
My name is ...	*asmee ...*
Pleased to meet you.	*mitsharf* (m)/ *mitsharfa* (f)
How are you?	*kee raak?* (to one person)
	kee raakum? (to a group)
I'm fine.	*la baas ilHamdu lillah*

EMERGENCIES

Help!	*'awen-nee!*
There's been an	*kayin akseedon*
accident.	
I'm lost.	*ana imwedder* (m)
	ana imweddra (f)
Go away!	*rooH qilnee khalleenee!*
Call a doctor!	*jeeboolee tabeeb!*
Call the police!	*jeeboolee il-booleeseeya!*
I've been robbed.	*sarqoolee Hwayjee*
Where are the toilets?	*ween kayin it-twaalet?*

Where are you from?	*mineen inta* (to a man)
	mineen intee (to a woman)
I'm from ...	*ana min ...*
I like/don't like ...	*ana inHebb/manHebbish*
Just a minute.	*dageega waaHida*

DIRECTIONS

Where is ...?	*ween kayin ...?*
Go straight ahead.	*rooH deerekt*
Turn left.	*door a-gosh*
Turn right.	*door a-limeen*
at the (next) corner	*fil kwan (illee jayy)*
at the traffic lights	*fi dhaw aHmer*
behind	*waraa*
in front of	*guddaam*
far (from)	*ba'eed ('ala)*
near (to)	*greeb (min)*
opposite	*mgaabil*
here	*hnaa*
there	*temma*
this address	*haada l-adrees*
north	*shmaal*
south	*janoob*
east	*sharq*
west	*gharb*
beach	*il-bHar*
bridge	*il-qantra*
castle	*il-qala'*
my hotel	*oteel taa'ee*
island	*jazeera*
main square	*is-saaHa li-kabeera*
mosque	*il-jaami'*
museum	*il-matHaf*
old city	*limdeena ligdeema*
palace	*il-qasr*
ruins	*il-athaar*
sea	*il-baHr*
square	*is-saaHa*
street	*it-treeg*
village	*al-qarya*

HEALTH

I'm ill.	*ana mreedh/a* (m/f)
My friend is ill.	*saHbee/saHibtee mreedh/a* (m/f)
It hurts here.	*yuwja'ni hinaa*

I'm ...	*ana mreedh/a bi ...* (m/f)
asthmatic	*il-fadda*
diabetic	*Hloowa*
epileptic	*l-epilepsee*

I have ...	*'andee ...*
diarrhoea	*kirshee tijree*
fever	*skhaana*
headache	*wjee'it ir-raas*

I'm allergic ...	*'andee Hasaseeya ...*
to antibiotics	*min antbioteek*
to aspirin	*min asbireen*
to bees	*min naHl*
to nuts	*min looz*
to peanuts	*min kakaweeya*
to penicillin	*min penisileen*

antiseptic	*anteesepteek*
aspirin	*asbireen*
condoms	*preservateef*
contraceptive	*wasaa'il mana' il Haml*
hospital	*sbeetaar*
medicine	*dwaa*
pharmacy	*fermasyaan*
pregnant	*Hebla*
prescription	*warqit at-tabeeb*
sanitary napkins	*alwees* (brand name)
stomachache	*wjee'it il-maada*
sunblock cream	*kreema did ish-shams*
tampons	*tampax*

LANGUAGE DIFFICULTIES

Do you speak English?
   titkallim ingleeziyya?
Does anyone here speak English?
   skhoon yeHder feekum yitkallim ingleeziyya?
How do you say ... in Algerian Arabic?
   kifaash tagooloo ... bi lahja dzayreeya?
What does ... mean?
   waash ta'nee ...
I understand.
   fehimt
I don't understand.
   ma fehimtish
Please write it down.
   mumkin tiktibhaalee
Can you show me (on the map)?
   mumkin twarreenee (fi l- khareeta)?

NUMBERS

Arabic numerals are simple to learn and, unlike the written language, run from left to right. Pay attention to the order of the words in numbers from 21 to 99. When followed by a noun, the pronunciation of *meeya* changes to *meet* for the numbers 100 and 300 to 900, and the noun is always used in its singular form.

0	*sifr*	·
1	*waaHid*	١
2	*zooj*	٢
3	*tlaata*	٣
4	*reb'a*	٤
5	*khamsa*	٥
6	*sitta*	٦
7	*sab'a*	٧
8	*tmaanya*	٨
9	*tis'a*	٩
10	*'ashra*	١·
11	*Hedaash*	١١
12	*tenaash*	١٢
13	*tletaash*	١٣
14	*rbetaash*	١٤
15	*khmestaash*	١٥
16	*sittaash*	١٦
17	*sbe'taash*	١٧
18	*tmentaash*	١٨
19	*tsa'taash*	١٩
20	*'ashreen*	٢·
21	*waaHid wi 'ashreen*	٢١
22	*teneen wi 'ashreen*	٢٢
30	*tlaateen*	٣·
40	*reba'een*	٤·
50	*khamseen*	٥·
60	*sitteen*	٦·
70	*sab'een*	٧·
80	*tmaneen*	٨·
90	*tis'een*	٩·
100	*meeya* (*meet* before nouns)	١··
200	*meeteen*	٢··
1000	*alf*	١···
2000	*alfeen*	٢···

How many?	*gaddaash?*

PAPERWORK

name	*ism*
nationality	*jinsiyya*
date/place of birth	*tareekh/maHal il-milâd*
sex (gender)	*jins*
passport	*paspor*
visa	*veeza*

QUESTION WORDS

Who?	*shkoon?*
What?	*waash?*
When?	*winta?*
Where?	*ween?*
How?	*keefaash?*
Which?	*aana Hooma?*

SHOPPING & SERVICES

I'd like to buy ...	*inHebb nishree ...*
How much is it?	*aash Haal?*
I don't like it.	*ma y'ajibneesh*
May I look at it?	*mumkin inshoofu?*
I'm just looking.	*ga'ad inshoof bark*
It's cheap.	*heeya rakheesa*
It's too expensive.	*heeya ghaaleeya bizaaf*
No more than ...	*mush akthaar min ...*
I'll take it.	*nishreeha*

Can you give me ...?	*tnajjemshee t'amelee ...?*
a discount	*takhfeedh*
a good price	*sooma mleeHa*

Do you accept ...?	*taakhudh ...?*
credit cards	*kart kredee*
traveller cheques	*sheekaat siyaHiyya*

more	*akthir*
less	*agall*
smaller	*asghar*
bigger	*akbar*

I'm looking for ...	*ana inHawwas 'ala ...*
a bank	*banka*
the bazaar/market	*is-sooq*
the city centre	*wist il-blaad*
the (...) embassy	*as-sifaara (...)*
the post office	*il-bosta*
the telephone centre	*haatif il-'umoomee*
the tourist office	*maktab is-siyaaHa*

I want to change ...	*inHebb insarrif ...*
money	*draahem*
travellers cheques	*sheekaat siyaHiyya*

Where is an internet café?	*ween kayin internet kafay?*

TIME & DATES

What time is it?	*sheHaal is-saa'a drook?*
It's (8 o'clock).	*drook (it-temaanya)*
in the morning	*fi s-sbaaH*
in the afternoon	*fi l-'asheeya*

in the evening	*fi l-leel*
today	*il-yoom*
tomorrow	*ghudwa*
yesterday	*ilbaaraH*
day	*yoom*
month	*sh-har*
week	*semaana*
year	*'aam*
early	*bikree*
late	*rotaar*
daily	*kull yoom*

Monday	*inhaar it-itneen*
Tuesday	*inhaar it-tlaata*
Wednesday	*inhaar il-arba'*
Thursday	*inhaar il-khmees*
Friday	*inhaar ij-jema'*
Saturday	*inhaar is-sibt*
Sunday	*inhaar il-Hadd*

January	*janfee*
February	*feefree*
March	*meghress*
April	*abreel*
May	*maayoo*
June	*jwaan*
July	*jweeyee*
August	*oot*
September	*sibtamber*
October	*uktoober*
November	*nofamber*
December	*deesamber*

TRANSPORT
Public Transport

When does the ... leave/arrive?	*winta iqella'/tuwsil ...?*
boat	*il-baboor*
bus	*il-kaar*
ferry	*il-ferry*
plane	*it-tayyaara*
train	*it-treen*

I'd like a ... ticket.	*ana baghee/bagheeya teekee ...*
one-way	*maashee*
return	*maashee oo jayy*
1st-class	*daarija oola*
2nd-class	*daarija taanya*

I want to go to ...
  inHebb inrooH ...
The train has been delayed.
  it-treen er-rotaar
The train has been cancelled.
  naHaaoo it-treen

Which bus goes to ...?
  aana Hooma il-kaar yeddi li- ...?
Does this bus go to ...?
  Haad il-kaar yeddi li ...?
Please tell me when we arrive in ...
  min fadlek gullee waqtillee nuwsiloo fi ...
What is the fare to ...?
  sheHaal it-teekee li ...?
Stop here, please.
  waqif hnaa min fadlek
Wait!
  istanna!

the first	*il-awwil/oola* (m/f)
the last	*il-aakhir*
the next	*il-qaadim*
airport	*layropor*
bus station	*is-stasyoon il-kaar*
bus stop	*laree*
city	*limdeena*
platform number	*noomroo raseef*
ticket office	*il-geeshee*
timetable	*jadwal awqaat*
train station	*lagaar*

Private Transport

I'd like to hire a/an ... *inHebb nikree ...*

car	*lowto*
4WD	*too terran*
motorbike	*mooter*
bicycle	*beskleet*
camel	*jimal*
donkey	*Hmaar*
guide	*geed*
horse	*Hsaan*

Is this the road to ...? *Haad it-treeg teddi li ...?*
Where's a service *ween il-kiyosk?*
  station?
Please fill it up. *'abbeehaalee min fadlek*
I'd like (30) litres. *inHebb (tlaateen) leetra*
diesel *diyaysel*
leaded petrol *leesans normaal* (regular)
  leesans sooper (super)
unleaded petrol *leesans son plom*
(How long) Can I *mumkin inwaggif lowto hnaa*
  park here? *(Hatta winta?)*
Where do I pay? *ween inkhallis?*
I need a mechanic. *Haajti bi mekanisyan*
The car has broken *lowto taaHit on pan ('and ...)*
  down (at ...)
The car won't start. *lowto mayikhdimsh*
I have a flat tyre. *il-pnou menfoosh*
I've run out of petrol. *wfaalee leesans*
I've had an accident. *'amelt akseedon*

TRAVEL WITH CHILDREN

Is there (a/an) ...? *kayin ...?*
I need (a/an) .... *Haajti bi ...*
  car baby seat *kursi taa' draaree li lowto*
  child-minding *kresh*
    service
  children's menu *menyoo taa' draaree*
  disposable nappies/ *koosh*
    diapers
  infant milk formula *Haleeb draaree*
  (English-speaking) *babysitter (illi titkallim bi*
    babysitter *l-ingleeziyya)*
  highchair *kursee taa' draaree*
  potty *kasreeya*
  stroller *karoosa*

Are children allowed? *tiqbloo draaree?*

FRENCH

While French has no official language status in Algeria, it is still widely spoken, particularly in urban areas. A few words and phrases could come in handy if you find yourself in a bind.

In French, an important distinction is made between *tu* and *vous*, which both mean 'you'. The informal *tu* is only used when addressing people you know well, or children. When addressing an adult who is not a personal friend, *vous* should be used unless the person invites you to use *tu*.

ACCOMMODATION

I'm looking for *Je cherche ...*   zher shersh ...
a ...

campground	*un camping*	un kom·peeng
guesthouse	*une pension*	ewn pon·syon
	(de famille)	(der fa·mee·ler)
hotel	*un hôtel*	un o·tel
youth hostel	*une auberge*	ewn o·berzh
	de jeunesse	der zher·nes

Where is a cheap hotel?
  Où est-ce qu'on peut trouver un hôtel pas cher?
  oo es·kon per troo·vay un o·tel pa shair
What is the address?
  Quelle est l'adresse?
  kel e la·dres
Could you write it down, please?
  Est-ce que vous pourriez l'écrire, s'il vous plaît?
  e·sker voo poo·ryay lay·kreer seel voo play

Do you have any rooms available?
Est-ce que vous avez des chambres libres?
e·sker voo·za·vay day shom·brer lee·brer

I'd like (a) ...	*Je voudrais ...*	zher voo·dray ...
single room	*une chambre à un lit*	ewn shom·brer a un lee
double-bed room	*une chambre avec un grand lit*	ewn shom·brer a·vek un gron lee
twin room with two beds	*une chambre avec des lits jumeaux*	ewn shom·brer a·vek day lee zhew·mo
room with a bathroom	*une chambre avec une salle de bains*	ewn shom·brer a·vek ewn sal der bun
to share a dorm	*coucher dans un dortoir*	koo·sher don zun dor·twa

How much is it ...?	*Quel est le prix ...?*	kel e ler pree ...
per night	*par nuit*	par nwee
per person	*par personne*	par per·son

May I see it?
Est-ce que je peux voir la chambre?
es·ker zher per vwa la shom·brer

Where is the bathroom?
Où est la salle de bains?
oo e la sal der bun

Where is the toilet?
Où sont les toilettes?
oo·son lay twa·let

I'm leaving today.
Je pars aujourd'hui.
zher par o·zhoor·dwee

We're leaving today.
Nous partons aujourd'hui.
noo par·ton o·zhoor·dwee

CONVERSATION & ESSENTIALS

Hello.	*Bonjour.*	bon·zhoor
Goodbye.	*Au revoir.*	o·rer·vwa
Yes.	*Oui.*	wee
No.	*Non.*	no
Please.	*S'il vous plaît.*	seel voo play
Thank you.	*Merci.*	mair·see
You're welcome.	*Je vous en prie.*	zher voo·zon pree
	De rien. (inf)	der ree·en
Excuse me.	*Excuse-moi.*	ek·skew·zay·mwa
Sorry. (forgive me)	*Pardon.*	par·don

What's your name?
Comment vous appelez-vous? (pol)
ko·mon voo·za·pay·lay voo

Comment tu t'appelles? (inf)
ko·mon tew ta·pel

My name is ...
Je m'appelle ...
zher ma·pel ...

EMERGENCIES

Help!
Au secours!
o skoor

There's been an accident!
Il y a eu un accident!
eel ya ew un ak·see·don

I'm lost.
Je me suis égaré/e. (m/f)
zhe me swee·zay·ga·ray

Leave me alone!
Fichez-moi la paix!
fee·shay·mwa la pay

Call ...!	*Appelez ...!*	a·play ...
a doctor	*un médecin*	un mayd·sun
the police	*la police*	la po·lees

Where are you from?
De quel pays êtes-vous? der kel pay·ee et·voo
De quel pays es-tu? (inf) der kel pay·ee e·tew

I'm from ...
Je viens de ...
zher vyen der ...

I like ...
J'aime ...
zhem ...

I don't like ...
Je n'aime pas ...
zher nem pa ...

Just a minute.
Une minute.
ewn mee·newt

DIRECTIONS

Where is ...?
Où est ...?
oo e ...

Go straight ahead.
Continuez tout droit.
kon·teen·way too drwa

Turn left.
Tournez à gauche.
toor·nay a gosh

Turn right.
Tournez à droite.
toor·nay a drwa

at the corner	*au coin*	o kwun
at the traffic lights	*aux feux*	o fer

behind	*derrière*	dair·ryair
in front of	*devant*	der·von
far (from)	*loin (de)*	lwun (der)
near (to)	*près (de)*	pray (der)
opposite	*en face de*	on fas der

beach	*la plage*	la plazh
castle	*le château*	ler sha·to
island	*l'île*	leel
main square	*la place centrale*	la plas son·tral
mosque	*la mosquée*	la mos·kay
museum	*le musée*	ler mew·zay
my hotel	*mon hôtel*	mon o·tel

old city	la vieille ville	la vyay veel
ruins	les ruines	lay rween
sea	la mer	la mair
street	la rue	la roo
village	le village	ler vee·lazh

HEALTH

I'm ill.	Je suis malade.	zher swee ma·lad
It hurts here.	J'ai une douleur ici.	zhay ewn doo·ler ee·see

I'm ...	Je suis ...	zher swee ...
asthmatic	asthmatique	(z)as·ma·teek
diabetic	diabétique	dee·a·bay·teek
epileptic	épileptique	(z)ay·pee·lep·teek

I'm allergic to ...	Je suis allergique ...	zher swee za·lair·zheek ...
antibiotics	aux antibiotiques	o zon·tee·byo·teek
aspirin	à l'aspirine	a las·pee·reen
bees	aux abeilles	o za·bay·yer
nuts	aux noix	o nwa
peanuts	aux cacahuètes	o ka·ka·wet
penicillin	à la pénicilline	a la pay·nee·see·leen

antiseptic	l'antiseptique	lon·tee·sep·teek
aspirin	l'aspirine	las·pee·reen
condoms	des préservatifs	day pray·zair·va·teef
contraceptive	le contraceptif	ler kon·tra·sep·teef
diarrhoea	la diarrhée	la dya·ray
medicine	le médicament	ler may·dee·ka·mon
nausea	la nausée	la no·zay
sunblock cream	la crème solaire	la krem so·lair
tampons	des tampons hygiéniques	day tom·pon ee·zhen·eek

LANGUAGE DIFFICULTIES

Do you speak English?
Parlez-vous anglais? par·lay·voo ong·lay
Does anyone here speak English?
Y a-t-il quelqu'un qui ya·teel kel·kung kee
parle anglais? par long·glay
How do you say ... in French?
Comment est-ce qu'on ko·mon es·kon
dit ... en français? dee ... on fron·say
What does ... mean?
Que veut dire ...? ker ver deer ...
I understand.
Je comprends. zher kom·pron
I don't understand.
Je ne comprends pas. zher ner kom·pron pa
Could you write it down, please?
Est-ce que vous pouvez es·ker voo poo·vay
l'écrire? lay·kreer

Can you show me (on the map)?
Pouvez-vous m'indiquer poo·vay·voo mun·dee·kay
(sur la carte)? (sewr la kart)

NUMBERS

0	zero	zay·ro
1	un	un
2	deux	der
3	trois	trwa
4	quatre	ka·trer
5	cinq	sungk
6	six	sees
7	sept	set
8	huit	weet
9	neuf	nerf
10	dix	dees
11	onze	onz
12	douze	dooz
13	treize	trez
14	quatorze	ka·torz
15	quinze	kunz
16	seize	sez
17	dix-sept	dee·set
18	dix-huit	dee·zweet
19	dix-neuf	deez·nerf
20	vingt	vung
21	vingt et un	vung tay un
22	vingt-deux	vung·der
30	trente	tront
40	quarante	ka·ront
50	cinquante	sung·kont
60	soixante	swa·sont
70	soixante-dix	swa·son·dees
80	quatre-vingts	ka·trer·vung
90	quatre-vingt-dix	ka·trer·vung·dees
100	cent	son
1000	mille	meel
How many?	Combien?	kom·byun

PAPERWORK

name	nom	nom
nationality	nationalité	na·syo·na·lee·tay
date/place of birth	date/place de naissance	dat/plas der nay·sons
sex/gender	sexe	seks
passport	passeport	pas·por
visa	visa	vee·za

QUESTION WORDS

Who?	Qui?	kee
What?	Quoi?	kwa
What is it?	Qu'est-ce que c'est?	kes·ker say
When?	Quand?	kon
Where?	Où?	oo

Which?	*Quel/Quelle?*	kel
Why?	*Pourquoi?*	poor·kwa
How?	*Comment?*	ko·mon

SHOPPING & SERVICES

I'd like to buy ...		
Je voudrais acheter ...		zher voo·dray ash·tay ...
How much is it?		
C'est combien?		say kom·byun
I don't like it.		
Cela ne me plaît pas.		ser·la ner mer play pa
May I look at it?		
Est-ce que je peux le voir?		es·ker zher per ler vwar
I'm just looking.		
Je regarde.		zher rer·gard
It's cheap.		
Ce n'est pas cher.		ser nay pa shair
It's too expensive.		
C'est trop cher.		say tro shair
I'll take it.		
Je le prends.		zher ler pron

Can I pay by ...?	*Est-ce que je peux*	es·ker zher per
	payer avec ...?	pay·yay a·vek ...
credit card	*ma carte de*	ma kart der
	crédit	kray·dee
travellers	*des chèques*	day shek
cheques	*de voyage*	der vwa·yazh

more	*plus*	plew
less	*moins*	mwa
smaller	*plus petit*	plew per·tee
bigger	*plus grand*	plew gron

Where can I	*Où est-ce qu'on*	oo es·kon
find ...?	*peut trouver ...?*	per troo·vay ...
I'm looking	*Je cherche ...*	zhe shersh ...
for ...		
a bank	*une banque*	ewn bonk
the bazaar	*le bazar*	ler ba·zar
the ... embassy	*l'ambassade*	lam·ba·sahd
	de ...	der ...
the hospital	*l'hôpital*	lo·pee·tal
the market	*le marché*	ler mar·shay
the police	*la police*	la po·lees
the post office	*le bureau de*	ler bew·ro der
	poste	post
a public phone	*une cabine*	ewn ka·been
	téléphonique	tay·lay·fo·neek
a public toilet	*les toilettes*	lay twa·let

TIME & DATES

What time is it?	*Quelle heure est-il?*	kel er e til
It's (8) o'clock.	*Il est (huit) heures.*	il e (weet) er
It's half past ...	*Il est (...) heures*	il e (...) er
	et demie.	e day·mee

in the morning	*du matin*	dew ma·tun
in the afternoon	*de l'après-midi*	der la·pray·mee·dee
in the evening	*du soir*	dew swar
today	*aujourd'hui*	o·zhoor·dwee
tomorrow	*demain*	der·mun
yesterday	*hier*	yair
day	*jour*	zhoor
month	*mois*	mwa
week	*semaine*	se·men
year	*année*	a·nay
early	*tôt*	to
late	*en retard*	on rer·tar
daily	*quotidien* (m)	ko·tee·dyun
	quotidienne (f)	ko·tee·dyen

Monday	*lundi*	lun·dee
Tuesday	*mardi*	mar·dee
Wednesday	*mercredi*	mair·krer·dee
Thursday	*jeudi*	zher·dee
Friday	*vendredi*	von·drer·dee
Saturday	*samedi*	sam·dee
Sunday	*dimanche*	dee·monsh

January	*janvier*	zhon·vyay
February	*février*	fayv·ryay
March	*mars*	mars
April	*avril*	a·vreel
May	*mai*	may
June	*juin*	zhwun
July	*juillet*	zhwee·yay
August	*août*	oot
September	*septembre*	sep·tom·brer
October	*octobre*	ok·to·brer
November	*novembre*	no·vom·brer
December	*décembre*	day·som·brer

TRANSPORT
Public Transport

What time does	*À quelle heure*	a kel er
... leave/arrive?	*part/arrive ...?*	par/a·reev ...
boat	*le bateau*	ler ba·to
bus	*le bus*	ler bews
plane	*l'avion*	la·vyon
train	*le train*	ler trun

I'd like a ...	*Je voudrais*	zher voo·dray
ticket.	*un billet ...*	un bee·yay ...
one-way	*simple*	sum·pler
return	*aller et retour*	a·lay ay rer·toor
1st class	*de première*	der prem·yair
	classe	klas
2nd class	*de deuxième*	der der·zyem
	classe	klas

I want to go to ...		
Je voudrais aller à ...		zher voo·dray a·lay a ...

The train has been delayed.
Le train est en retard.   ler trun et on rer·tar
The train has been cancelled.
Le train a été annulé.   ler trun a ay·tay a·new·lay

the first	*le premier* (m)	ler prer·myay
	la première (f)	la prer·myair
the last	*le dernier* (m)	ler dair·nyay
	la dernière (f)	la dair·nair
platform	*le numéro*	ler new·may·ro
number	*de quai*	der kay
ticket office	*le guichet*	ler gee·shay
timetable	*l'horaire*	lo·rair
train station	*la gare*	la gar

Private Transport

I'd like to hire	*Je voudrais*	zher voo·dray
a/an...	*louer ...*	loo·way ...
car	*une voiture*	ewn vwa·tewr
4WD	*un tout-terrain*	un too te·run
motorbike	*une moto*	ewn mo·to
bicycle	*un vélo*	un vay·lo

Is this the road to ...?
C'est la route pour ...?   say la root poor ...
Where's a service station?
Où est-ce qu'il y a   oo es·keel ya
une station-service?   ewn sta·syon·ser·vees
Please fill it up.
Le plein, s'il vous plaît.   ler plun seel voo play
I'd like ... litres.
Je voudrais ... litres.   zher voo·dray ... lee·trer
petrol/gas
essence   ay·sons
diesel
diesel   dyay·zel
(How long) Can I park here?
(Combien de temps)   (kom·byun der tom)
Est-ce que je peux   es·ker zher per
stationner ici?   sta·syo·nay ee·see?
Where do I pay?
Où est-ce que je paie?   oo es·ker zher pay?

I need a mechanic.
J'ai besoin d'un   zhay ber·zwun dun
mécanicien.   may·ka·nee·syun
The car/motorbike has broken down (at ...)
La voiture/moto est   la vwa·tewr/mo·to ay
tombée en panne (à ...)   tom·bay on pan (a ...)
The car/motorbike won't start.
La voiture/moto ne   la vwa·tewr/mo·to ner
veut pas démarrer.   ver pa day·ma·ray
I have a flat tyre.
Mon pneu est à plat.   mom pner ay ta pla
I've run out of petrol.
Je suis en panne   zher swee zon pan
d'essence.   day·sons
I had an accident.
J'ai eu un accident.   zhay ew un ak·see·don

TRAVEL WITH CHILDREN

I need a/an ...
J'ai besoin ...   zhay ber·zwun ...
car baby seat
d'un siège-enfant   dun syezh·on·fon
child-minding service
d'une garderie   dewn gar·dree
children's menu
d'un menu pour enfants   dun mer·new poor on·fon
disposable nappies/diapers
de couches-culottes   der koosh·kew·lot
infant milk formula
de lait maternisé   de lay ma·ter·nee·zay
(English-speaking) babysitter
d'une baby-sitter (qui   dewn ba·bee·see·ter (kee
parle anglais)   parl ong·glay)
highchair
d'une chaise haute   dewn shay zot
potty
d'un pot de bébé   dun po der bay·bay
stroller
d'une poussette   dewn poo·set

Are children allowed?
Les enfants sont permis? lay zon·fon son pair·mee

Also available from Lonely Planet:
Middle East and *French Phrasebooks*

LANGUAGE

Glossary

Abbasids – Baghdad-based ruling dynasty (AD 749–1258) of the Arab/Islamic empire
adrar – Tuareg for mountain; see also *msak* and *tadrart*
Aghlabids – Arab dynasty based in Kairouan who ruled Tunisia (AD 800–909)
agora – main public square of ancient Greek cities
aïn – well or spring
akerbai – loose-fitting *Tuareg* pants
akhle – haphazard network of sand dunes without discernible pattern
Al-Andalus – Muslim Spain and Portugal
Algerian War of Independence – the 1954–62 war against the French that led to Algerian independence
Allah – God
Almohads – puritanical Muslim group (1147–1269), originally *Berber*, that arose in response to the corrupt Almoravid dynasty
Almoravids – Muslim group (1054–1147) that ruled Spain and the *Maghreb*
Amazigh – *Berbers*, especially from the *Kabylie* region
aquifers – layers of rock holding underground water
ashaersh – *Tuareg* turban
assif – watercourse, river

bab – gate or door
bahr – ocean
Bani Hilal – tribes of Upper Egypt who invaded the *Maghreb* in the 11th century, causing great destruction and Arabising the region
banu – see *beni*
baraka – divine blessing or favour
Barbary – European term used to describe the North African coast from the 16th to the 19th centuries
barchan – crescent-shaped sand dune
basilica – court or assembly building (Roman) or church (Byzantine)
ben – son of (also *ibn*)
beni – 'sons of', often precedes tribal name (also *banu*)
Berbers – indigenous inhabitants of North Africa
bey – provincial governor in the Ottoman Empire
bordj – fort (literally 'tower')
burnous – warm over-robe worn by men and women

caliph – successor of *Mohammed*; ruler of the Islamic world
Camel Period – period of Saharan rock art from 200 BC to the present
capital – decorated top part of a column
capitol – main temple of a Roman town, usually situated in the *forum*

cardo – main road running north–south through a Roman city
casbah – fort, citadel; often also the administrative centre (also spelt *qasba*)
cavea – seating area in a Roman theatre
chergui – dry, easterly desert wind
cipolin – white marble with veins of green or grey
corniche – coastal road
corsairs – pirate bands in the 15th century and beyond
croix d'Agadez – *Tuareg* cross of stylised silver with filigree designs
cryptae – Roman promenade or underground corridors
curia – municipal assembly in Ancient Rome

dar – traditional town house
decumanus – main road running east–west through a Roman city
dey – the Ottoman army's equivalent of a sergeant who assisted the *pasha*
divan – council of senior officers who advised the *pasha* in Ottoman times
djedid – new
djellaba – popular flowing garment; men's *jellabas* are usually made from cotton or wool, women's come in light synthetic fabrics
djemaa – mosque

eid – feast (also spelled *aïd*)
erg – sand dunes or sand sea
emir – Islamic ruler, military commander or governor

Fatimids – Muslim dynasty (AD 909–1171) that rose to prominence in the 10th century
FIS – Islamic Salvation Front (Front Islamique du Salut) who won the first round of elections in 1991 and were then made illegal
foggara – underground channels leading to water
forum – open space at the centre of Roman towns
frigidarium – cold room in Roman baths complex
funduq – hotel

galabiyya – full-length loose-fitting robe worn by men
gare routière – bus station
gare terminal – ferry terminal
gîte – trekkers' hostel, sometimes a homestay
guelta – natural springs

haram – literally 'forbidden'; sometimes used to denote a sacred or forbidden area, eg the prayer room of a mosque
haj – pilgrimage to Mecca; one of the five pillars of Islam

hamada – plateaus of rock scoured by wind erosion

hammam – bathhouse

haram – prayer hall of mosque

High Plateaus – the 600m-long series of plateaus averaging 1200m above sea level, separating the Atlas Mountains of the coastal hinterland and the Saharan Atlas

hittists – literally those who hold up or hit the wall; used to refer to young unemployed men in Algeria

Horse Period – period of Saharan rock art from 1000 BC to AD 1

Ibadis – an offshoot of the *Kharajite* sect found only in the villages of the *M'Zab* Valley in Algeria, Jerba, Zanzibar and in Oman

ibn – son of (also *ben*)

Idrissids – Moroccan dynasty which established a stable state in northern Morocco in the 9th century

iftar – breaking of the fast at sundown during *Ramadan*; breakfast (also spelt *ftur*)

ijtihad – individual interpretation of sacred texts and traditions

imam – man schooled in Islamic law; religious leader of Muslim community

janissaries – professional soldiers committed to a life of military service who became rulers of Ottoman Libya

Kabylie – *Berber (Amazigh)* region east of Algiers

Kharijites – puritanical Islamic sect, which broke away from the mainstream Sunnis in AD 657 and inspired *Berber* rebellions from the 8th to the 10th century

khutba – sermon delivered by *imam*, especially at Friday noon prayers

ksar – castle, palace, fortified stronghold

laconica – sweat baths in a Roman baths complex

La Vache Qui Pleure – *Crying Cows*; famous rock-art site near Djanet

madhhab – school of Islamic law

madrassa – school of the *Quran* and Islamic law

Maghreb – (literally 'west') area covered by Morocco, Algeria, Tunisia and Libya

Maliki – one of four major schools of Islamic thought and the predominant one in Algeria; preaches the primacy of the Quran (as opposed to later teachings)

maqbara – cemetery

marabout – holy man or saint; also often used to describe the mausoleums of these men

Merenids – Moroccan dynasty (1269–1465), responsible for the construction of many of Morocco's *medrassas*

mihrab – vaulted niche in the wall of a mosque indicating direction of Mecca

minbar – the pulpit that stands beside the *mihrab* in a mosque

Mozabites – *Ibadi* people who inhabit the *M'Zab* Valley

msak – *Tuareg* for mountain; also *adrar* and *tadrart*

muezzin – man who calls the faithful to prayer from the minaret

muqarna – decorative plasterwork

musée – museum

M'Zab – region of five oases centred around Ghardaïa and home to a community of *Ibadi* Muslims

nargileh – water pipe or *sheesha* for smoking

natatio – entrance hall to Roman baths complex

Numidians – tribe from present-day Algeria, once controlled Northern Tunisia; founders of the cities of Bulla Regia, Sicca (El-Kef) and Thugga (Dougga)

nymphaeum – building with fountains; dedicated to nymphs

oued – riverbed, often dry (sometimes wad or wadi) except after rains

palaestra – exercise area in Roman times

palmeraie – palm grove

pasha – Ottoman governor appointed by the sultan in Constantinople

Pastoral Period – period of Saharan rock art from 5500 BC to 2000 BC, also known as the Bovidian Period

peristyle – colonnade or portico of columns surrounding a building or courtyard

petroglyphs – millennia-old rock carvings

Phoenicians – a great seafaring nation based in modern Lebanon, which dominated trade in the Mediterranean in the 1st millennium BC; founders of Carthage

pictographs – millennia-old rock paintings

pied-noir – literally 'black foot'; name given to French settlers in Algeria and their descendants (also called colons)

Prophet (Mohammed), the – founder of Islam, who lived between AD 570 and AD 632

Punic – ancient Phoenician people in North Africa

Punic Wars – three wars waged between Rome and Carthage in the 3rd and 2nd centuries BC, resulting in the destruction of Carthage by the Romans in 146 BC

qahwa – thick Arabic coffee

qibla – the direction of Mecca, indicated by a *mihrab*

Quran – sacred book of Islam

rai – world-famous Algerian music that originated in Oran

Ramadan – ninth month of lunar Islamic calendar, during which Muslims fast from sunrise to sunset

ras – headland

Round Head Period – period of Saharan rock art from 8000 BC to 6000 BC

Rustamids – *Ibadi* dynasty that ruled much of northern Algeria from Tahirt, from AD 761 to AD 909

sahn – courtyard of mosque

scaenae frons – façade behind the stage in Roman theatre

seif – Arabic for 'sword'; also the name for sand dunes with long, sweeping ridges

serir – basins, formed by wadies, in which salt is left after water has evaporated

sharia – street or road

sheeshah – water pipe or *nargileh* for smoking

sheikh – tribal chief

sherif – descendant of the *Prophet*

Shiites – one of two main Islamic sects, formed by those who believed the true *imams* were descended from the prophet's son-in-law Ali (see also *Sunnis*)

Sidi – saint

souq – market or bazaar

Sufi – follower of Islamic mystical orders that emphasise dancing, chanting and trances in order to attain unity with God

Sunnis – one of two main Islamic sects, derived from followers of the Umayyad caliphate (see also *Shiites*)

suras – verses or chapters in the *Quran*

taajeelah – *Tuareg* bread cooked under hot sand

tadrart – *Tuareg* for mountain

tagine – lamb dish with tomato and paprika

taguelmoust – *Tuareg* veil

Tamashek – *Tuareg* language

Tamazigh – *Berber* language

taxiphone – an inexpensive metered phone service

taxi brousse – shared taxi

taxi collectifs – shared taxi

Tell – narrow coastal strip and mountainous hinterland of northern Algeria

tende – *Tuareg* dance

tepidarium – warm room in a Roman baths complex

tifinagh – letters of the *Tuareg* alphabet

Tuareg – nomadic *Berbers* of the Sahara, also known as the Blue Men because of their indigo-dyed robes

Umayyads – first great dynasty of Arab Muslim rulers (AD 661–750), based in Damascus

ville nouvelle – new city; town built by the French alongside existing towns

wilaya – province

Wild Fauna Period – period of Saharan rock art from 10,000 BC to 6000 BC

zawiya – religious college or monastery

zeriba – palm hut

Behind the Scenes

THIS BOOK

This 1st edition of *Algeria* was researched and written by Anthony Ham, Anthony Sattin and Nana Luckham with contributions by Zahia Hafs and Jane Cornwell. The Health chapter was adapted from material written by Dr Caroline Evans. The guide was commissioned in Lonely Planet's Melbourne office and produced by the following:

Commissioning Editors Will Gourlay, Tashi Wheeler
Coordinating Editor Laura Gibb
Coordinating Cartographer Sophie Richards
Coordinating Layout Designer Cara Smith
Managing Editor Suzannah Shwer
Managing Cartographer Shahara Ahmed
Assisting Editors Elisa Arduca, Andrea Dobbin, Kate Evans, Rosie Nicholson, Stephanie Ong, Gina Tsarouhas
Assisting Cartographers Hunor Csutoros, Jessica Deane, Daniel Fennessy, Joshua Geoghegan

Cover Designer Jim Hsu
Indexer Gennifer Ciavarra
Project Manager Rachel Imeson, Craig Kilburn
Language Content Coordinator Quentin Frayne

Thanks to Sally Darmody, Brigitte Ellemor, Raphael Richards, Averil Robertson, Kathryn Stapley, Rabah Toubal, Celia Wood

THANKS
ANTHONY HAM

A big thank you to my co-authors, Anthony Sattin and Nana Luckham, whose intrepid travel, wise counsel and outstanding writing made them a coordinating author's dream. At Lonely Planet, Will Gourlay is an editor and friend with whom I hope to work many times in the future. Special thanks also to Laura Gibb who was a pleasure to work with and whose editorial interventions

---

LONELY PLANET: TRAVEL WIDELY, TREAD LIGHTLY, GIVE SUSTAINABLY

The Lonely Planet Story

The story begins with a classic travel adventure: Tony and Maureen Wheeler's 1972 journey across Europe and Asia to Australia. There was no useful information about the overland trail then, so Tony and Maureen published the first Lonely Planet guidebook to meet a growing need.

From a kitchen table, Lonely Planet has grown to become the largest independent travel publisher in the world, with offices in Melbourne (Australia), Oakland (USA) and London (UK). Today Lonely Planet guidebooks cover the globe. There is an ever-growing list of books and information in a variety of media. Some things haven't changed. The main aim is still to make it possible for adventurous individuals to get out there – to explore and better understand the world.

The Lonely Planet Foundation

The Lonely Planet Foundation proudly supports nimble nonprofit institutions working for change in the world. Each year the foundation donates 5% of Lonely Planet company profits to projects selected by staff and authors. Our partners range from Kabissa, which provides small nonprofits across Africa with access to technology, to the Foundation for Developing Cambodian Orphans, which supports girls at risk of falling victim to sex traffickers.

Our nonprofit partners are linked by a grass-roots approach to the areas of health, education or sustainable tourism. Many projects we support – such as one with BaAka (Pygmy) children in the forested areas of Central African Republic – choose to focus on women and children as one of the most effective ways to support the whole community.

Sometimes foundation assistance is as simple as restoring a local ruin like the Minaret of Jam in Afghanistan; this incredible monument now draws intrepid tourists to the area and its restoration has greatly improved options for local people.

Just as travel is often about learning to see with new eyes, so many of the groups we work with aim to change the way people see themselves and the future for their children and communities.

significantly improved the book. Michael Dreelan and Claire McWalter were my companions on my first illicit foray into Algeria. Thanks also to my Algerian friends (and clients) with whom I worked so many years ago and who taught me so much about their country – for obvious reasons they shall remain nameless. *Shukran* as always to my friends and family in Australia and Spain, and especially to my mother and friend, Jan, who gifted me with a nomadic soul. And to Marina who is the perfect travelling companion and the most supportive of partners – *la proxima vez vamos juntos al desierto mi amor*. This book is dedicated to Tom Parkinson, an outstanding author who was an Algerian pioneer for Lonely Planet, but who tragically died while this book was being written.

NANA LUCKHAM

Thanks first of all to my co-authors, and to Will Gourlay for sending me on this adventure. In London, Patrick Smith, John Marks, Vesna Maric and Shahrezad Razavi provided excellent pre-departure advice. In Algeria my thanks go to Sophie and Aidan for their company on my first night in the country, to the supremely connected Toufiq Boughali for all his help and advice in and around Ghardaïa, to Mustafa Chenni, an excellent tour guide to Ghardaïa, to Yousef for his music and company around the Grand Erg Oriental, to Sahli Abdelkader for the great dinner, lute playing and sightseeing in Taghit, to Claudia Bahedi in Tamanrasset and to Tahar Bouaka in Djanet. Thanks also to Brahim and Mohammed 'Kerase' for a beautiful, unforgettable trip into the Sahara and to my father for making my foray into the desert so much more enjoyable – thanks Hedge!

ANTHONY SATTIN

Thanks to Tom Hartwell, Carolyn McIntrye and Meriem Taibi for invaluable pretrip assistance and introductions. In Algeria, I was helped, encouraged, driven and fed by many people – the old cliché about Algerian hospitality is true – but special thanks to BH Yacine, Jean-Pierre and Karima Sami of Ile d'Occient, Mohand Akli Ikherbane, Abdallah Benmansour, Hisham and Mohamed Slimane, Hebri Belattar, Abdelhamid Benadda, Mohamed Ghemri and family, and Farouk Stambouli.

OUR READERS

Many thanks to the travellers who wrote to us with helpful hints, useful advice and interesting anecdotes:

Candice Font, Riad Hartani, Robert Leger

ACKNOWLEDGEMENTS

Globe on title page ©Mountain High Maps 1993 Digital Wisdom, Inc

SEND US YOUR FEEDBACK

We love to hear from travellers – your comments keep us on our toes and help make our books better. Our well-travelled team reads every word on what you loved or loathed about this book. Although we cannot reply individually to postal submissions, we always guarantee that your feedback goes straight to the appropriate authors, in time for the next edition. Each person who sends us information is thanked in the next edition – and the most useful submissions are rewarded with a free book.

To send us your updates – and find out about Lonely Planet events, newsletters and travel news – visit our award-winning website: **www.lonelyplanet.com/contact**.

Note: we may edit, reproduce and incorporate your comments in Lonely Planet products such as guidebooks, websites and digital products, so let us know if you don't want your comments reproduced or your name acknowledged. For a copy of our privacy policy visit www.lonelyplanet.com/privacy.

Index

INDEX

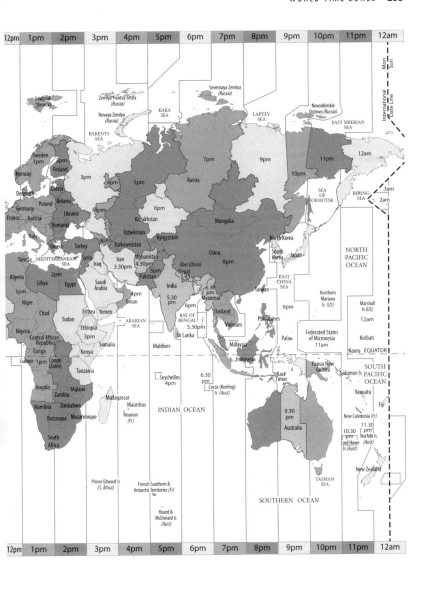

MAP LEGEND

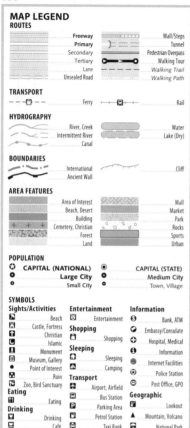

LONELY PLANET OFFICES

Australia

Head Office

Locked Bag 1, Footscray, Victoria 3011

☎ 03 8379 8000, fax 03 8379 8111

talk2us@lonelyplanet.com.au

USA

150 Linden St, Oakland, CA 94607

☎ 510 893 8555, toll free 800 275 8555

fax 510 893 8572

info@lonelyplanet.com

UK

72–82 Rosebery Ave,

Clerkenwell, London EC1R 4RW

☎ 020 7841 9000, fax 020 7841 9001

go@lonelyplanet.co.uk

Published by Lonely Planet Publications Pty Ltd

ABN 36 005 607 983

© Lonely Planet Publications Pty Ltd 2007

© photographers as indicated 2007

Cover photograph: Locals with camels in the desert, Frans Lemmens/ APL/Corbis. Many of the images in this guide are available for licensing from Lonely Planet Images: www.lonelyplanetimages.com.

Printed through The Bookmaker International Ltd

Printed in Hong Kong